Corporate Law and Climate Change

This book provides an analysis of the impact of the climate crisis on corporate law and theory in the coming decades as the world seeks to meet the target of net zero carbon emissions by 2050.

Net zero targets are a particular challenge for an economy such as Australia which has a historical reliance on fossil fuels, and powerful interests arguing for the continued use of coal and gas. The book examines four recent corporate case studies in Australia. The first two follow the Adani group of companies and coal in Queensland and Rio Tinto and the destruction of ancient rock shelters in the midst of iron ore mining in WA. The book then covers the pension fund member Mark McVeigh, issuing proceedings against REST super in relation to long-run investment decisions and the need to take into account climate risk. Finally, it discusses Sharma, a representative action taken by school children against the Federal government in relation to expansion plans in relation to fossil fuels alleging breach of the duty of care. These case studies highlight some of the key trends and challenges in the intersection between corporate activity and the need to account for climate risk and adaptation, with Australia as a G20 economy having much to contribute to the global debate.

The book will be of interest to students and researchers in the field of climate and environmental law, as well as corporate law and theory.

Dr Andrew Clarke has written widely in corporate law, governance, torts law, and risk. Andrew is an Adjunct Professor in the School of Law at Southern Cross University NSW, in the Institute of Innovation, Science and Sustainability at Federation University Victoria, and in the College of Comparative Law, China University of Politics and Law, in Beijing. Andrew was Foundation Dean in the College of Law and Justice at Victoria University in Melbourne between 2007 and 2016, and thereafter Chair of Corporate Law until the end of 2023. Andrew is currently the Principal Lawyer at Ballarat Grampians Community Legal Service.

Routledge Research in Corporate Law

Available titles in this series include:

Shareholder Activism and the Law
The Future of US Corporate Governance
Ekrem Solak

The Law and Governance of Decentralised Business Models
Between Hierarchies and Markets
Edited by Roger M Barker and Iris H-Y Chiu

The Enlightened Shareholder Value and Corporate Social Responsibility
A theoretical and qualitative analysis
Taskin Iqbal

Adjudicating Global Business in and with India
International Commercial and Investment Disputes Settlement
Leïla Choukroune and Rahul Donde

Business, Law and Human Rights in Africa
Oyeniyi Abe

Small and Medium Enterprises, Law and Business
Uncertainty and Justice
Jan Winczorek and Karol Muszyński

Legal and Ethical Standards in Corporate Insolvency
Elizabeth Streten

Corporate Group Legitimacy
Reconceptualising The Corporate Group
Peter Underwood

Corporate Law and Climate Change
Theory, Risk, Governance
Andrew Clarke

Corporate Law and Climate Change

Theory, Risk, Governance

Andrew Clarke

Routledge
Taylor & Francis Group
LONDON AND NEW YORK

First published 2025
by Routledge
4 Park Square, Milton Park, Abingdon, Oxon OX14 4RN

and by Routledge
605 Third Avenue, New York, NY 10158

Routledge is an imprint of the Taylor & Francis Group, an informa business

British Library Cataloguing-in-Publication Data
A catalogue record for this book is available from the British Library

Library of Congress Cataloging-in-Publication Data
Names: Clarke, Andrew (Lawyer), author.
Title: Corporate law and climate change: theory, risk, governance / Andrew Clarke.
Description: Abingdon, Oxon [UK]; New York, NY: Routledge, 2024. | Series: Routledge research in corporate law | Includes bibliographical references and index.
Identifiers: LCCN 2024016996 (print) | LCCN 2024016997 (ebook) | ISBN 9781032204772 (hardback) | ISBN 9781032204796 (paperback) | ISBN 9781003263746 (ebook)
Subjects: LCSH: Climatic changes–Law and legislation–Australia. | Corporation law–Australia.
Classification: LCC KU1509.5.C53 2024 (print) | LCC KU1509.5 (ebook) | DDC 344.9404/6342–dc23/eng/20240416
LC record available at https://lccn.loc.gov/2024016996
LC ebook record available at https://lccn.loc.gov/2024016997

ISBN: 978-1-032-20477-2 (hbk)
ISBN: 978-1-032-20479-6 (pbk)
ISBN: 978-1-003-26374-6 (ebk)

DOI: 10.4324/9781003263746

Typeset in Times New Roman
by Deanta Global Publishing Services, Chennai, India

Contents

Acknowledgements

I would like to acknowledge and thank Dr Stella Clarke, and my three daughters Rebecca, Jasmine and Imogen for their ongoing support and encouragement. This book is dedicated to them.

I want to acknowledge the support and encouragement of Professor Alan Benstead, Dr Steve Higgins, Dr Adrian Chandler, Professor Martin Partington, Professor David Feldman, Professor Harry Geddes, Professor John Farrar, Professor John Devereux, Professor Anona Armstrong, Dr Madeline Taylor, Dr Matt Harvey, Dr Chris Brien, Dr Yongqiang Li, Sherene Ozyurek, and Kathleen Raponi. Special thanks to Professor Rodger Fernandez, Leslie Glick KC, David Denton KC, Miriam MacDonald, Peter George, John Cain, Lazaros Zikou, Denis Nelthorpe, Judge Philip Misso, and Ian Boyle for their support and insights over the last several years. Many thanks to Murray Greenway and Debra Hutchinson for research assistance, and to Audrey and David Clarke for their dedication.

And finally, thanks to the outstanding team at Routledge; it has been a pleasure working with you.

Andrew Clarke,
March 2024

Introduction

Introduction

Australia and the climate emergency: a signal case in point

That there is a current climate emergency is beyond dispute in scientific terms. It is ascribed to the release of excessive carbon dioxide—about 51 billion tonnes every year—into the earth's atmosphere.[1] From a longitudinal perspective, the production of carbon dioxide has risen sharply ever since the late 18th century when the Industrial Revolution began, slowly at first but with increased acceleration from the post-war, mid-20th century onwards.

The period between 1770 and 1800 also corresponded with two crucial and related developments: first, Australia's European settlement, and second, the advent of the company as the pre-eminent business entity for commercial dealings and profit making. Companies have therefore essentially been a constant feature of Australia's economic, social, and political development ever since the European arrival first in 1770 by way of a preliminary site visit, and then in earnest from 1788 onwards. Many of the biggest and best-known Australian origin companies, achieving global scale, have been focused on the fossil fuel and resources sector, and have, as such, been major emitters of carbon dioxide. Within the foundations of the Australian context, companies have therefore been a major contributor to the causes of climate change and the resulting climate emergency.

Building on this foundational matrix, Australia's post-First Nations, Euro-centric, neo-liberal orthodoxy has provided a signal case in point combining four critical factors. First, it is coextensive with the global epoch of industrialization. Second, it has involved large-scale environmental destruction and degradation due to mining and extractive industries. Third, it has coincided with the epoch of modern climate change and, fourth, it has been predominantly informed by the emergence of corporate law and governance theories—rules and governance largely in the guise of the Anglo-US paradigm.

1 Bill Gates, *How to Avoid a Climate Disaster*, Allen Lane, 2021, 3.

DOI: 10.4324/9781003263746-1

The challenges posed by the climate emergency for company law and corporate governance

The climate crisis provides a fundamental challenge to corporate law orthodoxy, particularly as regards the intersection of social, economic, and environmental components with a future-oriented approach. How can reform position companies do better?

This challenge will include conceptual analysis and it will encompass an array of practical actions. The aims and objectives of *Corporate Law and Climate Change* are bounded within the parameters of that project. As such, it will include looking afresh at the theoretical base of companies and the practical use (and abuse) of the rules and processes. As the economy pivots in fundamental ways to meet net zero carbon emissions, and to grapple with climate risk (which includes financial and insurance components), companies will necessarily be at the foreground of this global project. Net zero by 2050 is a clarion call for accountability among corporations as key actors in the modern mercantile world.

This book analyses two intersecting elements within the paradigm of the scientifically established climate emergency:

- The corporation itself—how can the theory and practice of corporate law turn itself to providing sustainable solutions?
- Corporate governance—how should companies operate in an optimal way? What are the elements of law reform that should be examined?

These two constructs will occupy key terrain at the core of the solutions-enabled approach.

Companies delivering climate solutions

Given their popularity and importance as business entities, companies will necessarily play a key role in delivering climate solutions. The company is the pre-eminent commercial legal entity in advanced economies including Australia, the USA, and the UK. Companies attract disproportionate investment, the most risk capital from the largest number of investors, and far more than other business structures. They are invariably the largest private enterprises in developed economies by market value and by number of employees. The company is, however, a so-called 'creature of statute'; it is given legal status only via a process of registration. There is, therefore, a public dimension to what companies do, as well as their long-established private, for-profit motive.

Companies in Australia are governed by complex rules, principles, mechanics, and balancing of interests. The point now emerging, and arguably for the first time in corporate law history, is that those matters are threatened by a fundamental shift of parameters. This is because the coordinates of the wider ecosystem within which companies operate are transforming at phenomenal speed. In particular, the social context now combines with scientific evidence warning against business-as-usual as the planet moves towards dangerously high greenhouse emissions. This aggregates questions of social license together with the evolving scientific facts and consensus.

Corporations law

First, as regards corporations law which encompasses the mechanics, rules, and architecture of corporations embedded within the inquiry, what is a company and how does it operate to make a profit? The issues will involve whether we can and need to move away from a shareholder primacy model of corporate success? Or can there be a workable hybrid model that combines shareholder priorities with competing stakeholder concerns? What rules need to change and how can corporate law theory provide a robust platform to argue for these necessary changes? Private law companies are afforded generous public law advantages and yet this is rarely acknowledged within the contemporary commercial environment and the wider business habitat.

Corporate governance

Second, corporate governance, which is a 30-year international movement, is still in some degree of flux. It focuses on issues of accountability and stakeholder participation with an increasing examination of the social and the environmental 'bottom lines', the concerns of which are embedded within the questions why do companies exist for, for whom do they provide benefit? and to whom do they/should they owe responsibility? These questions in turn coalesce around the more fundamental question, how should a sustainable 21st company operate and by which increasingly international standards should it be held to account?

Given the ubiquity of corporations, they are seen as natural emanations of commercial activity. Their pervasive nature and popularity mask some important enquiries. How have they come to enjoy the privilege of incorporation and its allied benefits? Why are they given the twin pillars of limited liability for shareholders and separate entity status for the company, when other business entities do not enjoy the same fundamental advantages? How have then been so successful in promoting shareholder primacy above all else? These are each questions worthy of close analysis in the 2020s, but they take on urgency, especially given the climate emergency.

Corporations and their proxies have achieved a remarkable and durable effect: that they are part of the natural order of things and of the nature of business itself. Their ability to distract, obfuscate, and deflect from scrutiny is itself an act of ongoing temerity, if not genius. They hide in plain sight, enabled and underwritten by public rules and government largesse. This book examines long held but often obscured assumptions about corporations. Solutions lie first in shining light on the corporate realities and the unevenness of the business landscape, and then in law reform, more effective regulation, and scientifically informed legal innovation.

Australia as a renewables superpower?

The economic opportunity for Australia represented by the climate emergency allows the country to shift its political and economic axis. The emerging green economy and its elongated battle to emerge, particularly in a fossil-fuel enmeshed nation such as Australia, is a particular focus. Current corporate law and governance underwrite and enable the seemingly intractable industrial and post-industrial economy. How does Australia belatedly embrace the green economy and the kind of nation state sketched by experts such as Ross Garnaut?[2] The urgent, 21st-century challenge of making the transition to sustainability is enmeshed within this simple-to-state but wickedly difficult-to-navigate scenario.

The scope and structure of *Corporate Law and Climate Change*

Corporate Law and Climate Change (CLCC) examines established elements of company law—namely the attitudes encoded towards the assessment of risk and theory, and its governance in the rapidly emerging investment conditions. It examines these issues considering four recent Australian-based case studies and formulates points of conjecture and debate. These matters collectively are referred to in the book as the 'corporate climate'. This commercial ecosystem is more nuanced than may have been previously assumed to be the case. These evolving forces—which are social, scientific, and global in nature—together comprise a tipping point for understanding the theory of companies, for the assessment of risk by boards, and the governance of companies.

The economy will undergo a major transition in the impetus to achieve sustainability. The company will be a critical component at the centre of the forthcoming transformation. For some companies and industries (and indeed nations) resistant to acknowledging such current tectonic shifts, these issues are seen as illegitimate threats and fearmongering. By contrast, other companies are embracing the evolving order, viewing the situation in terms of opportunities for a paradigm change. As such, the social and the scientific forces are becoming global imperatives which threaten to constrain and undermine previously assumed corporate freedoms to legitimately operate in an enormous array of profitable fields which, in turn, provide the company, as a legal and commercial entity, with strong and ubiquitous appeal. Navigating these emergent threats and opportunities is the focus of *CLCC*.

Corporate Law and Climate Change is comprised of three Parts and contains ten chapters. The three parts are:

- Part One—contains an Introduction, Chapter 1, and Chapter 2. The latter provides an historical context to the development of key companies and of corporate techniques.

2 Ross Garnaut, *Superpower: Australia's low-carbon opportunity*, La Trobe University Press, 2020.

- Part Two—contains Chapters 3 to 6 and focuses on four Australian corporate case studies. These provide challenges, ideas, and solutions for corporations as discussed in Part Three
- Part Three—contains four chapters with an orientation on the future and the global project of achieving net zero carbon emissions by 2050. What will be the role of Australian corporations and the nation's corporate law and governance in achieving net zero by 2050?

References

Ross Garnaut, *Superpower: Australia's Low-carbon Opportunity*, La Trobe University Press, 2020.

Bill Gates, *How to Avoid a Climate Disaster*, Allen Lane, 2021.

1 Corporate law, climate change, and financial risk

1.1 Corporate law in Australia: a complex history of public and private law

1.1.1 The Constitution of 1901

A longitudinal view of the origins of Australian corporate law saw it symbiotically restricted and delayed as a federal project by the nature and wording of the Commonwealth Constitution. The Commonwealth was created in 1901 by the consent of the UK parliament. This was the result of a decade or more of debate, conventions, and consultation in the colonies and was enabled by the acquiescing role of the UK parliament to the UK sovereign. The Commonwealth is a creature of statute with enumerated powers in s.51 of the Constitution. Remarkably and surely by oversight, the framers of the Australian Commonwealth Constitution, 1901 did not give the Commonwealth regulatory or administrative power over new corporations. Section 51(xx) of the Constitution provides that:

> 51. Legislative powers of the Parliament
>
> The Parliament shall, subject to this Constitution, have power to make laws for the peace, order, and good government of the Commonwealth with respect to:
>
> (xx) foreign corporations, and trading or financial corporations formed within the limits of the Commonwealth.

This final sentence with its comma, and it reference to the past tense in the word 'formed' has proven to be the foundational issue of statutory interpretation whose resolution took a century of debate, litigation, and political manoeuvring. As a result, there is in addition to the usual type of case law about what it is companies do, a series of constitutional-related cases which provide the narrative to the Australian Commonwealth's fundamental lack of power as regards corporations. Hence, public law in the guise of constitutional law has provided a brake on the development and adventurism of corporate law as a national project. This has led to corporate law as narrowly focused on private contractual rights and shareholder primacy.

DOI: 10.4324/9781003263746-2

1.1.2 The development of corporate law in Australia

As a result of the constitutional limitations, the development of corporate law has been sporadic and its oversight has been through several informal but distinct phases:

1.1.2.1 Phase 1: 1901–1960—'piecemeal' development

Corporate law within the new Commonwealth was off to an uncertain start, given that the Commonwealth lacked the necessary power within s.51 (xx) of the Constitution to regulate companies. As a result, the Australian states each developed their own 'piecemeal' version of corporate law oversight. This approach was in place until the 1950s. After the Second World War, however, economic activity was increasingly national and so a form of national company law was needed.

1.1.2.2 Phase 2: 1960 to 1980 – the guiding hand of 'uniformity'

The solution eventually arrived and was based on Victoria's Companies Act 1958 (Vic). Each state used this Act as a starting point or template and modified it according to their own particular state needs. These were the Uniform Companies Acts variously passed by NSW, Qld, Victoria, WA, Tasmania, and SA in 1961 and 1962.

The schemes, however, grew unwieldy across the next two decades, and did so for several reasons:

- Each of the states amended their Acts, so that any notion of national 'uniformity' and consistency became diluted.
- There were episodes of corporate fraud with the growth of the stock market, requiring a national response.
- The international financial markets were becoming more complex, making it clear that a national approach was required.

By the late 1970s, it was again recognized that a political and legal solution with a nationally harmonious approach was a necessity if the Australian economy was to prosper in an increasingly connected world.

1.1.2.3 Phase 3: 1980 to 2000 – the era of 'cooperation'

Two decades of so-called uniformity were followed by a decade of the new model known as cooperation. The cooperative scheme involved a complex grid of legislative arrangements by the states and territories underpinned by the Companies Act 1981 (Cth). New problems emerged in the 1980s. These included the fact that any state at any stage could withdraw from the agreement. There were different bureaucratic arrangements in each state and territory as well as national regulation. The 1980s (infamous now for their 'greed is good' mantra including in Australia) had another series of corporate excess and fraud, including the stock market crash of 1987 and its aftermath.

As a result, the Hawke-led Labor government passed the Corporations Act 1989 (Cth). Before it came into law, NSW challenged its constitutional validity. It was clear that the Constitution was not able to provide an appropriate platform or legally robust supporting mechanism for 'cooperative federalism' for corporate law. It would not be until the year 2000 that the referral by the states provided a comprehensive political, legal, and commercial solution to enable the Commonwealth to pass the Corporations Act 2001, and in the same year the ASIC Act, setting up the regulator.

The Commonwealth's power over corporations remains conditional. There are two control mechanisms in the gift of the states: the corporate scheme needs to be renewed every five years; and if four of the six states (a numerical majority) so decide, the scheme can in theory be terminated. This arrangement has resulted in Australia's corporate law being modest in scope and focused on for profit entities as the dominant modus operandi.

1.1.3 Statute in the context of corporate law: a complex architecture but elusive in terms of principle

The post-World War 2 nation state has seen the relentless rise of statute and delegated legislation in both Australia and the UK. The apparently innocuous drafting oversight in the Australian Constitution created two distinct and persistent effects. Firstly, it resulted in constitutional gridlock where the Commonwealth was without power. This meant that corporate law in Australia was a state-by-state matter, and that it operated in small markets, thereby lacking an ambitious range. Secondly, Australian corporate law did not develop any grand design, let alone vision, because it did not have a national corporate law in mind. It took a century from 1901 to 2001 for there to be a Federal comprehensive corporate law. The current law reflects this long-standing piecemeal and atomized approach. As Bottomley et al. note regarding the Corporations Act 2001, it 'is an amalgamation of over a century of ideas about the nature of corporate activity and how it should be regulated'.[1] The authors go on to opine that:

> partly because of its history, the Corporations Act contains a mixture of drafting styles. Some provisions are worded in an open-textured manner that law down broad principles, allowing courts and regulators the opportunity to exercise interpretive discretion. Other provisions are lengthy, detailed and technical, attempting to deal with a particular issue in precise terms and to minimise the scope for regulatory or judicial discretion. In some instances this might be because Parliament has attempted to 'cover the field' of a

1 Stephen Bottomley, Kath Hall, Peta Spender and Beth Nosworthy, *Contemporary Australian Corporate Law*, Cambridge University Press, 2018, 37.

> particular problem. Another reason is that the legislation simply reflects the complexity of modern corporate and commercial transactions.[2]

Allied to the fact that the legislation is labyrinthine, is the long-held common law practice that the courts are in the first instance required to interpret the company's rules and regulations. As Christopher Bevan notes:

> The courts will attempt to give 'business efficacy' to the company's rules and regulations. Normally those rules are regulations are interpreted strictly. As many words and phrases are standard in most companies' constitutions and replaceable rules, courts may well follow previous decisions in their interpretation where they are on all fours with those under consideration. However, the courts will distinguish previous decisions where necessary.[3]

1.1.4 The 'conservative corporate law' of Australia

The Corporations Act 2001 is complex, multi-faceted, organic rather than organized, and without an overarching narrative, theme, or set of principles. As Jonathon Charkham has noted, a nation's corporate governance reflects a particular history and the collision of localized social, economic, political, and cultural vectors.[4] This is clearly the case in terms of Australia's 21st-century corporate law and governance provision. The public law limitations in the Constitution have enabled the narrow private law approach of the statute to flourish. Victoria Brumfield refers to 'Australia's conservative corporate law'[5] and notes that it 'remains in some ways stuck in the mindset from 30 years ago'.[6] As such, Australia's corporate law operates within proscribed theoretical confines, and is a clear example of shareholder primacy in action.

1.1.5 Australian corporate governance: is it any less conservative than corporate law?

Corporate governance in Australia is multi-faceted and includes the corporate law and self-regulation codes, the clearest example being the Corporate Governance Principles and Recommendations (CGP&R), published by the Australian Securities Exchange (ASX). Some scholars argue that this form of regulation is

2 Bottomley et al, n 1, 39–40.

3 Christopher Bevan, *Corporations Law*, 8th ed., Lawbook Company, 2011, 48.

4 Jonathon Charkham, *Keeping Better Company: Corporate Governance Ten Years On*, 2nd ed, Oxford University Press, 2005.

5 Victoria Schnure Baumfield, Chapter 12 'The Australian Paradox: Conservative Corporate Law in a Progressive Culture,' in Beate Sjafjell and Christopher M. Bruner (eds), *The Cambridge Handbook of Corporate Law, Corporate Governance and Sustainability*, Cambridge University Press, 2019, 161–75.

6 Baumfield, n 5.

more progressive than the corporate law.[7] It will be argued however, that similarly to corporate law, the sources and practices of corporate governance promote shareholder primacy as the dominant corporate paradigm. This is exemplified by the discussion in Chapter 4 regarding the 4th edition of the CGP&R.

1.2 The operating context of Australian companies, corporate law, and governance

1.2.1 The numerous advantages provided to corporations: strong economic dimensions

Companies in Australia have been afforded a range of distinct advantages over other potential business entities. These include at least 15 preferences. Companies:

- Can range from one member to many members; there is no effectively no upper limit for a public company in terms of size; the Commonwealth Bank of Australia has in the order of eight hundred thousand shareholders.
- Are separate legal entities from day one of their registration/incorporation.
- Have the legal capacities of an adult individual without legal impairment.
- Are provided with potential perpetual succession—they can theoretically outlive the current owners many times over.
- Provide their owner/member/shareholders with limited liability (referenced to the amount unpaid on shares).
- Provide mechanisms for financial returns to members through dividend income and the capital appreciation of shares.
- Provide mechanisms such that the shares can be transferred.
- Have their official start date as per the certificate of registration.
- Are given the imprimatur of state approval or a 'licence to operate' as per the registration process.
- Have automatic national reach under the Corporations Act 2001 (Cth)
- Have the benefits of a dedicated specialist national regulator, ASIC, paid for by the Commonwealth.
- Can borrow from third party lenders and enjoy the potential ability to raise share capital from members.
- Have national geographic reach to trade and operate under uniform rules within the whole of Australia.
- Have an advantageous taxation rate; the corporate rate of tax at 30% for large companies and 25% for those with revenues less than \$50 million[8] is less than the higher rates of tax for individual taxpayers.
- Enjoy flexibility of size and type, and thereby include micro, family, public, and listed companies.

7 Baumfield, n 5.

8 Australian dollar has been used across the book unless otherwise specified.

1.2.2 Companies: their political and social dimensions

In terms of Anglo-Australian corporate law theory, John Parkinson highlighted the thesis of corporate responsibility which is necessarily attendant with the exercise of corporate power.

Parkinson, a founding UK-based legal academic of theories about corporate social responsibility (CSR),[9] notes that large companies, especially valuable companies which are publicly listed on the stock exchange and which employ many people, are different from other interest groups in society because they have real 'social decision-making power' or influence in two ways:

- Directly through interest groups to make representations to government to influence government policy.
- Structurally because of the crucial role that boards and managers exercise over production, investment, and employment decisions which, in turn, shape the economic and political environment within which Governments make policy.[10]

These factors give large corporations enhanced bargaining power and particular special influence.[11] The question then is, how should large corporations act within this framework?

Parkinson notes that 'corporate freedom of action is bounded by law (the rights of employees, environmental controls, and so on) and constrained by markets, but within this limitation there is a core of real business discretion'.[12] Given its size and complexity, the corporate market is dynamic and includes mature players, mid-sized players, new entrants, and start-ups. As such, corporate minnows, gazelles, and behemoths operate in the same basic field of regulation.

1.2.2.1 Regulating multi-national companies

Multi-national corporate groups (MNCs) add another layer of regulatory complexity. This has been sheeted home by recent revelations in Australian about the use of confidential government tax information on-sold by international consulting firms. This has added to a sense of social disconnection with elite, well-resourced participants being subject to different rules and regulatory enforcement. This has a corrosive effect on public trust, particularly as regards large corporations. This came about as an extreme case of 'government dependence on business'[13] given the tunnelling out of the public service. John Parkinson notes three forms of problematic

9 CSR or corporate social responsibility is discussed in Chapters 4 and 8.

10 John Parkinson, *Corporate Power and Responsibility: Issues in the Theory of Company Law*, Oxford University Press, 1993, 19.

11 Parkinson, n 10, 20.

12 Parkinson, n 10, 19.

13 Parkinson, n 10, 19.

symbiotic dependence where business can get the upper hand in its relationship with government. These are:

- 'Inducements in the form of market and political benefits' for example, tax concessions and subsidies.
- The argument 'that governments must be cautious in their regulatory policies, avoiding 'excessive' regulation that might damage profitability; government that 'go too far' may be subject to direct pressure industry to dilute regulatory regimes'.
- '[C]orporate ambition that extends beyond influencing the detail of regulation'; in this regard, Parkinson cites M.D. Reagan who noted that 'corporations are not only much concerned to protect their own immediate legislative interests, but are reaching out in an attempt to create a business-oriented political and social framework within which all public decision-making would be constrained. Instead of the society channeling business decisions within the bounds of public interest, the corporations seek to channel public-interest decisions within business-interest bounds'.[14]

This last scenario captures some of the malfeasance at large in the recent international tax episode concerning PWC.[15] The same basis premise applies: is there the regulatory will to rein in behaviour as regards climate change?

1.2.3 Pressures on corporate law and governance in the next decade

In this book it will be argued that corporate law will come under pressure in the next decade. The activities that companies undertake in responding to addressing climate concerns and how they go about achieving those aims will be as crucial to progress as an established legal specialist ambit such as environmental law, with its essentially limited, post-application focus on the granting of licenses, approvals, and conditions.

The modern company in Western nations such as the UK and Australia is a descendant of trading techniques first given a level of sophistication some 2,000 years ago by the Roman Empire. Entering transactions and binding contracts, the limited liability of owners, risk taking, capital ventures, and collaborative projects—each of these are critical features of the company. The company is by far and away the most popular business vehicle; it covers the full spectrum of size and capacities from the one-person company to the million-member entity, and the complex multi-national corporate web. The company lies at the fulcrum of commercial activity in a modern mercantile economy. Its centrality is such that the work done by and on behalf of companies will be pivotal to a scientifically approved and sustainable social, political, and economic order.

14 M.D. Reagan, *The Managed Economy* (1963), at 129-130, as quoted in Parkinson, 21.

15 PWC Australia is alleged to have given advice to the government and then on-sold this confidential information to private clients.

There will be some comparative analysis, mainly with the UK. The so-called Anglo-Australian axis of corporate law is useful from a historical perspective, given the symbiotic development of aspects of this area of the law.

1.2.4 Corporations: invested with perpetual succession (at least in theory)

By contrast, the corporation is established via the incorporation process with perpetual succession being at least a theoretical possibility in terms of its future as a distinct legal entity. Perpetual succession is a bedrock condition of the corporate form; the company as a separate legal entity may outlive its current directors and shareholders and may still be around in centuries to come. A level of financial acuity and savvy stewardship is, of course, required by successive boards and senior managers. This topic is returned in the discussion on sustainable corporations in Chapter 9.

1.3 Climate change and the advent of the climate change movement

The start of the modern-day climate movement is often attributed to Rachel Carson's book, *Silent Spring* in the early 1960s.[16] Carson's seminal, academic work questioned the wide-spread use in the post-WW2 period of fertilizer sprays and insecticides. Her theories were rebuffed by special interest groups and she was subject to widespread and orchestrated personal and professional disparagement. The 1960s was also the period when corporate law in Australia, whilst state by state in format, was championing the rights of shareholders.

1.3.1 The post-WW2 acceleration of carbon emissions

Companies have long been part of the problem in creating global heating, particularly since WW2 and the nostalgia for the high-growth decades of the 1950s–1980s,[17] but they must also now be part of the solution in getting to net zero by 2050. Effective companies—those producing goods and services with net zero (or better) emissions—will be at the forefront of necessary innovation to meet this scientific goal. For this to occur, there needs to be guidance in the form of effective regulation and oversight, governance, and corporate law. This requires long-term consistent, project-based, political will. This book examines how to make companies fit for their 21st-century purpose—which is to make a profit, but also crucially to provide solutions to the existential challenge. It critiques the theory and practice of corporations (both for-profit and NFP), and the relevant law, governance, and regulations. It outlines some of the ways that these facets can be better aligned to enable companies to succeed in achieving this society-wide goal. How can

16 Rachel Carson, *Silent Spring*, Houghton Mifflin, 1962.
17 Thomas Piketty, *Capital in the 21st Century*, Belknap, 2014.

innovation and adaptation via the company be mobilized in such a way as to meet this challenge in a low growth economy which seems to be prevalent in the 2020s?

1.3.2 The paradoxical arguments plaguing the climate emergency debate: science versus politics

Global heating is regarded by the scientific community as an emergency. It affects all aspects of modern life including social, economic, political, security, and legal. The disparity, though, is a fundamental one. Its scientific basis has led to wicked political and economic problems. Science is observational and data driven. Politics is increasingly partisan and passionate in the forms of populism seen in many countries. Within this paradoxical realm sits the corporate form.

1.3.3 Climate change and the clash between science and belief

Climate change scepticism has seen the science of climate change converted into questions of belief. As such, climate change has moved into the political realm and an increasingly fractious discourse. The starkest example of this was the Trump administration's decision to remove the US from the Paris Agreement of 2015, followed by the Biden administration reinstating US involvement in it in 2021.

What were considered issues of personal belief are now substantial matters of scientific fact. Whilst the politics is still volatile, the science has moved steadily and inexorably in one direction. As will be discussed, financial risk has recently begun to move in tandem with this scientific trajectory. This set of interrelated, international market-based financial and risk developments will necessarily impact the economic model of nation states, and in turn the role of companies, corporate law theory, and governance.

1.3.3.1 Recognition of the climate crisis: politics catching up with the scientific consensus

President Barack Obama, in the 2013 State of the Union, put it in simple binary terms between believing in a series of coincidences or relying on evidence-based science and scientific information produced by qualified experts at scale. He said:

> for the sake of our children and our future, we must do more to combat climate change. Now, it's true that no single event makes a trend. But the fact is the 12 hottest years on record have all come in the last 15. Heat waves, droughts, wildfires, floods – all are now more frequent and more intense. We can choose to believe that Superstorm Sandy, and the most severe drought

in decades, and the worst wildfires some states have ever seen were all just a freak coincidence. Or we can choose to believe in the overwhelming judgment of science - and act before it's too late.[18]

1.4 From climate change to the climate emergency

1.4.1 The persistence of business as usual

The issue of climate change has largely been dealt with in two realms to date: the scientific, and more broadly, current and political affairs. Science has to this point led the way, but even then the scale and urgency of the problem has been widely recognized for only a few years. As David Attenborough notes, 'the term Anthropocene was only proposed in 2016 by a group of eminent geologists'.[19] Until very recently, the literature in the law and business categories has been largely focused on 'business as usual', and the status quo. It reflects a steady-state view of economics and society more broadly.

Furthermore, the specialisation approach is historically dominant in law; climate change represents a paradigm shift for which existing legal categories and cataloguing are not yet prepared. Emerging corporate law theory links law with economics, societal values, sustainability, and climate change.[20] It is predicted that this field will become far more prominent in coming years; an inter-disciplinary approach will be critical. For law, it represents the challenge of seeing historically narrow and apparently stand-alone areas of endeavour as more inter-connected and cross-cutting.

1.4.2 The recognition of the climate crisis

The ecological 'world clock' is at one minute to midnight. As the IPCC notes, time is of the essence,[21] and 'the 2020s will indeed be the decisive decade in addressing today's Climate Emergency'.[22] Indeed, 'the scale and urgency of the climate challenge is clear. The risk is not linear, we need a step change'.[23] It is 'the defining issue of our time … demanding an unprecedented sense of urgency, courage and shared vision'.[24]

18 The State of the Union Address, Remarks by President Obama 12 Feb 2013 https://obamawhitehouse.archives.gov/the-press-office/2013/02/12/remarks-president-state-union-address.

19 David Attenborough, *A Life on our Planet*, Penguin, 2020, 215.

20 Beate Sjafjell and Christopher M. Bruner (eds), *The Cambridge Handbook of Corporate Law, Corporate Governance and Sustainability*, Cambridge University Press, 2019.

21 https://www.ipcc.ch/report/sixth-assessment-report-cycle/.

22 Jonathon Porritt, *Hope in Hell: A decade to confront the Climate Emergency*, Simon and Schuster, 2020t, xv. See also Christina Figueres and Tom Rivett-Carnac, *The Future We Choose: Surviving the Climate Crisis,* Manilla Press, 2020.

23 Pollinationgroup.com.

24 Porritt, n 22, foreword.

By contrast, the so-called 'hockey stock graph' developed by the US climate scientist Michael Mann remains the single most compelling and pertinent illustrations of the point[25]; the last two recent centuries and recent decades within those centuries confirm compounding effect of CO_2 emissions,[26] rising temperatures,[27] and other linked phenomena. There is a compounding factor at play. After six decades since *Silent Spring*, the world has finally moved on to acknowledge that there is a climate emergency. That is, a rate of change which is measurable, unprecedented, unpredictable, but widely thought to be highly dangerous if not checked and balanced.

Indeed in Australia, several senior ex-armed services members and security practitioners in an open letter wrote that having 'witnessed up-close the devastation of war and crisis, we consider that climate change now represents the greatest threat to the future and security of Australians'.[28] This intervention was because of political gridlock in Australia on sufficiently recognizing the climate emergency as late as 2022. The resort by politicians is a useful device for broadening the arguments. The importance of neutral voices is also referred to in President Obama's State of the Union address in 2013 where he refers to such a group within the US context:

> I propose we use some of our oil and gas revenues to fund an Energy Security Trust that will drive new research and technology to shift our cars and trucks off oil for good. If a nonpartisan coalition of CEOs and retired generals and admirals can get behind this idea, then so can we. Let's take their advice and free our families and businesses from the painful spikes in gas prices we've put up with for far too long.[29]

This statement now appears prescient, given it was more than ten years ago. The US presidential election of 2024 appears to offer a stark choice: a return to the future with increased oil, gas, and coal production, or continuing with the project of global renewables leadership. Corporations occupy the spaces within both camps.

25 Michael E. Mann, *The New Climate War: the fight to take back our planet*, Scribe, 2021.

26 Micha Tomkiewicz, *Climate Change: The Fork at the End of Now*, Momentum Press, LLC, 2011, 19, shows this in relation to carbon dioxide concentrations as observed at Mauna Loa Hawaii between 1950 and 2010, and similarly at the South Pole.

27 Micha Tomkiewicz, n 26, showing mean annual global temperatures at page 20. The global temperature data starts to be collected in the 1880s, the first time there is a wide geographic distribution of mercury thermometers (invented by Gabriel Fahrenheit in 1714).

28 Lisa Cox, 'Climate crisis is greatest threat to Australia's future and security, former defence leaders warn', *The Guardian*, 23 March 2022.

29 The State of the Union Address, Remarks by President Obama, 12 Feb 2013 https://obamawhitehouse.archives.gov/the-press-office/2013/02/12/remarks-president-state-union-address.

1.4.3 Resistance to the climate crisis

Whilst the science seeks to promote a one planet approach, there is a persistent multi-nation view of the economics and politics of the problem which seeks always to project scepticism and the folly of doing more than one's share. Successive aggregated states of the climate reports have spelt out the folly of this approach, and as engendering a too little, too slow collective outcome.

The complexity of the climate crisis is increasingly recognized. As the climate scientist, Micha Tomkiewicz, has observed:

> the issue of anthropogenic causality of climate change is a complex issue and encompasses vast domains of our intellectual, physical, moral, political, and economic world … and … the observations from which we draw much of our understanding span an equally broad spectrum.[30]

The multi-faceted challenges of the climate emergency are such that it has been described by Timothy Morton as a 'hyperobject'—that includes 'entities of such vast temporal and spatial dimensions that they defeat traditional ideas about what a thing is in the first place'.[31] The climate emergency and the challenge of net zero by 2050 is both an imaginative construct of the present, and yet it is future-focused and abstract. Many people are working in the direct interface or space of the emergency—for instance, climate scientists, bureau of meteorology experts, academics, and designers of built structures. Others, such as farmers and those living in fire or flood prone areas, are exposed to it on a regular basis. For many others, they may not be direct participants, but thinking and worrying about the climate emergency takes up a lot of psychological energy on a day-to-day basis.

It is also an unprecedented issue at community and nation-state levels. It has distracting, punitive effect. It carries a high cost to capital in all its variations—whether it be economic, social, political, or environmental. As a subject, it defies boundaries; it is increasingly present on nightly summative news bulletins with their reports of storm and fires, of cyclones and hurricanes and record-breaking heat. This can be relegated by the consumers of news merely to weather discussion, or it can be acknowledged as part of an emerging and accelerating set of tipping points and climate switches. The global weather in 2023 has been scientifically verified by the US-based National Aeronautics and Space Administration's (NASA) Goddard Institute for Space Studies (GISS) as the hottest year on record.[32] As Gavin Schmidt, director of GISS has advised:

> The exceptional warming that we're experiencing is not something we've seen before in human history. It's driven primarily by our fossil fuel

30 Micha Tomkiewicz, n 26, xxii.

31 Timothy Morton, *Hyperobjects: Philosophy and Ecology after the End of the World*, University of Minnesota Press, 2013.

32 https://www.nasa.gov/news-release/nasa-analysis-confirms-2023-as-warmest-year-on-record/

> emissions, and we're seeing the impacts in heat waves, intense rainfall, and coastal flooding.[33]

The climate emergency fills questions about the future. It concerns young people in an often traumatic, dystopian way. It is like no other conversation we have had because it has no boundaries and no simple solutions. It is endured by every living creature on the planet. It affects every human being and it has many victims, particularly those people suffering front-line effects in poor nations but with very little contribution to the cause of the issue.

The climate emergency is complex and unprecedented because it presents a global challenge requiring a country-by-country effort, and a whole-of-society approach. The crisis demands a multi-faceted, inter-generational strategy comprising not less than tangible, credible, and measurable actions, together with robust accountability mechanisms. At this point, this is not likely.

Whilst the stated target of net zero by 2050 is now widely accepted as the timeline relevant to addressing the climate crisis, it may be urgent to many stakeholders, but for others it is a long time to set in motion doubt and obfuscation. This has resulted in a political fault line which has coalesced in Australia around the target of net zero carbon emissions by 2050 which the science tells us entails action on a continuum. The issue, however, is that political cycles are typically very short run, particularly in Australia where they are three years or less, four years in the US, and five years in the UK. Political instability, however, means that short-term electioneering and increasingly fractious debate dominate, as opposed to the elucidation of longer-term policy. Developing policy outcomes that survive the next administration is increasingly fraught and unpredictable.

The Paris 2016 UN Conference Of the Parties (COP) commitments are a case in point. President Obama signed up in 2016, only for Donald Trump to declare the US out in 2017, and then President Joe Biden re-joined in 2021. This leads to wildly varying positions ranging from climate action being viewed as a first order priority, to Trumpian denialism. This does not bode well for the 2050 target, because three decades encompasses multiple election cycles and it leads to a selectivity of political approach, rather than focusing on the scientific consensus. As the climate scientist Micha Tomkiewicz has noted:

> because many of the issues relate to rather long-range projections ('end of now'), the public discussion invites cherry picking- pursuing a certain agenda, choosing the evidence to support that agenda, and ignoring evidence that points in other directions. Such a process creates polarized positions that reinforce and feed on each other. This kind of dynamic reduces the issue to one of arbitration.[34]

33 NASA, n 32.
34 Micha Tomkiewicz, n 26, xxii.

Net zero by 2050 may be an organizing principle, but the level of complacency it entails is disturbing. A just-in-time mindset is proving hard to shift.

1.5 Linking corporations and nations to the climate emergency

The field of 'sustainability-related study of corporate law and governance' is very recent and can be traced to the work of Beate Sjajfell and Christopher M. Bruner.[35] Their edited *Handbook* contributes an Australian perspective to the project. They refer to 'the convergence of crises that we as a global society face' and they identify three of these being:

> the environmental emergencies ultimately threatening humanity's existence, notably climate change and catastrophic biodiversity loss; the undermining of the economic bases for functioning societies, combined with rising inequality, leading to populism and unrest; and the lack of resilience and resulting instability of our financial systems, making new financial collapses more likely.[36]

1.5.1 Climate change and the Australian export economy: the reality of the multiplier effect

The Australian context is particular and the numbers behind Australia's climate change problem are revealing. Australia has just 0.3% of the worlds' population, but it produces 1.2% of the world's CO_2 emissions.[37] This is a quadrupling effect which makes it among the highest per capita polluters in the world. Australia is producing four times its 'fair share' on a per individual basis. By any equitable measure, this is not sustainable.

1.5.2 The major emitters of CO_2: nation states

Nation states are the major emitters, and the biggest three national emitters are the USA, China, and India. Emissions are highly concentrated. As Ian Goldin notes, 'in fact, just three countries—the US, China and India—and the European Union account for more than two thirds of global carbon emissions.'[38]

Recognition of this concentration needs to be factored into finding effective, efficient, and time-critical solutions. Goldin rejects the idea of finding slow and

35 Beate Sjafjell and Christopher M. Bruner, Chapter 1, 'Corporations and Sustainability,' in Beate Sjafjell and Christopher M. Bruner (eds), *The Cambridge Handbook of Corporate Law, Corporate Governance and Sustainability*, Cambridge University Press, 2019, 1–12, 1.

36 Sjajfell and Bruner, n 35, 1.

37 See for example, Matt McDonald, 'How to answer the argument that Australia's emissions are too small to make a difference, *The Conversation*, 18 June 2019. https://theconversation.com/how-to-answer-the-argument-that-australias-emissions-are-too-small-to-make-a-difference-118825.

38 Ian Goldin, *Rescue: From Global Crisis to a Better World*, 2021, 174.

cumbersome global solutions that assume wide-spread equality in terms of the creation of the problem. As such, he argues for a targeted participatory model. He writes that:

> Insisting we reach global consensus on these hugely important issues can lead to gridlock, as the more participants there are in global negotiations the harder it is to reach consensus. Most problems can be resolved by much smaller groups, including coalitions of a critical mass of countries, cities, companies and communities.[39]

Many cities around the world have declared net zero targets, as have councils, states, and provinces within federal systems. This demonstrates the potential for a widespread political buy-in at all three levels of government within a nation state such as Australia with its distinct local, state, and federal arenas of powers.

1.5.3 Enlisting tangible climate action by the major corporate carbon emitters

There is clearly some overlap between the biggest national emitters and the biggest corporate emitters. The US has since WW2 had the biggest proportion of multinational corporations. On the other hand, nations such as China and Russia have state-owned enterprises which dominate the economy and produce the most carbon. The biggest corporate CO_2 emitters, however characterized, have been dominant in terms of the problem of rapidly rising CO_2 emissions. For instance, it was reported in 2017 that 'just one hundred companies have been the source of more than 70% of the world's greenhouse gas emissions since 1988.'[40] The Carbon Majors Report detailed the concentration of emissions produced by the largest global companies and 'pinpoints how a relatively small set of fossil fuel producers may hold the key to systemic change on carbon emissions.'[41]

The concentration of big emitting companies highlights the relevance of the thesis put forward by Ian Goldin. Quick, effective change and quick wins can be produced by ensuring the key players and the protagonists occupying the central area of concern come together and vary their behaviour. The solution starts at the core, not the periphery—being the many minor emitters—and not with the whole because it is unrealistic to get everyone inside the room to agree. This latter all-or-nothing approach has led to a degree of fatalism in Australia. This is worth noting in two domains. First, Australia has long argued that it is a minor emitter responsible for a little over 1% of CO_2. Successive conservative governments have thereby argued that the many bigger national players, particularly China, need to do more before Australia acts. There is no sense in Australia, as a G20 nation, setting an example to the rest of the world, given this orthodoxy. Second, at a

39 Goldin, n 38, 174.

40 Tess Riley, 'Just 100 companies responsible for 71% of global emissions, study says', *The Guardian*, 10 July 2017.

41 Riley n 40.

more local level, an ETS or Emissions Trading Scheme was proposed in 2009 in Australia by the Rudd Labor government but was rejected by the Greens party because it was not considered good enough; this has since been referred to as 'the perfect being the enemy of the good.' The politically charged 'climate wars' in Australia have wracked the polity ever since, and demonstrate the folly of seeking idealism in the first iteration of innovation, rather than adopting a test, observe, and improve model much more aligned with a scientific approach.

As such, early compromise by the core constituency political actors is a far better approach than an unachievable purity benchmark which delays the project. It also references the whole political and economic discourse. The cohort of Australian voters sought finally to put this debate into the historical archives by electing the Labor government in May 2022.

1.5.4 Corporate emitters concentrated in certain industries: the fossil fuel behemoths

The Carbon Majors Report identified four investor-owned companies within the top 12 corporate emitters in the 27-year period covering 1988 to 2017. These were Exxon Mobil in 5th place, responsible for 1.98% of emissions in this period; Royal Dutch Shell in 9th place, responsible for 1.67% of emissions; BP PLC in 11th place, responsible for 1.53% of emissions in this period; and Chevron in 12th place with 1.31% of global emissions.[42] Two of these are UK based, and two are US based. The domination of the Anglo-US economies is clear by reference to these fossil fuel companies. Australia, similarly, reflects a fossil fuel bias. BHP Billiton comes in 20th place, responsible for 0.91% of emissions, and Rio Tinto in 24th place, responsible for 0.75% of emissions in this longitudinal period.[43]

Many of the major emitters are state-owned enterprises including China Coal, the number one polluter responsible for 14.32% of emissions; India Coal at number six, responsible for 1.87%; and Russia Coal at number eight responsible for 1.86%.[44] The list is comprised of fossil fuel entities covering coal, oil, and gas. The national significance of coal is illustrated by the fact there are several national coal companies in the top 40 polluters including Poland Coal, Kazakhstan Coal, and Ukraine Coal.[45] Coal is endemic in terms of geography and systemic in terms of political economy.

1.5.5 The two-thirds problem: advanced nation states and global corporations

It is clear from an analysis of carbon emission at the nation state and the corporate level respectively, that there is a two-third, one-third divide. The core constituency

42 Riley n 40.
43 Riley n 40.
44 Riley, n 40.
45 Riley, n 40.

of nations and of companies make up about 70% or just over two thirds of the problem in their respective fields. They need therefore to be part of the solution. They need to be the first movers in setting out plans for and achieving net zero. The case is political, economic, and financial, and it is also a moral imperative. The leading emitters need to lead by example. Failing to do so simply delays the problem and exacerbates the issue for future generations.

The IPCC 2023 Summary for Policymakers also confirms this differential in emissions.[46] Emissions are essentially a high SES or socioeconomic status problem. Affluent nations produce disproportionate emissions across the five areas of carbon emissions discussed by Bill Gates which include plugging in, making things, growing things, getting around, and keeping cool and staying warm.[47] As the IPCC 2023 Synthesis Report makes clear, in 2019, 35% of the global population lives in countries where the per person annual emissions of carbon dioxide are more than 9 tonnes, whereas 41% of people live in countries emitting less than three tonnes per capita. Put another way, the 10% of households with the highest per person emissions contribute 35–45% of household-based carbon emissions, whereas the bottom 50% contribute just 13–15%.[48]

1.6 New and emerging versions of risk: climate-related financial risk

This chapter acknowledges the apparently existential nature of climate change, the 'hyperobject' nature of this challenge, and its effect upon the evolution of commercial activity, most pressingly, the company. Law, as an evidence-based discipline, should as a preliminary matter be open to being informed by the present weight of scientific consensus. The climate emergency is now widely acknowledged as a scientific reality (and increasingly as a political one, too) but Australia has until recently represented a salient case of a modern political economy in denial. Incumbency and vested interests, particularly in relation to the long-held hegemony of the fossil fuel industry, means that successive Australian governments have operated in defensive mode and to implicitly protect those interests.[49]

This remains the case even though most of the Australian population takes climate change seriously; for example, Australia has the highest percentage take-up of renewables in the way of solar panels in the world, and possibly also has the requisite resources to be a renewable energy superpower.[50] This is the fraught

46 IPCC, 2023: Summary for Policymakers. In: *Climate Change 2023: Synthesis Report. Contribution of Working Groups 1,2, and 3 to the Sixth Assessment Report of the Intergovernmental Panel on Climate Change* [Core writing team, H. Lee and J. Romero (eds)]. IPCC, Geneva, Switzerland, pp. 1–34.

47 Bill Gates, *How to Avoid a Climate Disaster: the solutions we have and the breakthroughs we need*, Allen Lane, 2021.

48 IPCC, 2023: Summary for Policymakers, n 46, Paragraph A.1.5.

49 Judith Brett, 'The Coal Curse: Resources, climate and Australia's future', *The Quarterly Essay*, 2020, 1–78.

50 Ross Garnaut, *Superpower: Australia's Low Carbon Opportunity*, La Trobe University Press, 2019.

national debate around the four corporate case studies which form the focus of this book. Therefore, Australia offers valuable lessons about the social, economic, and political challenges now relevant to corporate law and theory.

A key challenge of the climate emergency, as referred to, is the pace and scale of change. The narrative vectors are numerous and simultaneously engaged in one form or another and include the scientific, environmental, social, political, commercial, financial, economic, and legal elements. They have different trajectories and speeds. As we see in Chapter 5, the concept of legal climate-related risk, particularly for directors is emerging quite rapidly. Whilst some of these vectors remain as lag factors on nations like Australia adopting more urgent action, particularly the political realm with its short-term, party-political mind-set, some areas such as the financial and insurance realms are moving at a rapid pace.

The scientific and the financial realms as regards the climate emergency have increasingly begun to move in lockstep. Internationally, this is evidenced by investor titans such as Blackrock moving out of fossil fuel investments.[51] In Australia, it is evidenced in more prosaic ways by flood insurance premiums rising steeply, or insurance not being available at all to home owners.

1.6.1 Developing global best practice

Global best practice starts with regional ambition and a viable project. The EU's CBAM or carbon border adjustment mechanism is one such example. It came into force in October 2023. It is 'the first phase of the world's first system to impose CO_2 emissions tariffs on imported steel, cement and other goods as the EU tries to stop more polluting foreign products from undermining its green transition.'[52] Whilst the EU bloc will not collect any carbon dioxide emission charges at its borders until 2026, October 2023 is significant because it

> marks the start of an initial phase of the Carbon Border Adjustment Mechanism (CBAM) when EU importers will have to report the greenhouse gas emissions embedded during the production of imported volumes of iron and steel, aluminium, cement, electricity, fertilisers and hydrogen. Importers will from 2026 need to purchase certificates to cover these CO_2 emissions to put foreign producers on a level footing with EU industries that must buy permits from the EU carbon market when they pollute.[53]

51 Larry Fink, 2022 Newsletter to CEOs, https://www.blackrock.com/corporate/investor-relations/larry-fink-ceo-letter.

52 Philip Blenkinsop and Kate Abnett, 'EU launches first phase of world's first carbon border tariff', Reuters, 30 Sept 2023, https://www.reuters.com/business/environment/eu-launches-first-phase-worlds-first-carbon-border-tariff-2023-09-30/.

53 Blenkinsop and Abnett, n 52.

As to the rationale for the measure the European Economy Commissioner Paolo Gentiloni has said the aim is to:

> encourage a worldwide shift to greener production and to prevent European manufacturers relocating to countries with lower environmental standards. It is also meant to prevent them from losing out to foreign competitors while they invest to contribute to meeting EU targets to cut the bloc's net emissions by 55% by 2030 from 1990 levels. The European Commission says the border levy is in line with World Trade Organization rules in that it treats foreign and domestic firms alike and allows deductions from the border fees for any carbon prices already paid abroad. 'CBAM is not about trade protection. It is about protecting the EU's climate ambition – and seeking to raise the level of climate ambition worldwide.'[54]

As a result of the EU initiative, other governments are stepping up in this area of carbon pricing. For example, the Australian government is consulting on the idea of an Australian version with the consultation period running until October 2024.

1.7 Conclusion: the role of corporations in meeting net zero emissions by 2050

Examination of corporate law theory has been supressed in large part due to the binary which operates at the core of companies. That is, limited liability of the owners, and the separate legal entity status of the company. These two, essentially closed structures sit at the heart of companies. This pronounced architecture has driven a particularly narrow view of companies. Indeed, it can be argued that form has given rise to function. This was not the case until the latter part of the 19th century as is examined in Chapter 2. The essential mechanics of the limited company system today are essentially global. They are so ingrained that the company is assumed by many to be agnostic, and that is not informed by values or political dimensions. The history of the foundational concepts is traced in Chapter 2. They reveal several contested influences. Hence, the modern legal fiction that the structure of companies provides a value-free paradigm. That structure brilliantly appealed, at the same time, to the captains of industry and to the working class. It covered left and right political dimensions. It provided the illusion of the alignment. This is much like China's Evergrande corporation where employees have been encouraged to become active investors and would-be entrepreneurs. Part 2 covering Chapters 3 to 6 refers to several case studies in which the scope of the emerging climate risk is being realized as having clear financial implications. In particular, the emerging concept of climate-related financial risk is explored in Chapters 5 and 6.

54 Blenkinsop and Abnett, n 52.

References

David Attenborough, *A Life on our Planet*, Penguin, 2020.

Christopher Bevan, *Corporations Law*, 8th ed., Lawbook Company, 2011.

Judith Brett, 'The coal curse: Resources, climate and Australia's future,' *The Quarterly Essay*, 78, 2020, 1–78.

Victoria Schnure Brumfield, 'Chapter 12: The Australian Paradox: Conservative Corporate Law in a Progressive Culture,' in Beate Sjafjell and Christopher M. Bruner (eds), *The Cambridge Handbook of Corporate Law, Corporate Governance and Sustainability*, Cambridge University Press, 2019, 161–175.

Mark Butler, *Climate Wars*, Melbourne University Press, 2017.

Rachel Carson, *Silent Spring*, Houghton Mifflin, 1962.

Jonathon Charkham, *Keeping Better Company: Corporate Governance Ten Years On*, 2nd ed, Oxford University Press, 2005.

Christina Figueres and Tom Rivett-Carnac, *The Future We Choose: Surviving the Climate Crisis*, Manilla Press, 2020.

Ross Garnaut, *Superpower: Australia's Low Carbon Opportunity*, LaTrobe University Press, 2019.

Joelle Gergis, *Sunburnt Country: The History and Future of Climate Change in Australia*, MUP, 2018.

Ian Goldin, *Rescue: From Global Crisis to a Better World*, Sceptre, 2021.

IPCC, Intergovernmental Panel on Climate Change, 2021. https://www.ipcc.ch/report/sixth-assessment-report-cycle/.

IPCC, Summary for Policymakers. In: *Climate Change 2023: Synthesis Report. Contribution of Working Groups 1,2, and 3 to the Sixth Assessment Report of the Intergovernmental Panel on Climate Change* [Core writing team, H. Lee and J. Romero (eds)]. IPCC, pp. 1–34. https://www.ipcc.ch/report/ar6/syr/downloads/report/IPCC_AR6_SYR_SPM.pdf.

Michael E. Mann, *The New Climate War: The Fight to Take Back Our Planet*, Scribe, 2021.

Timothy Morton, *Hyperobjects: Philosophy and Ecology after the End of the World*, University of Minnesota Press, 2013.

John Parkinson, *Corporate Power and Responsibility: Issues in the Theory of Company Law*, Oxford University Press, 1993.

Thomas Piketty, *Capital in the 21st Century*, Belknap, 2014.

Pollinationgroup.com.

Jonathon Porritt, *Hope in Hell: A decade to confront the Climate Emergency*, Simon and Schuster, 2020.

Beate Sjafjell and Christopher M. Bruner (eds), *The Cambridge Handbook of Corporate Law, Corporate Governance and Sustainability*, Cambridge University Press, 2019.

Beate Sjafjell and Christopher M. Bruner, 'Chapter 1: Corporations and Sustainability,' in Beate Sjafjell and Christopher M. Bruner (eds), *The Cambridge Handbook of Corporate Law, Corporate Governance and Sustainability*, Cambridge University Press, 2019, 1–12.

Micha Tomkiewicz, *Climate Change: The Fork at the End of Now*, Momentum Press, LLC, 2011.

2 Corporate law history, hubris, and failing to assess risk

Trends from the East India Company to Kodak

2.1 Hubris and failing to assess risk: the symbiotic nature of legal and corporate history

Tthe study of companies which have succumbed to the gravity of ignominious calamity and financial collapse invariably involves a unique and complex narrative of how smart, motivated people can chart a journey to success, only to then witness a collapse, through overconfidence, not paying attention, or hubris. It involves failing to take account of risk; however, it is described in relation to the company. It may be financial or reputational and it may vary over time in terms of its characteristics. This chapter examines key developments in this wider context of history, hubris, and failures pertaining to risk. It applies these important general markers to the particularities of two well-known corporations, the EIC and Kodak.

The company is today a ubiquitous trading and business entity. It has not always been thus. The narrative of legal history and the development of the company are inextricably linked. That legal history has been reduced to a minor formal theme in contemporary legal education represents a closing of a deeply important imaginative realm to understanding the past and affording flexible thinking about the future and its inexorable challenges. Legal history in general, and corporate law history in particular, has become a liminal topic within a crowded curriculum.

The themes of pooled resources amongst individuals, allowing for the entity to be more dynamic than the sum of its parts, is a foundation principle of the business or social organization. It is a strategy based on the combined strength in numbers, the pooling of resources, and with the wisdom of the crowd as a prevailing theme. Risk is shared, and rewards too. The binary nature of these themes is also apparent for the wisdom of the crowd may give rise to stubborn and inflexible groupthink. Individuals with dominant personalities or poor risk assessment may drive the business in fundamentally wrong directions.

There is a fundamental tension between the pooling of resources amongst individuals (a version of high trust and collegiality) and the desire for limited liability for the individual (and the fact that a shareholder can lose their investment to zero, but not beyond that exact point). As a mechanism between these two polarities is the confirmation of the company as a separate and distinct legal entity. These three linked themes—pooling of resources, separate entity status, and limited liability—may appear as naturally occurring and fundamental as any in law, but

DOI: 10.4324/9781003263746-3

their journey to being as key markers of the corporate landscape is idiosyncratic, and the subject of happenstance due to messy, non-linear historical developments.

The climate emergency provides renewed impetus for reflexive corporate practice. Understanding and appreciating company law history allows us to better understand what may be possible in the epoch of climate change and to further appreciate the concept of stranded assets, and the 'stranded company' particularly in the next three decades as corporations and economies navigate the journey to a net zero world.

2.2 The British East India Company—a case study in corporate power

The key facts about the East India Company (EIC) are familiar to many generations of corporate law students. Their profundity, however, is worthy of further examination, given the urgent demands of the 21st century, and in recognition of the role that companies must play vis-à-vis the climate emergency. Given the range and importance of themes relevant to the EIC, the discussion is divided into four themes, namely: beginnings, zenith, decline, and legacy issues.

2.2.1 The historical and contextual importance of the East India Company: corporate practice being ahead of corporate law theory

The argument to be advanced in this chapter by reference to the East India Company is that the company was a legal device in practical and commercial terms for quite some time before it was later formally conceptualized and drawn in detail via legislation. Corporate law theory was essentially *ex post facto*. This reflected the economic and political realities of the late 1500s and the 1600s. There was much work to be done abroad, and competition to grasp the fabled riches on offer was fierce. The East Indies, or the Far East as they were then variously referred to, encapsulated a wide geographic and imaginative realm, from modern India and Bangladesh in the western region, to the modern-day archipelago of Indonesia in the east. To a relatively impoverished Europe, this huge swathe of the world promised untold mammon and wealth far greater than existed with the geographical confines of Europe.

For the English, the East India Company was the way to fix a pressing problem of the nascent state. At the end of the 1500s, the Dutch had outflanked the English and were far better established in the Far East.[1] The EIC was the business vehicle to take on the Dutch. Hence, the practice of international mercantilism came first, and well ahead of developed principles of company law. Getting the company working efficiently, and becoming highly profitable, were the twin first orders of business. As such, the 17th and 18th century were largely about the practice of generating efficient profit. This coincides with the advent of the EIC in the year 1600, and its

1 William Dalrymple, *The Anarchy: The Relentless Rise of the East India Company*, Bloomsbury, 2019.

ebullient trajectory to its zenith at the end of the 1790s. The EIC was the corporate poster child of this nearly 200-year period.

By contrast, the 19th century gave rise to pause, for the theory behind the corporate form and the broad application of company law was only belatedly developed in that century. This coincided with the growth of a wider range of corporations generally and with the decline of the EIC in particular.

2.2.2 The beginning of the EIC: from a modest start in London, 1599

The rise of the company, as a means of doing business and of making profit on an international basis, particularly from the late 1500s onwards, was symbiotically linked with two other key features which enabled, underpinned, and reinforced one another. These were imperialism and sailing ship technology, respectively.

2.2.2.1 Imperialism and European nation state projections of power

Imperialism was not a singular project. Rather, it involved multiple emanations of international power and conquest—versions of Imperialism—by various European nations such as Holland, Spain, Portugal, France, and England. These were projections of statecraft, and of royal consequence beyond the confined geography of Europe. Nationalism and internationalism went hand in hand. The idea of domestic Englishness developed in tandem with projections of international power, as it did likewise for other European powers. They effectively treated the rest of the world as a franchise to be divided, conquered, and carved up. There was a competitive frenzy of imperialist outreach as historical enmities within the close quarters of Europe meant that long-warring nations cast an increasingly global net.

2.2.2.2 The use of the trade winds and the development of sailing ship technology

The second feature was the advances in navigation and sea power. It can be seen in hindsight that long-range, sea trade routes did much to build and consolidate the jostling and ruthlessly competing modern 'Empires', each with European bases and headquarters. The geographer and historian Lewis Dartnell traces the maritime history of Portugal from the 1400s.[2] As the Portuguese sailed farther south, tracking essentially down the west coast of Africa, they would be slowed down if they simply followed the same route home. They discovered, by trial and error, that if they headed far enough west out into the Atlantic Ocean, the currents and the prevailing winds would carry them home quickly and in relative safety, given time at sea increased the odds of mishap and malnutrition. The Portuguese referred to this technique of fast passage as 'the *volta do mar*—the turn, or return of the

2 Lewis Dartnell, *Origins: How the Earth Made Us*, Penguin, 2018, particularly Ch 8, 'The Global Wind Machine and the Age of Discovery'.

sea'.[3] Hence, increasing knowledge of the different wind bands and ocean currents[4] revolutionized long-distance navigation from Europe to Africa and beyond. These large bands or 'stripes' of prevailing wind, which went, depending on the latitude, in a strong east to west, or west to east direction, and north to south and south to north direction, were brilliant natural conveyor belts allowing the looping of the Earth's vast sea-water surfaces and oceans to be navigated in astonishingly short periods. Trip times were able to be cut by impressive amounts. These naturally occurring features of geography and meteorology at the core of the Earth's systems revolutionized long-range mercantile trade, travel, and—by extension—versions of the emerging corporate entity. The pattern of winds were a primary feature and an implicit, intangible asset of the mercantile enterprise able to adapt and to take advantage of this beneficence.

Hence, the *volta do mar* became, for the Anglicized world, and for the English at least, the trade winds. These were the super-efficient, sea-bearing highways which increased travel speeds exponentially. As such, they also increased profits and reduced risk. The trifecta of corporate success was, in turn, undergirded by the basics of physics, geography, and oceanic systems.

These contextual conditions gave rise to a new form of competition. The versions of companies with 'East India' in their designation comprised a confederation, an oligopoly, and the first loose version of an international franchise. No fewer than five or more European nations set up an East India trading arm, Portugal, Spain, England, Holland, and France. At the end of the 1500s, an intricate history of more localized maritime seafaring gave rise to long-range and hazardous ventures. There were several East India companies emanating out of Europe. In this sense, it was the first consortium and oligarchy dividing up an international market. In fact, the British version of the East India Company was somewhat late to the party. It had been roundly reduced to by-stander status by two combining effects. The first was that the Dutch were well ahead in naval and military terms, and had established themselves in the then Far East, particularly Indonesia. The second was the lack of focus because England's attention had been to the west of the Atlantic, and on North America. By the late 1590s, the conditions were ready for a southerly and south-easterly bound focus towards modern India.

2.2.3 The formal establishment of the EIC

Early companies such as the EIC were established in very limited ways. They could be set up by royal charter granted by the Crown, or they could be established via a private act of parliament. The EIC was an example of the former. It was a

3 Dartnell, n 2, 219.
4 Dartnell, n 2, 250.

large foreign trading company, as was the Hudson Bay Company.[5] As Bottomley et al. note,

> the principal advantage of incorporation by charter was that it was accompanied by an exclusive right to conduct trade in a specific geographical area. These monopoly rights and special privileges were the main reason for seeking incorporation, as a recompense for the risks involved in undertaking large-scale foreign trading ventures.[6]

The EIC royal charter was granted by Queen Elizabeth I on 31 December 1600 to the original 218 petitioner investors.[7]

The EIC began with four vessels refitted and setting sail from the Thames Docks. The oceans to the west of Africa were the equivalent of new motorways being 'discovered' and delivered on the need for rapid southward sailing speed. The distances to be travelled were formidable. More than 7,000 nautical miles between London and Cape Town in South Africa. Added to this was another 6,500 nautical miles between Cape Town and Kolkata/Calcutta in the east of India. It is no wonder therefore that the East India Company used the remote island of St Helena[8] located in the west of the South Atlantic, later famously the last outpost of Napoleon, to substantially speed up the return trip. The EIC adopted the *volta do mar* technique to its advantage to ensure its return trips on sailing ships laden with valuable treasures, taxes, and 'loot'[9] made it safely back to the EIC headquarters in Leadenhall St, London and distributed in kind to its shareholders.[10]

2.2.3.1 The pooling of resources

The pooling of resources provides for two critical advantages. It enables growth and it spreads risk. The first EIC charter was granted to more than 200 investors. The nature of the business—provisioning sailing ships to make the hazardous journey to the other side of the world and their safe return—required intensive capital and the ability to embrace long term risk. This provided for scale. The company could, in theory, grow rapidly. The multiplier effect in the case of the EIC was extreme. It went from a modest entity housed in the London docks to the first global corporate multinational, and arguably the first ruler of modern geographical of India. It turned known concepts upside down; it became 'a state in

5 Stephen Bottomley, Kath Hall, Peta Spender, and Beth Nosworthy, *Contemporary Australian Corporate Law*, Cambridge University Press, 2018, 4.

6 Bottomley et al, n 5, 4.

7 Dalrymple, n 1, 9.

8 Dartnell, n 2, 222.

9 Dalrymple, n 1, 139-140.

10 In the case of Australia, the so-called 'roaring 40s' provided a quick trip for European ships seeking to make it to Java and East Asia. If, however, the vessel travelled too far, too fast, disaster struck and so many a ship ran aground on the coral reefs off the west coast of Australia. The Batavia is the most infamous of these instances, known as 'The Island of Angry Ghosts'.

the guise of a merchant'.[11] The company became the preferred business vehicle in this respect. It overtook the more established concept of partnership. This takeover of the commercial and mercantile realm by the company entity began in earnest in the 19th century.

2.2.3.2 Exploiting ambiguities in the EIC's foundation documents

William Dalrymple makes the point that the charter was more generous and expansive than the founders had hoped, and they took full advantage of the gaps and ambiguities in the documents to build the influence and reach of the fledgling company. Crucially the charter provided a generous start-up concession, in the form of 'freedom from all customs duties for their first six voyages'.[12] It also gave the EIC a

> British monopoly for fifteen years over 'trade to the East Indies', a vaguely defined area that was soon taken to encompass all trade and traffic between the Cape of Good Hope and the Strait of Magellan, as well as granting semi-sovereign privileges to rule territories and raise armies.[13]

The potential powers and the economic geography of the company's charter were enormous as the Crown would later realize. Indeed, the charter's wording

> was sufficiently ambiguous to allow future generations of EIC officials to use it to claim jurisdiction over all English subjects in Asia, mint money, raise fortifications, make laws, wage war, conduct an independent foreign policy, hold courts, issue punishment, imprison English subjects and plant English settlements.[14]

The company seemed to perfectly occupy the lacuna in the elongated period created by the decline of the divine right of Kings and Queens, and the rising of the modern parliamentary system of the nation state of Britain. For more than 150 years from its inception in 1600, the EIC went largely unchecked. It was an entity of its era.

By the middle of the 19th century, however, it was out of political largesse, Crown granted goodwill, and time. It was seen as a legal creature of a bygone era, and fundamentally out of step with the times. It had assumed enormous might. As Dalrymple notes, 'the wording of the EIC's charter left open from the beginning the possibility of it becoming an imperial power, exercising sovereignty and controlling people and territory'.[15] Each of these had occurred as the EIC had grown largely unchecked. The scale, influence, and excess of the EIC provides lessons for governments and corporations alike.

11 Dalrymple, n 1, 3, quoting Edmund Burke.
12 Dalrymple, n 1, 9.
13 Dalrymple, n 1, 9.
14 Dalrymple, n 1, 9.
15 Dalrymple, n 1, 9.

2.3 The zenith and decline of the EIC

The EIC grew so big and powerful, and did so quickly, that a fall was inevitable. There was literally not enough world for it to grow at the rate it had for nearly two centuries from 1600 to the 1790s. As a company it was like some super athlete ahead of its time, setting records which could only be aspired to by subsequent generations. In this regard, its story contains lessons for companies now and into the future. Its zenith and fall were marked by the fact that it was no longer simply a corporate structure. It had become a complex hybrid organization which defied simple categorization. It was no longer merely a company, nor was it a formal political entity like a nation state. It occupied the uncertain but flexible space within these polarities. It required new concepts and new language to sufficiently proscribe its ambit in the latter 1700s when its power was such that it challenged the English state. The EIC with its HQ in London, and its vast reach across India, was the equivalent of a global superpower with few checks on its acts abroad, and little accountability for its panoply of powers. It needed to be reined in and controlled, and that is what the English state and the succession of reigning monarchs set about doing until the company's demise was complete in the 1870s.

2.3.1 Becoming a company state: the two stages of development

In his book *The Anarchy*, William Dalrymple traces two distinct stages of development of the EIC. The first stage between 1600 and the mid-1700s saw the company

> which had started off as an enterprise dominated by privateers and former Caribbean pirates ... transformed itself ... into a relatively respectable international trading corporation, with a share price so reliable its stock was regarded almost as a form of international currency.[16]

By the 1760s, the company 'was transformed a second time, not just as a vehicle of trade operating from a scattering of Indian coastal enclaves, but as the ruler of a rich and expansive territorial empire extending across South Asia.'[17] In this regard

> a business empire had now emerged from its chrysalis, transformed into an autonomous imperial power, backed by a vast army, already larger than that of the British Crown, and was poised now to exercise administrative control over 20 million Indians. A body of merchants had been transformed into the de facto sovereign rulers of much of northern India.[18]

The vaulting ambition of the EIC was noted contemporaneously by the famous classical economist, Adam Smith, who referred to the hegemonic binary of the

16 Dalrymple, n 1, 201.
17 Dalrymple, n 1, 201.
18 Dalrymple, n 1, 202.

EIC, in its guise as a Company State, as being 'a strange absurdity'.[19] Such was the EIC's domination, that the 'stage was set for the most extraordinary corporate takeover in history'.[20] India was described as

> groaning under the Anarchy. Laws have no power of sanction, morals are corrupt to the ultimate degree, the people groan under a multitude of vexations, all caused by the decay and confusion into which this once-great empire has fallen, with legitimate rulers having neither credibility of authority.[21]

As such, it was a splintered geography and set of fiefdoms in the 1790s simply not able to resist the EIC's strategy of domination. In effect, in that decade, a corporation had subsumed a continent.

2.3.1.1 The essential 'takeover' of India by the EIC

The EIC was afforded a series of advantages which together afforded it unprecedented power. It was a company operating in uncharted territory with many of the powers, and few of the accountabilities, of nation states. First, it had been given charter status by the Crown with monopoly rights. The charters were typically granted for 20 years at a time. This meant that time was of the essence. Heightened risk taking and a 'devil may care' attitude became part of the company's operating DNA. The company was not imbued with the theoretical nicety of perpetual succession. It needed to project power, generate a profit, and to make its mark in short order. Secondly, it was adept at splicing its fortunes with the financial backing of powerful players, including members of the royal family and parliamentarians. This was a form of nascent but effective lobbying and regulatory capture. Thirdly, it was able to establish and grow its own military force. The assumption of corporate power was thereby not merely by economic logic, or the power of monetary persuasion, but was enforceable by military might. And fourthly, the EIC benefitted from the classic agency gap—the managers and personnel on the ground in places far-flung from England could do as they pleased—and so they acted first and only explained, as needed, months later. The truth and reality of events could be softened, if not expunged by the passage of time and the latest harvest of profiteering.

In the EIC's role in India, this was not merely a commercial takeover in the narrow sense of one company assuming control of the shares of another. It was a commercial entity in name, appearance, and style, subsuming the formal and informal vestiges of power sufficient to run a vast swathe of world geography. It was, in effect, a total subjugation of a myriad of people by an ostensibly simple for-profit entity. It included all aspects of governing, including revenue and tax raising. It enveloped the exercise of power in all its guises—settlement of disputes,

19 Dalrymple, n 1, 202.
20 Dalrymple, n 1, 202.
21 Dalrymple, n 1, 144.

security issues, and military might. The usual constitutional aphorism of peace, order, and good government vested in a state polity had been assumed by the EIC and transmogrified into a 'whatever-it-takes' version of the same. This is the cautionary tale of what occurs when a private company assumes a position of such dominant public authority.

2.3.2 Defying 'commercial gravity' for more than two centuries: the EIC as an outlier company

At its simplest, imperial ascendancy by England was achieved via the corporation, and by way of the trade winds. The business model of the EIC was both brilliant and ruthless. The company was granted royal charter by Elizabeth I. The preferred business entity was the company. Its choice, in turn, of the elite vehicle of its time for maximizing profits was the sailing ship. It also chose cut-throat managers and built considerable armies on the ground in India comprising English and Indian troops. It cut deals and traded in takeovers by force. It perfected elements of being a protection racket by extracting high prices for businesses to be free of harassment and for the settlement of disputes. It drove very hard bargains whenever it could but it could not keep defying gravity. It was a complex version of a one-company corporate bubble, and the South Sea Bubble of the 1720s was an early warning sign.

The world's geography and natural attributes of circulating sea currents and prevailing winds, combined with the artifice of the legal entity, provide the EIC with an early version of super profits. It was a corporate example of being an 'outlier', making optimal use of the combination of fortunate timing, location, opportunity, and context. The EIC was the right company at the right moment in history, and in a related context, Malcolm Gladwell has identified striking patterns which can combine to underwrite success for individuals.[22] The EIC willed itself into the middle pages of the history books. It was grandiose and belligerent, and if there was a gap to be exploited or an opportunity to be compounded, its protagonists did not hesitate. Those executives on the ground in India, acted first and sought permission later.

2.3.3 The slow demise of the EIC: 1790 to 1870

By the 1790s, the ruling elites in metropolitan London were clearly vexed by the distant corporate behemoth child which the EIC had become. The world was for turning and the headquarters of the Empire would relentlessly reassert dominion over the EIC across the course of the next six decades. In effect, the EIC had become an ignoble and dangerous version of the corporate enterprise, altogether too powerful, unpredictable, and dangerous. Effecting accountability would involve a

22 Malcolm Gladwell, *Outliers: The Story of Success*, Penguin, 2008, 75.

series of checks and balances, but reining back in the hitherto uncontrolled entity would also nearly bring down both the nation and its imperial project.

By 1833, the EIC had lost its Charter to trade, and in 1859, its assets in India were nationalized.[23] The EIC ceased its operations in 1874, with very little fanfare.[24] The EIC was 'finally wound up, ending the anomaly whereby a corporation had governed a subcontinent'.[25]

2.4 The 19th century company: corporate law theory seeking to catch up with corporate techniques

While companies until the latter part of the 19th century were often complex international trading agglomerations, like the East India Company, and with their own founding act of Parliament, the basic parameters of the corporate form were in place. They were comprised of many stockholders or owners, were run by managers, and benefited from the labour and endeavours of employees and others. The famous case of *Salomon v A Salomon & Co Ltd*[26] in 1897 set up the conditions for the small or high street company, and so the 20th-century growth of companies was enabled. The basic architecture was in place. Owners (being also referred to as shareholders or members) invested risk capital. Directors or managers ran the company on their behalf, and the company was conceived of as a separate entity able to enter contracts, sue, and be sued. Limited liability for owners was also particularly attractive, as Richard Posner notes:

> uncertainty increases the expected value of a company's stock, particularly a new company's, because the sky is the limit to the value the stock may attain (think of Google), but the potential loss is cut off at zero. (This asymmetry is the unintended consequence of limited corporate liability- that is, of the fact that the shareholders cannot be sued for the losses of the corporations.) So go for it—reach for the stars.[27]

The East India Company was arguably the first global company and the first to allow its shareholders to 'reach for the stars' by investing in the limits of the then-known world. As noted, the British East India Company was just one of several European versions of the same type of enterprise,[28] so that the 1600s and the nascent corporate form went together. That founding ethos, exemplified by the EIC, still finds echoes in the behaviour and actions of modern companies, such as Rio Tinto discussed in Chapter 4.

23 Dalrymple, n 1, 390.

24 Dalrymple, n 1, 391.

25 Niall Ferguson, *Empire: How Britain made the Modern World*, Penguin, 2003, 178.

26 *Salomon v A. Salomon and Co. Ltd*, [1897] AC 22.

27 Richard A. Posner, *A Failure of Capitalism: The Crisis of '08 and the Descent into Depression*, Harvard University Press, 2009, 85–6.

28 Ferguson, n 25, 20–4.

2.4.1 The development, decline and fall of commercial arrangements other than the company

Across the nearly three centuries of the East India Company's existence as a major trading organization, commercial and mercantile entities developed in fundamental ways. By its demise in the 1870s, the EIC had in effect been central to establishing a widely adopted if not globally relevant precedent to the effect that the company was thereafter regarded as the pre-eminent business entity. In the UK and in Australia this was, and certainly remains the case.

2.4.1.1 Pre-cursor business entities: merchant guilds, the charter company, and the joint stock company

In the EIC's earliest days around 1600, other types of business entities were dominant, and these were variously the merchant guilds, the joint stock company, and the charter company. The EIC was originally established in this latter form. Merchant guilds

> were not corporations ... but they had many of the characteristics of corporations such as the ability to own property. The guilds were broadly similar to modern trading associations in that the traders operated individually under the auspices of the guild, much as a lawyer practices through his or her membership of the state law society.[29]

Chartered corporations were granted charters of incorporation by the Crown. In the case of the EIC this provided exclusivity of rights and an effective monopoly of wide scope; as noted, the Charter granted in 1600 gave the EIC no less than the 'the exclusive right to conduct trade between England and the East Indies, Asia and parts of Africa'.[30]

Joint stock companies were a hybrid form of entity combining elements of the company and the partnership.[31] They had several features later adopted by corporations including a board of directors, internal rules, and a separate trading name.[32] In terms of architecture they

> were often set up as a partnership with a management committee holding the property under a trust (known as a 'deed of settlement'), with members taking shares (or rights) to a percentage of the profits if any were in fact made.[33]

29 Jason Harris, *Company Law: Theories, Principles and Applications*, LexisNexis, 2012, 7, referencing the Australian legal regulatory system.

30 Harris, n 29, 7.

31 Paul Redmond, *Corporations and Financial Markets Law*, Thomson Reuters, 2017, 27.

32 Harris, n 29, 7.

33 Harris, n 29, 7.

In this sense, partnership principles and notions of modern company law have been intrinsically linked.

2.4.2 The partnership concept as central to commercial legal history and the development of the company

If the criterion for commercial entity success had simply been reduced to the efficient pooling of resources, the partnership may have proven ascendant. The benefits of the partnership as a business vehicle were well tested because they were private and confidential, they efficiently shared risk, and they bore, as a signifying hallmark, fiduciary duties as between the partners. Indeed, in the Australian context the eminent High Court jurist Dixon J, later Chief Justice, noted in Birtchnell's case in 1929 that 'the relation between partners is, of course, fiduciary. Indeed, it has been said that a stronger case of fiduciary relationship cannot be conceived than that which exists between partners'.[34]

Crucially, the popularity of partnerships pre-dated companies. In the race for ascendancy, however, they lost out to the company from the middle of the 19th century onwards due to potential unlimited liability for partners. The gap between companies out front, with partnerships lagging someway behind, only widened as the take-up of companies accelerated from the beginning of the 20th century in the wake of the Salomon case.[35] The most famous corporate litigation established limited liability and separate entity status, and propelled the growth of the nascent high street enterprise which is today the backbone of the modern UK and Australian economies. So much so that whilst partnership law in Australia is state and territory based, there is a nationally applied criteria applied as to the allowable size of partnerships. The biggest partnerships in Australia are capped at 1,000 for accountants, as it happens. These limitations are set out in statute; to the ignominy of those who champion the choice of partnerships, the rules as to partnership size are set out in the Corporations Act 2001 (Cth). By contrast, the Commonwealth Bank of Australia (CBA), as the most widely held company, has more than 800,000 shareholders.

The paradox is that corporate law, applies rules to partnerships. As to the possible size of a partnership or firm in Australia, the nationally applicable set of criteria are as follows:

> **CORPORATIONS ACT 2001 - SECT 115**
> **Restrictions on size of partnerships and associations**
>
> (1) A person must not participate in the formation of a partnership or association that:
>
> a) has as an object gain for itself or for any of its members; and
> b) has more than 20 members;

34 *Birtchnell v Equity Trustees, Executors and Agency Co Ltd* [1929] HCA 24, (1929) 42 CLR, 384, 407.

35 Salomon's case, n 26.

unless the partnership or association is incorporated or formed under an Australian law.

Note: For the effect of a contravention of this section, see section 103.

(2) The regulations may specify a higher number that is higher than the number specified in paragraph (1)(b) for the purposes of the application of that paragraph to a particular kind of partnership or association.
(3) An offence based on subsection (1) is an offence of strict liability.

As s.115(2) provides, there can be exceptions to the limit of 20 partners. These exceptions apply to professional firms including:

- Lawyers; and
- Accountants.

Note that this section refers to associations also. Section 115(2) refers to regulations specifying the number of partners in different partnership contexts. This is set out in the Corporations Regulations as follows:

CORPORATIONS REGULATIONS 2001 - REG 2A.1.01
Size of partnerships or associations

(1) For paragraph 115(1)(b) of the Act, the number prescribed for a kind of partnership or association is the number specified in the following table for that kind of partnership or association:

Item	*Kind of partnership or association*	*Number*
1	(a) Actuaries, medical practitioners, patent attorneys, sharebrokers, stockbrokers or trademark attorneys (b) Partnerships or associations of the kind specified in subregulation (2)	50
2	Architects, pharmaceutical chemists or veterinary surgeons	100
3	Legal practitioners	400
4	Accountants	1 000

(2) For paragraph (b) of item 1 of the table in subregulation (1), the partnership or association is one that:
a) has as its primary purpose collaborative scientific research; and
b) includes as members:

i. at least 1 university; and
ii. at least 1 private sector participant;

whether or not it also includes government agencies or publicly funded research bodies.

(3) In subregulation (2):

"private sector participant" means an entity that obtains the majority of its revenue from sources other than Commonwealth, State or Territory appropriations.

From the information set out in s.115 CA2001, it is clear that different professions are afforded different levels of flexibility. Legal partnerships can comprise 400 partners; accountants by contrast, can have up to 1,000 partners, as noted. This configuration can be significant for international and global businesses. The so-called 'Big Four' accounting firms[36] are examples of globally configured businesses with strong Australian 'branches'.

The historical dimension provides confirmation that commercial entities can wax and wane in terms of popularity. What suits one epoch may not survive another. The climate emergency gives rise to new conceptions of the corporate form. In this regard, Australian corporate law has a useful legislative precedent; this is 'the introduction of No liability (NL) mining company in response to the Victorian mining boom'[37] in the mid-to-late-19th century. These entities are discussed in Chapter 7.

2.4.3 The emergence of the 'twin pillars' of corporate law

The twin pillars of modern corporate law are the separate entity status of the company and the limited liability of members.

2.4.3.1 The separate legal entity status of the company

The EIC ceased its operations in 1874, and just two decades later, the House of Lords confirmed the contours of the modern corporation in the Salomon case.[38] As such, the EIC

> represented a bridge between the older, guild-based, quasi-public enterprises confined to towns and professions, and the future modern corporation, separate from tis diverse membership base and trading for its own benefit shared amongst the members, although at the sole discretion of the management.[39]

Whilst the Salomon litigation solved a developing problem—the legal rights of the high street one person incorporated business; it unwittingly created a set of future problems which exists to this day. These include where to draw the line with outlier cases, particularly as regards the role of companies within corporate groups.[40] Separate entity status also references perpetual succession and the theoretical existence of the corporation to the ends of time. Whilst a nicety not taken advantage of by many companies, it is no coincidence that early adopters of

36 The Big Four accounting and advisory service firms (KPMG, Ernst & Young (EY), Deloittes, and PricewaterhouseCoopers (PwC)) are the four biggest professional services networks in the world, offering audit, assurance services, taxation, management consulting, advisory, actuarial, corporate finance, and legal services.

37 Harris, n 29, 12.

38 Salomon's case, n 26.

39 Harris, n 29, 8.

40 Janet Dine, *The Governance of Corporate Groups*, Cambridge University Press, 2000.

separate legal personality included monasteries. How to protect assets and grow the value of the enterprise was as recognisable a challenge to monasteries as it was to guilds and local government bodies.[41] The idea of ownership that goes beyond the lifetime of the current members is a powerful practical and spiritual prophylaxis.

2.4.3.2 The limited liability of members

The unlimited nature of partner liability means that the form has remained largely as relic of 19th century business practice. The spectre of potential personal bankruptcy hovers for each unlimited partner.

By contrast, the UK Companies Act 1855 provided confirmation of limited liability, and the nascent ability of small companies to set up outside the standard of the royal charter.

Whilst the liability of the member of a company limited by shares, on the other hand, may be called in at any time, depending on the relevant contract between the company and the shareholder, its floor is zero. A member can lose their investment, but no more than that, as Richard Posner, the US judge and law and economics scholar notes.[42] The two sides of the ownership equation are thus in place for shareholders; from zero to infinity. No other business can compete with this compelling mathematical construct reserved for the corporation. There are of course problems with limited liability and separate entity status. Corporations seek to bend the rules to their advantage. As Dalrymple notes:

> If history shows anything, it is that in the intimate dance between the power of the state and that of the corporation, while the latter can be regulated, the corporation will sue all the resources in its power to resist.[43]

Limited liability has been elevated in the 21st century to steadfast doctrine in Australia, even if in the colonial era it was a haphazard developmental journey.[44] To question it is seen as highly contentious. It was not always thus and need not be so in future. A degrowth economic model, for example, would mandate its review. Recognition of the climate emergency and the link with the corporation means that it is quite aptly ripe for reconsideration, but it would also require review of the regulatory mindset regarding companies, and unprecedented political will.

41 Phillip Lipton, Abe Herzberg, and Michelle Welsh, *Understanding Company Law*, 20th edn, Lawbook Co, 2020, 5–6.

42 Posner, n 27.

43 Dalrymple, n 1, 394.

44 Phillip Lipton, 'The Introduction of Limited Liability into the English and Australian Colonial Companies Acts: Inevitable Progression or Chaotic History?' *MULR*, 2018, vol. 41, 1279–323.

2.4.4 The development of Australian corporate law in the 20th century

At the end of the 19th century, the Salomon case provided a fundamental pivot point for corporate law in both the UK and Australia. It popularized the small, closely held family company as the new thread of wealth building and employment security. From the modest beginning, the House of Lords' decision has reverberated throughout the common law world and has ever since provided the central narrative in the untrammelled growth and continuous expansion of the corporation as the runaway commercial entity of choice. In this respect, the Australian corporate market has been a signal case in point, and the influence of the case was matter of binding common law in the whole of the 20th century before the national Corporations Act 2001 (Cth) was enacted.

As such, the last 120 years or so since the Salomons case has seen the explosion of companies, from micro businesses, family companies, and publicly listed corporations dominating the stock exchange. The advantages provided by the founding principles of separate entity status and limited liability have blossomed and expanded, giving rise to further legal and commercial advantages. These processes have been to the great advantage of companies but have also been to the effective detriment of other potential business entities. The practical initiatives have tipped the scales firmly in favour of the corporation; indeed, as early as the year 1911, the US philosopher and President of Columbia University, William Murray Butler wrote:

> I weigh my words, when I say that in my judgment the limited liability corporation is the greatest single discovery of modern times, whether you judge it by its social, by its ethical, by its industrial or, in the long run, after we understand it and know how to use it, by its political, effects. Even steam and electricity are far less important than the limited liability corporation, and they would be reduced to comparative impotence without it.[45]

Whatever the salience of these observations, the advantages of the limited liability company have been added to by the Australian corporate law arrangement and project. Provision over the last century, and particularly so with the advent of the Corporations Act 2001, have favoured the corporate form. Two decades in to the 21st century, the context for profit-seeking business entities in Australia is and remains firmly in place in favour of companies. They have been afforded distinct advantages over other potential business entities.

Addressing the climate crisis calls for renewed examination of the assumptions underpinning the corporation. A more politically astute and socially informed journey will be part of the new corporate landscape and the suite of demands placed on directors between now and 2050, and indeed beyond that line in the sand.

45 William Murray Butler, 1911, http://conversableeconomist.blogspot.com/2017/07/the-limited-liability-corporation-is.html.

2.5 The corporate legacy issues attributable to the EIC

2.5.1 The failure by the EIC directors to adequately assess corporate risk

The advent of corporate risk grew alongside the development of the East India Company. The challenges faced by the company were apposite, UK based investors, distant markets, and linking them were vessels operating at their seaworthy limits, and managers and employees delegated with high degrees of trust. Corporate law has embedded fiduciary concepts alongside related limiting devices such as the agency gap, and the notion of moral hazard. Alignment of interests are extant, and executive pay issues germinate from such conditions. The foundations of the modern corporation were tested and retested in the two and a half centuries of domination by the East India Company.

2.5.2 The advent of limited liability—and the creation, in turn, of competitive corporate law

As Jason Harris notes 'limited liability was a hotly contested issue in the 19th century. There were strong supporters and opponents to the introduction of limited liability'.[46] It became law in the UK in the mid-19th century in the Limited Liability Act 1855 (UK). Insurance companies and banks were excluded from its ambit.[47] Two main reasons are given for its introduction. The first was a domestic business factor. That is, small proprietors were being disadvantaged by unlimited liability and this was restricting entrepreneurial activity'.[48] The exposure of owners to unlimited liability—and the loss of assets and the prospects of bankruptcy—added to the asymmetries of contemporary small businesses. This UK-derived facet was added to by an early example of competitive, international, corporate law provision. In the case of limited liability this was evidenced by the fact that 'several European countries and a number of American states had allowed limited liability for some time'.[49] This is an example of law reform and innovation based on an international comparative approach, developing best practice by reference to solutions in other jurisdictions.

2.5.3 From the unlimited liability of partners to the limited liability of shareholders

In terms of basic historical analysis, corporations grew out of partnerships. Whereas partnerships saddled the individual partners with potential total liability of the business, the crucial inflexion point was the formal introduction in the middle of the 19th century in England of the limited liability of shareholders. As

46 Harris, n 29, 11.
47 Harris, n 29, 11.
48 Harris, n 29, 11.
49 Harris, n 29, 11 citing P Blumberg, *The Multinational Challenge to Corporation Law: The Search for a New Corporate Personality*, Oxford University Press, 1993.

variously owners, members and equity holders in the company, the shareholders were afforded the peace of mind unique to limited liability. The limit of liability is the total amount to be paid for the shares. If there are ten one-dollar shares, the liability is ten dollars, and not a cent more.

By contrast, partnerships held partners to account in theory to their last dollar or pound, and their last hectare or acre. The threat of debtor's prison loomed large. The 19th-century legislation was the first to formalize the limited liability of shareholders. This was not the result of simple linear events but a mess of competing issues and interests.

2.5.4 The lesson of hubris from the EIC corporate playbook

The East India Company has generated its own folklore. Its launch on the very last day of 1600 has meant that its 400th anniversary would give rise to a new round of analysis. And so it has come to be. Historical accounts paint an array of views, ranging from depicting the might of English imperiousness, to the worst of venal excess and corrupting overreach.

In the last two decades since the year 2000, the instances of greed, malfeasance, and war-mongering have been predominant themes in examining the EIC.[50] This is a reflection of seeking to understand contemporary issues of corporate excess, such as the dot com bubble of the late 1990s, and just a decade later, the Global Financial Crash of 2008–9. This sense that the edifice of capitalism itself was liable to collapse, and in need of major reform was a crucial theme For instance, Nick Robins writing in 2006 of his own professional journey notes that:

> As the new millennium opened, market euphoria was still in the air, though with hindsight the crazed dot.com bubble had already peaked on the last day of 1999. I was entering the world of socially responsible investing as the speculative surge started to implode, revealing malpractice on a scale not seen 1929. [the Great Depression].... Across the world, inquiries got underway to discover if it was just a few 'bad apples' at Enron, Worldcom and Tyco who were to blame, or whether the entire 'barrel' of corporate capitalism was at fault.[51]

Unfortunately, the GFC was imminent, and precipitated in its wake widespread and ongoing critique of a version of hyper-capitalism without due restraint. For example, William Dalrymple in concluding *The Anarchy* observes that:

> As the international subprime bubble and bank collapse of 2007–9 have so recently demonstrated, just as corporations can enrich, mould and positively shape the destiny of nations, so they can drag down their economies. In

50 Dalrymple, n 1.

51 Nick Robins, *The Corporation that Changed the World: How the East India Company Shaped the Modern Multinational*, 2006, Pluto Press, x.

> all, US and European banks lost more than $1 trillion on toxic assets from January 2007 to September 2009.[52]

Indeed it can be said that modern capitalism is roiling in a heavy sea as it lurches from crisis to crisis. The peaks and troughs are ever more extreme. Economic inequality and inordinate profit-taking are driving these vertical rises and steep, vertiginous falls.[53] The synergies between concepts of Empire and new forms of excessive capitalism remain. Dalrymple argues that US imperialism is heavily linked to surveillance-capitalism:

> as recent American adventures in Iraq have shown, our world is far from post-imperial, and quite probably never will be. Instead Empire is transforming itself into forms of global power that use campaign contributions and commercial lobbying, multinational finance systems and global markets, corporate influence and the predictive data harvesting of the new surveillance-capitalism rather than—or sometimes alongside—overtly military conquest, occupation or direct economic domination to effect its ends.[54]

2.5.4.1 The decadence and monstrosity of the East India Company

The recent account of the rise and fall of the EIC, *The Anarchy* by the esteemed Scottish historian, William Dalrymple paints a bleak picture of ongoing barbarity and Tarantino-esque violence, interspersed with periods of nation building. Takeovers by armed force, extraction of protection money, looting, and gouging local communities; it is not an easy read in many places. The presumed civility of economic theory and corporate law principle is not part of the account. Ever present is the motive of the EIC operatives (and by extension, its shareholders): the making of vast wealth by whatever means possible. Of course, this is a contested history, but this version paints a large canvas in swathes of red and crimson, marked by internecine warfare, barbarities visited upon local warlords, and violence of shocking scale and intent.

The lesson for governments and regulators is one of caution with the need for vigilant oversight. Of the state paying attention and being prepared to regulate and to step in from time to time, as required. To play an active role as societal guardian in relation to the potential tyranny of an approach favouring the shareholders of an essentially private fiefdom but afforded too much freedom. To bear in mind the fact that with corporate power comes responsibility, and that granting monopoly rights with very light-touch regulation and little working knowledge of operations on the ground sets the conditions for eventual mayhem. In the case of the EIC, the government in London was many steps removed from the action. The allowed the EIC managers to act only as necessary, to report in a *de minimis* way, and to craft

52 Dalrymple, n 1, 395.
53 Thomas Piketty, *Capital in the 21st Century*, Belknap Harvard, 2014.
54 Dalrymple, n 1, 397.

the correspondence. Delay and obfuscation were the order of the day, given the geography and the extant technology. The inverted hierarchy was multi-layered and included the senior managers, executives, directors, shareholders, and only then, the government.

The EIC to this day also suffers a reputational malaise. It has a degree of notoriety unmatched by other corporations. Its shadow is powerful and ever present, so much so that it can be mistaken as consigned to history. Its lessons are with us in plain view. Hence it bears re-examination for companies and corporate law, now and into the future. Its legacy is a multi-faceted case study in corporate power and excess. The lessons require generational renewal, lest they be forgotten or parlayed to the sidelines.

2.5.5 Modern-day corporate techniques and devices developed by the EIC

The company invention allowed an inversion to take place. The markets of China and India were ascendant societies and economies in the 16th and 17th century but by the 19th century, this had been reversed. The nations with corporate and seagoing capacity had become dominant. The theory and power of empire was enacted through the means of corporate control. There are several corporate techniques which the East India Company developed that are now part of corporate law. The first is the supremacy of shareholders within the rubric of the Anglicized company. Shareholders are the pre-eminent stakeholders in the company's fortunes, sitting comfortably ahead of employees, customers, or creditors. Shareholders provide risk capital in return for financial rewards, whether as dividends, extra shares, or an increase in the tradable value of shares. This has historically meant that the (Anglo-US-Australian) model of the company has been firmly one of shareholder primacy. By contrast, in nations such as Germany and Japan, the primary stakeholders have been employees.

Fundamental consequences flow from this orientation of the company. If this is the dominant narrative or motif, then essentially the means justify the ends. The company's overwhelming purpose is to enrich shareholders. How this happens, and its moral efficacy, is secondary. Where it happens also does not matter, and if it takes place in far flung corners of the world, geographically this is in no way an issue; in fact, it has the advantage of being out of sight and out of mind. This mode of operating was perfected by the East India Company. It traded in opium and spices; it featured a military and a police force; it was arguably the first public-private international consortium. It had essentially free reign whilst it engorged its shareholders in the UK and Europe. Shareholder primacy and nascent globalization went hand in hand and were reinforced by corporate law theory. The directors were directed by law to act in the best interests of the company. The company was an artificial legal entity. It had a legal personality, but no legal conscience. The early 20th case in the House of Lords, *Percival v Wright*[55] confirmed that 'the com-

55 *Percival v Wright* [1902] 2 Ch 421.

pany', in turn, meant the shareholders as a group. A brilliant circularity had been achieved, and this circulation finds faithful repetition in a key provision today of the Corporations Act 2001 (Cth).[56]

2.5.5.1 The EIC as the first company 'too big to fail', bailouts, and shocks to the state

The EIC was the first recipient of a mega bailout. This occurred in 1772 as result of famine in Bengal and huge losses incurred by the company. The monopoly rights vested by the royal charter meant that the EIC and the nation state were intertwined. This ran the risk that the company could drag the nation 'down into an unfathomable abyss'.[57] Echoes of this occurred in the wake of the GFC in Iceland in the three years from 2008 when the collapse of several of the nation's banks nearly brought down the national economy.

2.5.5.2 The EIC as a political power, a lobbyist of influence, and a self-interested advocate

Given its scale and provenance, the EIC mastered news means of lobbying government and the crown. It became an adept self-interested advocate, brilliant at exploiting loopholes and limitations in its founding documents. It used its charter to maximum effect. Where there was a gap or ambiguity, this was not an obstacle but a creative opportunity to be exploited. In this practice, it was the same blueprint that lawyers later devised to skirt limitations in the modern Memorandum and Articles of Association and the *ultra vires* doctrine.

2.5.5.3 The evolution of enterprise risk as first traced by the EIC

Risk for the EIC had started out as simple and linear. It focused on the safe passage of sailing ships and their return to London. The EIC's growth was in large part because of it becoming audacious exponent of the art of takeover, whether by stealth or by force. By the end of the EIC's dominance in the 1850s, it was managing the risk associated with political and mercantile power on a vast scale. It literally involved governing a vast continent. No company has ever stretched the nature and gradient of risk to such limits. From simple project risk to one enveloping the nation state and governmental risk, it was clear that the nation state, whether England or India, needed to reassert its hegemony over the brigands in charge of the EIC.

56 Section 181(1) Corporations Act (2001) Cth provides that (1) A director or other officer of a corporation must exercise their powers and discharge their duties: (a) in good faith in the best interests of the corporation.

57 Dalrymple, n 1, 395.

2.5.5.4 The EIC as the first multi-national company MNC

The EIC provides multi-layered lessons and insights including the fact that its corporate complexity was an early manifestation of the corporate group. The MNC requires a powerful home base. In response, the host nation needs in response to provide a clearly regulated domain. These issues were first raised by the EIC's rampaging success and remain elusive. As Dalrymple notes:

> The corporation- the idea of a single integrated business organisation stretching out across the seas- was a revolutionary European invention contemporaneous with the beginnings of European colonialism that upended the trading world of Asia and Europe.[58]

The potential of the corporation and the peril of corporate excess were embodied in the EIC.

2.5.5 The failure of regulation to reign in the EIC

Through a series of factors, the EIC was able to avoid the strictures of legislation and regulation. This is perhaps the foremost lesson of the EIC experiment. A company freed from moral, social, or legal responsibility is liable to run amok, especially when it is operating a long way from home. The EIC was the beneficiary over nearly two centuries of a nascent form of self-regulation. There were no developed codes, standards, or competitors. For much of that period it operated in a field of one. It was largely hegemonic and brilliant at exploiting the time and distance of operating many thousands of kilometres away, when the speed of communication (and by extension, accountability) could only operate as fast as sailing-ship speed.

The EIC example presses home the point that the government of the company's HQ is a vital cog in the proper and sustained oversight of the company. Alongside the invention of the company there remains the vexed issue of accountability:

> The 300-year-old question of how to cope with the powers and perils of large multinational corporations remains today without a clear answer: it is not obviously apparent how a nation state can adequately protect itself and its citizens from corporate excess. No contemporary corporation could get away with duplicating the violence and sheer military might of the East India Company, but many have attempted to match its success at bending state power to their own ends.[59]

The EIC is a case study in both corporate creativity and the fact that for much of its history, it operated outside any form of effective oversight.

58 Dalrymple, n 1, 394.
59 Dalrymple, n 1, 395.

2.5.5.1 *Was the EIC a* sui generis *company?*

One of the ongoing debates is how to categorize the EIC. This is problematic because the EIC was, in several respects, a *sui generis* company within its 250-year epoch. Its time as a legal entity was a combination of military, political, commercial, and economic power. It was the first global multi-national company. It was the first company to advance and perfect sophisticated forms of lobbying of political power. In its organizational complexity, it embraced both public and private power, particularly as regards having its own army. As such, it was for a considerable period, an entity essentially interchangeable with the contours of the nation state, and as such, it was increasingly a challenge to the expression of orthodox political power in the UK and in India. As noted, it was the recipient of a major government bailout having the advantage of public funds to alleviate essentially private financial distress. In its gargantuan size and reach, it was the archetypal example of being a company being 'too big to fail'.[60] It also stands as an example of corporate greed and excess, and the use and abuse of state and private power when the lines of responsibility are not clear. It was a ruthless manifestation of money-making in locations far removed from the owners. In this way, it was an example of hyper-capitalism—or profit at any cost. Each of these features is worthy of further consideration in the current period when the world is addressing the less than three-decade window to the 2050 deadline.

2.5.5.2 *The relevance of the EIC to the role of corporations in addressing the climate emergency*

The key point is that the climate emergency requires the mobilization of resources to meet it. The centrality of effective regulation to meet the climate emergency is a case in point. A company which is not sufficiently regulated will not have the ability to know when to stop. When is enough, enough? The company does not have a will or a conscience. There is no inherent self-correcting mechanism. By degrees, as the EIC advanced into a super-power, the state in effect retreated. The EIC treated its charter as a licence simply to maximize profit. There were no fetters or guardrails.

By contrast, if a nation state commits to climate neutrality by a certain date, typically 2050, then the regulatory agenda can be aligned with this aim. The United Nations and other international bodies can at least call out recalcitrance and disregard. This accountability is predicated on the finding of a scientifically informed climate emergency that is based, in turn, on an existential threat for the collective of nation states.

In turn, the nation state has levers it can use vis-à-vis companies housed in its jurisdiction. It can provide incentives and mete out disincentives. It can clearly

60 This phrase assumed resonance in the wake of the GFC.

delineate its economic priorities and its preferred pathways to reaching net zero by 2050.

2.6 The case of Kodak Eastman Company case study: the titan of the photography industry

The Kodak Eastman company became famous by developing a ground-breaking technology and device widely used for recording time and events. Its core business of film and cameras meant that it was recording the present and memorializing the past. Its fatal flaw was to take its eye off the future.

The EIC was a corporate titan whose footprint covered much of the world's shipping routes of the 17th to 19th centuries. In doing so, it linked Europe to the Far East. Out of the two-and-a-half-century juggernaut of corporate activity emerged the contours of the modern nation state of India. The EIC also tracked the rise, zenith, and fall of British imperial power. This was the company as central to the tectonic shifting of power within nascent globalization.

By contrast to the EIC, Kodak arose rapidly and in a dizzying fashion as part of the American economic ascent in the 1880s, and laid the social and cultural foundations along with other iconic, American-based corporations and brands for super power status in the 20th century. Jonathon Mantle's survey of 50 corporations which 'changed the world' between the EIC which commenced in 1600, up to Google in 1998, includes no fewer than 26 firms founded in the USA.[61]

The time linkage between the demise of one and the rise of the other is worthy of mention. The genesis of Kodak-Eastman was just a few years after the EIC went into dissolution. The EIC had experimented with many of the techniques that multi-national corporations (MNCs) have continued to develop, practice and perfect. The EIC's legacy is pervasive and wide ranging. By contrast, the case of Kodak Eastman is more singular. It was focused on a product that, for an extended period was dominant, but the company failed to see the technology changes on the horizon. Its demise was a late 20th-century example of fast moving in innovation and consumer choices.

2.6.1 The rise of the Eastman Kodak corporation

The whimsy of nostalgia is strong in the current US epoch. Tom Steyer, a candidate seeking nomination to be the presidential candidate in 2020 on the Democratic side, recounted with glorified reverie the country's dominance in the 20th century:

> America's eye for innovation and passion for solving big problems ushered in an era of unprecedented wealth creation and prosperity in the 20th century. If we hope to lead and reap the rewards of technological and economic

61 Jonathon Mantle, *Companies that Change the World: From the East India Company to Google Inc.*, Quercus Publishing Plc, 2008, 61.

superiority in this century, we now must win the race for climate technology that is already underway.[62]

The story of the Kodak company reflects this same rise, challenge, and fall. The Eastman Dry Plate Company was commenced by George Eastman in 1881. In 1884, he patented a paper-based film and four years later invented the Kodak camera. The company was renamed Eastman Kodak in 1892 and thereafter Kodak was a global brand for a century until:

> by the 1990s, in common with many of the great companies that began life in the 1880s and triggered the 'American century,' a company that had once been an American treasure had become a bureaucratic, sluggish and complacent corporation, constantly and unfavourably compared with Japan's Fuji. The company also had losses to match. Towards the end of the first decade of the 21st century, Kodak was still a company in turn-around. The billion dollar-plus loss of 2005 was halved in 2006, but the fight was on to reinvent the company for the age of consumer digital imaging and graphic communications.[63]

2.6.2 The demise of Kodak in 2013: seeking to maximize the litigation value of its historic patents

The direct and broad-based historical context relevant to Kodak filing for Chapter 11 Bankruptcy in 2013 was the global financial crisis of 2008. As Ayotte and Skeel note: 'The financial crisis generated increased attention on the importance of liquidity, and the dramatic consequences that can follow from illiquidity'.[64] They

> define a firm as liquid when it can borrow against its full value, or sell its assets for full value, on short notice. Firms that suffer from illiquidity may be forced into premature liquidation or going-concern sales at prices below their fundamental values.[65]

They observe that liquidity issues have become a major driver of Chapter 11 cases:

> Since the financial crisis, liquidity problems have been cited as the cause behind both the decisions to file for bankruptcy and the outcomes of many Chapter 11 cases.[66]

62 Tom Steyer and Abigail Ross Hopper, 'Voices: America is losing its superpower status to China. There's only one way we can get it back', *The Independent*, 15 February 2022.

63 Jonathon Mantle, n 61, 62.

64 Kenneth Ayotte and David A Skeel, 'Bankruptcy Law as a Liquidator Provider', *The University of Chicago Law Review*, Vol. 80, No 4, Fall 2013, 1557–623, 1559.

65 Ayotte and Skeel, n 64, 1560.

66 Ayotte and Skeel, n 64, 1559–60.

Kodak, the iconic film and imaging company suffered from this phenomenon. This was an ignominious end given it was part of the American imagination and central to the projection of international cultural power, in the same way as Walt Disney was for motion pictures.

Unfortunately for its directors, Kodak became a by-word for corporate complacency. The board did not appreciate, either through hubris or negligence, that it was involved in a fast-moving, technologically driven, highly competitive industry. It refused to embrace change and to acknowledge these tectonic shifts. As such, the company completely failed 'to capitalize on the trend away from traditional film and toward digital imaging'.[67] Instead, it adopted an idiosyncratic, circuitous, and high-risk strategy. Essentially the company 'shifted focus to monetizing its portfolio of imaging patents through litigation, licensing, and patent sales'.[68] This strategy simply exacerbated liquidity problems and left the company prey to the aggressive tactics of its competitors. As Kodak Eastman's financial position became more precarious 'it found that companies like BlackBerry, Apple, and HTC employed delay tactics to starve the company of cash and gain advantage in litigation'.[69]

With nowhere to turn, Kodak responded and in January 2012 filed for Chapter 11 bankruptcy. This was part of a belated strategy 'to buy time and free up cash, allowing Kodak to maximize the sale and litigation value of its patent portfolio and to reorganize around its core printing business'.[70] This was the last roll of the dice. As Ayotte and Skeel note, 'Kodak's lead bankruptcy lawyer explained to the court on the first day of the case: "We're here for liquidity"'.[71]

The GFC had fatally exposed Kodak's strategic failings. Whilst it owed and controlled a valuable portfolio of patents, it had become an illiquid company. It believed in its own iconic status. The irony for Kodak was that it 'filed for Chapter 11 bankruptcy protection, having succumbed to a digital revolution in photography that it helped to start'.[72] It was a company whose board was infused with misplaced optimism even at that point as 'the company's managers still hoped to escape from bankruptcy and have another shot at greatness by selling part of a portfolio of patents that experts valued as high as US $4.5 billion'. [73]

2.6.3 The contrasting fortunes of Fuji Xerox

Kodak's demise can be contrasted with one its main competitors, Fuji. Fuji Photo Film Co Ltd commenced in Japan in 1934 and thereafter was the Asian-based

67 Ayotte and Skeel, n 64, 1559–60.
68 Ayotte and Skeel, n 64, 1559–60.
69 Ayotte and Skeel, n 64, 1559–60.
70 Ayotte and Skeel, n 64, 1559–60.
71 Ayotte and Skeel, n 64, 1559–60.
72 Mark Harris, 'Snapping Up Kodak: The Shocking patent deal that nearly sank a technology giant', IEEE SPECTRUM.IEEE.ORG, *North American*, Vol 51, Issue 2, Feb 2014, 31.
73 Mark Harris, n. 72, 31.

competitor to Kodak. Whereas Kodak dominated photographic film sales in the US, Fuji did so in Japan. Until the Second World War, it made three types of film—photographic, motion pictures, and X-ray. After the war, it expanded into other technical fields like medical printing. In 1962, Fuji Xerox Co Ltd was set up as a joint venture between Fuji Photo Film Co Ltd and the UK-based company, Rank Xerox. This Anglo-Japanese joint venture meant that Fuji was a more diversified company, as opposed to Kodak with its fixation on physical film and its founder's hegemonic influence. Ultimately, the Fuji board was more strategic and savvier than Kodak's. For example, it became successful in the US market after sponsoring the Summer Olympics in Los Angeles in 1984. Kodak, by contrast, had passed up this same opportunity. Kodak also struggled to gain market share in Japan, Fuji's home base.

The 21st century saw the sharp rise in consumer demand for digital cameras and technology, and yet Kodak was still fixated on producing and selling physical rolls of film. Fuji embraced digital technology and together with its diversified business and more international outlook (embedded by business arrangements including the joint venture), it successfully navigated the first two decades of the new century. By the early 2000s, when Kodak was seeking to build a large, but little-profitable, digital camera business, the era of the smart phone had arrived and such devices would soon include a camera as a standard operating feature.

2.6.4 The aftermath of the Kodak corporation

Today, Kodak trades on and its share price is around $4. True to its original DNA, it is still focused on producing physical products such as movie film and hobbyist camera film, particularly given the advent of a strong 'nostalgia' market. The lessons of an ignominious Chapter 11 bankruptcy have been taken on board, however, and the company offers a diversified range of products including digital cameras. It is no longer a behemoth company, its iconic days are long gone; it is as much a corporate curiosity and a real-time reminder of a bygone era of US technological and cultural ascendancy. Its roller-coaster lifecycle reflects, perhaps like few other companies, the rise, zenith, and fall of American influence.

2.7 Conclusion: Legacy issues for the 21st century corporation

The two companies are interesting case studies in the rise and decline of once-mighty corporate entities. The fact that they still exist as corporations, and trade on, albeit in far reduced form from their respective heydays, is testament to the practical force of perpetual succession. Some companies find their brand deeply imprinted within the social and cultural psyche of the nation within which they were founded, and this is the case with the EIC and the UK, and Eastman Kodak and the US, respectively.

The 19th century marked both the EIC's greatest achievement as a virtual controller of a nation state, and its tumultuous rendering and demise. The grandeur of its corporate ambition made it an early form of sovereign risk. Its projection of power, through diplomacy, advocacy, and its vast army, meant that it was a direct threat to the nation state from whence it had emerged. In this sense, its defenestration was inevitable.

The 20th century represented the zenith for Kodak Eastman. After its charismatic founder George Eastman died by suicide in 1932, the company essentially did not move on from his 19th-century vision of a physical hand-held camera. This was 1888 and the camera was 'pre-loaded with enough film for 100 exposures, was released into the market at a price of $25 with the slogan coined by Eastman, 'You press the button, we do the rest'.[74]

In the third decade of the 21st century, the business and conditions of the 20th century are fading fast. The period from 1945 to 2000 was, in retrospect, a time of relative stability and prosperity comprised of high prices and buoyant asset classes; of cheap money and stable employment for life; of big employee numbers engaged in manufacturing; and of bountiful Fordist-style production lines. The clarity of time has ascertained that decades after the Second World War provided an ahistorical kink of unprecedented prosperity, as Thomas Piketty outlines comprehensively in his magnum opus, *Capital in the 21st Century*.[75] The slow growth since 2000 is much aligned with long-run historical norms.

In the wake of the globalization epoch apparent in the 1990s, much of the developed world has witnessed several inter-connected tremors that have caused financial contagion on a global basis. These have been the Asian financial crisis, the dotcom bubble, and the GFC amongst others. The elongated medical and financial contagion brought about by COVID-19 may in fact top them all, given the aftermath of high, if not hyper, inflation around the world caused by excessive government stimuli and post-pandemic shocks such as the Russian invasion of Ukraine.

Within the midst of the increasing pace of globalization comes the most pressing enunciation of the 'one planet' ethos which is encapsulated by the climate emergency and the stark realization there is no planet B. The lessons of adaptability, and the focus on rapid change—both borne out by the response to COVID-19—provide the requisite hallmarks of success.

What is indisputable is that the challenges and promise of this century have replaced the competing historical narratives of the past century. This is an inevitable consequence of the decades turning over. It is no doubt a third-decade phenomenon throughout history rendered via the calendar.

In any event, there is a new challenge. It is the hyperobject of climate change, the verities of the climate emergency, and the economic positioning that these existential challenges that some countries are stepping up to meet, and others are being forced to embrace. For companies, this juncture has been described in colourful terms as essentially, 'decarbonise or die'.[76] There is no middle ground or point of

74 Jonathon Mantle, n 61, 61.

75 Thomas Piketty, n 53, 2014.

76 Nick O'Malley, 'Decarbonise or die, world's biggest investor warns business', *The Age*, 18 January, 2022.

neutrality. For existing companies, the choice is put in stark terms as a question and challenge: 'as your industry gets transformed by the energy transition, will you go the way of the dodo, or will you be a phoenix?'[77] The binary is presented as extinction or reinvention and rising from the ashes of calamity.

For new companies, the road ahead is also clear, according to Larry Fink, head of the world's largest fund:

> The next 1000 unicorns won't be search engines or social media companies, they'll be sustainable, scalable innovators—startups that help the world decarbonise and make the energy transition affordable for all consumers.[78]

Never have the fates of existing companies and nation states been more interlocked and symbiotic. Corporations may not have the physical armies of companies like the EIC, but through multi-country, customers, employees, and marketing reach exact a highly influential leverage. Ultimately the power and influence of corporations can be overcome by the nation state of origin enacting laws to curb them. Nowhere is this truer than the anti-trust laws of the US. If this regulatory capacity is not used, then the winner-takes-all approach may prevail.

The EIC's reach was trimmed and redacted over time by statecraft; an early form of this was to end the company's royal charter. Combined with laws enacted by parliament, the company was constricted over decades by the parliament and sovereign operating in tandem. Inattention to changing dynamics over time was the death knell of both the EIC and Kodak. The EIC proved to be the signal case disproving the aphorism that an entity was 'too big to fail'. Kodak's brand—cool one decade, cold the very next—has been witnessed by many companies in the tech era. These corporate headwinds remain in the epoch of the climate emergency. They are added to and exacerbated by the multi-dimensional nature of that emergency which covers all aspects of a corporation's personality including its current operations, future, competitive pressures, access to finance, and the overall viability of its business. Various of these vectors are examined in Part Two, comprising the next four chapters which cover four Australian corporations, respectively.

In this sense, the lessons from EIC are highly pertinent. The EIC at its zenith and prime remains today as an abiding imaginative cultural construct and a corporate entity admired and reviled in roughly equal measure. In the challenges it faced and the solutions it found, its legacy is multi-faceted and complex. It also provides a multi-layered blueprint or template for modern global corporations. In this respect, it provides salutary lessons in excess. Kodak Eastman provides a more localized specific example of a company obsessed by its own narrow product range and

77 Larry Fink, 2022 Newsletter to CEOs, https://www.blackrock.com/corporate/investor-relations/larry-fink-ceo-letter.

78 Fink, n 77, https://www.blackrock.com/corporate/investor-relations/larry-fink-ceo-letter. The term 'unicorn', in this context is a US business-specific reference, which encompasses rapidly growing businesses, typically with pre public-flotation values of $1bn.

tunnel-vision success. Historic hubris affected both entities. A lack of oversight and accountability together with failing to consider the risks and challenges of changing trading conditions deeply affected each of them. These are abiding themes of corporate failure but are often overlooked, as every decade brings with it its own narrative phenomenon of corporate excess and inattention. Curiosity, humility, and not resting on one's laurels: these qualities apply to the corporation, to the board collectively, and to individual directors and to do that over successive generations of management remains an elusive task.

References

Stephen Bottomley, Kath Hall, Peta Spender, and Beth Nosworthy, *Contemporary Australian Corporate Law*, Cambridge University Press, 2018.

William Dalrymple, *The Anarchy: The Relentless Rise of The East India Company*, Bloomsbury, 2020.

Lewis Dartnell, *Origins: How the Earth Made Us*, Penguin, 2018.

Janet Dine, *The Governance of Corporate Groups*, Cambridge University Press, 2000.

Donald H. Dunn, *Ponzi: The Incredible True Story of the King of Financial Cons*, McGraw Hill, 1975.

Niall Ferguson, *Empire: How Britain made the Modern World*, Penguin, 2003.

Malcolm Gladwell, *Outliers: The Story of Success*, Penguin, 2008.

Ross Grantham and Charles Rickett (eds), *Corporate Personality in the 20th Century*, Hart Publishing, 1998.

Jason Harris, *Company Law: Theories, Principles and Applications*, LexisNexis, 2012,

EJ Hobsbawm, *The Age of Capital 1848–1875*, Abacus, 1975.

EJ Hobsbawm, *The Age of Empire 1875–1914*, Abacus, 1987.

David S. Landes, *The Wealth and Poverty of Nations*, Abacus, 1998.

Phillip Lipton, 'The introduction of limited liability into the English and Australian Colonial Companies Acts: Inevitable progression or chaotic history?' *MULR*, 41, 2018, 1279–1323.

Phillip Lipton, Abe Herzberg, and Michelle Welsh, *Understanding Company Law*, 20th ed, Lawbook Co, 2020.

Jonathon Mantle, *Companies that Changed the World*, Quercus, 2008.

Arthur Macgregor, *Company Curiosities: Nature, Culture and the East India Company, 1600–1874*, Reaktion Books, 2018.

John Merriman, *A History of Modern Europe: From the Renaissance to the Present*, WW Norton and Co, 1996, 465. See also Lawrence James, *The Rise and Fall of the British Empire*, 1994, Chapter 3.

Bernard Porter, *Empire and Superempire: Britain, America and the World*, Yale University Press, 2006.

Richard A. Posner, *A Failure of Capitalism: The Crisis of '08 and the Descent into Depression*, Harvard University Press, 2009.

Paul Redmond, *Corporations and Financial Markets Law*, Thomson Reuters, 2017.

Nick Robins, *The Corporation that Changed the World: How the East India Company Shaped the Modern Multinational*, Pluto Press, 2006.

Robert Wearing, *Cases in Corporate Governance*, Sage, 2005.

3 The corporate climate I

Coal and politics, the Adani Group of companies, and the emergence of stranded assets

3.1 The case study: the Adani Group of companies and coal resources located in the Galilee Basin

The Adani Group discussion focuses on the fossil fuel sector—oil, coal, and gas—with particular emphasis on thermal coal within the Galilee Basin of Queensland. Coal is widely regarded now as the 'weakest link' of the three main fossil fuels because it is the most exposed to climate change. Its use and burning creates copious amounts of carbon dioxide and is a central issue for leading thermal coal suppliers such as Australia and Russia, and to end users such as China and India. As such, coal is at the leading edge of the climate emergency. As an industry, it is vulnerable to becoming part of a suite of formerly valuable assets which may be 'stranded' or exposed to the point where the industry participants cannot readily or easily secure finance or insurance, and where individual companies cannot make a profit, or predict the short or long-term future with any degree of stability or assurance.

Of the four case studies discussed in *Corporate Law and Climate Change*, the Adani-related matter is the longest running, and has been the most overtly political in nature for much of that period. It has involved several aspects including litigation. It has been as much a national saga as a case study.

3.1.1 The multi-faceted basis of the Adani case study

The Adani group of companies refers to the multinational conglomerate based in India. The Adani website refers to Adani Australia being 'a multi-dimensional energy and infrastructure company, dedicated to delivering energy solutions for an advancing world'.[1] It also refers to Adani Mining Pty Ltd as 'an Australian mining company that operates out of regional Australia'.[2] Given the complex group basis of the Adani business, the references here are to Adani Mining Pty Ltd within the Australian context, and the Adani Group more broadly.

1 Adani Enterprises, https://www.adanienterprises.com/businesses/mining-and-mdo/australia.

2 Adani Enterprises, n 1.

DOI: 10.4324/9781003263746-4

As such, the Adani case study is a reference to current and ongoing investment in coal mining in the Galilee Basin in the outback region of Queensland, Australia. The Adani matter has become shorthand for several contested propositions:

- The increasingly political and contested nature of fossil investment in Australia.
- The environmental impact of large-scale, open-pit mines on threatened native animal species, habitats, and groundwater.
- The role of government in providing infrastructure or infrastructure support for key enabling assets such as rail lines, roads, and port access to enable export by ships.
- The effect on off-shore iconic world-heritage areas, such as the Great Barrier Reef, which is contiguous to much of the Queensland coast.
- The role of the various layers of government in their capacities as licence providers, legislators, and regulators.
- The commercial viability of existing and new coal mines, and of current and future coal-fired electricity generation.
- The broader acceptability—economic, political, and social—of new investments in coal mines.

There are also the complex political and legal dimensions of the Australian context including the fact that mining licenses are granted by the States, but matters which are core to the projects, such as environmental protection and export licenses, are matters of Commonwealth power, and therefore relevant to the federal political debate. This positions local issues such as maintaining jobs and employment prospects in particular towns and regions, against global perspectives, such as the responsibility for scope 3 carbon emissions arising from exported fossil fuels. In turn, this involves the fact that coal projects with local, state, national, and international dimensions give rise to the need to examine all the links in the relevant supply chains.

The Adani case study also calls to question transitional social and economic issues. For example, how fast can the economy move towards net zero carbon emissions, and what is the wider future of coal and coal-based employment? How can legacy issues be managed at the same time as innovation sweeps across the social landscape? Corporate decisions regarding efficient capital allocation sit at the heart of this rapidly moving area, with the fossil fuel sector being transformed by the investor and insurance market, with questions of emerging risk at their core. Will investors and lenders view these ventures as economically and socially acceptable ventures in which to invest long-term risk capital across the course of the next several decades? Increasingly, the answer to these questions is problematic, as evidenced by the Adani case study.

3.1.2 The Galilee Basin, Queensland: the extent of proposed coal mining and corporate activity

The Galilee Basin is in the Queensland interior, west of the coastal city of Townsville. It is part of a very large land mass of about 250,000 square kilometres including the Cooper Basin to the south-west and the Bowen Basin to the east. The fact that the Galilee Basin contains vast deposits of coal has been known for many years. Corporate interest and investment activity, by contrast, has been more recent and has been in play since about 2008.

The key issue is that the Galilee Basin is regarded by critics of coal mining as containing a potential 'carbon bomb'. Total carbon emissions from the extraction and export of the theoretically available thermal coal will have global impact, given its scale. The potential development of the region has coincided with the rising awareness of climate change and the climate emergency, the politicization of climate action, and the rapidly problematic nature of funding new coal mines, as the rise of renewables and their comparative cost fundamentally changes the power generation and electricity landscape.

The only current coal mine in the Galilee Basin operated by Adani is Carmichael and occupies about 27,000 hectares. It was slated to produce 60 million tonnes of thermal coal per annum, but that has not been achieved, and it operating at around ten million tonnes per annum.[3] The strategy involves sending it by rail to the deepwater port at Abbott Point, near Bowen in northern Queensland, and exporting it by ship to India and other Asian destinations without causing damage to the world heritage listed Great Barrier Reef. Securing finance and insurance for the multitude aspects of the project has proved difficult. Climate change, politics, renewables, and financing barriers with new long-term fossil fuel projects have resulted in a perfect corporate storm. The Carmichael mine was 'supposed to be the first of many. Yet there is little sign of more coal to come, with many projects shelved, lapsed, or discontinued, and uncertain futures for those that remain'.[4] The company's ambitions remain in place but there is a level of stasis and gridlock as the wider social awareness of the climate emergency intensifies.

3.1.3 The case for Adani's coal production plans in the Galilee Basin

Adani Australia proclaims in its corporate literature that it is 'a multi-dimensional energy and infrastructure company, dedicated to delivering energy solutions for an advancing world'.[5] It is keen to downplay thermal coal as its focal point. In its literature, it variously refers to other more politically palatable considerations. For instance, it refers to providing infrastructure, as noted above. Elsewhere it refers to 'providing energy solutions in Australia and the Asia Pacific region from thermal and renewable energy'.[6] This couples a strategy which combines traditional fossil fuels at one end of the spectrum with new generation technology at the other.

3 Graham Readfearn, 'After Adani: whatever happened to Queensland's Galilee basin coal boom?', *The Guardian Australia,* 9 January, 2022, https://www.theguardian.com/australia-news/2022/jan/09/after-adani-whatever-happened-to-queenslands-galilee-basin-coal-boom.

4 Readfearn, n 3.

5 Adani Australia, Energy solutions for an advancing world, Mining, Rail and Port - Australia | Adani Enterprises Ltd.

6 Adani website, n 5.

It adds to the impression of scale and corporate capacity, such that Adani can simultaneously operate successfully at divergent points of the asset's spectrum. The Adani website refers to the Carmichael project being a 'thermal mine and rail project'.[7] Each of these claims dilutes the clear reference to, and focus on, increasingly problematic thermal coal extraction. The claims the company makes are bold:

> we will create jobs and help fund major infrastructure upgrades to hospitals, schools and roads by contributing billions of dollars in taxes and royalties to the Australian economy'[8] and as regards the 'transport [of] coal from the Galilee Basin to countries in Asia, including India, delivering thousands of jobs in the process.

Adani also makes a claim for being a community builder, given the geographical reach of the project:

> By delivering 10 million tonnes per annum mine, combined with a 200km narrow gauge rail line that connects with existing rail infrastructure through to the Port of Abbott Point, communities like Townsville, Rockhampton, Mackay, Bowen, Gladstone, Central Highlands and the Isaac regions are ideally positioned to receive new jobs and contract opportunities for local workers and businesses.[9]

These types of hubristic statements resulted in political brinksmanship and complexity at the federal level particularly before the 2019 election in which the Adani development proposal of the Galilee basin was a major issue and 'emblematic of attitudes to climate change'[10] and economic development. The then Labor opposition was accused of

> seeming to equivocate on the Adani mine [and this stance] allowed the [Conservative LNP Liberal National Party] government to present itself as the major political party favouring growth in employment and incomes in the coalmining regions, and in the state of Queensland in which coalmining was proportionately most important.[11]

As such, climate change was pushed to the background.

3.1.4 The case against coal mining investment by Adani

The case against Adani has been multi-faceted, including political, economic, environmental, and accounting critiques. These arguments have crossed over and intersected between contexts. It has been a 15-year imbroglio.

7 Adani website, n 5.
8 Adani website, n 5.
9 Adani website, n5.
10 Ross Garnaut, *Superpower: Australia's Low-carbon opportunity*, LaTrobe University Press, 2019, 170.
11 Garnaut, n 10, 170.

3.1.4.1 Climate science

The main argument against further coal projects is the increasingly robust climate science. The conflation of Australia's exposure to climate risk and Adani is clear to climate scientists. On the wider issue of Australia's exposure to damaging climate change, Joelle Gergis, an ANU-based climate scientist, notes that Australia's

> dramatic natural climate variability means that climate events are becoming even more extreme as the planet begins to warm. Australia is also a nation heavily reliant on its large agricultural sector, which in turn is highly sensitive to weather and climate extremes.[12]

Gergis provides a comprehensive critique of the Adani Carmichael Mine; the starting position is that 'to give ourselves just a 50% chance of staying within the two degrees Celsius Paris Agreement target, nearly 90 percent of the world's existing coal reserves must be left in the ground'.[13]

These concerns include, in terms of scale, the fact that the Carmichael mine 'will be one of the biggest in the world, including six open-cut pits and five underground mines across an area five times the size of Sydney Harbour'.[14] In terms of carbon dioxide pollution, 'at peak production, the Adani Carmichael coalmine will generate up to 120 million tonnes of carbon dioxide annually- more than the annual emissions from fossil fuel burning in over 100 countries'.[15] As for the mine's projected operating span, 'over the course of the mine's estimated sixty-year lifespan, it would cumulatively generate a colossal 4.6 billion tonnes of planet-cooking carbon dioxide emissions'[16]

3.1.4.2 Environmental issues

Ground water loom as a key factor given that it is 'of huge concern to local farmers is the fact that the mine will use approximately 12 billion litres of water each year, which threatens to dry up the aquifers necessary for agriculture in the Great Artesian Basin'.[17]

The potential effect on the Great Barrier Reef with the export terminal located at Abbott Point means 'there are grave concerns that the enormous scale of the coal exports may damage the Great Barrier Reef, as the terminal is located on the coastline of the UNESCO-listed World Heritage Area'.[18]

12 Joelle Gergis, *Sunburnt Country: The History and Future of Climate Change in Australia*, MUP, 2018, 219.
13 Gergis, n 12, 260.
14 Gergis, n 12, 261.
15 Gergis, n 12, 261.
16 Gergis, n 12, 261.
17 Gergis, n 12, 261.
18 Gergis, n 12, 261.

As such, environmental and cultural values are pitted against economic considerations and the profit imperative. Australian history demonstrates that the latter factors will invariably predominate.

3.1.4.3 The economic analysis

The economic analysis has concentrated on the opportunity costs of development in the Galilee Basin and the proposition, asserted by Ross Garnaut, that the Galilee Basin 'is the best solar country in eastern Australia and just about as good as any in the world'.[19] Garnaut, too, has previously made the point that 'Australia is the most vulnerable country of the developed world when it comes to climate change'.[20] The Galilee Basin is therefore claimed by proponents of both fossil fuels and renewables. To this point fossil fuels have won the battle for ideological supremacy given their myriad advantages. Such resources are obvious and in the ground at or near the surface, they are fixtures of the geology of the country itself, part of the historical national narrative, and incumbent in terms of the political and economic status quo, particularly in a resource-rich state such as Queensland. As such, the political and economic pitch for developing fossil fuels has been favoured well ahead of the liminal, elite alternative which involves the speculative nature of the costly development at scale of unreliable alternative renewable sources of power. This occurs in other nations with similar contextual issues. For example, in Alberta, Canada, a province with a strong fossil fuel sector, opposition to the federal government's plans to decarbonize the national electricity grid refer to the unreliability of renewables headlined by a campaign warning 'no one wants to freeze in the dark'.[21]

3.1.4.4 Community-based opposition

There has been broad-based community opposition from groups such as StopAdani, whose focus is to stop the Carmichael mine. It argues that

> if allowed to go ahead, Adani's Carmichael coal mine will unlock the Galilee Basin—one of the world's largest untouched coal reserves—paving the way for at least eight more coal mines to be built. All at a time when scientists are warning we can't build any more fossil fuel infrastructure if we want to avoid catastrophic global heating.[22]

StopAdani refer to several key risks:

19 Garnaut, n 10, 187.

20 Garnaut, n 10, 219.

21 Corporate Knights, Rick Spence, 'Zero: Alberta's fearmongering media blitz to try to delay federal climate action, *Climate*, Winter 2024, 31 Jan 2024, Alberta premier Danielle Smith's campaign to delay federal climate action (corporateknights.com).

22 StopAdani website, https://www.stopadani.com/.

> Adani's Carmichael coal mine would be the biggest coal mine in Australian history and open a new coal basin. In addition, Adani's mine will violate the land rights of the Wangan and Jagalingou people; drain tens of billions of litres of water every year -threatening the survival of the ancient Doongmabulla Springs; drive the extinction of endangered species such as the Black-Throated Finch; and lead to hundreds more coal ships travelling through the Great Barrier Reef every year.[23]

The StopAdani website notes that 'if all these mines go ahead the Galilee Basin alone could produce over 5% of global carbon emission by 2030'.[24] The potential scale of emissions from large fossil projects in Australia, including thermal coal and natural gas, is globally significant.

3.2 The background to and context of the Adani case study

Whilst fossil fuels are somewhat benignly described as 'remnants of trees and other plants that died as early as 600 million years ago',[25] they have generated maximum political heat in contemporary Australia for more than two decades.

3.2.1 The industrial economy in Europe: the centrality of coal

Coal has a prosaic genesis in terms of its later economy-wide centrality. It was used domestically long before it powered the machines of the Industrial Revolution. In the late 1500s, wood predominated as the source of domestic heating in England, and the use of coal at this point was limited. It has been observed that 'the early rise of coal is not a story about industry it is a tale of domestic needs and comforts, of individual, private choices',[26] until the late 16th century witnessed a rapid transition to the use of coal from wood:

> In 1570 there was still little sign of any major divergence from the traditional use of wood as fuel. Less than forty years later, in 1607, a case brought by the Crown in the Star Chamber stated as fact that 'sea coal'—a name for the coal that arrived in London by ship from Newcastle—was 'the ordinary and usual fuel … almost everywhere in every man's house.' A single generation had made the switch.[27]

As such, 'the domestic expansion of coal use in the Elizabethan period helped spur the country's mining industry and the later adoption of coal as the fuel of

23 https://www.stopadani.com/adanis_big_coal_problem.

24 https://www.stopadani.com/adanis_big_coal_problem.

25 Micha Tomkiewicz, *Climate Change: The Fork at the End of Now*, Momentum Press, LLC, 2011, 17.

26 Ruth Goodman, *The Domestic Revolution: How the Introduction of Coal into Our Homes Changed Everything*, Michael O'Mara Books limited, 2020, xvii.

27 Goodman, n 26, xvii.

manufacturing, which transformed first Britain and then the world.'[28] This was a precursor to coal's widespread industrial use in the 18th to 20th centuries. It was the fuel which drove the Industrial Revolution and continues to drive much of the world's industry and heating.

3.2.2 The nation-building role assumed by the coal industry

In Australia's case, given that the Industrial Revolution coincided with European settlement, and that coal was plentiful and easily extracted, it became part of the foundation myths of the new political arrangement and has since become coincidental with tropes of national progress. The narrative of coal in Australia has been relentlessly promoted. From the nascent industrial base of the 19th century, to the 21st-century globally connected trading marketplace, it has positioned itself at the centre of the nation building project, as an assets backed by corporate behemoth and governments alike, and almost singly responsible for underwriting the nation's wealth and wellbeing. So much so, that critiquing its destructive capacity as a CO_2-producing fossil fuel has until very recently been an antagonism akin to somehow being anti-Australian.

3.2.3 The land mass of viewed as an economic resource and the consequential effects

It is just over 250 years since Captain James Cook first landed on the shores of Botany Bay just south of Sydney in New South Wales. The colony founded on the basis of the *terra nullius* doctrine, which is now thoroughly discredited as a fiction, was from its inception a brutal society operating in effect as a penal colony, and it was soon industrial in scale, particularly as regards the farming of sheep and cattle, and the plundering of whales and seals.[29] The significance of this is that the entire extent of Australia's modern economy is contained by the epoch of the Industrial Revolution which is widely regarded as having started in England in about 1760. Australia, in its guise as a modern colonial nation state, has never known a world other than that built on the concept of the rational economic investor modelled on the theories of Adam Smith (1723–1790) and the allocation of capital to monetize the land and its resources. This dominant economic and political foundation has been the constant context for the development and oversight of the Australian company, and of the country's corporate law and governance.

European colonization has meant that Australia's dominant economic profile has been that of a super pit, whether that was gold in the state of Victoria (in Ballarat and Bendigo) or in WA (in Kalgoorlie and Coolgardie) in the 19th century. The model of resource exploitation was set in place and created a series of consequential

28 Goodman, n 26, xviii.

29 Robert Hughes, *The Fatal Shore: History of the Transportation of Convicts to Australia, 1787–1868*, Pan Macmillan, 1988.

effects on the landscape, including widespread salinity, land degradation, and the loss of habitat. Along with habitat loss, Australia also has a poor record when it comes to the preservation of native species in that

> native animals and birds had been able to maintain a reasonable balance' for thousands of years under the stewardship of First Nations people. By contrast, the European colonists considered that 'the whole continent of Australia was found not possess a single animal worthy of perpetuation.[30]

The idea of perpetuity—a theory apposite for the corporate entity by the middle of the 19th century in England—was not gifted to the natural world in Australia. The new colony and ancient continent were soon variously a quarry, a farm, and an industrial zone.

Exploitation of natural resources was so ingrained that by the 20th century it was part of the national folklore. The land was a resource to be exploited, including coal in NSW (particularly in the Hunter Valley) and iron ore in the Pilbara Region of WA. A founding colonizing myth involved wealth derived from wool where it was for a time a pound in currency for a pound in weight and wool's champion John Macarthur (1767–1834) was regarded as the colony's foremost entrepreneur.

3.2.4 Mineral exploration and speculation: the case of Poseidon Mining

The period since the 1960s has coincided with the enormous increase in the economic and political influence of the fossil mining industry, particularly coal, as outlined in Judith Brett's seminal essay.[31] Mining, speculation, and excessive risk-taking have gone together in the Australian economic narrative, particularly in the last six decades. The nascent national stock market witnessed the Poseidon Mining company, a small Adelaide-based nickel miner go through a price bubble in 1969, only to see the share price crash in 1970. Regular booms followed by busts have been a feature of corporate activity, and particularly of the mining sector, in Australia.[32]

3.2.5 Australia's place as the world's third largest exporter of CO_2 emissions

Since the year 2000, however, there has been widespread awareness that the burning of fossil fuels is a key driver of anthropogenic or human-induced global warming. As a result, the mining industry's extended role in this long-running saga begins to look less like economic triumph, and more like an increasing risk with widespread potential liability. Australia is the third largest exporter of emissions after the United

30 Michael Cannon, *Life in the Country: Australia in the Victorian Age: 2,* Currey O'Neil Ross Pty Ltd, 1983, 223.

31 Judith Brett, 'The Coal Curse: Resources, climate and Australia's future', *The Quarterly Essay*, Issue 78, 2020, 1–78.

32 Trevor Sykes, *The Bold Riders: Behind Australia's Corporate Collapses*, Allen and Unwin, 1994.

Arab Emirates and Russia.[33] Whilst politicians refer to Australia's 1.2–1.5% total of global emissions, by comparison, scope 3, the total of a country's emissions, including its domestic and international or exported emissions (including coal, oil, and gas), increases this figure markedly to approximately seven%,[34] in line with relevant deposits.[35] The dominant neo-liberal narrative underpinning this economic model has given rise to a particularly enduring form of shareholder primacy within Australia's corporate law and governance.

The ongoing centrality of mineral extraction, and the burning of fossil fuels, shows no signs of abating. The 'sheep's back' has been emphatically replaced by digging and drilling, whether this includes proposals for natural gas exploration in the Great Australian Bight (off the SA coast) or Scarborough off the WA coast, or the proposed series of mines in the Galilee Basin of Queensland. Each of these fossil fuel projects have been met with widespread environmental and social opposition.[36] As Judith Brett observes that whilst 'Australians were generally happy to ride on the sheep's back. Many of us are not at all happy to be riding in a coal cart.'[37] There is increasingly a disconnect between the political and corporate sectors respectively, and the Australian society more broadly in which, for example, domestic rooftop solar take-up is amongst the highest in the world and an issue of widespread community passion.[38]

3.2.6 The Australian paradox: a G20 nation with a very simple economy

This overlooks the fact that the luck of 'the lucky country'—to use Donald Horne's phrase[39]—is based on happenstance of geological location. Countering this is the well-established principle of economics that raw commodity prices are volatile. A national economy such as Australia's which relies on the strength and stability of such base-level prices (without adding value by way of processing and manufacturing) is heavily exposed to international trading conditions, and to uncontrollable issues of global supply and demand. But Australia has been lucky more than once; it has been able to pivot as one sector declined and another

33 The Australia Institute, 'New analysis: Australia ranks third for fossil fuel export', 19 August, 2019, https://australiainstitute.org.au/post/new-analysis-australia-ranks-third-for-fossil-fuel-export/.

34 The Australia Institute, n 33.

35 Brett n 31, 18, notes for example that Australia has 9% of the world's deposits of black coal. The focus on scope 3 is a cornerstone issue for some mining companies. In terms of BHP see https://www.bhp.com/-/media/documents/investors/annual-reports/2019/bhpscope3emissionscalculationmethodology2019.pdf?la=en.

36 https://www.stopadani.com/why_stop_adani.

37 Brett, n 31, 40.

38 Renew Economy: Clean Energy News and Analysis, Sophie Vorrath, 'Australia again tops global solar per capita, as world installs 240GW of PV in 2022', 19 April 2023, https://reneweconomy.com.au/australia-again-tops-global-solar-per-capita-as-world-installs-240gw-of-pv-in-2022/#:~:text=Taking%20this%20into%20account%2C%20the,at%20the%20end%20of%202022.&text=above%2017%25%20and%20the%20Netherlands,%25%2C%E2%80%9D%20the%20report%20says.

39 Donald Horne, *The Lucky Country*, Penguin, 1964.

became available. When wool prices collapsed in the 1960s, abundant iron ore was 'discovered' and has been able to fill the void ever since. This puts Australia, as a G20 country, in a paradoxical position: it has an economy characterized with a high simplicity index and has positioned itself as a price taker more akin to basic or developing economies. This contrasts with other G20 nations such as Germany and Japan with their strengths in manufacturing and value adding resulting in high complexity, affording their economies relative protection from price volatility.

3.2.7 Political issues and the nexus with corporate activity

The political dimensions of the Adani case study have gone to the heart of the idea of Australia- progress, jobs and prosperity versus uncertainty, idealism, and failure. The Adani corporate case study is something of a mirror of the wider climate change crisis. It is long-term and intergenerational. It is complex and variable according to local geography, natural resources, and social and economic history.

3.2.7.1 The climate change dimensions of the 2019 federal election

The political fault lines related to the Adani case peaked in Australia in the lead-up to the May 2019 federal election. In the more than month-long election campaign, the famous environmental campaigner and former leader of the federal Greens political party, Bob Brown led a motorcade from the southern states more than two thousand kilometres north to Queensland visiting coal towns along the way. This galvanized issues across several fault lines and essentially false dichotomies including the city versus regional and remote areas, mining and tangible industries versus metropolitan-based services sectors, and of course the hard-working, blue-collar authenticity versus white-collar rent-seeking. It galvanized an abiding political binary which occupied centre-stage during the 2019 federal election campaign. It was both essentialist and relentless in its stereotyping. It set up the nation in a tribal fashion. It pitted the mining-related, heart-of-the-nation outback, regional and remote 'north' versus the interfering, city-centric, metropolitan 'south'; this was essentially a male typology set against the feminine 'other', and weaponized to devastating effect by the political right, especially the right wing of the conservative Liberal National Party (LNP) coalition.

For Mark Butler, the then Labor shadow minister for climate change, there was a tendency to position the Labor party behind more objective financial metrics and third-party decision-making, to avoid taking a clear position. These included assertions that new coal projects are 'simply not financially viable',[40] as regards 'coal price projected to be in the doldrums for years',[41] and lenders being 'subject

40 Mark Butler, *Climate Wars*, Melbourne University Press, 2017, 118.
41 Butler, n 40, 118.

to intense lobbying campaigns by environmental groups to refuse finance to new coal mines'.[42] Further, it asserted that matters turn on 'the Indian government's policy of phasing out thermal coal imports over the next few years.'[43] Labor was in a bind and was outmaneuvered.

The motorcade which travelled during the election campaign from south to north gave stark illustration to the deep political fault line. With the benefit of retrospective analysis, it is widely recognized to having tilted the balance of power in several regional Queensland seats, and pivotally helped to re-elect the overtly pro-coal, conservative Liberal National Party government at the May 2019 federal election. The coal industry, and Queensland's overt support of it, had become the linchpin for the Conservatives to hold onto power and to win the so-called miracle election.[44] It was vindication of the approach taken by the fossil fuel lobby.[45] The opposition to new coal mines had been effectively weaponized.[46]

3.2.7.2 The changing dynamic of federal politics in Australia: the 'climate change election' of May 2022

Less than six months after the federal election of May 2019, much of the east coast of Australia and the iconic forested areas of the Great Dividing Range suffered a fire. This coincided with Prime Minister Morrison being on a secret holiday in Hawaii. Greg Mullins, the retired former fire commissioner of NSW, publicly eviscerated the PM. Mullins noted that his expert panel had been warning of such a catastrophe and had been trying without success to meet with the PM and senior members of the government. Morrison returned to Australia but dismissed the need to discuss climate change. Now was not the time, he intoned. Across the summer of 2019–20 the so-called Black Summer bushfires raged and destroyed many thousands of acres and killed an estimated three billion native animals. The renowned US climate scientist, Michael Mann, was on holiday in Australia during that period and it was then he 'truly came face to face with the climate crisis'.[47] He noted too the role of the Murdoch media 'replete with "false-alarm" climate framing'[48] and the media's role more generally in taking a lukewarm view of the climate science thereby aiding the denialism of the then conservative LNP government.[49]

By March 2020, Australia and the world was coping with rapid spread of COVID-19 and the bushfires were relegated in the public consciousness. Across much of

42 Butler, n 40, 118.

43 Butler, n 40, 119.

44 Morrison was championed by Trump as a right-wing hero who had won against the political odds; a miracle man whom he was seeking to emulate at the 2020 US Presidential election.

45 Indeed, among the then Prime Minister Scott Morrison's many marketing-style stunts across his political career was to stand in parliament with a lump of coal and to pronounce 'this is coal, don't be afraid, this is coal'.

46 Judith Brett, n 31.

47 Michael E. Mann, *The New Climate War: the fight to take back our planet*, Scribe, 2021, 44.

48 Mann, n 47, 220.

49 Mann, n 47, 175–7.

2021, the spectre of Australia going to COP 26 in Glasgow without a commitment to net zero by 2050, held much of the political attention. Reluctantly, and just a few weeks before the Conference, PM Morrison secured a net zero commitment from the LNP party room. There was no updated target for 2030 for Australia, despite this being a central requirement of the COP meeting. It remained at 26–28% above 2005 emissions. The PM's mantra was that Australia would meet and beat this target. It would not legislate a target or strategy to get there. Instead, it produced a modest 20-page booklet.[50] The slogan underpinning this approach was 'technology not taxes'. It became apparent that the National party, the junior coalition member, had extracted many concessions for their agreeing to sign up to the target. Nothing substantial happened in the way of the government advancing new policy. Instead, the east coast of Australia endured more catastrophic climate change events in the summer and early part of 2022. There were no fires this time, but floods. The northern NSW town of Lismore was inundated twice in short succession.

The nation had seen enough and the LNP government lost the election held on 21 May 2022 after nine years in power led by three Prime Ministers.[51] It was the climate change election, and Labor hoped to finally end nearly two decades of climate disagreement in Australia. The Labor party won government by a very narrow majority, securing 77 of the 151 sets in the lower House of Representatives, just one seat more than the mathematical requisite majority of 76. To advance the argument that the May 2022 election was indeed the climate change election, two other phenomena were apparent. Firstly, the Greens won a record four seats in the House of Representatives. It took its total of lower house seats from one to four and it did so by winning seats in central Brisbane suburbs. This is remarkable given that Brisbane is the capital of Queensland. The tectonic plates had shifted since the 2019 election. Secondly, the Conservative party lost several formerly blue-ribbon seats in its traditional heartlands of wealthy metropolitan suburbs in Melbourne and Sydney and even in Perth, a state like Queensland with an economy heavily focused on mining. These seats were won by independent, non-aligned candidates, and were in part funded by Climate 200, a group put together by Simon Holmes à Court. The so-called Teal independent seats were secured by female candidates whose platforms comprised a powerful set of issues—gender equality, particularly as regards equal pay and safe workplaces, the establishment of a federal anti-corruption commission, and most crucially for present purposes, real, deep, and abiding commitment to acting on climate change. The political realm in Australia had just gone though one of its most consequential changes in more than 50 years.

Action on climate change is now a centrifugal issue in Australian federal politics. The Labor government has set 43% as the reduction target by 2030, and legislated this interim target and the net zero by 2050 target. The Greens and the

50 Australian Government, 'The Plan to Deliver Net Zero: The Australian Way' Commonwealth of Australia, 2021, https://www.dcceew.gov.au/sites/default/files/documents/the-plan-to-deliver-net-zero-the-australian-way.pdf.

51 This was the last Saturday possible, given that the term of parliament is a maximum of three years.

Teal independents have higher ambitions across a range of policy settings and are actively advocating that they will hold the government to account.

3.3 Financial analysis of Adani

As the Environmental Defenders Office notes, 'Adani's proposed Carmichael mine has become a touchstone for Australia's climate change efforts'.[52] While Adani continues to operate in Australia, there are also wider lessons for fossil fuel companies from the Adani Group's thermal coal exploits. Even though Adani indicates that there is a strong, diverse, and ongoing market for fossil fuels into the future, the financial analysis of the company itself and of coal investment more broadly have been called into question.

3.3.1 The Adani group of companies: the forensic accounting critique and the precarious fortune of the complex corporate structure

In the wake of the 2019 federal election and the fault lines exposed by continued fossil fuel investment, there was some belated academic analysis of the Adani corporate group structure. This commenced in 2019 with a deal of analysis in the field of forensic accounting undertaken by Professor Sandra van der Laan at the University of Sydney and the research focused on the group company's structural and financial framework. The conclusion was that the group company was structurally complex and commercially opaque.[53] As such, it was potentially an insolvent group of companies.[54] This flew in the face of the group's apparent success, its ambitious plans in Australia, its iconic status in India, and the charismatic projections of its founder, Gautam Adani. As a result, Professor van der Laan's analysis did not garner significant ongoing attention. However, in 2023 these concerns were given renewed impetus by the New York-based market analyst, Hindenburg Research.

3.3.2 The Hindenburg report of January 2023 and the Adani riposte

As the result of a two-year investigation, Hindenburg Research published a 51-page report on 24 January 2023 alleging that 'conglomerate Adani Group has engaged in a brazen stock manipulation and accounting fraud scheme over the course of decades' with the corporate group also suffering from "near-term liquidity pressure"'.[55]

52 https://www.edo.org.au/adani-and-the-galilee-basin/.

53 ABC, The World Today, Stephen Long, 'Adani Mining is in a perilous financial position, expert warns', quoting Professor Van Der Laan, 24 July 2019, https://www.abc.net.au/listen/programs/worldtoday/adani-mining-is-in-a-perilous-financial-position,-expert-warns/11341632.

54 Professor Sandra Van Der Laan, https://www.sydney.edu.au/business/about/our-people/academic-staff/sandra-vanderlaan.html#collapseBio.

55 Hindenburg Research, 'Adani Group: How the World's 3rd richest man is pulling the largest con in corporate history', 24 January, 2023, https://hindenburgresearch.com/adani/.

Gautam Adani, founder of the Adani Group was assertive and combative in his response and the company produced a 413-page riposte within a few days.[56] Despite this corporate strategy of defence and counter-attack, the stock price and Gautam Adani's wealth both fell dramatically and in tandem. At the 2023 AGM in July, some six months after the first reports into the governance of the group, Gautam Adani asserted:

> As all of you are aware, on the eve of our Republic Day this year, a US-based short-seller published a report to short our stocks just as we were planning to launch the largest Follow-on Public Offering in India's history. The report was a combination of targeted misinformation and discredited allegations, the majority of them dating from 2004 to 2015. They were all settled by the appropriate authorities at that time. This report was a deliberate and malicious attempt aimed at damaging our reputation and generating profits through a short-term drive-down of our stock prices.[57]

In referencing India's Republic Day, which falls on January 26 each year since 1950, Mr Adani was conflating the nation with the Adani corporate group, such that an attack on Adani was at least sub-consciously an attack on the Indian nation and its people. A good deal of Gautam Adani's speech implicitly links the capacity of the corporate group to grow as part of India's destiny:

> While economic cycles are getting increasingly hard to forecast, there is little doubt that, India—already the world's 5th largest economy—will become the world's 3rd largest economy well before 2030 and, thereafter, the world's 2nd largest economy by 2050. It is well understood that for any economy to implement policy and lay the foundation of growth, a stable Government is critical, and we have seen this impact with the implementation of several structural reforms that are critical for strong, sustainable, and balanced growth. This stability, coupled with India's demographics and continued expansion of internal demand, is a potent combination. Our nation's demographic dividend is expected to drive consumption and accelerate the growth of a tax-paying society at a record pace. The United Nations Population Fund projects that India's median age will be just 38 years even in 2050. Over this period, India's population is expected to grow by approximately 15% to 1.6 billion, but the per capita income will accelerate by over 700% to about 16,000 US dollars. On a purchasing power parity basis, this per capita metric will be 3 to 4 times higher.[58]

56 Adani Response to Hindenburg, 29 Jan 2023, https://www.adani.com/-/media/Project/Adani/Invetsors/Adani-Response-to-Hindenburg-January-29-2023.pdf.

57 Adani Enterprises Ltd, Annual General Meeting (AGM), 2023, July 18 2023, Address to shareholders by Gautan Adani, 1-13,3, https://www.adanienterprises.com/-/media/Project/Enterprises/Investors/corporate-governance/Others-Dynamic/AEL-AGM-2023-Transcript-Final.pdf.

58 Adani Enterprises Ltd AGM, n 57, 5.

The nation's economic prosperity is directly connected to the company's aspiration to be at the core of India's future projected success and economic might, and the following extract from the speech essentially rejects international criticism as an overhang of outdated colonialist thinking from an epoch prior to India's independence:

> And we have the statistics to prove it. Following our independence, it took us 58 years to get to our first trillion dollars of GDP, 12 years to get to the next trillion, and just 5 years for the third trillion. I anticipate that within the next decade, India will start adding a trillion dollars to its GDP every 18 months. This puts us on track to be a 25 to 30 trillion-dollar economy by 2050 and will drive India's stock market capitalization to over 40 trillion dollars—approximately a 10-fold expansion from current levels.[59]

India positions itself as a 21st-century power in competition for the number one economic spot with China, thereby overriding 20th-century hegemonic nations such as the UK and latterly the US. The speech is as much political as commercial. There is just one mention of Australia by Gautam Adani at the Adani AGM of 2023:

> Our national and international partnerships are proof of our governance standards. The scale of our international expansions is validated by our success in Australia, Israel, Bangladesh, and Sri Lanka.[60]

Given other developments outlined in this chapter, this appears to be an optimistic assessment of the company's operations in Australia. Despite that being the case, the Adani corporate group occupies space at the very centre of the political and public power dynamics of the modern Indian nation, as evidenced by the close relationship between company CEO/Chair, Gautam Adani and the Indian Prime Minister, Narendra Modi. In this respect Adani is arguably in some respects becoming to India what that the East India Company was to Britain in the 18th and 19th centuries, and similar to the role the global tech behemoths such as Apple and Amazon have occupied since the late 20th century in relation to the US projection of global power.

3.3.3 The complexity of the debate in Australia concerning the extraction, use and export of different types of coal

Coal, as a type of fossil fuel, is not a singular commodity in Australia (or indeed elsewhere that it occurs) in terms of deposit types or end use. There are two basic types of coal identified by reference to colour: brown and black. Brown coal is the more CO_2-emitting, and as such the more polluting of the two types. Hence it is

59 Adani Enterprises Ltd AGM, n 57, 5.
60 Adani Enterprises Ltd AGM, n 57, 6.

often referred to as 'dirty coal'. It is used in Australia at some power stations, such as Yoy Lang in Victoria. It is not exported. Black coal, in turn, consists of two basic types: thermal and coking coal. Thermal coal, like brown coal, is used in power stations to generate electricity and it is the focus of the opposition to coal in places such as the Bowen Basin.

By contrast, coking or metallurgical coal is combined with iron ore to make steel. Coking coal is therefore in quite a different economic category. The use and deployment of coking coal goes to the heart of a paradox and is a wicked problem. It is a material which is currently required to build sustainable infrastructure, including wind turbines and wave machines and for improving solar technology. Coking coal is vital to steelmaking. It is a necessary component, therefore, in the journey to sustainability and the net zero emissions target. As such, the future of coking or metallurgical coal is quite different to that of its counterparts.

There is also a debate about the emergence of a green steel industry. Its potential merit is in not having to use coking coal to make it. Whilst green steel is lauded as a concept, the technology is still in its formative stages, and it is estimated that it will not be scalable for companies to produce for some time. New generation corporate entrepreneurs like Mike Cannon-Brookes and Andrew Forrest are championing this emerging technology.

Hence, there is no singularity about the fossil coal per se. It is not a monolithic product, and debate about it needs to recognize the different types of coal and the quite different uses to which it is put. That being the case, the arguments referencing coal as a problematic fossil fuel and resource are essentially connected to the extraction and use of brown coal, and the extraction, use and export of thermal black coal, respectively.

3.3.4 Coal in Australia as a ubiquitous source of 'firming power'—a rapidly changing price point

One of the ongoing elements of economic and political complacency in Australia is the abundance of coal and the ease by which it can be mined, monetized and exported. Indeed, as Micha Tomkiewicz notes:

> If the only driving force in choosing among fuels is the price per unit of energy, then the incentive will be to use coal, the fuel with the highest CO_2 intensity and thus the greater climatic consequences. Coal is also the fuel with the most adverse environmental consequences, yet it is the least expensive fuel … and the fuel with the largest reserves.[61]

The ubiquity of coal has been central to the argument in Australia and, until recently, it was the cheapest source of electricity. The rise of renewables sources of power has challenged this orthodoxy, but it has long been supported by political ideology

61 Micha Tomkiewicz, n 25.

and by generous publicly-funded subsidies. Twentieth-century economics and entrenched political stasis meant that the use of coal was not challenged until very recently. The current and projected costs of renewables are now widely viewed as cheaper than coal. Joelle Gergis notes the financial point, too, in terms of funding new coal projects versus renewables. She references the fact that BlackRock, 'the world's largest infrastructure group' argues that Australia is 'denying gravity' by encouraging and making new investments in coal. This is because renewable energy is, at the very least, 'financially competitive with coal'.[62]

The prospects for new brown coal and black thermal coal projects are bleak, given the funding uncertainty. Projects are long-term in nature, such that their horizons coincide and overlap with the 2050 timeline. Obtaining competitive project finance and ancillary project capacity, including insurance, and largesse from governments, will be increasingly fraught. As the price of renewables—wind, solar, and pumped hydro—and storage continues to fall, the baseline economic proposition and the accounting necessity of making a profit, will be increasingly problematic. Banks, insurance companies, superannuation and pension funds will be averse to requests. International investment behemoths such as BlackRock with US$10 trillion funds under management has already expressed through Larry Fink, its renowned CEO, a clear signal to the global market that it will no longer invest in coal.[63] Divestment announcements of this type send a powerful signal to the market. Coal's carrying capacity as central plank of the Industrial Revolution is teetering; the 250-year journey is in steep, if not quite yet terminal, decline.

3.3.5 The rapidly evolving investment outlook for fossil fuel corporations

For much of the 21st century, the reference to coal, oil, and gas—the trinity of fossil fuels—provides a fundamental fault line in Australia. Conservative governments placed these industries—including the exploration for mining and extraction of its use domestically and export internationally—at the centre of the political and economic debate in Australia. They referred to the size and scale of the export income and the number of jobs they created. They linked the existence of community assets such schools and hospitals to these industries. Indeed, the conservative coalition government lauded a gas-led recovery in 2021 as the pathway out of the COVID-19 pandemic. This reverence for fossil fuels has camouflaged the rapidly changing financial case for such industries, and the companies backing them. This has been most apparent in the case of coal. Coal was long considered the financial equivalent of 'black gold'. It was money found in the ground, monetizable around the world, and it would alleviate poverty and provide homes and businesses in places such as India and Africa with abundant electricity.

62 Gergis, n 12, 261.

63 CBS News Moneywatch, Stephen Gandel, 'BlackRock to sell $500 million in coal investments in climate change push', 14 Jan 2020, https://www.cbsnews.com/news/blackrock-puts-climate-change-first-in-its-its-investment-strategy/.

Alongside this concerted political and economic narrative, however, the financial case for coal has slipped backwards. The financial viability of coal has been called into question because accessing project finance and insurance has become increasingly more difficult. The viability of large-scale and long-term capital projects necessarily requires a big-picture, long-run, and highly objective analytical approach. Whilst there may be corporate intent in evidence, the ability of companies to access affordable finance and insurance is increasingly problematic. Capital allocations and flows which price risk are reluctant to back new coal projects. As a result, coal has gone from being the backbone industry of the Australian national economy, to one associated with high risk, expensive finance, and hard to secure insurance.

3.3.5.1 The percentage of thermal coal in the energy grid

Coal provides about 60% of the generation of the Australian electricity grid. Australia is arguably operating at or about the point of 'peak coal'. Its recent, relatively high cost of production, coupled with its high emissions of carbon dioxide provide a double disincentive to increasing its use. Renewables have grown rapidly from supplying 20% of the power grid in 2019 to 35% in December 2021.[64] Labor has projected a figure of more than 70% renewables use by 2030. The hegemony of coal is fast disappearing, as its former primacy is inverted by renewables. The pace and scale of this phenomenon is changing the power dynamics—both in terms of electricity production and political narrative—of the nation.

3.3.5.2 The ongoing and contested nature of fossil fuels in the transition economy

The contested issues relevant to such companies and group structures are numerous and inter-connected. They include their profitability and solvency, the level of concessions and subsides they receive from various levels of government, the amount of tax they actually pay in Australia, the social license to either to commence, or to continue to operate, the number of people they employ (particularly in ongoing jobs), the overall contribution they make to the national economy, and the regional social networks in which they generally operate.

3.4 Related corporate case studies

Adani is not an isolated case of an Australian-based corporate entity which is reliant on thermal coal, struggling in the marketplace as the take up of renewable increases.

64 Adam Morton, 'The early closure of Australia' biggest coal plant caught Angus Taylor by surprise-but it shouldn't have,' *The Guardian Australia Online*, 18 February 2022.

3.4.1 Energy supplier AGL and the disorderly transition of Australia's biggest corporate CO_2 emitter.

AGL—formerly The Australian Gas Light Company—was one of the first companies to be established in the then colony of NSW in the early 1800s. From the moment of European arrival in 1788, the primary focus, as noted was on running a penal settlement with Foucauldian levels of control and order, rather than a market-based economy. The English, sponsoring state provided much of the colony's funding, such that private investment was little-needed in the first few decades. This changed with the establishment of some early corporate enterprises offering basic goods and essential services, such as power supply, banking, and agricultural trading services, and several of these companies are still in existence today. They include AGL in the energy sector, Westpac Bank (which started as the Bank of New South Wales) in banking, and the Australian Agricultural Company in agri-services.[65] These iconic companies are on the ASX200, the Australian Securities Exchange's list of the largest 200 publicly listed, blue-chip companies.

AGL is currently navigating significant legacy and transition issues. It is Australia's largest greenhouse gas emitter, being responsible for more than 8% of total annual national emissions. It operates three large but ageing and inefficient coal-fired power plants. These are increasingly unreliable and susceptible to becoming stranded assets. They are due to be phased out of operation by the year 2045.

The other major aspect of AGL's business is supplying power to more than four million customers across the eastern seaboard of Australia. Given this bifurcation of the basic elements of the business, the AGL board recently considered that its preferred strategy would be to spit the company into two parts, separating the legacy issue of coal generation from the future-oriented sector of supply-side energy. The corporate demerger required the passing of a special resolution by shareholders, being 75% of the votes cast at a shareholder meeting. The largest shareholder in AGL is the technology entrepreneur and founder of Atlassian, Mike Cannon-Brookes who holds, through his family company, Grok Ventures, 11.3% of the voting shares. Grok along with other shareholders had sufficient votes—25% or more—to block the passing of the special resolution to demerge the company into two different entities, and so it did not take place.

3.4.1.1 The spectre of takeover activity and board renewal

Instead, Cannon-Brookes sought to takeover AGL via a consortium with backing from a Canadian-based group. The takeover offer was twice rebuffed by the AGL board.

The AGL share price reflects these embedded corporate complexities. It is a company with a divided focus and with a problematic plan. In the end play,

65 Jason Harris, *Company Law: Theories, Principles and Applications*, LexisNexis, 2012, 11.

Cannon-Brookes has succeeded in having four directors appointed to the board.[66]AGL provides an example of the multiple strategies that former-era fossil fuel companies face, including climate activism on the share register, a changing board, dynamic, divestment pressures, and takeover challenges.

3.4.2 Origin Energy: another big energy corporation widely seen as a climate transition laggard

AGL is not alone in terms of the disorderly transition where customers, shareholders, and employees are liable to suffer. The largest coal-fired power station in Australia is Eraring in Lake Macquarie, NSW. It uses black thermal coal and generates nearly 3,000 MW of power.[67] Eraring has been operating fully since 1984 and provides about 20% of NSW's electricity generation. It was due to close in 2032. In February 2022, Origin Energy, a large, listed company and the owner of Eraring indicated that Eraring would be decommissioned in 2025, some seven years earlier than planned and this caused political consternation for the LNP government.[68] Origin gave notice to the Australian Energy Market Operator (AEMO) on this basis, and the company set out that that its decision was strategic, economic, and reflected:

> the rapidly changing conditions in the national electricity market, which are increasingly not well suited to traditional baseload power stations.[69]

The Chief Executive Officer of Origin, Frank Calabria said:

> the reality is the economics of coal-fired power stations are being put under increasing, unsustainable pressure by cleaner and lower cost generation, including solar, wind and batteries.[70]

In May 2022, there was a change of government as the Albanese-led Labor party was elected.

66 Peter Hannam, *The Guardian Australia,* 'Mike Cannon-Brookes succeeds in shaking up the AGL board, 15 Nov 2022, Mike Cannon-Brookes succeeds in shaking up AGL board | AGL | The Guardian.

67 Adam Morton and Peter Hannam, 'Australia's largest coal-fired power station, Eraring, to close in 2025, seven years early', *The Guardian Australia Online*, 17 February 2022.

68 Adam Morton, 'The early closure of, Australia' biggest coal plant caught Angus Taylor by surprise-but it shouldn't have', *The Guardian Australia Online,* 18 February 2022, https://www.theguardian.com/environment/2022/feb/18/on-coal-plant-closures-the-energy-industry-has-learned-to-keep-angus-taylor-out-of-the-loop.

69 Morton and Hannam, n 67.

70 Morton and Hannam, n 67.

3.4.3 The contrasting fortunes of new and emerging boom companies

By contrast to businesses focused on thermal coal and methane gas, there will be companies in the renewables sector which create or deal with rapidly increasing asset prices. These will potentially generate so-called 'super profits' and will likely grow rapidly in valuation, particularly as the market for their products matures. At their optimal settings, they will likely create a virtuous circle between the company, its investors, and delivering improvements to the wider public good constituted by contributions to climate solutions, either directly or implicitly. They will be the Australian version of the US-based corporate unicorn[71] and will likely include lithium batteries, solar panels, advanced manufacturing, battery storage, solutions for off the gird self-sufficiency and electrification of the home, heating, cooling, and family transport.

Australian versions of innovative corporations will emerge. They may not rival the US corporations such as Tesla, Google, Apple, or Amazon in terms of size and scale but they will be significant. Just as Australia was firstly fortunate to produce fine wool for burgeoning export markets, and secondly to become a minerals extraction powerhouse, its third lucky chapter is arguably nigh. Abundant wind and solar resources, along with rare-earth and strategic minerals, provide Australia with an advantage endowed by nature, such that corporations can in turn harness this bounty. The Australian Government's Intergenerational Report 2023 notes in this respect:

> The mining sector is expected to evolve as the world transitions to net zero and reduces its reliance on the fossil fuels and emissions-intensive commodities Australia exports. Australia's critical minerals and other resources could potentially become key exports for the global net zero transformation.[72]

The Commonwealth Department of Science, Industry, and Resources will publish and update the list of 'critical minerals', defined as

> Australia's Critical Minerals List includes minerals that are essential to our modern technologies, economies and national security, and whose supply chains are vulnerable to disruption. The list is based on global technology needs, particularly for emissions reduction, advanced manufacturing and defence. The Australian Government is establishing a process to update the list. This will help ensure it responds to global strategic, technological, economic and policy changes.[73]

71 This refers to companies not yet publicly listed but with an imminently anticipated market capitalization more than $1bn.

72 Intergenerational Report 2023: Australia's future to 2063, https://treasury.gov.au/sites/default/files/2023-08/p2023-435150.pdf, 4.

73 Australian Government, Department of Science, Industry and Resources, Australia's Critical Minerals List, June 2023, https://www.industry.gov.au/publications/australias-critical-minerals-list.

These include lithium and nickel, of which Australia has abundant quantities.

3.4.4 The hypothesis that Australia can become an economic superpower through renewables

This emerging economic and corporate thesis of Australia potentially being a renewables superpower has been sketched out by the well-known Australian economist, Ross Garnaut.[74] The climate emergency provides a serendipitous opportunity for Australian corporations—existing, new, and emerging—to thrive within the matrix of a southern hemisphere country with a world-leading 21st- century story to tell. Professor Garnaut was also commissioned in 2008 by the federal Labor government to produce a comprehensive national Climate Change Review.[75] The review recommended an emissions trading scheme (ETS) which was in place briefly and proved successful at curbing emissions but by 2013, there was a change of government with the incoming conservative LNP government describing the ETS as a carbon tax, with its slogan of 'axe the tax', and Australia thereafter endured a hyper-partisan stasis on climate policy. All momentum stalled, such that by 2019, Ross Garnaut described 'climate change as a diabolical problem with a saving grace'.[76] The saving grace was that he still optimistically perceived there to be a strong base of support for reform.[77] The other point, more fundamentally, was that Australia's unique geology and geography mean that its place in a post-carbon world economy could be unlimited in scope.[78] Other experts have made similar points about the economic and social opportunity for an effective climate policy. For example, Nicky Ison has noted of Australia's opportunity, 'we can replace coal power with renewables and storage, electrify everything, create a renewable export industry and grow clean energy supply chains'.[79] Since the Labor government was elected in 2022, after nine years in opposition, it has framed the climate change emergency as a job-creating economic opportunity for Australia, and relied on expatriate experts with international experience such as Dr Saul Griffith (who spent much of his career in the US including as an adviser in the Biden administration in the US) whose ideas regarding essentially in due electrifying everything are central to the Labor government's climate solutions ambitions.[80]

74 Garnaut, n 10, 15.
75 Garnaut, n 10, 15.
76 Garnaut, n 10, 15.
77 Garnaut, n 10, 16.
78 Garnaut, n 10, 183.
79 Nicky Ison, 'Australia can swiftly end the climate wars and become a renewables superpower. Here's how', *The Guardian Australia*, 25 May 2022, https://www.theguardian.com/australia-news/commentisfree/2022/may/25/australia-can-swiftly-end-the-climate-wars-and-become-a-renewable-superpower-heres-how.
80 Saul Griffith, *The Big Switch: Australia's electric future*, Black Inc., 2022.

3.4.5 The ongoing links between fossil fuels and politics

The corporation, Whitehaven Coal, is a prime example of the inter-connected nature of coal, corporate activity, and political power in Australia. The Chairperson of Whitehaven is Mark Vaile, a former leader of the federal National Party and holder of the office of Deputy Prime Minister, in a previous Conservative-coalition LNP government. Indeed, the relationship between members of the National Party and corporate coal interests is an abiding one. This linkage is not limited to one political party or side of politics. Both major parties, Labor and Liberal/ LNP, whether federally, or in their state guises, are criticized for being too close to carbon intensive industries. The capture of state governments by the fossil fuel industry is also apparent. For instance, is the case of the recently retired Premier of WA, Mark McGowan who has shortly after leaving office taken on roles with two corporations BHP and Mineral Resources.[81]

It is also alleged that when Premier in 2019, Mark McGowan telephoned Tom Hattan, the then head of the statutory, independent WA authority, the Environmental Protection Agency, to withdraw climate guidelines which were opposed by gas companies. Mr Hatton has said of the extraordinary phone call:

> There is a view that industry is important to the state's economy. I can understand why he felt he needed to take the concerns of some of those companies seriously. I think it was inappropriate and certainly did not respect the statutory independence of the EPA.[82]

The alleged call has also been criticized by a former Labor Premier, Carmen Lawrence. She noted that if true, it was 'certainly improper', 'ethically questionable', and 'illustrated the power that fossil fuels have to influence the government' in the resources-rich state.[83]

Bill Hare, the Perth-based head of Climate Analytics, noted the alleged call was problematic in terms of the abiding power of oil and gas interests in WA:

> I don't think it's well understood on the east coast. It seems quite apparent that the state capture is fairly well complete, and at least de facto supported by the federal government.[84]

The climate emergency still appears to give way to economic imperatives, particularly in the resource- intense states of Australia

81 Adam Morton, 'Mark McGowan phone call allegation puts fossil fuel influence in WA under spotlight', *The Guardian*, 9 October 2023.

82 Morton, n 81.

83 Morton, n 81.

84 Morton, n 81.

3.5 The implications of the Adani and related case studies for corporate law theory, risk, and governance

The ongoing nature, and the broader ripple effect of the Adani saga regarding coal projects in the Galilee Basin, demonstrates several factors. First is the unique power of governments to provide support—both explicit and implicit—to unsustainable businesses because of ideology. The political license provided by the federal government may have trumped the lack of a social license to operate.

3.5.1 The Australian economic situation: simplicity, vulnerability, and volatility

It can certainly be validly proposed that Australia is an outlier case—a first-world economy with an abiding reliance on wealth generated by fossil fuel extraction and export. It may be vulnerable to a legacy of stranded assets, and if this is significant enough it may become a stranded economy, in the sense that its present exports will fail to find markets, and its relative wealth as a G20 nation will slip down the rankings. These case studies provide lessons from Australia which may potentially have wide-spread relevance for other advanced and developing economies.

The approach adopted to date has resulted in a particular legacy. Australia has a very simplistic economy as judged against other similar economies by reference to The Harvard University's Centre for International Development which has an Atlas of Economic Complexity in which it ranks national economies by complexity.[85] The top five countries by complexity are Japan, Switzerland, South Korea, Germany, and Singapore. By stark contrast, Australia comes in 93rd place, after Uganda and just ahead of Pakistan. This reflects the high degree of simply extracting and exporting fossil fuels in their raw state, with no value-adding. As such, Australia suffers a diminished manufacturing sector, and economic profile very different to other G20 countries and to its traditional trading partner the UK in 8th place on the complexity index.

3.5.2 The local as global: the counting of exported or scope 3 emissions

Emissions fall in three categories, scope 1 being direct from the company's activities, scope 2 are based on necessary inputs into making the activities happen, and scope 3 emissions refer to the those created by assets not owned or controlled by the reporting organization or to emissions caused by the end-use of a company's products, for example the use of Australian coal, gas, and oil in overseas markets. The three types of emissions taken together account for the totality of emissions. Clearly measuring, publishing, and acknowledging levels of scope 3 emissions is a sensitive issue for companies, sectors, and nations because it can provide a forensic comparative international lens that would otherwise not be applied. As research by the Australia Institute Research notes:

85 Harvard University Centre for International Development (CID), Atlas of Economic Complexity, 'Country and Product Complexity Rankings', https://atlas.cid.harvard.edu/rankings

> Australia's exported fossil fuel CO_2 potential is more than double Australia's total domestic emissions. This makes Australia the world's third largest fossil fuel exporter in CO_2 terms. It is behind only Russia and Saudi Arabia. The vast majority of the export CO_2 is coal, although gas has been increasing dramatically.[86]

Australia as a nation and many of its major carbon emitters have to date been reluctant to disclose scope 3 emissions. There has been little evidence of leading by example as an advanced first-world economy.

By contrast, the European Carbon Border Adjustment Mechanism (CBAM) developed by the European Commission is a mechanism for levelling up carbon emissions and setting a high benchmark for other nations to aspire to.[87] However, even in this regard, Australia is reserving its position in 2024 in terms of developing its own scheme, as was discussed in Chapter 1.6. The big, bold reform steps to tackle the climate crisis remain elusive in Australia.

3.5.3 Public money and profiteering: the abundant public subsidies propping up the fossil fuel industries

In terms of solving the climate crisis, physics and hard sciences need to trump the social sciences of politics, economics, and law. In Australia, there has been resort to weak self-regulation for companies, no disclosure requirements as regards emissions (although this is proposed by the Australian Treasury to change for certain large corporations by mid-2024[88]), and the narrative that corporations are somehow in charge of reducing emissions on their own and will therefore come up with technological solutions and lead the nation's 'journey' to net-zero.[89] It is a form of magical thinking and stands in contrast to an approach with a rigorous framework of mandated rules, targets, and best practice. Given the political quagmire, this latter approach is being driven largely by the market:

> Investors, however, continue to press companies for greater commitments. While most top ASX-listed businesses have set their own targets to neutralise their own emissions by 2050 or earlier, shareholders are increasingly calling for further measures, including taking account for emissions caused by

86 The Australia Institute, Tom Swann, 'Scope of the Reporting: Submission on national greenhouse and energy reporting amendment (Transparency in Carbon Emissions Accounting) Bill 2020', April 2020, 1–12, 5, https://australiainstitute.org.au/wp-content/uploads/2021/10/P898-NGER-Transparency-and-Scope-3-bill-submission.pdf.

87 European Commission, Taxation and Customs Union, Carbon Border Adjustment Mechanism, https://taxation-customs.ec.europa.eu/carbon-border-adjustment-mechanism_en.

88 Climate Works Centre, Charlotte Mills and Steve Kelly, 'Mandatory climate-related financial disclosures for Australian companies, explained', 30 Oct 2023, Mandatory climate-related financial disclosures for Australian companies, explained - Climateworks Centre.

89 Australian Government, 'The Plan to Deliver Net Zero', n 47.

> customers of their products, aligning their future strategies with their climate targets, and to start allocating the money required.[90]

Whilst this approach is sought, bringing it to fruition in the Australian corporate sector is slow and seemingly complex:

> In a first-of-its-kind analysis, Climate Action 100+, a group of 545 investors managing a combined $70 trillion of assets, last month determined none of the 12 Australian companies assessed had disclosed how it would align future investments with stated emissions-reduction aims. Australian companies were "second only to the European companies" in setting net-zero targets, Climate Action 100+ director Laura Hillis said, but few were backing their pledges financially.[91]

A key reason for stasis is that Australian governments—whether labor or conservative, and at local state and national level—provide a range of generous tax concessions for research and development and for unproven carbon sequestration methods such as carbon capture and storage. The dilemma is that the tax concessions provided to multi-national companies involved in industries with a high degree of financial climate risk means there may be no tax at all collected from them.

In addition to a weak tax collection system, there are generous subsidies and rebates provided to emissions-intensive industries. The Australia Institute's analysis supports a finding that there is in the order of $11.6bn in the 2021–2 financial year, an increase of $1.3bn on the previous year, provided by governments in Australia to fossil fuel companies by way of subsidies and rebates. This locks in power and advantage to incumbent industries. It reinforces the status quo, it makes innovation more difficult, and the threshold conditions to be met new market entrants become more complex and expensive. Of this totality of factors, Rod Campbell, Research Director at the Australia Institute observes:

> It is perverse that Australian governments continue to subsidise fossil fuel production and consumption while communities across the country are bearing the costs of disasters exacerbated by fossil fuel use. This is bad economics and even worse climate policy. We are witnessing Australia's flood-stricken communities trying to pick up the pieces while fossil fuel interests are cashing in the tune of over $22,000 a minute. Worse still, these subsidies are growing and show no sign of slowing down. It is the Federal Government driving increases in fossil fuel subsidies, with $6.7 billion worth of new measures committed since the 2019 election. The big increases are not hidden, but are central government policies such as the 'gas-fired recovery' and more money for ever-failing technologies like carbon capture

90 Nick Toscano, '"We will take action": Investors target ASX's climate-laggard directors', *The Sydney Morning Herald,* 26 April, 2021, https://www.smh.com.au/business/companies/we-will-take-action-investors-target-asx-s-climate-laggard-directors-20210423-p57lv5.html.

91 Toscano, n 90.

> and storage. It is long past time for these irresponsible budget measures to be reversed and these resources directed to combating climate change and preparing Australians for its consequences.[92]

Furthermore, the opaque nature of political donations law means that wealthy fossil fuel enterprises can wield largely unaccountable power and influence by gaining ready access to political leaders.

3.5.4 Project finance risk in an era of rapid energy transition

Another risk is transition risk. This was identified in 2015 by the G20 Financial Stability Board and then Chair of the FSB and Governor of the Bank of England, Mark Carney, and it focuses on the shift away from emissions-intensive operations to a low-carbon economy, a shift that will occur over years and have 'the potential for long-tail risks to be significant, uncertain and non-linear'.[93] In this regard, by late 2016 there has been 'seismic disruption in asset values in the American coal industry … the combined market capitalization of America's four biggest coal companies had plummeted by 99 percent since 2010, with three of them (Peabody, Arch and Alpha) filing for bankruptcy'.[94] The Australian Energy Council has noted that the financing of coal projects is increasingly problematic. [95]

As Mark Butler, the former Labor shadow minister, notes 'the re-pricing of these assets is not the only risk that flows from this profound economic transition. There are dramatic impacts on jobs and local communities'.[96] The paradox is that the site of impact and economic vulnerability is also likely to be the locus of opportunity; this is the Adani situation writ large with the Galilee Basin simultaneously both a coal super pit and the potential site for a world-leading solar grid.

92 Australia Institute, 'Australian fossil fuel subsidies surge to $11.6billion in 202-22', 28 March 2022, https://australiainstitute.org.au/post/australian-fossil-fuel-subsidies-surge-to-11-6-billion-in-2021-22/.

93 Mark Carney, Chair, Bank of England, 'Breaking the tragedy of the horizon- climate change and financial stability', *Lloyd's of London*, 29 Sept 2015, 1–16, 10. https://www.bankofengland.co.uk/speech/2015/breaking-the-tragedy-of-the-horizon-climate-change-and-financial-stability.

94 Mark Carney, Chair, Bank of England, 'Resolving the Climate Paradox', Arthur Burns Memorial lecture, Berlin, 22 Sept 2016, 1–15, 9. https://www.bankofengland.co.uk/-/media/boe/files/speech/2016/resolving-the-climate-paradox.pdf.

95 Australian Energy Council, Submission to Senate Standing Committee on Environment and Communications, 'The retirement of coal fired power stations,' 10 November 2016, https://www.energycouncil.com.au/media/tawbmnlr/16-11-10-aec-submission-senate-inquiry-retirement-of-coal-fired-power-stations.pdf.

96 Butler, n 40, 118.

3.5.5 The emergence of the climate-related financial risk: the exposure of 'stranded assets'

Financial analysis makes it clear that the investment tide is going out on coal with the rise of risk and uncertain returns such that fossil fuel assets, which were previously valuable assets, may be of little or no value and impossible to raise finance against or to insure. Recent international analysis by German-based academics has focused on economics of coal investment by Adani and others in the Galilee Basin:

> We parameterize coal mining in the Galilee Basin based on the Carmichael coal mine and export project specifics. We construct three coal demand scenarios with varying climate policy ambitions based on bottom-up coal sector data of the major coal consuming countries in Asia. We find that, even under most optimistic assumptions, new coal mines in the Galilee Basin are not economically viable in the long-run and prone to become stranded assets.[97]

The environmental scientist Tim Flannery has argued that 'the fossil fuel industry continues to survive only because it has financial backers and companies willing to insure it. Over the past few years, significant advances have been made in choking off these vital resources'.[98] Access to finance and insurance are key parts of 'fossil fuel's support network'.[99] Once these become problematic divestment or exiting fossil fuel investments begins. This movement was begun in 2010 by environmentalist Bill McKibben on US university campuses, and by 2015 'it was reportedly the fastest growing divestment movement in history'.[100] This has created a snowball effect because 'as one large investor after another has announced its withdrawal from fossil fuels, the pressure grows. At the very least, the divestment movement has brought into increasing question the social licence of the fossil fuel industry to operate'.[101]

There is an increasingly complex but steadfast connection between factors such as social licence, finance, risk, and insurance. As Flannery notes, 'risk and insurance are intimately linked, and as the fossil fuel industry faces increasing regulatory and other risks, the pool of insurers available to it is shrinking'.[102] The rapid emanation of climate-related financial risk means that coal is in the cross hairs in the first instance, but gas and oil will become vulnerable too in the transition economy as the price, reliability and scale of renewables improves. The stranding analogy may

97 Christian Hauenstein, Franziska Holz, Lennart Rathje and Thomas Mitterecker, 'Stranded Assets in the Coal Export Industry? The Case of the Australian Galilee Basin', DIW, Berlin, 2022. https://www.diw.de/documents/publikationen/73/diw_01.c.840655.de/dp2003.pdf

98 Tim Flannery, *The Climate Cure: Solving the Climate Emergency in the Era of COVID-19*, Chapter 10, 'Cutting off Fossil Fuel's Support Network', *Text Publishing*, 2020, 11–115, 112.

99 Flannery, n 98, 112.

100 Flannery, n 98, 112.

101 Flannery, n 98, 113.

102 Flannery, n 98, 113.

therefore be applied in an increasing number of potential settings to include assets, companies, market sectors, and even nation states.

For companies, this raises the scenario that the combination of shareholders, third party financing, and insurance, respectively, may simultaneously desert old-style companies which are not paying sufficient attention to the climate emergency zeitgeist. Governments, of course, can play a key role as rule-setters. Their regulatory capacity should be on full display with a suite of incentives for solutions driven companies and disincentives for laggards and recalcitrant actors. Corporate regulation is discussed in Chapter 9.

The fate of corporations will be intrinsically linked with emerging asset classes, including the unprecedented scale of potential stranded assets. These will be created and exposed in rapid time, given the unpredictable nature of the market, its increasingly connected international parameters, effects, and its search for global solutions. There have been many examples of companies such as Kodak missing the seismic shifts in consumer needs and expectations. That a whole asset class as ubiquitous as coal may fall into this category is testament to the pace and scale of change. Coal has seen its status in Australia as 'black gold' and worthy of government support and high-order corporate risk and return, move quickly to a situation where it is fast becoming more expensive and riskier to remove from the earth in which, for millions of years it has laid dormant and compacted by time immemorial. Instead, regions such as the Galilee Basin that are 'home to fossil fuel industries [are] well-positioned to host new clean industries if supported by the right policies'.[103]

3.6 Conclusion

3.6.1 A lucky country with a simple economy

The lucky country thesis was made famous by Donald Horne in the 1960s.[104] Australia suffered from a mediocre polity but had been blessed from its inception in the 18th century with the happenstance to produce fine wool and then it found gold in the 19th century. Since then, its luck has been maintained twice over in the 20th century by iron ore and coal. Each has been underwritten latterly by demand from China. Coal exports really took off in the 1990s. This rose from 100 million tonnes in the 1980s, to 150 million tonnes by 1996; to 250 million tonnes by 2010, and 300 million tonnes by 2013. This is described by Judith Brett as a coal rush 'magnified by changes in the way coal is mined. The deep mines and coal pits of

103 Adam Morton, '"Highly implausible" that new Galilee Basin coalmines would be profitable study finds', *The Guardian Australia*, 27 May 2022, https://www.theguardian.com/australia-news/2022/may/27/highly-implausible-that-new-galilee-basin-coalmines-would-be-profitable-study-finds.

104 Horne, n 39, as Hugh Mackay's Introduction notes of Horne's key phrase 'Australia is a lucky country, run mainly by second-rate people who share its luck', The Lucky Country by Donald Horne - Penguin Books Australia.

the past have been replaced with open-cut mega-mines, which strip the vegetation and topsoil and compete with agriculture for access to the land'.[105]

Adani and exports to India have become a key part of that narrative in the 21st century. This timing should have been unfortunate given that climate change should have been a central concern of governments in Australia. Instead, government largesse provided the framework for a new layer of complacency, and the early 2000s saw iron ore become the staple of Australian exports. Australia has been lucky several times over, but it has resulted in a great complacency. Most economies move from simplicity to complexity, and from low-productivity areas such as agriculture and mining to high-productivity sectors such as advanced manufacturing. Indeed, The Atlas of Economic Complexity, the Harvard-based global index measuring complexity by reference to national economies puts Australia beyond 90th place amongst more than 130 countries.[106] As such, Australia is a G20 country and political system with the equivalent of a struggling, third-world mono-economy. This makes Australia particularly vulnerable to price fluctuations in raw materials such that it is a price taker, not a price setter. It is stuck in a simplicity loop and this provides fundamental constraint for building resilient corporate capacity. Judith Brett has reported that in June 2018, there were about 36,000 people working in the coal-mining industry, whereas there were about 44,000 people employed in the car manufacturing industry. This latter industry no longer exists there, and its demise was overseen by the LNP government. It had been the focal point of high-end manufacturing—this included 'cars, engines, electrical and other components, as well as trucks, buses and products for the automotive after-market'.[107] Australia's long-run complacency has given rise to an economy and polity being forced to adjust. Economies operating at stall speed, in an era of global competitiveness, gives rise to the danger of the stranded nation concept encompassing sovereign risk.[108]

3.6.2 The corporate law and corporate governance dimensions of the climate change crisis

These political changes will have major consequences for corporations and the Australian business sector. This is both a challenge and an opportunity for companies ranging from start-ups to long-established, listed entities. In general, companies engaging in solutions-driven climate change initiatives will have a clearer road map, both in the medium term to 2030, and the longer term to 2050. Companies in legacy areas, such as coal, will have deeply problematic futures. All companies will need to review their governance and structures. Boards which better reflect

105 Brett, n 31, 18.

106 Harvard University, Growth Lab, The Atlas of Economic Complexity, .

107 Brett, n 31, 13.

108 Stephen Martin, Committee for Economic Development of Australia (CEDA) CEO, 'GFC and Sovereign Risk', https://www.ceda.com.au/NewsAndResources/News/Economy/GFC-and-sovereign-risk.

society, particularly as regards gender parity, will be vital. The project of finding climate change solutions and necessary reform and innovation will combine robust sustainable corporations with cutting-edge governance. The just and sustainable society implicit in the commitment to net zero by 2050 will be powered by companies who are able to link excellence and sustainability in their operations, together with compelling social engagement initiatives and clear-eyed strategy.

3.6.3 The Third Carbon Age

The US theorist Donna Haraway suggests that society is now experiencing the Third Carbon Age wherein:

> every imaginable, and many unimaginable, technologies and strategic measures are being pursued by all the big global players to extract every last calorie of fossil carbon, at whatever depth and in whatsoever formations of sand, mud or rock, and with whatever horrors of travel to distribution and use points, to burn before someone else gets at that calorie and burns it first.[109]

Adani's role in the Galilee basin is an example of this possibility. Have the economic and financial metrics finally deserted coal and other fossil fuel investments, or will Haraway's gloomy prognosis prove to be correct?

3.6.4 Links between the Adani and the other case studies

Adani is the first of four case studies discussed in *Corporate Law and Climate Change*. It raises issues some of which are *sui generis* and others which find expression in related commercial and corporate contexts. Adani sets the scene for some emerging themes. These surround the inescapable consequences for corporations grappling with a changing climate and the remediation necessary to address the climate emergency. These features find expression and clarity in the three-decade global project of net zero by 2050.

Solutions must necessarily focus on fossil fuels. Australia is one of the world's largest exporters of fossil fuels. In this respect, it has much in common with Saudi Arabia and Russia and yet it is also a modern market economy with a functioning democracy. Australia is a major global emitter if the totality of its emissions is considered, with its exported or scope three emissions. Given these fundamental features—an historically leading fossil fuel producer, an advanced market economy, and a century of world-leading electoral practice, including compulsory voting—what occurs in the next three decades matters at an international level. It represents a bellwether set of emerging economic and social issues for much of the world, whether by reference to it being an advanced economic model or to nascent and advancing economic systems in the process of construction and deliberation.

109 Donna J Haraway, *Staying with the Trouble: Making Kin in the Chthulucene*, Duke University Press, 2016, 47.

The Adani case study is pivotal within this national rubric. It links to the social licence aspects of the Rio Tinto case study in the next chapter. Is there a social licence for carrying on with coal production? Is there a social licence for corporations who do not treat ancient rock art with due respect? These issues can be both singular and emblematic of wider consequences.

The financial implications of Adani include the access to capital markets. This issue is also playing out in the aftermath of the McVeigh case study which is discussed in Chapter 5. The application of novel duties, such as the duty of care applied to a minister of the Crown in Sharma's case discussed in Chapter 6, are also likely to have reverberations for directors of coal and other companies.

Adani has been at the fulcrum of political change in Australia. Taken together, the four case studies are symptomatic of seismic changes taking place in Australia. They demonstrate that the economic and social model is evolving rapidly. In turn, this fundamentally affects how companies will need to act and react in the race to achieving net zero by 2050. The Adani case provides an elongated and ongoing case study of the challenges, pitfalls, and opportunities for corporations within the Australian context.

References

Judith Brett, 'The Coal Curse: Resources, Climate and Australia's Future', *Quarterly Essay, Black Inc. Books*, 78, 2020, 1–78.

Mark Butler, *Climate Wars*, Melbourne University Press, 2017.

Michael Cannon, *Life in the Country: Australia in the Victorian Age: 2*, Currey O'Neil Ross Pty Ltd, 1983.

Rachel Carson, *Silent Spring*, Houghton Mifflin, 1962.

Tim Flannery, *The Climate Cure: Solving the Climate Emergency in the Era of COVID-19*, Text Publishing, 2020.

Joelle Gergis, *Sunburnt Country: The History and Future of Climate Change in Australia*, MUP, 2018.

Ruth Goodman, *The Domestic Revolution: How the Introduction of Coal into Our Homes Changed Everything*, Michael O'Mara Books Limited, 2020.

Saul Griffith, *The Big Switch: Australia's Electric Future*, Black Inc., 2022.

Donna J. Haraway, *Staying with the Trouble: Making Kin in the Chthulucene*, Duke University Press, 2016.

Jason Harris, *Company Law: Theories, Principles and Applications*, LexisNexis, 2012.

Donald Horne, *The Lucky Country*, Penguin, 1964.

Robert Hughes, *The Fatal Shore: History of the Transportation of Convicts to Australia, 1787–1868*, Pan Macmillan, 1988.

Sean Kelly, *The Game: A Portrait of Scott Morrison*, Black Inc., 2021.

Michael E. Mann, *The New Climate War: The Fight to Take Back Our Planet*, Scribe, 2021.

Lisa Miller, 'The Use of Case Studies in Law and Social Science Research', *Annual Review of Law and Social Science*, 14, 2018, 381.

Adam Morton and Peter Hannam, 'Australia's largest coal-fired power station, Eraring, to close in 2025, seven years early,' *The Guardian Australia Online*, 17 February 2022.

Anthony Sampson, *The Seven Sisters: The Great Oil Companies and the World They Shaped*, Viking, 1975.

Micha Tomkiewicz, *Climate Change: The Fork at the End of Now*, Momentum Press, LLC, 2011.

Robert Yin, *Case Study Research: Design and Methods*, 5th ed, Sage, 2014.

4 The corporate climate II

Rio Tinto and the social licence to operate

4.1 The case study: the Rio Tinto Corporate Group and the destruction of the rock shelters in the Juukan Gorge, Western Australia

4.1.1 The events of May 2020

In May 2020, caves and rock shelters in the Juukan Gorge in the Pilbara region of WA were destroyed by explosives detonated by the Rio Tinto Group 'while blasting in the area as part of its mining operations'.[1] This was done to 'make way for an expansion of Rio Tinto's Brockman 4 iron ore mine'.[2] The extraction of more tonnes of iron ore for export markets and the further monetization the landscape took place, in this instance, on sacred country of the traditional indigenous owners.[3] As Kate Galloway notes:

> The caves contained archaeological treasures evidencing human occupation spanning some 46,000 years. As such, they represent globally significant sites—sites far older than Stonehenge and the pyramids of Egypt. But more than that, the caves held ongoing spiritual significance for the traditional owners of the area, the Puutu Kunti Kurrama and Pinikura.[4]

The destruction 'attracted global attention'[5] and resulted in the wide-spread condemnation of Rio Tinto. The board, clearly taken aback by the level of vitriol, expressed regret in the international media.[6] Its then CEO and Chair both spoke in remorseful terms about the company's terrible mistake.

1 Kate Galloway, 'A legal lacuna: between cultural heritage and native title', *Australian Environment Review*, Sept 2020, 110–3, 110.

2 Nick Toscano, 'Three years on, Rio Tinto says Juukan disaster remains a deep stain', *The Sydney Morning Herald*, May 25, 2023. https://www.smh.com.au/business/companies/three-years-on-rio-tinto-says-juukan-disaster-remains-a-deep-stain-20230524-p5db1p.html

3 Elizabeth Pearson, 'Heartbreak in the Juukan Gorge: 'Embarrassingly out of Kilter' Law Destroys 46,000-Year-Old Aboriginal Sacred Sites', *Art Antiquity and Law*, Vol. 25, Issue 2 (July 2020), 147–58, 147.

4 Galloway, n 1, 110.

5 Galloway, n 1, 110.

6 See for example, BBC news, 'Mining firm Rio Tinto sorry for destroying Aboriginal caves', 31 May 2020, https://www.bbc.com/news/world-australia-52869502.

DOI: 10.4324/9781003263746-5

4.1.2 The legal paradox regarding the destruction of the rock shelters in the Juukan Gorge

Despite the clearly insensitive destruction of an ancient spiritual First Nations site, the technical legality of the company's actions was not in dispute. As Kate Galloway notes:

> To the astonishment of the general public- including a shareholder backlash- in destroying the obviously special caves Rio Tinto did not break the law. It had obtained the necessary permissions to destroy the culturally significant site under the *Aboriginal Heritage Act* 1972 (WA).[7]

The irony is that the indigenous or CATSI corporation established under federal legislation[8] is the unwitting, but ultimately flawed, corporate vehicle by which indigenous consent is gained. As such, the hegemonic reach of a corporation, such as Rio Tinto, is garnered by reference to another selective corporate entity comprised of some of the traditional owners, but not others. Read within this wider frame, the destruction by Rio Tinto[9] of the ancient indigenous rock art and globally significant artefacts is both shocking and a direct consequence of the theory of companies. Companies have the necessary capacity and legal personality to contract with one another and to be bound by those agreements.

The issue is simply reframed by corporate law where it positions separate legal-entity status of the company, contractual capacity, and the pursuit of profits for shareholders—collectively, the key elements of the shareholder primacy model of Australian corporate law—against the long-standing cultural sensitivity of a First Nations site of significance. Given its age of an estimated 46,000 years, the site is almost beyond the comprehension of a Eurocentric orthodoxy of time, let alone the very few decades (and arguably centuries) in which companies have been a dominant economic and social force.

Episodes such as this in the mining and extractive industries are, however, unfortunately commonplace; the Rio Tinto example perhaps being the most brazen. It obscures, however, a steady pattern of destruction of places of 'importance and significance'[10] by mining corporations.

Before demolishing the site, Rio Tinto cleared the caves and catalogued the materials found; this is reminiscent of the Dickensian, 19th-century colonialist epoch. It positions the curios of Empire as disembodied artefacts, and their creators as Other. It is as if the Western economic and scientific process of taxonomic referencing, cataloguing, and classification is somehow, in and of itself, equivalent to

7 Galloway, n 1, 110.

8 The *Corporations (Aboriginal and Torres Strait Islander) Act 2006* (CATSI Act).

9 The company is formally known as Rio Tinto International Holdings Ltd, a publicly listed company, listed in Australia and the UK and the world's second biggest mining conglomerate after another Anglo-Australian company BHP Limited.

10 Galloway, n 1, 111.

sufficient acknowledgment, and respect—in effect a memento mori—of an ancient spiritual place.

4.1.3 The immediate after-effects for Rio Tinto of its destruction of the Juukan Gorge

In the wake of the global backlash, Rio Tinto sought essentially to divest itself of moral and ethical culpability.[11] It did so via several legal avenues. These included contract law and issues of contractual validity, environmental law, and of advocating vociferously that they had secured all requisite licenses. Their defence was one of legal compliance by the corporate entity and its office holders. It also sought to rely on having met its obligation under native title legislation arguing that it sought and received permission from relevant indigenous owners. In this secondary technical sense, it was, it argued, also legally compliant. Despite the resorts by the company to legalism and box ticking compliance, these propositions did not cut through in the days and weeks following the destruction.

Rio was caught off-guard, the glare of the global spotlight shocking it out of its inward-looking operational stance. This is where, in this instance, the gap between the claims of legality on the one hand and the attribution or otherwise of social licence on the other became apparent. The suite of laws that Rio had relied on as a complete prophylaxis against critique had failed them. Instead of granting them unfettered permission to destroy ancient sites within the statutory limits, these laws have been described since the destruction by prestigious international analysis as 'outdated, insensitive and ineffective ... [and] criticized as more permissive of destruction than protective of Aboriginal Indigenous heritage'.[12] This is where the world sees Australia, and its resources-dominated corporate ethos, quite differently to how it perceives itself. The shortcomings of state and Commonwealth statutes which reflect a bias towards development over cultural sensitivity have been thoroughly exposed in the prolonged glare of the international spotlight.

Rio Tinto also relied on long-established legal principles within corporate groups. It assiduously sought to ring-fence the technicalities of the decision-making process relevant to the destruction from the corporate headquarters, and to attribute that process to the iron ore sub-division of the group. As such, the company attempted to define its actions as lawful, reasonable, and essentially inevitable given the range of structural issues evident in a complex conglomerate group. In doing so, it sought to promote the corporate complexity afforded by its group structure as a shield, protecting the Chief Executive Officer and the parent board from ongoing scrutiny or culpability. In particular, the company has deployed the corporate form within the group as a mechanism to isolate or seal off the actions of subsidiary from

11 Calla Wahlquist, 'Leaked tape reveals Rio Tinto does not regret destroying 46,000-year-old Aboriginal rock shelter to expand mine', *The Guardian*, 17 June 2020, https://www.theguardian.com/australia-news/2020/jun/16/rio-tinto-repeats-apology-for-blasting-46000-year-old-rock-shelter-to-expand-mine.

12 Pearson, n 3, 147.

the parent company. This has been to disconnect any responsibility between the boardroom decision on the one hand and its real-world consequences on the other. Such attempted imposition of traditional corporate distancing techniques has not, however, satisfied international shareholders in this instance.

The destruction of the rock shelters forced the announcement of the resignation of the group CEO, Jean-Sebastian Jacques, 'by mutual agreement' in September 2020, four months after the destruction and relentless criticism.[13] Two other executives also resigned, but all three were entitled to receive long-term bonuses.[14] Despite the mixed messages the corporation was conveying, the Chair of Rio, Simon Thompson announced:

> What happened at Juukan was wrong and we are determined to ensure that the destruction of a heritage site of such exceptional archaeological and cultural significance never occurs again at a Rio Tinto operation. We are also determined to regain the trust of the Puutu Kunti Kurrama and Pinikura people and other traditional owners. We have listened to our stakeholders' concerns that a lack of individual accountability undermines the group's ability to rebuild that trust and to move forward to implement the changes identified in the board review.[15]

Whilst the CEO went, the Chair of the Board remained. The accountability of corporate conscience to some limited extent had now been achieved, and the resignations were welcomed by superannuation funds and other institutional groups including the Australian Centre for Corporate Responsibility and the Australian Council of Superannuation Investors.[16] The CEO of Australia's biggest superannuation fund, AustralianSuper, Ian Silk, said he was 'satisfied that appropriate responsibility has now been taken by executives at Rio Tinto'.[17]

As it happened, Jean-Sebastian Jacques did not physically leave the company until May 2021, a year after the destructive blasts, and left with a large payout which caused a strong backlash from shareholder voting of more than 50% against the remuneration report. The proxy adviser CGI Glass Lewis in its advice to large institutional shareholders recommended their clients vote against the report:

13 BBC, Rio Tinto chief Jean-Sébastien Jacques to quit over Aboriginal cave destruction, 11 September 2020, https://www.bbc.com/news/world-australia-54112991. See also https://www.abc.net.au/news/2020-09-14/superannuation-forcing-change-rio-tinto-juukan-gorge/12659824?fbclid=IwAR251rRf7GBz7rDcazj08wbdIQeAM_3dMyATpEwFlJQ4jftyrd6dYl05E5Q.

14 Ben Butler, Lorena Allam and Calla Wahlquist, 'Rio Tinto CEO and senior executives resign from company after Juukan Gorge disaster', *The Guardian Australia*, 11 September 2020, https://www.theguardian.com/business/2020/sep/11/rio-tinto-ceo-senior-executives-resign-juukan-gorge-debacle-caves.

15 Butler, All and Wahlquist, n 14.

16 Butler, All and Wahlquist, n 14.

17 Butler, All and Wahlquist, n 14.

> we have severe reservations with the size of the awards vesting for former chief executive Jean-Sebastian Jacques under his 2016 long-term incentive plan in light of the events in the Juukan Gorge in the past fiscal year, and we are concerned with the opacity of disclosure on the decision-making related to remuneration sanctions made as a result.[18]

The chair of Rio's remuneration committee, Sam Laidlaw, defended the remuneration decision within a narrow legal argument:

> the penalties applied to the responsible executives were, in the best view of the board, the most that could be durably applied and legally defended in light of the executives' ultimately accountable for Juukan Gorge.[19]

This resort to narrow legalism by Rio, even in the wake of the relentless corporate social licence, responsibility, and conscience arguments raised by the events of May 2020 was still thoroughly ingrained one year on. It is an approach embedded in the corporate DNA.

By contrast, the chief executive of the National Native Title Council Jamie Low referred to the need for Rio to make structural changes, and the fact that 'the law needs to be strengthened. We can't rely on the goodwill of mining companies; we need the law strengthened. We can't rely on their word that things will get better'.[20] The problems with the laws supposedly designed to protect indigenous owners in Western Australia are fundamental. Two examples illustrate the point. First, the 'grant of mining rights by the state sets up an inherent conflict between traditional owners and miners over the use of the same land'.[21] This approach prioritizes development and the right, if not expectation, to mine the country and extract resources. As such, it positions indigenous groups in a reactive position. Second, 'there is no requirement that any Aboriginal person at all is involved in assessing places connected with sacred, ritual, or ceremonial sites of special significance'.[22] As such, no indigenous person or traditional owner is afforded expertise or custodian rights. Their evidence and stories are not heard. The law in this area, simply put, is not fit for purpose.

4.1.4 The rise of shareholder activism within the Rio Tinto corporate group

Prior to the events of May 2020, the company, Rio Tinto, was predictable, stable, profitable, and well regarded. Its shareholders were satisfied with the large profits being generated. There was, as is generally the case with miners, no scientific basis

18 Nick Toscano, 'Rio Tinto investors revolt against ex-CEO pay after cave blast crisis', *The Sydney Morning Herald*, May 6, 2021, https://www.smh.com.au/business/companies/rio-tinto-investors-revolt-against-ex-ceo-pay-after-cave-blast-crisis-20210506-p57pgo.html.

19 Nick Toscano 2021, n 18.

20 Butler, All and Wahlquist, n 14.

21 Galloway, n 1, 111.

22 Galloway, n 1, 111.

or particular social licence attached to its activities. It relied on geology, with its corporate strategy firmly in place. However, Rio Tinto's destruction of the ancient indigenous art and artefacts in the rock shelters changed that orthodoxy in the weeks following the detonation. It fundamentally misread the history and anthropology of the local area. This created, in turn, seismic consequences for stakeholders.

The first group affected were the First Nations' custodians. Second, the owners, as members and shareholders of the Rio Tinto Group were affected by reputational connection with the malfeasant company. Instead of the usual corporate law theory and practice of being essentially 'remote', and relatively disengaged shareholders, they were immediately transformed into powerful activists and advocates in direct opposition to the board and senior management. They insisted on swift and tangible accountability from the company's leadership group. As such they sought governance changes in the company, and this was achieved, at least in part, by the resignations of senior managers, and the CEO. This episode of intense pressure, giving rise to a set of response mechanisms is increasingly symptomatic of the activism that major companies will face. This is particularly the case when they act in a way to disrupt or destroy the hitherto implicit veil of corporate social responsibility.

4.2 The background to and context of the Rio Tinto corporate case study

The story of Rio Tinto and iron ore mining is intricately connected with Lang Hancock, father of Gina Rinehart, who one morning in November 1952, whilst flying his own light plane across the Hamersley ranges of WA at very low altitude given the stormy conditions, 'noticed what he thought was mineralisation on the rock wall. The rust red immediately signified one thing: oxidised iron'.[23] The geological find had to be kept a secret though because there were federal and state embargoes on iron exports still in place from prior to World War 2. Western Australia was a very poor state in the 1950s and early 1960s, with little mining activity. Hancock and his business partner, Peter Wright, finally succeeded in their lobbying efforts to get the embargoes removed. In 1961, Hancock travelled the globe seeking financial support. After he had also been to Rio's Australian headquarters in Melbourne, Hancock went to London to meet the Global Chair of Rio, Val Duncan, and persuaded him to visit the Pilbara and 'a few months later, in 1962, Rio Tinto, Hancock and Wright signed the momentous Hamersley iron ore royalty agreement'.[24] This provided royalties of 2.5% on every tonne of exported iron ore to Hancock and Wright. By contrast, 'Rio spent a fortune developing the mining and railway infrastructure that would extract the ore and transport it from

23 Adele Ferguson, *Gina Rinehart: the untold story of the richest woman in the world,* Macmillan, 2012, 7.

24 Ferguson, n 23, 11.

Mount Tom Price to the Port of Dampier'.[25] Rio has therefore been involved for more than six decades as a foundation participant in iron ore mining in WA since the industry's inception, and this deal along with others has 'transformed Western Australia and the national economy'.[26] Rio Tinto and iron ore extraction have been synonymous ever since, and this may partially explain the company's grave missteps when it came to the events in the Juukan Gorge in May 2020.

4.2.1 The Rio Tinto Group's sale of its coal assets

By contrast to its central and ongoing role in iron ore mining, Rio Tinto had sold it coal assets by 2018. This involved exiting its three coal mines based in Queensland at Hall Creek, the Valeria project, and Kestrel respectively. In the few years prior to that point, there was:

> speculation the company was moving away from coal because of pressure to address climate change. The company played down the carbon angle, saying the move was more about maximising the efficiencies of its different businesses.[27]

Hence, the company was clearly aware, at the board level, of issues relevant to its social licence to operate in relation to one fossil fuel central to its portfolio. Companies can of course present their plans and strategies to suit their own narrative. A lack of profit and poor prospects can be presented, perhaps more palatably to the market, as a deficit of efficiency. Either way, the coal assets of Australia and the world's then second biggest miner was to divest itself of carbon intensive assets. Thermal coal no longer fitted within the corporate strategy. Its competitor BHP has followed a similar path of divestment of increasingly problematic assets.

When Jean-Sebastien Jacques, the then CEO of Rio, was interviewed in March 2020, which was less than two years after the divestment by the company of its coal mines, (and just two months before the destruction of the caves in the Juukan Gorge) he observed that:

> It seems like a long time ago. It was the right decision. It was highly discussed at the time. We looked at it through two lenses. Did we believe this was a sunset industry or not? If so, was it better to exit or stay in and be the last man standing? We were able to exit the business for very good value and reallocate the capital.[28]

The company's decision-making process was characterized by first determining the nature of the wider industry itself and identifying efficient returns on capital.

25 Ferguson, n 23, 11.

26 Ferguson, n 23, 10.

27 Glenda Korporaal, 'The Jacques Solution', *The Australian–The Deal*, Issue 121, March 2020, 10–11.

28 Korporaal, n 27, 11.

Such a macro-economic approach, naturally aligned with longer-term thinking, was instrumental to the board's deliberations, and is part of the course of boards in optimizing their rent seeking. The currency of any corporation is the strategic optimization of returns for shareholders. In its assessment of coal, the board concluded that coal was not a priority and presented high risk. The market for coal assets has since proven volatile. As Jean-Sebastian Jacques noted:

> when we sold, people said we got very good value. A year later people said it was the dumbest decision we ever made. Another year on, people are saying it was 'magnificent.' If you were selling those assets today you wouldn't get close to the value of the assets that we did (when we sold them).

Whilst intermittent high prices in the market for coal assets have been elusive, volatile, and exacerbated by external global events including the Russian invasion of Ukraine, they have generally been heading in a downward direction as demand wanes and the price of renewables lowers.

4.2.2 The evolution of the ASX Corporate Governance Principles and Recommendations

Another issue relevant to the Rio episode in the Juukan Gorge has been the long-standing debate about social license embedded in the review process of the Australian Stock Exchange (ASX) key suite of Corporate Governance Principles and Recommendations (CGP&R) which are a market driven form of self-regulation operating on an 'if not, why not' basis and the assumption of compliance with standards set by competitors.

The 1st edition of the ASX CGP&R was published in 2003, the 2nd edition in 2007, and the 3rd edition in 2014. The foreword to the 3rd edition set out the ongoing impact of the Global Financial Crisis as the context for reform and consideration of a 4th edition:

> Since the release of the second edition in 2007, there has been considerable focus across the world on corporate governance practices in light of the events leading up to, and during, the Global Financial Crisis. In response, a number of jurisdictions have adopted new legislation regulating corporate behaviour and/or upgraded their corporate governance codes.[29]

Two events created ongoing impetus for the review of the 3rd edition of the ASX CGP&R. First, as noted above, was the continuing fallout from the Global Financial Crash of 2009–10.[30] Australia had avoided a recession, unlike most developed economies, and this extended the period from the previous recession in 1991 to

29 ASX Corporate Governance Council, *Corporate Governance Principles and Recommendations*, 3rd edn., Foreword Alan Cameron AO Chair, ASX Corporate Governance Council 27 March 2014, 4. https://www.asx.com.au/regulation/corporate-governance-council.htm.

30 Robert B. Reich, *Aftershock: The Next Economy and America's Future*, Vintage Books, 2011.

more than 20 years. This supposed golden age was a cause for successive federal governments of both the left (Labor) and the right (the Liberal National Party (LNP)) to express hubristic claims about the so-called 'clever country',[31] having succeeded the 'lucky country'.[32] Second however, it was clear time that there was a rising tide of corporate scandal and malpractice, particularly relevant to the big four Australian banks, as well as major insurance and financial organizations. The forces at work in this regard eventually yielded to a federally funded Banking Royal Commission.[33] This was initiated, belatedly and reluctantly, by the then conservative LNP Prime Minister, Malcolm Turnbull who was PM between 2015 and 2018. The resistance to this important initiative would be echoed by the techniques of vociferous, persistent, and astutely garnered opposition to the proposed introduction of a social licence to operate (SLTO) concept into the 4th edition of the ASX CGP&R.

The ASX determined that the need for responsive regulation was still relevant in 2017. In terms of contextualizing the timing of the review of the 3rd edition and its reasons for signalling the publication of the 4th edition the ASX Chair Elizabeth Johnstone noted that:

> In 2017, the ASX Corporate Governance Council ('Council') agreed that it was an appropriate time to commence work on a fourth edition of the Principles and Recommendations to address emerging issues around culture, values and trust, fuelled by recent examples of conduct by some listed entities falling short of community standards and expectations.[34]

The consultation process for the 4th edition was conducted between May and July 2018 to July 2018 with a view to publication in February 2019. It contained several changes, given the concerns about social licence with the focus for current purposes on Principle 3. The ASX Chief Compliance Officer Kevin Lewis went so far as to produce slides and a roadshow presentation to assuage sceptics as regards the remit of the proposed 4th edition of the ASX CGP&R.[35] The slides provided a direct comparison of the then current 3rd edition, Principle 3 with the proposed 4th edition, Principle 3:

31 Professor Ian Lowe, 'The Story: The Clever Country?' https://www.abc.net.au/science/slab/clever/story.htm. Prime Minister Bob Hawke in 1988 first referred to the phrase 'the clever country' in stressing the importance of science, innovation and technology to economic prosperity.

32 Donald Horne, *The Lucky Country*, Penguin, 1964.

33 *Royal Commission into Misconduct in the Banking, Superannuation and Financial Services Industry, Final Report,* February 2019.

34 ASX Corporate Governance Council, *Corporate Governance Principles and Recommendations*, 4th edn., Foreword Elizabeth Johnstone, Chair, ASX Corporate Governance Council 27 February 2019, https://www.asx.com.au/content/dam/asx/about/corporate-governance-council/cgc-principles-and-recommendations-fourth-edn.pdf

35 Kevin Lewis, ASX Chief Compliance Officer, ASX Corporate Governance Council, Presentation slides 'Proposed 4th edition of the Corporate Governance Principles and Recommendations', June 2018. https://slideplayer.com/slide/4594490/

> **Current: Principle 3: Act ethically and responsibly**
> A listed entity should act ethically and responsibly.
>
> **Proposed: Principle 3: Instil the desired culture**
> A listed entity should instil and continually reinforce a culture across the organisation of acting lawfully, ethically and in a socially responsible manner.[36]

This proposal, however, met with sustained critical resistance. For example, the leading international law firm, KWM published the following analysis:

> According to the ASX Corporate Governance Council, preserving a listed entity's "social licence to operate" requires that the entity's board and management '***must have*** *regard to the views and interests of a broader range of stakeholders than just the entity's security holders*'. The Council suggests that the other stakeholders which should form part of an entity's considerations include employees, customers, suppliers, creditors, regulators, consumers, tax payers and the local communities in which the entity operates. With respect, the assertion that directors "must have regard" to certain matters – while well-intended – is inconsistent with directors' statutory and general law duties. It may also create unintended confusion and have unintended consequences for directors who follow ASX's guidance.[37]

By September 2018, it was clear that peak bodies such as the Law Council of Australia and the Australian Institute of Company Directors had 'significant concerns about the ambiguous concepts of social license to operate and socially responsible manner used in the commentary to principle 3'.[38] Revealing the strength of political and industrial opposition to the social license proposal, the ASX published a communique in August 2018 in which it wrote:

> It is wrong to label the consultation draft as the work of 'left-wing activists' or 'social engineers'. It is the work of those who invest in, raise capital from, and provide professional support for, the market.[39]

36 Lewis, n 35, slide 8.

37 King and Wood Mallesons, Will Heath and Lauren Beasley, 'Insight: Proposed Fourth edition of ASX Corporate Governance Principles', *KWM*, 6 June 2018. https://www.kwm.com/au/en/insights/latest-thinking/proposed-fourth-edition-asx-corporate-governance-principles.html.

38 King and Wood Mallesons, Will Heath, Anthony Hong and Paula Mucha, 'Insight: Proposed Changes to the ASX Corporate Governance Principles: Stakeholder Submissions and Next Steps,' 7 September 2018 https://www.kwm.com/au/en/insights/latest-thinking/proposed-changes-to-the-asx-corporate-governance-principles.html.

39 ASX Corporate Governance Council Communique, 'Chair of Corporate Governance Council comments on the debate about the proposed fourth edition of the Principles and Recommendations,' 6 August 2018. https://www.asx.com.au/content/dam/asx/about/corporate-governance-council/cgc-communique-6august2018.pdf.

The ASX was evidently surprised and dismayed at how its role had been characterized.

4.2.3 The excision of corporate social responsibility from the 4th edition of the Corporate Governance Principles published by the Australian Securities Exchange

In February 2019, the Australian Securities Exchange published its 4th edition of *Listing Rules* and Principle 3 in its final form provided as follows:

> **Instil a culture of acting lawfully, ethically and responsibly:** A listed entity should instil and continually reinforce a culture across the organisation of acting lawfully, ethically and responsibly.[40]

Critically, two words were excised from the draft which had been proposed. The word 'desired' in terms of the corporation's culture, and the word 'social' in terms of the corporation's wider social responsibility. They were but two words and two simple concepts but their presence in the draft had exercised some of the most powerful forces in corporate Australia. This was despite the fact the Chair of the ASX had specifically referred to the fact the community standards had driven the need for the review and update.[41] Principle 3 was not so much watered down as defenestrated between proposal and finalization. Also, as a result of the consultation process, the following ASX Commentary was excised by the ASX:

> ***Commentary***
> A listed entity's "social licence to operate" is one of its most valuable assets. That licence can be lost or seriously damaged if the entity or its officers or employees are perceived to have acted unlawfully, unethically or in a socially irresponsible manner. Preserving an entity's social licence to operate requires the board and management of a listed entity to have regard to the views and interests of a broader range of stakeholders than just its security holders, including employees, customers, suppliers, creditors, regulators, consumers, taxpayers and the local communities in which it operates. Long term and sustainable value creation is founded on the trust a listed entity has earned from these different stakeholders. Security holders understand this and expect boards and management to engage with these stakeholders and to be, and be seen to be, "good corporate citizens".[42]

The ASX, however, realizing it was caught in an intractable position between the opposing forces of community standards on the one hand, and corporate demands

40 ASX Corporate Governance Council, Corporate Governance Principles and Recommendations, 4th edn, Principle 3.1, 1-40, 19. https://www.asx.com.au/content/dam/asx/about/corporate-governance-council/cgc-principles-and-recommendations-fourth-edn.pdf.

41 ASX Corporate Governance Council 4th edn, n 40.

42 ASX Corporate Governance Council, 4th edn, n 40.

on the other, sought to characterize the retreat from these concepts as being of no great moment:

> Importantly, the final version includes all of the key changes around culture and values proposed in the consultation draft, with some drafting changes reflecting feedback received in the consultation. Council considers it imperative that listed entities align their culture and values with community expectations to help arrest the loss of trust in business. Having listened carefully to the consultation feedback, Council has shortened the commentary and made changes to make it clearer that it is guidance and not intended to be prescriptive. Council has also replaced references in the commentary to 'social licence to operate' – for which there was considerable support from many stakeholders but opposition from others – with references to 'reputation' and 'standing in the community'. Council regards the concepts as synonymous.[43]

The fourth edition came into force for financial years (which in Australia run from 1 July to 30 June) commencing on or after 1 January 2020.[44] What had occurred during the consultation period was a concerted campaign against the inclusion of the term social licence. As has been since noted, its proposed inclusion 'met with such hostility that the ASX Corporate Governance Council removed it from the final version of the Principles'.[45] The ASX acknowledged the vexed nature of the issue:

> The proposed introduction of the term "social licence to operate" ("SLTO") into the Principles and Recommendations was unquestionably the most polarising issue addressed in the consultation feedback.[46]

To be clear, this chain of events demonstrates that 'social licence' or 'social licence to operate' within the Australian economic, legal, and corporate governance context concerns in particular the main mining and extractive industries, and as such, is directly linked to Australia's carbon emissions and to climate change. The ASX was, however, assiduous in seeking to neutralize the issue:

> Those who opposed the introduction of SLTO into the fourth edition argued that the term is vague and subjective, that it could mean different things to different stakeholders, and that its reach would likely vary over time. They noted that it could be confused or conflated with community opposition,

43 ASX Corporate Governance Council, COMMUNIQUE, 27 February 2019, Release of fourth edition of the ASX Corporate Governance Principles and Recommendations, https://www.asx.com.au/content/dam/asx/about/asx-media-releases/2019/cgc-communique-27-feb-2019.pdf.

44 ASX Corporate Governance Council, 4th edn., n 40.

45 Rosemary Teele Langford, 'Social Licence to Operate and Directors' Duties: Is there a Need for Change?' *(2019) 37 Company & Securities Law Journal 200*, (2018), 200.

46 https://www.asx.com.au/documents/regulation/cgc-consultation-response-fourth-edn.pdf.

> which in turn might expose listed entities to "social engineering agendas and objectives" that are not necessarily concerned with good corporate governance. Further, the notion of broader stakeholder accountability inherent in SLTO might actually conflict with the duties of directors, as they have been espoused by the courts and are traditionally understood in Australia.[47]

In the written response and summary of the consultation process dated 27 February 2019, the ASX listed four specific industries affected by social issues and the potential inclusion of SLTO:

> A number of respondents raised concerns about the application of SLTO to entities involved in industries that raise particular social issues, such as gaming, alcohol, tobacco and fast food.[48]

In the speech to launch the ASX 4th edition of the CGP&R which also took place on 27 February 2019, the ASX Chair applied some brilliant deconstruction of the SLTO concept:

> Almost all investor interest groups, accounting bodies and standards setters strongly supported the concept of 'social licence to operate' and the recognition of broader stakeholder accountability. However there were a range of other stakeholders who were troubled by the term 'social licence to operate'. They argued it is vague, subjective and elastic.[49]

The nub of the launch speech, and its real agenda was then revealed. The next paragraph of the published speech provided an insight into the forces at play; it exposed the core reason for the campaign of intense pressure which the ASX acknowledged. The fact that the opposition to social licence had been so hostile and polarizing was due to the submissions made to the ASX during the consultation period. As the Chair of the ASX noted of the submissions, they:

> pointed out the particular difficulties that it could cause for listed entities legitimately operating in particular sectors that some parts of society are opposed to – such as companies involved in the gaming, alcohol, tobacco, fast food, *coal and coal seam gas sectors*.[50] (emphasis added)

47 https://www.asx.com.au/documents/regulation/cgc-consultation-response-fourth-edn.pdf.

48 https://www.asx.com.au/documents/regulation/cgc-consultation-response-fourth-edn.pdf 27 February 2019.

49 ASX Corporate Governance Council Launch of The 4th Edition of The Corporate Governance Principles & Recommendations, Address by The Chair of The ASX Corporate Governance Council Elizabeth Johnstone, 27 February 2019, https://www.asx.com.au/content/dam/asx/about/corporate-governance-council/ej-speech-press-version.pdf.

50 ASX Corporate Governance Council Launch, Address by The Chair, n 47.

What is revealing is that the words 'coal and coal gas seam sectors' were included in the Chair's speech to launch ASX 4th edition, but not in the ASX's written response to the final form of the 4th edition of the CGP&R. The references to coal and coal seam gas sectors were tellingly removed from the written document. The mining lobby has been highly effective both politically and economically, at staving off any fetters on its freedoms to extract these fossil fuels from large swathes of the continent. Although gaming, tobacco, alcohol, and fast food were listed in both the speech, and the written document respectively, these industries raise fundamentally different issues to the coal and coal gas seam industries which were referenced in only the Chair's speech. One need only take a cursory review of the Australian political agenda of the last decade to observe the vociferous defence of fossil fuels,[51] and the adept campaign denying global heating, or any link between fossil fuels mined in Australia and climate change. By contrast, the same industry refers to reckless renewables. Without a hint of irony, the Chair of ASX concluded this part of her launch speech with the following observations:

> The Council saw the force in these arguments. Consequently, the Council has replaced the references in the commentary to 'social licence to operate' with references instead to 'reputation' and 'standing in the community'. The Council regards these concepts as essentially synonymous with 'social licence to operate', in the sense in which that term was used in the consultation draft. However, this modified terminology is more likely to be better understood and therefore more consistently applied by listed entities, their boards and other stakeholders.[52]

This was dexterous pivot. Further proof of the core agenda in the submissions is illustrated by the following extract from law firm KWM in its submission and related publications concerning the proposed ASX 4th edition. In its submission of 27 July 2018, KWM included the following paragraph:

> it is very difficult to measure whether a listed entity is acting in a socially responsible manner as what is required for an entity to act in a socially responsible manner changes on a day to day basis. *For example, would a listed entity which owns coal mines be required to cease operating on the basis that coal mining is not considered socially responsible anymore*? We assume that this is not the intended outcome of the Council. As such, we submit that the reference to 'a socially responsible manner' should be deleted.[53] (emphasis added)

51 Judith Brett, 'The Coal Curse: Resources, Climate and Australia's Future', *Quarterly Essay*, Black Inc. Books, Issue 78, 2020, 1–78.

52 ASX Corporate Governance Council Launch, Address by The Chair, n 49.

53 KWM Submission to the ASX Corporate Governance Council, 'Proposed fourth edition of the ASX Corporate Governance Principles and Recommendations', 27 July 2018, 1-10, 8, https://www.asx.com.au/content/dam/asx/about/corporate-governance-council/reviews-and-submissions/2018/king-wood-mallesons.pdf.

The specific reference to the coal mining industry was not merely hypothetical; it was the main point of opposition to the ASX proposal. Social licence did not make it into the 4th edition. The consultation draft for the 5th edition of ASX Corporate Governance Principles and Recommendations is due for release in February 2024,[54] and it is of interest to see if social licence is still as divisive a concept five years on.

4.3 Rio Tinto since the Juukan Gorge incident in May 2020

4.3.1 The narrative for Rio Tinto since the destruction of the Juukan Gorge caves in May 2020

May 2023 marked three years after the destruction of the ancient rock shelters in the Juukan Gorge. In that period, several major changes have taken place. These included two steps common to corporations who have faced major corporate governance issues and failures of good practice. This is the replacement of the Chair of the Board and of the Chief Executive Officer. Perhaps more fundamentally is acknowledgment of wrongdoing by the new Chair, Dominic Barton, who says of the destruction of the rock shelters that:

> it's something I am deeply, deeply apologetic for, and something that is a deep stain on our history that we have to deal with It's deeply felt within the organization, and I think we have got to use that to move us institutionally forward.[55]

This is as close to shame as a corporation can admit. It is of note that the Chair speaks for and on behalf of the company as a separate legal entity. It does rise to a renewed sense of stewardship and of the corporate history being a peopled narrative, and that people at the top of the entity must take responsibility for the company's deeds and misdeeds. Another development, and the most significant of them is that the traditional owners, the Puutu Kunti Kurrama and Pinikura (PKKP) people have spoken about accountability. The PKKP chairperson, Burchell Hayes, has said that 'the destruction of our most significant cultural heritage site should not have happened.'[56] As such, and with a view to the future, the PKKP have sought to exercise co-management rights with Rio Tinto 'that would give them a greater say over future works on their ancestral lands.'[57] Chairperson of the PKKP Land Committee, Burchell Hayes, has said:

54 ASX Corporate Governance Council, Update on the release of the 5th edition of the ASX Corporate Governance Principles and Recommendations Consultation Draft, 7 December 2023, https://www.asx.com.au/content/dam/asx/about/corporate-governance-council/7-dec-update-on-5th-edition-corporate-governance-principles-recommendations-consultation.pdf

55 Toscano 2023, n 2.

56 Toscano 2023, n 2.

57 Toscano 2023, n 2.

> To ensure that we will never experience this senseless feeling of loss and devastation in the future, we are driven towards achieving a co-management process of Country with mining companies. We have already started to see minor aspects of the co-management model working at Juukan Gorge, through rehabilitation works of some of the surrounding areas. We have always said that we are not opposed to mining, but it needs to be done in the right way, involving traditional owners, and first of all, gaining our free, prior and informed consent.[58]

This episode marks the end of narrow legalism in which obtaining a technical contractual sign-off—an apparently legal permission slip to destroy a human wonder—was a logical but indefensible reflection on the relevant legal regime. A properly constituted consultative model, as outlined by the PKKP chair, is the only sustainable way forward, and well-resourced corporations such as Rio Tinto need to observe these processes as high-order values and principles of responsible conduct. Corporate social responsibility is writ large in this approach.

4.3.2 The Jabiluka Mine site remediation/clean-up

The second issue currently relevant to Rio Tinto is the corporation's ongoing responsibility for remediation of the Jabiluka uranium mining site in the Northern Territory, contiguous to the World Heritage listed Kakadu National Park, the traditional owners of which are the Mirrar people.[59] The site involves large-scale mining extraction and several large reservoirs of highly contaminated 'acidic radioactive slurry'.[60] The issue in this case is that something like half a billion dollars will be required for the site clean-up.[61] However, powerful shareholder groups oppose this initiative.[62] Again there are complex corporate group structures in play. The mine is operated by listed company, Energy Resources Australia (ERA), a subsidiary company, which is in turn 68% owned by Rio Tinto.[63] A key concern is the potential issue of long-term environmental damage:

> ERA is required to remediate the mine site and return it to a state fit to be incorporated in the surrounding Kakadu national park, by 2026. There have been longstanding concerns about the risk of a uranium leak from the Ranger mine, amplified by its location at the eastern end of the remote national park in the Northern Territory.[64]

58 Toscano 2023, n 2.
59 Mirrar, https://www.mirarr.net/pages/mirarr.
60 Ben Butler and Ben Smee, 'Rio Tinto's plan to clean up Ranger uranium mine in doubt after hedge fund objects', *The Guardian*, 17 December 2019, https://www.theguardian.com/environment/2019/dec/17/rio-tintos-plan-to-clean-up-ranger-uranium-mine-in-doubt-after-hedge-fund-objects.
61 Butler and Smee, n 60.
62 Butler and Smee, n 60.
63 Butler and Smee, n 60.
64 Butler and Smee, n 60.

Though the contractual commitments last for just six years, the potential for damage is many years beyond that date. As a result, the Australian Conservation Foundation has opined that:

> The one future for the uranium sector in Kakadu is closure and a credible clean-up. This is required by law and expected by the community. Any moves to chase false profits, rather than face real responsibilities, are flawed and deeply unhelpful. The site needs to be rehabilitated to a standard where it could be incorporated into the surrounding Kakadu National Park – a very high threshold.[65]

4.3.3 Brand and reputation issues for Rio: ongoing or localized?

In the short-term, the destruction of the rock shelters in the Juukan Gorge affected the Rio corporate brand and did bring about a change of management style and rhetoric. Has Rio become a by-word for reputational loss? Only briefly. Its share price has recovered and it has new leadership. A company, given its separate entity status and access to perpetual succession, can reinvent its image by change at the top, particularly if both the CEO and the Chair of the Board vacate their positions in response to the crisis.

Rio did bear some consequences but these have been limited in time and scope. Paradoxically, Rio has become something of an example of a lightning-rod case study for corporations and other powerful economic interests in terms of the development restrictions they face post since the Juukan Gorge. This argument can be made considering the legislative developments referred to below.

4.3.4 The 2021 national review of state heritage protection laws and the need for improved standards

As noted, the Rio episode at the Juukan Gorge involved the lawful destruction because Rio sought and obtained permission of the relevant indigenous corporation. Such was the backlash against Rio, however, that the Commonwealth government intervened by conducting a review of the state-based heritage laws in 2021 examining all six sets of laws. The State of the Environment Report[66] aimed to identify the gaps and deficiencies in the current state heritage laws and to provide recommendations for improvement. The review was conducted by the then Commonwealth Department of Agriculture, Water, and the Environment, now called the Department of Climate Change, Energy, the Environment and Water

65 Peter Ker, 'Call to develop Jabiluka Mine slammed by traditional owners', *Australian Financial Review*, 12 February 2020, https://www.afr.com/companies/mining/jabiluka-mine-call-slammed-by-traditional-owners-20200211-p53zr0.

66 Department of Climate Change, Energy, the Environment and Water (DCCEEW), Australia: State of the Environment 2021, Heritage recognised under the EPBC Act, https://soe.dcceew.gov.au/heritage/environment/heritage-recognised-under-epbc-act.

(DCCEEW).[67] The DCCEEW report recommended the introduction of a more rigorous and consistent set of standards to align with the Environment Protection and Biodiversity Conservation Act 1999 (Cth).

4.3.5 The repeal of new environmental protection laws in WA: the hegemony of development interests

Despite the review by the Commonwealth, states have gone their own way. The state Labor government of WA has recently repealed the laws which were specifically enacted in response to the destruction of the Juukan Gorge.

As law firm, Clayton Utz, notes, the Aboriginal Cultural Heritage Act 2021 (WA) had only been in operation for five weeks when the premier of WA announced its repeal. As such WA:

> will return to the old system of managing and protecting Aboriginal cultural heritage. This means: a narrower definition of heritage ('Aboriginal site'); a Committee that determines whether a place meets the legal definition of an 'Aboriginal site' and receives the protection of the Act; an approval process whereby the Minister is responsible for granting consent to use land where doing so will damage Aboriginal heritage if it is in 'the general interest of the community'; and an approval that is tied to a specific owner of land and cannot be transferred. The Repeal Bill repeals the ACH Act and Regulations and reinstates the previous Aboriginal Heritage Act 1972 (WA) with several new amendments.[68]

This major change of political strategy was as the result of widespread resistance from the farming, agricultural, and mining sectors into what it characterized as overly restrictive new rules impacting on economic activity. It galvanized farmers and others in regional electorates. It focused on relatable examples of farmers not being able to put access crossings over waterways on their own properties. It implicitly gave rise to post-Mabo case fears (after the High Court litigation of 1992 which established native tite in Australia) about wide-spread land right claims. It has also coincided with the national referendum debate about the federal Indigenous advisory 'voice to parliament' in which untrue claims were commonplace. The power of the business-as-usual approach is obvious. In terms of mining, it continues to occupy space at the centre of the national economy; it is the equivalent approach of 'if a resource is there, why not exploit it?' This has been a constant imperative of progress in the nation, one founded in the same epoch as the Industrial Revolution.

67 Department of Climate Change, Energy, the Environment and Water (DCCEEW), https://www.dcceew.gov.au/about/who-we-are/structure.

68 Clayton Utz, Lucy Shea, 'WA's Aboriginal Cultural Heritage regime- Back to the future: what the repeal means', 10 August 2023, https://www.claytonutz.com/insights/2023/august/was-aboriginal-cultural-heritage-regime-back-to-the-future-what-the-repeal-means.

4.3.6 Rio Tinto redux? Riverlea and the Walker Corporation

Three years after Juukan Gorge and in WA's neighbouring state of South Australia, similar issues have arisen in the context of a proposed housing development, Riverlea, on a site of several hundred hectares located a half hour drive north of the Adelaide CBD.[69] The developer is the Walker Corporation. The proposal was granted major development status by the Labor government in 2007. Despite approval more than a decade ago, it has only been in the last year that a thorough and belated archaeological examination of the site has been conducted. Over the last decade, several artefacts have been found indicating a major indigenous campsite. In 2023, it was confirmed that the site contains several major indigenous burial grounds. The company has negotiated with the Kaurna Yerta Aboriginal Corporation, as the representative of the native title holders, which has approved the removal of the ancestral remains to a new location. The issue is, however, that other traditional owners strongly object to this compromise. Instead, they want the remains left in place. This posits apparently 'vacant land' as merely a potential resource to be developed generating a source of profit for decades to come. It simply fails to comprehend the complex concept of country, central to First Nations people. The argument is redolent of the *terra nullius* principle applied to localized areas. Legal title seeks to erase connections to country formed over hundreds of generations and many thousands of years.

This developing saga is another example of the modern, Western, legal construct of the corporation being used as a means of validating agreements with First Nations people. The legal theory behind the practice purports to be simple and conclusive; that is, the developer corporation negotiates and agrees a set of outcomes with a single, designated CATSI corporation. This may be the traditional way of doing business by companies within a Western, neoliberal framework. It is artificial and narrow when one of the parties is a CATSI corporation because it purports to give exclusive rights to the ascribed leaders (chair and directors) of the indigenous corporation identified as intrinsically and exclusively linked to the proposed development site, rather than to the collective of traditional owners of whom there may be many overlapping groups representing a complex social geography. It is a legal device aimed at simplification of the process, and based on an assumption of exclusive ownership rights, but it negates providing an authentic and comprehensive voice to the traditional owners so that their will can be fully expressed. It is a specious form of Othering. It seeks to deploy property, contract, and corporate law as unproblematically applicable to this complex process of obtaining the consent of First Nations-based groups consent.

In this case, the technical consent of the relevant indigenous corporation was secured within a legislative framework, even though the chair of the corporation was aware that indigenous burial grounds are often located nearby to campsites.

69 ABC News, 'Building on a burial site: Aboriginal ancestral remains found at SA housing project', 14 November 2023, www.abc.net.au/news/programs/730.

This important point of anthropological information was apparently ignored in the haste to secure approvals and consents.

It is an unfortunate truism that legislation designed to provide heritage protection regularly becomes, by default, used to facilitate development on behalf of corporations. There is scope to change the process by expanding the repertoire of techniques that are used to investigate the landscape before plans are made for infrastructure and before development approvals are granted. This would require political and regulatory will. The fact that new protective laws in WA which were designed to avoid another disaster like Juukan Gorge, have been hastily reversed, bodes very poorly for the aspiration of developing nationally consistent, best practice.

4.3.7 Rio and reversion to 'business as usual' just three years after Juukan

Just over three years later, the extraction industry in Australia has resumed business as usual and the Rio share price is at high and it is enjoying record levels of profit, with a dividend of US$16.8bn based on 'bumper iron ore prices'.[70] Whilst the Juukan gorge destruction was a shocking event, the economic rebound has been telling with the resumption of full-scale extraction of WA-based iron ore deposits.

In October 2023, the Australian Tax Office (ATO) Taskforce, which had been established in 2016 and was charged with recovering tax from mining and fossil fuel multinationals, announced that it had clawed back $6.4bn. This included the 'mammoth settlement'[71] of a decade-long dispute with Rio Tinto over its Singapore-based marketing hub. Rio agreed to pay $1bn in unpaid taxes. The ATO Deputy Commissioner, Rebecca Saint, referred to it as 'one of the largest settlements in Australia's tax history'.[72]

4.4 Related corporate case studies

4.4.1 Corporate asset sales: Broken Hill Proprietary Ltd (BHP)

Other corporate developments to have emerged since 2020 include the fact that large conglomerate mining corporations such as Rio Tinto's key competitor, BHP, have reviewed their portfolio of businesses holdings and assets, particularly if they entail fuels. The CEO of BHP, Mike Henry, has taken the company from being dual listed in the UK and Australia to being singly listed in Australia.

70 Reuters, 'Rio Tinto records record profit and US $16.8bn dividend on bumper iron ore prices', 23 Feb 2022, https://www.reuters.com/video/watch/rio-tinto-sets-record-dividend-as-profit-id743870946.

71 Lisa Visentin and Shane Wright, *Sydney Morning Herald*, 'ATO claws back record $4.6bilion in multinational crackdown', 21 Oct 2023, https://www.smh.com.au/politics/federal/ato-claws-back-record-6-4-billion-in-multinational-crackdown-20231021-p5edz3.html.

72 Visentin and Wright, n 71.

4.4.1.1 The oil business division of BHP

In early 2022, BHP has sold its petroleum division for $63bn to Woodside, making it one of the world's top ten producers of oil and gas.[73] Effecting a sale and divestment is the simplest corporate strategy to rid a company of problematic long-term carbon-intensive assets.

4.4.1.2 The coal and iron ore divisions of BHP

The coal and iron ore divisions of BHP may be next. Whilst Rio Tinto completely divested from coal in 2018, BHP is in the process of divesting from thermal coal. It is still invested in metallurgical coal which is used for steel making.

4.4.2 BHP's 'early closure' of the Mt Arthur thermal coal mine in NSW

Examples of stranded assets are becoming apparent. BHP, the world's largest miner, announced in June 2022 that it will close its thermal coal operations at Mt Arthur in the Hunter Valley of NSW on 30 June 2030. It had been aiming to sell the mine since August 2020, a period of nearly two years but this 'did not result in a viable offer'.[74] Part of the issue in selling was the obligation to remediate the mine site. Potential bidders wanted BHP to carry this obligation which is booked at US$700 million. Environmental groups calculate the actual figure to be far higher. The rehabilitation process is expected to take 10–15 years. The site currently employs two thousand people.

This is an example of several vectors creating the conditions for a previously valuable project to potentially become a stranded project or set of assets because of a fundamental shift in market conditions which jeopardize current and long-term financial viability. Even with companies bringing forward closure plans, this can be seen as insubstantial. For example, Carmel Flint, the national coordinator at the Lock the Gate Alliance said the organization was 'still of the view that the mine should close in 2026 as previously planned- the world can't afford to keep delaying climate action'.[75] Flint went on to say:

> It's taken too long for BHP to read the writing on the wall. Had the company committed to shutting down Mt Arthur instead of trying to sell it several years ago, it could have already spent that time retraining and supporting workers instead of delaying the inevitable. This is a very significant step by BHP, and the absence of buyers for the mine sends an incredibly strong

73 Anthony Marx, 'Carve-up of BHP would unlock value, says Citi', *The Australian*, Wednesday 1 June, 23.

74 Ben Butler and Lisa Cox, 'BHP to close NSW's largest coalmine in 2030 after failing to sell it', *The Guardian Australia* online, 16 June 2022, https://www.theguardian.com/business/2022/jun/16/bhp-to-close-nsws-largest-coalmine-in-2030-after-failing-to-sell-it.

75 Butler and Cox, n 74.

> message that thermal coal is in decline globally, as customer countries act on climate change.[76]

The signal to the global market was emphasized. This is quite a different narrative to the one which positioned Australia and its CO_2 emissions from public and private actors as insignificant and as justification for what is increasingly now characterized as recalcitrant delay.

Harriet Klater, the climate leader for Australia from the Australasian Centre for Corporate Responsibility,[77] was of the view that BHP had 'finally made the right call'. Klater went on to note that:

> The current US$700m provision for closure does not appear to match the enormous scale of the likely clean up bill. BHP has an opportunity to draw on the returns from current record-high thermal coal prices to properly fund high quality remediation. The International Energy Agency Net Zero scenario stated that there can be no new coal mines or extensions from 2021 so the decision to still seek a mine life extension from 2026 to 2030 is completely inconsistent with the Paris Agreement and limiting warming to 1.5 degrees.[78]

Stakeholder groups are well organized and pointed in their critiques. Elizabeth Sullivan from the Australian Conservation Foundation said that BHP's decision was:

> a welcome acknowledgment of the energy transition that is underway. As the world rapidly shifts to renewable energy, projects like Mt Arthur have become such a climate liability that companies can barely give them away. A closing date of 2030 is a big improvement on 2045, but earlier would be better for the climate.[79]

Previously predictable linear timelines are collapsing in on companies. The pressures from within Australia and beyond are increasing monthly. The pace of change is now unrelenting. Boards are faced with a series of unprecedented challenges in terms of their scale and urgency. Their steps and missteps are the subject of increasing, real-time critique. This phenomenon was accelerated in Australia by the issues relevant to the Rio Tinto corporate group in 2020.

76 Butler and Cox, n 74.
77 Butler and Cox, n 74.
78 Butler and Cox, n 74.
79 Butler and Cox, n 74.

4.4.3 The BHP subsidiary corporation, South32: selective asset deployment in the era of climate change and in the face of political incentives

South32 is a company listed on the ASX with secondary listings on the London and Johannesburg stock exchanges. It was demerged from BHP in 2015.[80] The company owns and operates a metallurgical coal mine at Dendrobium in the Illawarra area south of Sydney. South32 wanted to increase its extraction of metallurgical coal by 78m tonnes, and to increase the life of the mine to 2048 via the investment of more than one billion dollars. From an environmental perspective the mine site is located nearby two of Sydney's main dams, the Avon and the Cordeaux. In its assessment of the project in 2021, the Independent Planning Commission (IPC) of NSW was concerned with the widespread effect on water quality of the proposed expansion if it had gone ahead. The evidence to the IPC was that the expansion 'could cause irreversible damage to the Sydney and Illawarra drinking water catchments'.[81] The IPC as the specialist regulator blocked the expansion. In response, however, to the IPC's decision, the New South Wales state government 'declared the expansion to be "state significant infrastructure" due to the mine's role providing coal for the Port Kembla steelworks'.[82] As such, 'the declaration would have allowed South32 to submit a new environmental impact statement for a scaled down proposal to the state's planning department'.[83]

This action by the NSW government led to widespread concern expressed by local community organizations including the Lock the Gate Alliance and Protect our Water Catchment Incorporated. As Lisa Cox notes, 'the decision to overrule the IPC was strongly criticized by environment and climate groups, which accused the NSW government of being captured by the coal industry'.[84]

It ultimately took the protagonist company in question, South32, to reject the project based on commercial viability. In August 2022, the company announced to the Australian Securities Exchange (ASX) that it had 'abandoned plans to expand its Dendrobium metallurgical coalmine in the New South Wales Illawarra region'.[85] Its CEO Graham Kerr noted that:

> Our decision today follows an extensive analysis of the alternatives for Dendrobium together with the anticipated returns from the upfront capital investment which would be required. Over the past 18 months we have made significant progress actively reshaping our portfolio and this decision increases our capacity to direct capital toward other opportunities.[86]

80 South32, https://www.south32.net/.

81 Lisa Cox, 'Controversial $1bn Dendrobium coal mine expansion plan abandoned by mining company', *The Guardian*, 23 August 2022, https://www.theguardian.com/environment/2022/aug/23/controversial-1bn-dendrobium-coalmine-expansion-plan-abandoned-by-mining-company.

82 Cox, n 81.

83 Cox, n 81.

84 Cox, n 81.

85 Cox, n 81

86 Cox, n 81.

The secretary of the Illawarra- and Sydney-based environmental group Protect Our Water Catchment Incorporated, Deidre Stuart, said the project was 'never in the public interest and South32's decision to walk away was a terrific result for communities who had worked to oppose it'.[87] The irony is that South32 relied on economic analysis, despite the overt and ongoing political support from of the NSW government.

Community based local factors increasingly feature in the closure and remediation stages of such mine closures. The Lock the Gate Alliance sought measures including gradually rehabilitating the land once the mine closes to give workers ongoing employment, protecting the water catchment area from further degradation by the passing of legislation, and seeking a ban on any new or expanded projects near the mine site.[88]

The rhetorical power of jobs in the mining sector has always been significant, even though the number of ongoing jobs created is often contested. The importance of remediation of sites is ecologically necessary but ensuring it is done well to an adequate budget and is overseen properly is an ongoing regulatory challenge.

This corporate episode illustrates that political arguments in Australia are very powerful, even in the face of significant environmental and commercial issues. The danger is that governments, driven by political interests, can become too activist and ideological in the marketplace. In this case, the political imperatives were ultimately opposed by the conflation of commercial and local, social, and environmental issues. The case illustrates the practical obstacles to climate progress if governments seek to change the rules of the game. It ultimately took a combination of both environmental and financial considerations to halt this project and to avoid the folly 'development at all costs'.

4.5 The implications of the Rio and related case studies for corporate law theory, risk, and governance

4.5.1 The Anglo-Australian context: moving away from second mover advantage to disadvantage

Australia with its common law inheritance, and ability to adapt the considered thinking of legislation devised in the UK, has long prided itself on being legally progressive. It was always able to adapt and modify legislation formulated in another context and transplant it to the colonies, the nascent Federation, and later what was thought of as a younger, newer world somewhat liberated from the shackles of tradition.

This developmental approach performed successfully in several commercial law settings. The UK Partnership Act 1890 is a clear example, adapted by colonies in the 1890s, then becoming part of the laws of the various states in 1901. So too, corporate law: the famous House of Lords case dealing with the rise of the high-street

87 Cox, n 81.
88 Cox, n 81.

business model in *Salomon v A. Salomon and Co. Ltd*[89] is such an example in common law terms. The House of Lord's confirmation of the company as a separate legal entity and with the related protections of the corporate veil, has been dutifully adopted in Australia. A third and presently informative instance was another House of Lords UK case, *Percival v Wright* in 1902,[90] in which the court confirmed that the directors owed their duties to the company. Again, this legal principle has been enshrined in Australian legislation, and finds voice in s.181 of the Corporations Act 2001 (Cth). This ability to legislate based on a primary model initially developed elsewhere provided an inbuilt ability (and a ready advantage) for Australian law to build on, and to improve, the legal principles from their first formation. Australia was able to benefit from the practice of second iteration of the central legal ideas first developed in the UK. Adept adoption provided a spirit, if not of legal adventurism, then of law reform and of an informed comparative analysis.

With the advent of the Corporations Act 2001 (Cth) at the turn of the new millennium, Australian corporate law was for the first time truly national, set on solid Constitutional foundations, and set out comprehensively almost in a code-like fashion. It was intended to provide a flexible and efficient template for adapting law to fit the 21st century. However, more than twenty years later, Australian corporate law and governance, in key respects, are now some way behind the UK corporate governance and related law. It is caught in a mid-20th century grid. This comparative gap between the two national systems is increasingly apparent, even though the UK law is not considered radical in its scope, s.172 of the UK Companies Act 2006 is well-advanced on its Australian equivalent provision.

4.5.2 Comparing directors' duties between Australia and the UK

Whilst direct comparisons of statutes between countries must be careful to bear in mind the unique factors—social, economic, cultural, and legal—which make up that national context, contrasting key aspects of director focus and duty in particular reveals a distinct contrast. As noted, s.172 of the UK Companies Act 2006 refers to several stakeholder groups which have widened the contemporary prism through which directors view their role. Whilst the provision is criticized as providing optionality and little in the way of legal consequence, it is a quantum leap on the provision which goes to the same subject matter in the corporate law of Australia referred to in s.181 of the Corporations Act 2001 (Cth).

The late Polly Higgins, a UK barrister, has trenchantly voiced dissatisfaction with the UK provision:

> In the UK, as in many other countries, the duty to act in the interests of profit above other interests is enshrined in law. Section 172 of the Companies Act 2006 is the legal duty to promote the success of the company. When

89 *Salomon v A Salomon & Co Ltd* [1896] UKHL1, [1897] AC 22.
90 *Percival v Wright* [1902] 2 Ch. 421.

exercising the duty, the director is required to 'have regard' to various non-exhaustive list of 'factors' listed in s.172. To 'have regard' is a far lower legal standard to attain than to 'prioritize.' The difference is determinative: the former can be given the most cursory of considerations, whilst the latter demands a determination according to the importance of the factor. 'Success' is not defined in the Act.[91]

The full text of s.172 of the UK Companies Act 2006 is set out below, including this ambiguous wording:

Companies Act 2006

172 Duty to promote the success of the company

(1) A director of a company must act in the way he considers, in good faith, would be most likely to promote the success of the company for the benefit of its members as a whole, and in doing so have regard (amongst other matters) to—

a) the likely consequences of any decision in the long term,
b) the interests of the company's employees,
c) the need to foster the company's business relationships with suppliers, customers and others,
d) the impact of the company's operations on the community and the environment,
e) the desirability of the company maintaining a reputation for high standards of business conduct, and
f) the need to act fairly as between members of the company.

(2) Where or to the extent that the purposes of the company consist of or include purposes other than the benefit of its members, subsection (1) has effect as if the reference to promoting the success of the company for the benefit of its members were to achieving those purposes.

(3) The duty imposed by this section has effect subject to any enactment or rule of law requiring directors, in certain circumstances, to consider or act in the interests of creditors of the company.

Whatever the merits of, and the arguments for and against s.172 of the UK Companies Act 2006, the provision is referenced as a point of somewhat stark comparison with the relevant Australian law. Despite its arguable shortcomings,[92] s.172 remains a quantum leap ahead of its Australian counterpart provision; its conscious raising of various stakeholders appears radical next to the haiku-like brevity of s.181 of the Corporations Act 2001 (Cth) which adopts the principle set

91 Polly Higgins, *Eradicating Ecocide: Exposing the Corporate and Political Practices Destroying the Planet and Proposing the Laws to Eradicate Ecocide*, Shepheard-Walwyn, 2010, 4.

92 For example, see Brenda Hannigan, *Company Law*, 6th edn., OUP, 2021 or David Kershaw, *Company Law in Context, Text and Materials*, 2nd ed., OUP, 2012.

out in the 1902 UK litigation, *Percival v Wright*.[93] Section 181 has now been the central statutory provision in Australia for twenty years. It reflects classic early 20th-century jurisprudence. It provides as follows:

> **CORPORATIONS ACT 2001 - SECT 181**
> Good faith-civil obligations
> Good faith-directors and other officers
>
> (1) A director or other officer of a corporation must exercise their powers and discharge their duties:
>
> a) in good faith in the best interests of the corporation; and
> b) for a proper purpose.
>
> Note 1: This subsection is a civil penalty provision.

Whilst community expectations have gathered pace, s.181 has remained stolidly immobile. As such, Australia's provision is shareholder primacy in singular form. As such, it succinctly encapsulates Milton Friedman-style economic rationalism. It underwrites the link between corporate law and governance, and the wider economic model and effectively excludes community input. It has been conveniently co-opted by Australia's slate of extractive businesses and mining companies; it is coterminous with late-stage industrialism. It also freezes this vital aspect of corporate governance review and reform in the early decades of the 20th century, rather than of the 21st. The outcomes from the UK case *Percival v Wright*[94] are instructive. Australian common law has been a loyal adherent to the orthodox principle that the directors owe their duties to 'the company' which in turn is the current collective of shareholders. Only in very limited circumstances, will the courts recognize that the directors owe a duty to a particular shareholder, or to any other stakeholder, let alone to the environment or the wider host community in which the company operates and through whose support it benefits. As such, the common law of Australia has provided only some very limited exceptions for individual shareholders in constrained facts and circumstances.[95] This is because Australian courts operate, given their historical lineage, by reference to techniques of incrementalism, rather than adventurism and they leave, except for when exceptional courts are operating in exceptional circumstances, law reform and any related progressive leaps of the law, to the legislature.

The core duty for directors are expressed in the respective national corporate laws. What are the essential differences between the broad, multi-stakeholder provisions in s.172 in the UK as opposed to the narrow provision of s. 181 in Australian, and does it matter? Clearly, the law on the statute books of the two

93 *Percival v Wright,* n 91.
94 *Percival v Wright,* n 91.
95 Clarke A.D., *Corporations Law: Concepts, Cases and Culture*, OUP, 2021, 218–23.

advanced economies is quite different in tone, emphasis, and style. It matters in two important respects. Firstly, how courts might interpret the respective provisions. Secondly, and perhaps more fundamentally, how other relevant groups, including law review and law reform entities, can respond to and build on the provisions. In short, it goes to the important consideration of how the law in the 21st century can respond to seismic shifts in the social, economic, and legal fabric. Three forces are, firstly, the need to meet community expectations, secondly, the requirement to deliver justice, and thirdly, the necessity to underpin the validity and consistency of the rule of law. In essence, the law on the books is a vital indicator of the health of the law reform ecosystem.

4.5.3 The social effect: the effect on SLTO

To combat the climate crisis, ideally there needs to be a shift from social licence merely as a form of baseline permission or acceptance, and for it to be reformulated as social and environmental imperative in line with economic, social, and governance (ESG) perspectives. The issue in fossil fuel economies is that the mere mention of social licence is anathema to powerful interest groups with excellent lobbying access. The submissions to the ASX Corporate Governance Council in the lead up to the finalization of the 4th edition of Corporate Governance and Principles and Recommendations are clear evidence of this. The Governance Council received one hundred submissions in just under three months from a wide range of peak bodies, accounting and law firms, and powerful lobby organizations.[96] Another technique which is deployed in fossil fuel dominated economies, such as British Columbia in Canada, is to cloud and fog the meaning of social licence to suggest that it is a dangerously unstable idea:

> So, what are these organizations talking about? The answer is neither simple nor consistent across the spectrum of people and organizations using the term in their public communications. Project developers often talk about social licence as the outcome of a commitment to corporate social responsibility. Others often expect something deeper, akin to demonstrable community acceptance. Without definition and boundaries, social licence is no more than abstract rhetoric that has little meaning or, worse still, may frustrate genuine efforts to align interests because of the differing expectations it creates.[97]

96 ASX Corporate Governance Council, *Reviews and Submissions: Fourth edition of Corporate Governance Principles and Recommendations*, 27 February 2019, https://www.asx.com.au/about/regulation/asx-corporate-governance-council/reviews-and-submissions.

97 Business Council of British Columbia, 'Rethinking social license to operate- a concept in search of definitions and boundaries', *Environment and Energy Bulletin*, Vol 7 Issue 2, 28 May 2015, 1–10,1. The guest author was David Bursey, a partner with the law firm Bennett Jones LLP, https://bcbc.com/reports-research/rethinking-social-licence-to-operate-a-concept-in-search-of-definition-and-boundaries/.

Note the use of the concept of the Other in the quote. Another technique is to suggest that it is a nascent concept and that it involves another form of red tape for directors to navigate.[98] Collectively, these techniques amount to an effective form of advocacy because they remove the lexical creation of clear legal meaning and consequences in industries where they are most needed. Take the various sectors hinging on consumer 'freedom of choice' such as gaming, alcohol, tobacco, and the sugar in fast food. Each of these sectors is potentially 'addictive' via various mechanisms, and the business models in which they operate is predicated on this approach. The results for susceptible individuals are inevitably high health, medical, and social costs. Whether through 'irrational financial behaviour' relevant to gambling, the alcohol and sugar content relevant to alcohol, the nicotine and additives in tobacco, or the sugar, fat, and additives in fast, highly manufactured, and processed food, there are deep societal costs embedded in their use. To obfuscate, the producers place responsibility on individuals, but they pitch their marketing craft, global reach, and asymmetric resources directly to those same individuals, such that it is an inherently unfair contest. There may be no safe alternative to these products per se, so that the only safety mechanism is limited intake which reverts to individual responsibility. It is more apt therefore to say the social licence of such industries should be contingent and conditional, and that these very profitable, recession-proof businesses need to pay taxes, imposts, and other disincentives to counter their disruptive and high-cost effects which form the core of such mercantile models.

Similarly, coal and coal seam gas have been entrenched businesses sitting at the core of neoliberal economies. By contrast to the industries above, there are clear alternatives to their use in the way of renewables including wind, solar, and wave technologies. This is where the social and environmental imperative to scale-up these correlative renewable sectors is fundamental. If an industry with a deficit social licence or highly contingent licence is in direct competition with industries in which there is a social and environmental imperative, the state needs to intervene and to assist the latter sector. The binary is clear: coal and coal seam gas have a like-for-like replacement in renewables. This can be justified from several emerging perspectives. The analytical prisms provided by social, economic, scientific, and environmental considerations are clear. The one vector which presently trumps the others in Australia is the federal government's political and ideological preference for coal and coal seam gas. Indeed, the former conservative LNP government promoted a post-COVID, gas-led recovery with veterans form the fossil fuel sector. This trope is not restricted to one side of politics. Still, the Environment Minister approves new coals mines, and the Resources Minister approves a large-scale gas-fracking project in the Beetaloo Basin in the NT.

Additionally, federal governments from left and right subsidize fossil fuels to the order of billions of dollars annually. Indeed, even funds aimed at renewables are too often used to underpin fossil fuel projects. There is clear and sustained

98 Teele Langford, n 45, provides a comprehensive survey of these issues.

evidence of ideological capture. The powerful corporate interests are firmly vested in the political and economic fabric. Incumbency thinking provides direct connection between powerful corporations and industry peak bodies, on the one hand, and the two main political parties, on the other. This is achieved via lobbying and political donations, as well as significant marketing, advertising, and social media campaigns.

As noted, Australia has ridden its lucky breaks—with wool and agriculture, and then with mineral wealth. This has, however, come at a cost. The lucky country has morphed into the simple economy, as confirmed by the Harvard Atlas of Economic Complexity discussed in Chapter 3.[99] This has arguably created a sense of complacency and myopia. A national version of 'she'll be right mate', not looking far into the future and being reactive to current international events. Hence, Australia is often out of step with its G20 partners and competitors, and seemingly caught off-guard. By contrast, Australia was a key player in establishing the UN in the late 1940s.

The embedded nature of the economy centred on extractive industries and fossil fuels puts in peril the ability of Australia to deploy its inherent comparative advantage.[100] Whether there are clear and emerging alternatives to those long-dominant industries with at-best contingent claims to social licence, these new alternatives need every opportunity. However, the opposite occurs in Australia. Instead of encouraging electric vehicle (EV) take up, state governments have taxed them for using the road and governments of all stripes have failed to invest in sufficient infrastructure, such as charging stations. Australia needs to leapfrog beyond sclerotic decades-old debates about the social license to operate and instead shift to what might be called 'ESSE-I', that is Economic, Social, Scientific and Environmental-Imperatives. If the climate data and scientific evidence is clear, then the case for such a paradigm shift is compelling.

4.5.4 The ongoing hegemony of the economic licence to operate: an overarching feature of the neo-liberal economy in Australia

The long-established historically dominant theory of companies is a simple one: if there is a licence, it involves an imperative to be a money-making venture. The company is given due legal personality by the law as if it were in some respects an adult person. It can enter contracts and be held responsible by the courts as a legal actor with relevant legal responsibility. Whilst the company is a legal personality, with powers equivalent to an adult, it does not need to be reflective. Nor, if guidance is had from the formal law, or the Rio case study, does it require a conscience. That is an optional stance for the board to take on; it is additional and contiguous to the

99 Harvard University Centre for International Development (CID), Atlas of Economic Complexity, 'Country and Product Complexity Rankings', https://atlas.cid.harvard.edu/rankings

100 Ross Garnaut, *Superpower: Australia's Low-carbon opportunity*, LaTrobe University Press, 2019, 170.

core aim of increasing the wealth of shareholders. The legislation in Australian in the form of the Corporations Act 2001 (Cth) does not require it. Companies therefore are 'legal persons' invested with legal personality but ultimately, neither good faith nor good conscience is manifest in what they do, or how they go about doing it.

Dividends, capital growth, and bonus shares are the riches which drive corporations locally and globally. What was implicit in Charles Dickens' epoch of the 19th century, remains implicit in the contemporary era. Mass share ownership is a regarded as an Australian success story. This is evidenced by the growth and extent of superannuation funds. Australia's corporate law system is a faithful proxy of the Anglo-US model. Monetize all available assets at any cost to satiate the desire for shareholders to become wealthy. Under this model, another tonne of iron ore is the prize; the cost—whether social or cultural—is a minor concern. Mine, monetize, and ship to market. This is the trinity of concepts of Australia's extractive industries. This is part of what Dickens foresaw, 'the chaos and indifference of the modern industrial system'.[101]

The provenance of the profit of the company has to date been of little consequence. This has been the unquestioned and overarching philosophical and operating model until very recently. The notion of the company as compelled to do the right thing, and behave ethically, however, has more recently come to the fore. It is not mainstream yet, but its rise is apparent. This is encapsulated variously by references to corporate social responsibility and the concept of social licence to operate.

Environmental damage and climate change should make it clear that companies can no longer operate impervious to the negative impacts on their local communities and relevant ecosystems. Companies need increasingly to act in good conscience but how the law ensures this has not yet been established. There are many factors driving this change, including risk assessment more broadly, interconnected capital markets, and globally competitive standards. It may also be attributed to the acknowledgment of finite resources inherent in the challenge of navigating the 21st century. There is an articulation between climate change, land degradation, species collapse, and the failure to recognize or deal with the human rights of First Nations. We are reaching a consciousness of limits; we can no longer reach for the stars. Restraint comes into play. This gives rise to an unprecedented confluence of forces. Companies, particularly global mining entities, are operating within this array of intersecting vectors.

101 Peter Preston, Introduction to Charles Dickens, *The Mystery of Edwin Drood and other Stories*, Wordsworth Classics, 2005, xxi.

4.6 Conclusion: the patterns revealed by the fossil fuel corporate case studies

This chapter has covered the second of two case studies which focus upon present corporate industrial challenges dealing with Adani and with Rio Tinto, respectively. These are about the current and emerging corporate. This chapter focused on a notorious corporate event concerning the extraction of iron ore. Whilst the events of 2020 were shocking, the political and corporate responses since are telling. Three years later, there has been the resumption of business as usual. The Rio Tinto practices should be outliers, but they are not. They are mainstream. They are given full fiat by the economic licence to operate.

The issues extant in the Australian mining sector are widespread; they include the destruction of sites for mining purposes, and they also apply to the proper remediation of sites once mining has ceased. In each case, it is a question of relying on the narrow technical law, as opposed to a company acting more broadly morally, ethically, and in an environmentally sustainable way. Its 'personhood' is reflectively, profoundly (and usefully) defective, in fact, monstrous.

The problem is that the law appears to licence and underwrite economic development at all costs, such that companies are mandated to maximize profits and to not perceive the wider world in an informed or humanistic context. The lessons from the Rio Tinto example are that this narrow traditional form of corporate licence to profit must be challenged in the next three decades, given the global project of net zero by 2050.

References

ASX Corporate Governance Council, *Corporate Governance Principles and Recommendations*, 3rd ed, Foreword Alan Cameron AO Chair, ASX Corporate Governance Council 27 March 2014, 4. https://www.asx.com.au/regulation/corporate-governance-council.htm

ASX Corporate Governance Council Launch of The 4th Edition of The Corporate Governance Principles & Recommendations, Address by The Chair of The ASX Corporate Governance Council Elizabeth Johnstone, 27 February 2019. https://www.asx.com.au/content/dam/asx/about/corporate-governance-council/ej-speech-press-version.pdf

Judith Brett, 'The Coal Curse: Resources, Climate and Australia's Future', *Quarterly Essay, Black Inc. Books*, 78, 2020, 1–78.

Corporations (Aboriginal and Torres Strait Islander) Act 2006 (CATSI Act).

Clarke AD and Swain SR, 'Dickens and Grisham: Agents of Imperialism', *Australian Journal of Law and Society*, 15, 2000, 137–163.

Charles Dickens, *The Mystery of Edwin Drood and other Stories*, Wordsworth Classics, 2005.

Ross Garnaut, *Superpower: Australia's Low-carbon Opportunity*, LaTrobe University Press, 2019 170.

Brenda Hannigan, *Company Law*, 6th ed, OUP, 2021 or David Kershaw, *Company Law in Context, Text and Materials*, OUP, 2nd ed., 2012.

Donald Horne, *The Lucky Country*, Penguin, 1964.

Rosemary Teele Langford, 'Social Licence to Operate and Directors' Duties: Is there a Need for Change?' *Company & Securities Law Journal*, 37, 2019, 200.

Lisa Miller, 'The Use of Case Studies in Law and Social Science Research,' *Annual Review of Law and Social Science*, 14, 2018, 381.
Mirrar. https://www.mirarr.net/pages/mirarr.
Percival v Wright [1902] 2 Ch. 421.
Peter Preston, *Introduction to Charles Dickens, The Mystery of Edwin Drood and other Stories*, Wordsworth Classics, 2005.
Robert B. Reich, *Aftershock: The Next Economy and America's Future*, Vintage Books, 2011.
Adele Ferguson, *Gina Rinehart: The Untold Story of the Richest Woman in the World*, Macmillan, 2012.
Robert Yin, *Case Study Research: Design and Methods*, 5th ed, Sage, 2014.

5 The corporate climate III

Long-term risk, superannuation, and the McVeigh case

5.1 The case study: Mark McVeigh v REST Super and the long-term financial risk posed by climate change

5.1.1 A summary of the McVeigh case

The McVeigh case refers to the case brought by Mark McVeigh, a young superannuation account holder working in the retail sector against his superannuation or pension fund, REST. REST is a 50bn-dollar fund and is a major participant in Australia's three-trillion-dollar superannuation and pension fund sector. McVeigh's contention was that the corporate trustees of the REST fund needed specifically to take climate change into account, given the necessarily long-term nature of investments made within superannuation fund accounts.

Mark McVeigh was born in 1995 and the maturity date of his superannuation fund policy, which coincides with his 60th birthday, is therefore 2055, some five years beyond the broader Australia-wide target of net zero carbon emissions by 2050. As such, he sought clarification as to what climate risk strategies were relevant to and considered by the corporate trustees in making investment decisions within the wider portfolio and sought to be provided with this information. It was not forthcoming so Mark McVeigh issued legal proceedings in the Australian Federal Court in July 2018.

Just over two years later, the matter was settled at the defendant REST's instigation just before trial in November 2020 in favour of Mark McVeigh. REST issued a press release in November acknowledging the importance of climate risk and the centrality of it to the fund.

The McVeigh litigation and settlement has wider implications than the immediate case. It is regarded as a world first litigation process in terms of an individual account holder within a superannuation fund issuing proceedings against the corporate trustees of the fund in relation to the issue of climate risk.

The McVeigh-REST litigation and case settlement is arguably the fulcrum or pivotal cause of action giving rise to an emerging legal approach in Australia which positions climate change and climate risk at the centre of the economy, and the relevant legal challenges for corporations and their boards. The genesis of this litigation is found in Australian developments and in international factors.

DOI: 10.4324/9781003263746-6

5.1.2 The McVeigh litigation

Mark McVeigh was just 23 years old when he issued proceedings against his superannuation provider, REST.[1] Court documents confirmed he is employed in the retail sector, and contributes superannuation payments of 9.5 per cent of his salary to REST.[2] REST refers to the company, Retail Employees Superannuation Pty Ltd which is the corporate trustee of the Retail Employees Superannuation Trust.[3] McVeigh has been a member and beneficiary of the REST Trust since January 2013.[4] His membership is subject to a preservation age of 60 years. As such, he cannot access his superannuation account held by REST until January 2055, which coincides with his 60th birthday.[5] Given these facts, the question of long-term risk is central to the case. The preservation year of 2055 is also relatively close to the year 2050 which has taken on global significance as the marker for many nations and firms for achieving net zero emissions.[6]

5.1.2.1 The key legal documents: the concise document, July 2018

The pertinent facts and the nature of the claim were set out in two key documents filed on behalf of Mark McVeigh as plaintiff. The first was the Concise Document, filed in the Federal Court of Australia in July 2018.[7] Mark McVeigh sought a declaration and access to information under s.1017 of the Corporations Act 2001 (Cth).

The basis for establishing the claim relied on several provisions in the Corporations Act, and other statutes pertinent to superannuation. Paragraph 4 of the Concise Statement sets out seven contentions, the first two of which are as follows:

> At all material times REST was, and remains, governed by a board of directors (**Trustee Directors**) each of whom was bound by duties, including to:
>
> a) exercise their powers and discharge their duties with care and diligence: s 180(1) *Corporations Act*;
> b) exercise their powers and discharge their duties in good faith in the best interests of REST: s 181 *Corporations Act*.[8]

1 Concise Statement, *Mark McVeigh v Retail Employees Superannuation Pty Ltd*, 26 July 2018, http://climatecasechart.com/climate-change-litigation/wp-content/uploads/sites/16/non-us-case-documents/2018/20180723_NSD13332018_complaint-1.pdf, para 5. (McVeigh Concise Statement).
2 McVeigh Concise Statement, n 1, para 5.
3 McVeigh Concise Statement, n 1, para 1.
4 McVeigh Concise Statement, n 1, para 6(a).
5 McVeigh Concise Statement, n 1, para 6 (d).
6 United Nations Climate Change, Conference of the Parties 21, Paris, December 2015, https://unfccc.int/process-and-meetings/the-paris-agreement.
7 McVeigh Concise Statement, n 1.
8 McVeigh Concise Statement, n 1, para 4 (a) and (b).

These are the two key provisions in the Corporations Act dealing with the potential negligence of directors, and their requirement of acting good faith in relation to the company. In addition to the main director's duties set out in the Corporations Act, the plaintiff pleaded breaches of another Commonwealth statute, the Superannuation Industry (Supervision) Act 1993 (Cth) ('SIS Act'). The SIS Act essentially provided replication of the standards in the Corporations Act. For example, that trustee directors exercise 'due care, skill and diligence',[9] or variations on that word formula, in relation to several matters under the SIS Act, including their treatment of beneficiaries of the fund, and in relation to compliance with the licencing requirements. These matters reflect the essential content of s.180 (1) of the Corporations Act. Further, the SIS Act required the directors to act in the 'best interest' of the beneficiaries.[10] This 'best interest' formulation is essentially a replica of s.181 of the Corporations Act.

5.1.2.2 The amended concise document, September 2018

The Amended Concise Statement, lodged in September 2018, sought information that confirmed that REST was addressing what were referred to as 'climate change business risks'.[11] This was a compendium term comprising climate change, and including its physical impacts, and transition impacts since the financial year of 2016. This aligned the litigation document with the Paris 2015 COP21 agreement which came into force in November 2016.[12] The key point for determination was whether these elements taken 'individually or in any combination'[13] posed undue risk. The context related to REST's core business of long-term investment and was described in the Amended Concise Statement as 'material or major risks to the financial position of many of REST's investments'.[14] The litigation was world-leading, and 'attracted global attention'.[15] It involved consideration of investment time-horizons more than 30 years.

5.1.2.3 Legal concepts relevant to climate change litigation

As noted, the litigation documents filed by Mark McVeigh also hinged on several climate-related definitions which the Financial Stability Board (FSB) proposed

9 McVeigh Concise Statement, n 1, para 4 (d), referring to s 52A (2) (b) of the SIS Act.

10 McVeigh Concise Statement, n 1 para 4 (c), referring to s 52A (2) (c) of the SIS Act.

11 Amended Concise Statement, *Mark McVeigh v Retail Employees Superannuation Pty Ltd*, 24 September 2018, http://climatecasechart.com/climate-change-litigation/wp-content/uploads/sites/16/non-us-case-documents/2018/20180921_NSD13332018_complaint-1.pdf. (McVeigh Amended Concise Statement).

12 Paris 2015, n 6.

13 McVeigh Amended Concise Statement, n 11, para 9 (c).

14 Ibid.

15 Mark Bland, Partner, Mills Oakley, 'McVeigh v Rest- a new standard for managing climate change risks', November 2020, https://www.millsoakley.com.au/thinking/mcveigh-v-rest-a-new-standard-for-managing-climate-change-risks/.

within an international framework in 2015.[16] There were variously: 'climate change', 'physical impacts', and 'transition impacts' and these three concepts were essentially freighted from the international stage to the Australian litigation context. The fourth critical concept adopted in the pleadings in the McVeigh case was 'climate change business risks'.[17] By contrast, this was deployed as relevant to the defendant's business activities.[18]

5.1.3 Settlement of the McVeigh litigation

The proceedings in the McVeigh case were settled before trial in November 2020. The settlement was reported as being essentially in the plaintiff's favour and of significance, more broadly, as a key development in climate change litigation.[19] The asymmetry of the parties was noted; a by-then 25-year-old litigant had taken on a corporate enterprise with funds under management in excess of $50 billion.[20] The defendant superannuation fund, REST, issued a statement on 2 November 2020.[21] It noted the importance of the FSB international approach, and stated that 'consistent with the Task Force on Climate-related Financial Disclosures (TCFD), REST acknowledges that climate change could lead to catastrophic economic and social consequences and is an important concern of REST's members'.[22] This approach aligns domestic and national consequences with the benchmarks set out in international instruments. In terms of the three-trillion-dollar Australian superannuation sector[23] REST acknowledged that:

> Climate change is a material, direct and current financial risk to the superannuation fund across many risk categories, including investment, market, reputational, strategic, governance and third-party risks. Accordingly, REST, as a superannuation trustee, considers that it is important to actively identify and manage these issues, and continue to develop the systems,

16 Financial Stability Board, 'Proposal for a disclosure task force on climate-related risks', 9 November 2015, https://www.fsb.org/wp-content/uploads/Disclosure-task-force-on-climate-related-risks.pdf. (Financial Stability Board Proposal 2015).

17 McVeigh Amended Concise Statement, n 11, para 9 (c).

18 McVeigh Amended Concise Statement, n 11, para 9 (c).

19 *Business Insider*, 'A 25-year-old took on a $57 billion super fund over climate change and won. Experts see the case as evidence of "which way the wind is blowing"', by Jack Derwin, *Business Insider*, 5 November 2020, https://www.businessinsider.com.au/mark-mcveigh-rest-super-case-climate-change-investment-2020-11 (McVeigh, Business Insider).

20 McVeigh, Business Insider, and referenced as 'what can only be described as a David and Goliath battle'.

21 Rest website announcement, 'Rest reaches settlement with Mark McVeigh', 2 November 2020, https://rest.com.au/why-rest/about-rest/news/rest-reaches-settlement-with-mark-mcveigh, (Rest website announcement).

22 Rest website announcement, n 21.

23 Business Insider, n 19.

> policies and processes to ensure that the financial risks of climate change[24] are identified, considered, and mitigated and managed.[25]

This will have wide economic repercussions because of the size and reach of superannuation funds. Market analysis of the decision noted that:

> What is critical here are REST's expectations regarding the companies that it invests in, in their ability to assess and disclose their exposure to climate change risk, both physical and transitional risks. So it's almost the whole supply chain that's now being directed by a significant investor. That will drive further change within the Australian economy and Australian business.[26]

The settlement of the McVeigh case provided a keystone in the evolving theory and practical issues regarding climate risk, both short and long-term in reach, and national and potentially international in terms of effect. As was noted, the case 'despite not creating a legal precedent, sets a standard against which other superannuation funds will be measured'.[27] It formalized the fact that climate risk was a central concern for boards, directors, and trustees. Such risk was no longer an abstract concept, relevant simply to inchoate, long-term possibilities, but a live legal principle with present-day consequences to be actively managed. In summary, the McVeigh litigation can be contextualized by reference to developments in terms of legal risk for boards, directors, and corporate trustees. These national trends are underpinned by international climate science and by the UN-based consensus delivered by Paris COP21. In this sense, Australian legal opinion has moved in parallel with the international project.

5.2 The background to and context of the McVeigh case study

The background to this case covers international developments and Australian applications of those developments.

5.2.1 International developments and the emergence of a new risk model?

Given the fundamental challenge of climate change, it is now arguable that a fundamental review of established economic approaches is now taking shape with consideration of social foundations and ecological limitations and guided by international instruments. Its contours have particularly emerged since the Paris COP21. Although it may be seen as still in its relative infancy, it is developing rapidly. This is evidenced by the advent of climate change litigation such as the McVeigh-Rest case. This chapter examines some of the key concepts, principles,

24 Rest website announcement, n 21.

25 Rest website announcement, n 21.

26 Business Insider, n 19, quoting Brendan Bateman, a partner at law firm Clayton Utz.

27 Mark Bland, n15.

and techniques at the fulcrum of this emerging area in Australian commercial law, with a focus on superannuation and long-term risk.

5.2.1.1 The emergence of the post-Paris risk model

The emergence of the post-Paris risk model is predicated on four international events in the first two decades of the 21st century. The first of these, as discussed above, was the GFC which provided a prolonged sense of crisis (both internationally, and on a nation-by-nation basis) followed by a prolonged period of critique and introspection, which focused largely on the profound shortcomings of the status quo model of econometrics.

This was followed just a few years later by three international events in 2015, which together provide the mainframe for the evolving risk model. These are firstly, the Paris COP21[28] which established ecological limits within an agreed international set of mechanisms. Secondly, publication of the UN Social Developments Goals,[29] which provide a social floor or foundation for the model. And thirdly, the least known but arguably the most important in terms of developments in climate risk, the scoping paper published by the Financial Services Board[30] which established an international context for climate risk. Each of these documents is examined below.

5.2.1.2 The Paris COP21, December 2015

The COP21 held in Paris in 2015[31] was a momentous global occasion described by the UN as ‘a landmark in the multilateral climate change process because, for the first time, a binding agreement brings all nations into a common cause to undertake ambitious efforts to combat climate change and adapt to its effects’.[32] It gave rise to a broadly adopted international framework to cap carbon emissions to a maximum of 1.5 degrees of warming, together with national commitments. The UN website notes that:

> The Paris Agreement is a legally binding international treaty on climate change. It was adopted by 196 Parties at COP 21 in Paris, on 12 December 2015 and entered into force on 4 November 2016. Its goal is to limit global warming to well below 2, preferably to 1.5 degrees Celsius, compared to pre-industrial levels.[33]

28 Paris 2015, n 6.
29 United Nations, Social Development Goals, https://sdgs.un.org/goals, (United Nations SDGs).
30 Financial Stability Board Proposal 2015, n 16.
31 Paris 2015, n 6.
32 Paris 2015, n 6.
33 Paris 2015, n 6.

In this sense, COP21 has provided the mechanism for future Conferences of the Parties (COPs).[34] It can be argued that COP21 signalled a fundamental change of direction and focus; it gave rise to a fundamental economic pivot, imbued with global intent, and seeking nation-by-nation adherence. If the current Anglo-US economic model is econometric in theory and emanated out of Chicago, the emerging variation on that model is ecological, has its genesis in Paris, and is EU-centric in outlook.[35] The fulcrum moment was documentary in nature and was provided by the express terms and implied intent of the Paris 2015 Agreement.

5.2.1.3 The United Nations' Social Development Goals

The United Nations' Social Development Goals (SDGs) were published in 2015 by the UN's Department of Economic and Social Affairs and agreed to by some 193 countries, as part of the 2030 Agenda for Sustainable Development.[36]

These 17 goals or standards cover a range of fundamental topics including: no poverty, zero hunger, good health and wellbeing, quality education, gender equality, clean water and sanitation, affordable and clean energy, decent work and economic growth, industry innovation and infrastructure, and responsible consumption and production. They also include reference to climate action, life below water, life on land, peace, justice and strong institutions, and partnerships for the goals.[37] The UN SDGs set out a comprehensive set of interconnecting ideas. In this regard, the 17 goals are accompanied by 169 targets, more than 3,000 events, more than 1,300 publications, and over 5,500 actions. [38]

Crucially, the SDGs can be seen to provide the basis of the 'social floor'. which is an important element of the post-Paris arrangement. As the UN notes, '2015 was a landmark year for multilateralism and international policy shaping, with the adoption of several major agreements'.[39] The SDGs are an example of a cascade of documents originating from a broad-based international setting, in this case the UN, and onwards to being applied at the national and local levels. It is part of an increasingly apparent form of global-local convergence.

34 Such as the Glasgow-based COP26 of November 2021, which embedded the requirement reviews of national targets to be published in the following year, https://ukcop26.org/.

35 Exemplified by the so-called CBAM or carbon border adjustment mechanism, https://www.europarl.europa.eu/legislative-train/theme-a-european-green-deal/file-carbon-border-adjustment-mechanism#:~:text=On%2010%20March%202021%2C%20Parliament,and%20imports%20in%20selected%20sectors.

36 United Nations SDGs, n 29.

37 United Nations SDGs, n 29.

38 United Nations SDGs, n 29.

39 United Nations SDGs, n 29.

5.2.1.4 The Financial Stability Board (FSB) Proposal, November 2015

As noted above, the Financial Stability Board (FSB)[40] published its proposal, in the same month as Paris COP21, on behalf of its membership group comprising the leading G20 economies, and their central banks. It focused on the disclosure of climate-related risk. On first examination, the work of the Task Force may appear technical and subsidiary to the main political and economic machinations. However, the aim of the Task Force was 'to develop voluntary, consistent climate-related disclosures of the sort that would be useful to lenders, insurers, investors and other stakeholders in understanding material risks'.[41] It referred to the stability of the financial system, and the fact that 'policymakers have an interest in ensuring that the financial system is resilient to all forms of risk'.[42] This integrated an approach which went to the efficacy and durability of the financial and economic system. It combined consideration of two fundamental vectors: increased international cooperation in the wake of the GFC, together with a focus on climate change as a present and future imperative. It looked to the lessons of the past, and the consequences of failing to act presently, and in the future. It set out 'three broad categories' of 'possible climate-related risks', namely physical risks, liability risks, and transitions risks.

These were formally defined in the Financial Stability Board Proposal document as follows:

> **Physical risks:** the impacts on insurance liabilities and the value of financial assets that may arise from climate- and weather-related events, such as floods and storms that damage property or disrupt trade. In the financial sector, these losses have consequences most immediately for the insurance sector, but also extend more widely;
> **Liability risks:** the impacts that could arise if parties who have suffered loss or damage from the effects of climate change seek compensation from those they hold responsible. Such claims could come decades in the future, creating liabilities for carbon extractors and emitters and their insurers;
> **Transition risks:** the financial risks which could result from the process of adjustment towards a lower-carbon economy. Changes in policy, technology and physical risks could prompt a reassessment of the value of a large range of assets as costs and opportunities become apparent. The abruptness with which such re-pricing occurs could influence financial stability.[43]

The FSB Proposal adapted the concept of 'risk', a long-established general commercial and legal concept, and detailed it via sub-categories, and thereby extended

40 Financial Stability Board, https://www.fsb.org/. The FSB describes itself as 'an international body that monitors and makes recommendations about the global financial system', https://www.fsb.org/about/.

41 Financial Stability Board Proposal, n 16.

42 Financial Stability Board Proposal, n 16.

43 Financial Stability Board Proposal, n 16

its application to a range of scenarios. This process of lexical transmutation has given rise to the rapid advent of a new form of risk for boards. These three definitions of risk have informed the Australian legal analysis flowing from this international approach.

The FSB proposal also noted, somewhat presciently, that the 'potential risks to the financial sector from climate change are complex, and the understanding of them is still at an early stage'.[44] It observed that risk management in late 2015 was 'most active and sophisticated in the general insurance and reinsurance sectors where catastrophe risk modelling and capital standards take climate risks into account'.[45] Since then, other key aspects of the financial system, including legal risk, have followed the lead of insurance. Hence, a document which ostensibly began as a narrowly conceived commercial guideline, has since taken on widespread social, political, economic, and environmental consequences.

The FSB proposal, and the documents which have followed in its wake, have had a distinctive impact on the debate relevant to climate risk for corporations within national settings. In the case of the FSB, this output of documentation is ongoing (as it is with the United Nations COPs). For instance, the FSB's Taskforce on Climate-related Financial Disclosure (TCFD) published its Final Report in June 2017.[46] The FSB also publishes annual climate Status Reports on climate-related financial disclosures.[47] These publications are increasingly influential at the national, local and domestic levels. In particular, the TCFD framework has been instrumental in providing the framework for climate risk in Australia.

5.2.1.5 The features of the emerging post-Paris COP21 variation as regards the established risk model

Whilst the later econometric theory refers to scarcity and scarce resources, its critics argue that it became 'a value-free zone shaking off any normative claims of what ought to be'.[48] By contrast, the post-Paris approach centralizes scarcity and it is grounded in ecological terms. It also refers to the concept of an 'ecological ceiling',[49] or ecological limits. It seeks to ensure that long-term sustainability is

44 Financial Stability Board Proposal, n 16, 2.

45 Financial Stability Board Proposal, n 16, 2.

46 Financial Stability Board, Taskforce on Climate-related Financial Disclosure (TCFD), 'Final Report: Recommendations of the Task Force on Climate-related Financial Disclosures', 15 June, 2017, https://www.fsb.org/2017/06/recommendations-of-the-task-force-on-climate-related-financial-disclosures-2/.

47 Financial Stability Board (FSB), https://www.fsb.org/publications/?policy_area%5B%5D=149, and Taskforce on Climate-related Financial Disclosure (TCFD), https://www.fsb-tcfd.org/publications/#historical-materials.

48 Kate Raworth, *Doughnut Economics: Seven Ways to Think Like a 21st Century Economist*, Penguin, 2017, 34.

49 Raworth, n 48, 44.

built into the economic system. This system is referred to as 'regenerative and distributive'.[50]

5.2.1.6 *The ecological or 'doughnut' metaphor for an emerging form of 21st century climate risk: the social floor, and the ecological ceiling, respectively*

The Oxford-based economist, Kate Raworth, has referred to the new requisite paradigm as 'the doughnut model'[51] based on a pictorial representation and including the social 'floor' as the inner ring and the ecological 'ceiling'[52] as the outer ring. Climate science modelling and other core scientific disciplines, including ecology and botany, inform the model. It adopts an evidence-based approach predicated on scientific consensus to provide objective factual analysis to support the principles and related assumptions.

The doughnut model is based first on 12 social foundations, which are essentially informed by the UN SDGs discussed above.[53] These comprise eight basics of life—clean water, sufficient food, access to healthcare, access to education, decent housing, a minimum income from decent work, access to networks of information, and access to networks of social information.[54] The four social enablers that underpin the eight basic needs are gender equality, social equity, political voice, and peace and justice.[55] Collectively, these form the social foundation.[56]

The ecological ceiling in Kate Raworth's depiction of the doughnut model comprises nine elements, each of which should not be exceeded, lest they give rise to 'tipping points' the consequences of which, according to the preponderance of expert scientific opinion, are both dangerous and hard to predict.[57] These nine elements are climate change, ocean acidification, chemical pollution, nitrogen and phosphorous loading, freshwater withdrawals, land conversion, biodiversity loss, air pollution, and ozone layer depletion.[58] The model depicts that the 'overshoot of planetary boundaries' has in fact occurred in four of them to date: climate change, nitrogen and phosphorous loading, land conversion, and biodiversity loss.[59]

This depiction of floor and ceiling, in turn, creates the conditions for the new economy. This model aims to be sustainable, regenerative, and distributive and it operates within the space provided between the social foundation and the ecological ceiling. It refers to this as 'the safe and just space for humanity'.[60] The COP21,

50 Raworth, n 48, 44.
51 Raworth, n 48, 44.
52 Raworth, n 48, 44.
53 Raworth, n 48, 44.
54 Raworth, n 48, 45.
55 Raworth, n 48, 45.
56 Raworth, n 48, 45.
57 Timothy Lenton, Will Steffen and others, 'Climate Tipping Points- Too Risky to Bet Against', *Nature*, Comment, 27 November, 2019, https://www.nature.com/articles/d41586-019-03595-0.
58 Raworth, n 48, 44.
59 Raworth, n 48, 44.
60 Raworth, n 48, 44.

held in Paris in November 2015, provides a fulcrum point for the development of climate-related risk on a nation-by-nation basis. This was a momentous shift in global sentiment and coordinated action and expectation. It has set the modern anchor point for debate ever since. In the same month as the Paris COP summit, the Financial Stability Board published a proposal on behalf of its membership group, the G20 economies, and their central banks regarding the disclosure of climate-related risk. This proposal and documents which have followed in its wake have had a particular impact on the debate relevant to climate risk for corporations. Hence, pivotal international documents and proposals have had a profound effect on national economies since late 2015. This translation effect can be observed in the case of Australia. In particular, the McVeigh case study can be contextualized by reference to developments in terms of legal risk for boards, directors, and corporate trustees. These developments are underpinned by climate science and the UN-based consensus delivered by the Paris COP21. In this sense, Australian legal opinion has moved in parallel with the international project.

5.2.2 Key developments in Australia in climate risk analysis

In the Australian context, between 2016 and 2021 there have been a total of five Opinions published involving the eminent senior counsel, Noel Hutley QC. The instructing solicitor in each case was David Barnden, a leading climate change lawyer in Australia. Three such Opinions, published in 2016, 2019, and 2021 have focused on director liability for climate risks. These Opinions were sought and publicly provided by the Centre for Policy Development, a non-profit think-tank based in Sydney. Additionally, two Opinions on the liability of corporate trustees operating within the domain of superannuation funds have been published in 2017 and 2021. These two Opinions were sought, and publicly provided by Market Forces, an affiliate of Friends of the Earth and similarly a non-profit organization. The Opinions can be studied thematically by reference to the two subject areas, or by date. However so configured, the five Opinions, when taken together, provide a compelling sequence and narrative which demonstrates the shift over the five-year period (2016 to 2021) in climate change awareness, risk, and potential legal liability. Each of these Opinions will be examined, together with other relevant key developments.

Two of the Opinions (2016 and 2017) predate the issuing of proceeding in the McVeigh case in 2018. The Opinion of 2019 was published after the issue of proceeding (which took place in 2018), but prior to the settlement of the case in November 2020. The remaining two Opinions came after the proceedings were settled. They, too, demonstrate a clear trajectory requiring directors to take a serious, considered, and proactive approach to the strategic oversight and the management of climate risk.

5.2.3 Australian developments: linking climate risk to corporations and to directors' liability

Climate related risk for boards in Australia has proceeded apace since 2016. It combines several elements, including case law and legal settlements of disputes in more recent times. Climate change case law, as a global phenomenon, is encapsulated in the online domain maintained by the Sabin Centre at the University of Columbia.[61] The cases referred to in Parts V and VI are on this site and provide an Australian link to developments in the rest of the world.

In the commercial law context, however, the foundation has been heavily influenced to date by a sequence of three legal Opinions which together have comprehensively set out the law relevant to climate change as it affects key actors within the sphere of corporate law and trust law. These Opinions have in turn been instrumental in shaping the Australian case law which has followed them, so there has been a symbiotic development of the law.

5.2.3.1 The Hutley sequence of legal Opinions on the duties of directors

There are three legal Opinions which have provided a framework for focusing on evolving climate change risk as it affects directors. The first Opinion was published in 2016,[62] and the two others have followed in 2019 and 2021. The lead author in each Opinion is Noel Hutley QC, widely regarded as one of Australia's foremost silks, and bestowed with 'bet-the company' accolades. The three Opinions have been cowritten with Sebastian Hartford-Davis, a rising junior, and also a member of the NSW Bar. The Opinions are noteworthy for several reasons. Firstly, they provide statements of the law in the round, rather than as answers to specific enquiries. The Opinions were produced for The Centre for Policy Development (CPD) and The Future Business Council, and the instructing solicitors were Minter Ellison. Secondly, is the fact that the three sequential Opinions have been published online as an important feature of the wider discourse by a leading commercial firm and the CPD think-tank. This marks a worthy form of pro bono contribution within the broader business and legal community. Thirdly, the Opinions collectively form part of a dynamic and evolving narrative, given that they cover and report on five years of legal and related development. In each of these respects, they obviate the need for litigants to litigate each matter in detail. They set out the parameters of the law and can be seen to encourage settlement of disputes on that basis, as was the case in the McVeigh proceedings discussed in Part V.

The Opinions provide something of a template, the overriding commercial message of which is that boards of directors need to be proactive and to take very seriously their growing obligations as regard climate risk.

61 Sabin Centre, Columbia Law School, Columbia University, New York, Climate Change Litigation Databases, http://climatecasechart.com/climate-change-litigation/ (Sabin Climate Law Centre).

62 Noel Hutley SC and Sebastian Hartford- Davis, 'Memorandum of Opinion, Climate Change and Directors' Duties', 7 October 2016 https://cpd.org.au/wp-content/uploads/2016/10/Legal-Opinion-on-Climate-Change-and-Directors-Duties.pdf, (2016 Director Opinion).

5.2.3.2 The 2016 Opinion and climate risk and the rising likelihood of litigation

The Opinion in 2016 set the benchmark, and the subsequent opinions have borne out the key predictions of the first Opinion. The 2016 Opinion was 50 paragraphs over 20 pages in length. It came after the Paris COP21 and the FSB Draft of 2015. The Opinion took into account each of these international documents and in so doing identified climate risk as directly pertinent to the role of directors in Australia.

The 2016 Director Opinion concluded that 'climate risk disclosure is the subject of increasing litigation in the United States'.[63] The link between the US and potential developments in Australia was flagged where the Opinion noted 'sometimes, though not always, trends … in the American litigation market can influence litigation in Australia'.[64] This observation has turned out to be an accurate precursor to the increasing prevalence of climate change litigation in Australia. The focus on climate-related risk, which was first apparent in the general insurance and reinsurance sectors, has since migrated into several other aspects of the wider financial system.

5.2.3.3 The 2019 Supplementary Opinion, 26 March 2019

On 26 March 2019, Noel Hutley SC and Sebastian Hartford-Davis provided a Supplementary Memorandum of Opinion, titled 'Climate Change and Directors' Duties', also published by the Centre for Policy Development.[65] It comprises 22 numbered paragraphs in 12 pages. The authors note that 'there have been a number of significant developments in the period since 2016'.[66] They opine 'that we are now observers of a profound and accelerating shift in the way that Australian regulators, firms and the public perceive climate risk'.[67] They refer to three critical issues. Firstly, 'a series of coordinated interventions by Australian regulators, which will require in practice that increased attention be given to both the assessment and disclosure of climate risk'.[68] Secondly, 'acute interest … from investor groups,'[69] and thirdly, 'developments in the state of scientific knowledge'.[70] The collective effect of these factors is to 'elevate the standard of care that will be expected of a reasonable director'.[71] They conclude this part of the Opinion by noting that:

63 2016 Director Opinion, n 62, para 50.
64 2016 Director Opinion, n 62, para 50.
65 Noel Hutley SC and Sebastian Hartford- Davis, 'Supplementary Memorandum of Opinion, Climate Change and Directors' Duties', 26 March 2019, https://cpd.org.au/wp-content/uploads/2019/03/Noel-Hutley-SC-and-Sebastian-Hartford-Davis-Opinion-2019-and-2016_pdf. 2019 Director Supplementary Opinion).
66 2019 Director Supplementary Opinion, n 65, para 3.
67 2019 Director Supplementary Opinion, n 65, para 4.
68 2019 Director Supplementary Opinion, n 65, para 4.
69 2019 Director Supplementary Opinion, n 65, para 4.
70 2019 Director Supplementary Opinion, n 65, para 4.
71 2019 Director Supplementary Opinion, n 65, para 4.

> Company directors who consider climate change risks actively, disclose them properly and respond appropriately will reduce exposure to liability. But as time passes, the benchmark is rising.[72]

The reference to the rising benchmark serves as an apt metaphor for climate risk. As the Opinion observes:

> As time passes, it is increasingly obvious that climate change is and will inevitably affect the economy, and it is increasingly difficult in our view for directors of companies of scale to pretend that climate change will *not* intersect with the interests of their firms. In turn, that means that the exposure of individual directors to "climate change litigation" is increasing, probably exponentially, with time.[73]

The onset of these issues in the international realm has occurred in a short period of time. The compression within the Australian context has been even more acute. For instance, the 2019 Supplementary Opinion's forecast of an increase in climate change litigation has proven correct, as will be examined in terms of recent and ongoing cases.

5.2.3.4 Regulatory alignment

The theme of regulatory intervention referred to in the 2016 Director Opinion is further developed in the Opinions since then. For instance, the 2019 Director Supplementary Opinion noted that:

> there is now a striking degree of alignment between the Reserve Bank of Australia (RBA), the Australian Securities and Investment Commission (ASIC) and the Australia Prudential Regulation Authority (APRA) as to the financial and economic significance of climate risks.[74]

Within the Australian context, the two main regulators relevant to corporate oversight are ASIC and APRA. Their centrality to the financial and insurance sector is such that they were referred to as the 'twin peaks' of prudential regulation in the Banking Royal Commission Final Report of February 2019,[75] and it was recommended they be retained as such, given their importance.[76]

The 2019 Supplementary Opinion also noted an increasing bifurcation between the regulatory setting, and other relevant contexts. The authors observed that 'the regulatory environment has profoundly changed since our 2016 Memorandum,

72 2019 Director Supplementary Opinion, n 65, para 4.

73 2019 Director Supplementary Opinion, n 65, para 4.

74 2019 Director Supplementary Opinion, n 65, para 6.

75 Final Report, Royal Commission into Misconduct in the Banking, Superannuation and Financial Services Industry, 1 February, 2019, 1–530, https://treasury.gov.au/sites/default/files/2019-03/fsrc-volume1.pdf, (Banking Royal Commission Final Report).

76 Banking Royal Commission Final Report, n 75, 71.

even if the legislative and policy responses have not'.[77] This is an implicit acknowledgment of the advent of a curious gap between the formal law on the books, and the actual and experienced risk environment within the marketplace. This gap may reflect the speed of developments or the reluctance of the political realm to acknowledge the change in wider market dynamics.

5.2.3.5 Scientific knowledge and climate risk

There is an increasing link between scientific knowledge and consensus scientific opinion on the one hand, and the legal consequences within the civil liability realm on the other. In terms of advances in climate science, the 2019 Director Supplementary Opinion observes that:

> there have been some notable developments in the state of scientific knowledge, which inevitably bear upon the gravity and probability of climate risks which directors need to consider. We do not attempt to summarise those developments here, beyond pointing (as a first resource) to the October 2018 report of the Intergovernmental Panel on Climate Change ("IPCC"), *Global Warming of 1.5°C*, which summarises scientific findings concerning the differences in regional climate characteristics that will occur if the globe warms by 1.5°C from pre-industrial levels.[78]

Beyond the IPCC report, the authors also refer to 'the timeline for the realisation of physical climate risks is the subject of significant available scientific study',[79] the scientific 'consensus global warming is likely to reach 1.5°C between 2030 and 2052 if it continues to increase at the current rate',[80] and 'the well-documented risks'.[81] This scientific consensus carries legal significance. It provides references for boards in identifying legal and financial risk. The legal standard or test is broadly that of the 'reasonable' director. The publicly available level of knowledge, based on the UN documentation and elaborated in the Opinions, provides a comprehensive guide. Specifically, the 2019 Supplementary Opinion notes that scientific advances and regulatory developments, when viewed in tandem, 'are indicative of a rapidly developing benchmark against which a director's conduct would be measured in any proceedings alleging negligence against him or her'.[82] The conflation of science, economic considerations, commercial law, and legal risk are now highly consequential. The Opinions have been given further support by extrajudicial observations.

77 2019 Director Supplementary Opinion, n 65, para 6.
78 2019 Director Supplementary Opinion, n 65, para 10.
79 2019 Director Supplementary Opinion, n 65, para 12.
80 2019 Director Supplementary Opinion, n 65, para 12.
81 2019 Director Supplementary Opinion, n 65, para 14.
82 2019 Director Supplementary Opinion, n 65, para 6.

5.2.3.6 *Extra-judicial Analysis by former Justice of the High Court, Kenneth Hayne, September 2019*

After the 2019 Addendum Opinion, and prior to the 2021 Opinion, are the extra judicial remarks of Kenneth Hayne, former Justice of the High Court of Australia. Following his retirement from the High Court in June 2015,[83] Justice Hayne was appointed in December 2017[84] as the Royal Commissioner of the Royal Commission into Misconduct in the Banking, Superannuation, and Financial Services Industry.[85] This culminated in the Final Report published in February 2019.[86] Hence, the resonance of comments by Justice Hayne in late 2019 at the Centre for Policy Development's Business Roundtable on Climate and Sustainability.[87]

In his presentation, Justice Hayne examined climate change 'from the individual entity's point of view'.[88] This approach accords with the focus of classical economic theory based on the actions of the firm or business, acting as a rational business entity. It also coincides with the standard, established, and historical approach to the legal analysis of the company. In doing so, Justice Hayne distinguished his approach from a 'system-wide response',[89] whilst also confirming his view that, with input being offered more appropriately from other disciplines, a 'systemic response is essential'.[90]

Justice Hayne referred to two issues afflicting boards of directors of individual companies. He referred to these as 'learned helplessness and entrenched short-termism'.[91] Interestingly, having said that his approach was to be conducted at the individual firm level, he noted in relation to these two points of critique that 'the issue, of course, is global'. This is an implicit recognition of the evolving sequencing of climate change in the post-Paris COP21 environment.

This approach aligns the micro and the local, on the one hand, with the macro and the international, on the other. The traditional degrees of separation and the historically informed techniques of distancing are being compressed, if not collapsing altogether. Informed legal analysis now must now invariably consider both sets of information, given the symbiotic nature of the linkages. Tellingly, Justice Hayne then went on to connect international trends to local and more immediate matters, where he observed 'that what we are now considering is individual responses by entities and by their directors (separately and collectively)'.[92]

83 https://www.hcourt.gov.au/justices/current/justice-hayne-ac.
84 Banking Royal Commission Final Report, n 75, 3.
85 Banking Royal Commission Final Report, n 75, 3.
86 Banking Royal Commission Final Report, n 75, 3.
87 Justice Kenneth Hayne, Centre for Policy Development, Climate Change Round Table, 21 November 2019 in Sydney, 1-5,1. https://cpd.org.au/2019/12/full-text-of-kenneth-hayne-ac-qc-remarks-to-cpd-climate-roundtable/, (Justice Hayne 2019 CPD Roundtable)
88 Justice Hayne, 2019 CPD Roundtable, n 87, 1.
89 Justice Hayne, 2019 CPD Roundtable, n 87, 1.
90 Justice Hayne, 2019 CPD Roundtable, n 87, 1.
91 Justice Hayne, 2019 CPD Roundtable, n 87, 3.
92 Justice Hayne, 2019 CPD Roundtable, n 87, 3.

5.2.4 The 2021 Supplementary Opinion, April 2021

The third of the Opinions focused on director' duties relevant to climate change was published in April 2021.[93] It emphatically endorsed the issues identified in the 2016 and 2019 Opinions and went on to advance them. Whereas the 2016 Opinion had focused on 'the existence of the duty; that is, what directors could and should be doing on climate change to discharge their duty of care and diligence',[94] it noted that 'the pendulum has swung'[95] and that it 'is now uncontroversial'.[96] In addition, they noted that:

> In 2019, we observed that the risk of liability for directors on this front was rising exponentially. In 2021, it appears to us that the focus is increasingly on *how* the duty is discharged.[97]

The five-year period between the first and the 2021 Director Further Supplementary Opinion represents a paradigm shift for directors moving from basic risk awareness in 2016 to undertaking complex, strategic risk oversight and management in 2021. As regards companies making commitments to 'net zero' carbon emissions by a certain date,[98] this 'brings into focus an acute litigation risk'.[99] The 2021 Directors Further Supplementary Opinion deals in detail with the legal concept of 'greenwashing'.[100] It is apparent from this approach that new concepts and evolving lexical terms are relevant to the climate crisis and net zero by 2050 economics in terms of creating liability and influencing asset prices. This is clear from the 2021 Directors' Duties Opinion which provides a legal, contextual, and working definition 'of "greenwashing" which we understand to mean inaccurate climate-related statements and disclosures, including flawed climate scenario analysis and "net zero" commitments that are misleading or made without a reasonable basis'.[101]

It is apparent that key concepts within the post-Paris COP21 environment are developing at different rates and within multiple contexts. For example, the legal concept of greenwashing which is focused on overly optimistic future projections, differs from the more established use of the term within the realms of marketing, for instance, whereas it is characterized as a decoy or diversionary

93 Noel Hutley SC and Sebastian Hartford Davis, 'Climate Change and Directors' Duties', *Further Supplementary Memorandum of Opinion*, The Centre for Policy Development, 23 April 2021, https://cpd.org.au/wp-content/uploads/2021/04/Further-Supplementary-Opinion-2021-3.pdf (2021 Director Further Supplementary Opinion).

94 2021 Director Further Supplementary Opinion, n 93, para 49.

95 2021 Director Further Supplementary Opinion, n 93, para 49.

96 2021 Director Further Supplementary Opinion, n 93, para 49.

97 2021 Director Further Supplementary Opinion, n 93, para 49.

98 2021 Director Further Supplementary Opinion, n 93 para 3. Typically, the target for net zero carbon emissions is 2050.

99 2021 Director Further Supplementary Opinion, n 93, para 6.

100 2021 Director Further Supplementary Opinion, n 93, para 5. The term 'greenwashing' is referred to seven times in the 2021 Director Further Supplementary Opinion.

101 2021 Director Further Supplementary Opinion, n 93 para 5.

tactic used by companies and firms to curry favour with markets and customers.[102] Terms are materializing apace, including climate risk, net zero, carbon neutrality, tipping points, and stranded assets.[103] The three Opinions provide valuable public information, and provide important information for commercial and other organisations. They reduce the need for litigation and provide clarity for boards and directors. Their utility will be explicit and implicit. The reach of the Opinions, in the latter sense, is clear in relation to the legal liability of corporate trustees, discussed below.

5.2.5 Other Australian developments: long-term climate risk assessment and the liability of corporate trustees

The sequence of three Opinions on climate risk relevant to boards and directors form part of a broader emerging field relevant to the risk settings for other key commercial actors, including corporate trustees. This is the case with two further Opinions produced by Noel Hutley SC and the barrister, James Mack in 2017 and 2021 respectively.

5.2.5.1 The Memorandum of Opinion on Trustee Duties of 2017

The Memorandum of Opinion titled 'Superannuation Fund Trustee Duties and Climate Change Risk' was published in June 2017.[104] The instructing solicitors were Environmental Justice Australia, based in Melbourne.[105] The 2017 Trustee Opinion was provided for Market Forces which was described as 'an affiliate project of Friends of the Earth who are a non-profit organisation'.[106]

The 2017 Trustee Opinion referred[107] to the 2016 Director Opinion[108] which had addressed the law relevant to Australian company directors and climate change risk. By contrast, the 2017 Trustee Opinion focused 'on the breadth of superannuation fund trustee duties and climate change risk',[109] and the role and duties of trustee directors as regards those risks. They concluded that 'trustee directors should source, consider and weigh relevant information relating to climate change risk and record their decision-making processes, including any considerations of climate change

102 Guy Pearse, *Green Wash: Big Brands and Carbon Scams*, Black Inc., 2012.

103 See, for example, in the Australian economic context, Alan Finkel, 'Getting to Zero: Australia's Energy Transition', *Quarterly Essay*, Issue 81, 2021, 1–103.

104 Noel Hutley SC and JE Mack, Memorandum of Opinion, 'Superannuation Fund Trustee Duties and Climate Change Risk', Environmental Justice Centre, 15 June 2017, https://www.envirojustice.org.au/sites/default/files/files/20170615%20Superannuation%20Trustee%20Duties%20and%20Climate%20Change%20(Hutley%20%26%20Mack).pdf (2017 Trustee Opinion).

105 2017 Trustee Opinion, n 104, para 1.

106 2017 Trustee Opinion, n 104, para 1.

107 2017 Trustee Opinion, n 104, para 1.

108 2016 Director Opinion, n 62.

109 2017 Trustee Opinion, n 104, para 1.

risks'.[110] Reference to the phrase 'source, consider and weigh' provides a tripartite suite of functions. The appropriate standard of care is that of 'due care, skill and diligence'.[111] The 2017 Trustee Opinion refers to the 'prudent' trustee director.[112] The focus is on financial risk. That is, 'a trustee director should perform their duties and exercise their powers in the best *financial* interests of beneficiaries'.[113] This conclusion is a result of the statutory scheme relevant to superannuation[114] and of the court's interpretation of the scheme. The key point of analysis relevant to actors within the commercial sector was that:

> there is an inherent harmony between the *financial* effect associated with climate change risks and the cardinal requirement of a trustee to act in the best *financial* interests of beneficiary. It follows that climate change risks can and should be considered by trustee directors to the extent that those risks may intersect with the financial interests of a beneficiary of a superannuation fund. This situation is most likely to arise if a trustee director is making a significant decision related to investments that are exposed to climate change risk.[115]

The 2017 Trustee Opinion prioritized consideration of financial risk within a given 'factual matrix'.[116] In this regard it noted that

> it is the treatment of climate change as a *financial* risk (as distinct from the treatment of climate change as an environmental, social or governance issue) that trustee directors ought to consider in an appropriate case when fulfilling the requirements imposed.[117]

This analysis can be viewed in two possible ways. Firstly, it shifts environmental social governance (ESG) considerations to the sidelines. Based on this argument, it converts ESG to a liminal suite of issues within this context. Secondly, however, it can be seen to expand the remit and importance of climate change as a financial risk factor which is, in turn, central to decision-making within long-term investment schemes, such as superannuation funds. The 2017 Trustee Opinion, for instance, predicted that the Australian Prudential Regulatory Authority (APRA) would conduct the regulatory functions conferred on it by the relevant statutory scheme[118] 'on the basis that climate change presents a financial risk'.[119] That prediction has

110 2017 Trustee Opinion, n 104, para 3.3.
111 2017 Trustee Opinion, n 104, para 5.
112 2017 Trustee Opinion, n 104, para 2.3 and para 13.
113 2017 Trustee Opinion, n 104, para 6.
114 In the case of superannuation this is the *Superannuation Industry (Supervision) Act 1993* (Cth), (SIS Act).
115 2017 Trustee Opinion, n 104, para 10.
116 2017 Trustee Opinion, n 104, para 11.
117 2017 Trustee Opinion, n 104, para 15.
118 SIS Act, n 114.
119 2017 Trustee Opinion, n 104, para 15.

proven to be prescient as subsequent events have proved, and accurate as the 2021 Trustee Opinion confirms.

5.2.5.2 The Memorandum of Opinion Superannuation Trustee Duties and climate change, 16 February 2021

This Opinion was published in February, 2021 (the 2021 Trustee Opinion).[120] By contrast to the 2017 Trustee Opinion, its title removed the words 'Fund' and 'Risk' respectively. It was an updated Opinion 'having regard to … developments'[121] since the 2017 Trustee Opinion. It noted that its observation in the 2017 Trustee Opinion, as regards the expanded role of the regulator, APRA, had proven accurate. That is, APRA 'has continued to make public statements consistent with [the] simple proposition'[122] that 'climate change presents a financial risk'.[123] APRA had explicitly disclosed and publicly clarified how it would conduct its regulatory functions. So, too, had the Australian Securities and Investments Commission (ASIC)[124] and the Actuaries Institute.[125] Each regulator confirmed that climate change gave rise to material and systemic financial risk.

The 2021 Trustee Opinion also referred to the approach of the four large Australian-based superannuation funds,[126] and by a major superannuation consultancy[127] as being consistent with that of the regulators. One of those four superannuation funds was REST, against which Mark McVeigh issued proceedings.[128] In this respect, the 2021 Trustee Opinion noted that:

> REST, another large superannuation trustee, in November 2020, in the context of a settlement of a Federal Court proceeding which challenged its compliance with obligations of prudence and disclosure, stated that climate change is a material, direct and current financial risk to the superannuation fund. Further, REST committed to achieving a portfolio wide net zero by 2050 target, advocating for companies and governments to align with the climate goals of the Paris Agreement, incorporating climate risks into its risk management framework, aligning the fund's disclosure practices to the TCFD, and to disclosing *all* portfolio holdings.[129]

120 NC Hutley and JE Mack, Memorandum of Opinion, 'Superannuation Trustee Duties and Climate Change', Environmental Justice Centre, 16 February 2021, https://equitygenerationlawyers.com/wp/wp-content/uploads/2021/04/Hutley-SC-Mack-Superannuation-Trustee-Duties-and-Climate-Change-Memo-2021.pdf, (2021 Trustee Opinion).

121 2021 Trustee Opinion, n 120, para 1.

122 2021 Trustee Opinion, n 120, para 1.

123 2021 Trustee Opinion, n 120, para 1.

124 2021 Trustee Opinion, n 120, para 3(a).

125 2021 Trustee Opinion, n 120, para 3 (c).

126 2021 Trustee Opinion, n 120, para 3 (d), (f), and (h).

127 2021 Trustee Opinion, n 120, para 3 (g).

128 2021 Trustee Opinion, n 120, para 3(h).

129 2021 Trustee Opinion, n 120, para 3(h).

The 2021 Trustee Opinion noted that 'climate change scenario analysis' or the 'stress testing' of plans and climate and financial risk would be the 'new normal'.[130] Additionally, 'trustees should expect that, increasingly, every investment turn will require an engagement with the financial risk posed by climate change'.[131] It was clear that climate risk and financial risk were symbiotically intertwined, and increasingly so. The 2021 Trustees Opinion made it clear that trustees and directors ignored these new touchstones at their peril.

5.3 Post case-study events

5.3.1 The emergence of climate change litigation in Australia

It was the novelty of the McVeigh case and the 'David versus Goliath' dimensions of it that made it the subject of worldwide scrutiny. The case was settled, so the issues were not tested publicly, but the fact that the large, well-resourced defendant was the party to finally relent just before trial marked the beginning of the acceptance of the climate science and its entanglement with long-term investment and legal risk for boards. Justice Hayne refers to climate science as being based on 'scientific observation and extrapolation'.[132] Courts can no longer ignore the propensity of data pointing to a climate emergency. Litigation will be increasingly used in the context of that emergency to hold to account carbon emitters and their boards. As the law firm KWM has observed, the McVeigh case was the first in Australia in what has become a growing trend on the part of plaintiffs aiming 'to influence corporate behaviour and governance, rather than seeking damages'[133] which has been the traditional common law remedy. This highlights the fact there are multiple techniques and aims, including litigation, now being used in relation to the climate crisis and these are discussed in Chapter 6.

5.3.1.1 The political paradox: the growing gap between the marketplace for risk and the political sphere

The paradox is that between 2016 and 2021, the formal law on the books had not changed, and the political debate was shrouded in the notion that climate change was largely seen, as former Justice Hayne has referred to it as 'a matter of belief or ideology',[134] as opposed to one scientific consensus. It was only in the very last few weeks before COP26 in Glasgow that the government committed to net zero by 2050 as an aim, and in so doing, joined the Labor Opposition and each of the States

130 2021 Trustee Opinion, n 120, para 10(b) iii.

131 2021 Trustee Opinion, n 120, para 11.

132 2021 Trustee Opinion, n 120, 4.

133 King and Wood Mallesons, Will Heath et al, 'Insight: A big week for the fossil fuel sector: climate activism hits global courts and boardrooms', 1 June 2021, https://www.kwm.com/au/en/insights/latest-thinking/climate-activism-hits-global-courts-and-boardrooms.html

134 Justice Hayne, 2019 CPD Roundtable, n 87, 4.

and Territories. In October 2021, climate change was a debate which could enter the public realm having been long-relegated to the partisan, political sidelines.

5.3.1.2 The nexus between international events and national responses

The legal architecture of systems such as superannuation,[135] pension funds, directors' duties, and the enunciation of risk has largely been nationally based in the latter half of the 20th century and the first decade of the 21st century. Its development has been part of the province of nation states, but the world is now witnessing, in relation to the climate emergency, the development an international architecture and benchmarks against which formerly hegemonic nation states are expected to align their national arrangements. The G20 nations are a case in point with the growing influence of the Financial Stability Fund (FSB). The FSB's ongoing development of climate-related Financial Disclosure is a clear, indeed signal, example of the internationalization of formerly, nationally determined standards. Expectations are moving towards mandatory schemes. As such, member states are increasingly required to align with the internationally determined instrument and to report back. There is a form of concordance around doing the right thing by one's nation state peers, if not a nascent form of shaming. As a result, particularly those states subject compliance with domestic agendas, such as Labor in Australia, have begun the process of translating these international requirements. The work of the FSB is intensifying. It provides an update of compliance on the website.[136] This in turn generates urgency on a domestic level The Australian context of climate risk as set out by Hutley SC is emblematic of this approach. It refers to the FSB international standards and domestic vectors, such as the attitude of the relevant regulators. As such, the contours of climate risk are being sketched and filled in despite government attitudes and of the law on the books. The hegemony of national governments and their assumed control of domestic commerce is a relic of the 20th century.

5.3.1.3 The emergence of the annual UN Conference of the Parties as an international audit of climate change progress

The annual Conference of the Parties provides a forum for nations to compare their efforts for political leaders to emerge or to retreat depending on their political and economic stances respectively and for new concepts such as the 'loss and damage' fund at COP27 held in Sharm-el-Sheikh, Egypt in November 2022.

Australia was seen as a laggard state, if not a pariah by some for its role as major exporter of cola oil and gas and its dismissal of concerns regarding considering scope 3 or actual place-of-use of exported goods which in turn create carbon emissions. With a change of federal government in May 2022, the new centre-left

135 2021 Trustee Opinion, n 120, para 8.
136 Financial Stability Board, n 47.

government seeks to burnish its improved climate credentials. It has legislated a 43 per cent target by 2030, a requirement for nation states set out by COP26 held in Glasgow in November 2021.

The core question in Australia, however, is in relation to whether the government will continue to allow new coal, oil, and gas projects with projected long-term life-cycles which go close to and beyond 2050. The political labels have been both plentiful and misleading including reference to clean coal, that Australian coal is somehow superior, that the world needs coal and there is no alternative, and he gas-led recovery after COVID. This has created a convenient veil for political parties, for governments and for major corporate emitters with a pastiche language entwined by jargon, obfuscation, and euphemism.

5.3.1.4 The advent of scientific method and consensus concerning climate warming and the urgent need for action by nation states and corporations

These opinions give rise to the intersection of law with science and scientific. The scientific hypothesis and consensus become the foundation for legal evidence and meets the civil standard of balance of probabilities. It places the director squarely within the reasonable person test. Ignorance is no excuse.

Where the law refers to broad-based principles, for example, the reasonable director, the competent response, and so forth, the law is changing from within. The content of these principles is changing to reflect the lifting of the set of expectations of the community and of the courts. These are inevitably flexible standards which vary (as in usually rise) over time. This is evident in Australia from the McVeigh case and its context, both prior to and since the settlement of the litigation. The defendant drew a line in the sand. It limited its ongoing publicity (negative) and put out a public statement pivoting from a fund paying insufficient attention to climate risk, to one putting such considerations at the core of its short- and long-term business strategies.

The responses to climate change are varied as climate scientist Michael Mann has observed.[137] On a continuum, there are several basic positions. Of course, one stance is to deny there is a problem at all and that the issue is a Disney fantasy, a conspiracy, or similar. If the climate science is accepted, one extreme is of impending doom and catastrophe comprising the doomsayers who see any progress as too late, given the end is nigh. At the other extreme is a radical repositioning of society and advocating the end of capitalism. This is the hair shirt position. In the middle is what we might call redirected capitalism. It is solutions-driven within emerging social and economic considerations underpinned by the need to achieve net zero by 2050. No longer can companies do business as if the playing field is undifferentiated. Redirected capitalism provides signposts for companies, market signals. The rules of the market are nuanced and provide for incentives and

137 Michael E. Mann, *The New Climate War: the fight to take back our planet*, Scribe, 2021, Chapter 8: 'The truth is bad enough', 179–224.

disincentives against an index of success which puts ecological sustainability as a pervasive value.

5.4 Related corporate case studies

5.4.1 The superannuation fund HESTA and its exit from thermal coal

Another large superannuation fund is undergoing scrutiny as regards its long-term investment strategy. It has indicated it wants to exit thermal coal but will remain in oil and gas investment via companies such as Santos. It refers to the need for an orderly transition and views oil and gas as part of that staging process. Its view is that it wants to change companies by being on the inside as a major investor.

5.4.2 Origin Energy and the new paradigm for valuing assets

How a corporation is seen to be handling the climate crisis will be key consideration in valuing it and its assets. Climate laggards will be valued as low, climate innovators high. For those firms analysed as suffering from untapped climate solutions, they are beholden to the market. An example of this occurred in late 2023 with the Australian-listed company Origin Energy. It was subject to a takeover by a Brookfield-led consortium endorsed by the Origin board. Brookfield is a Canadian infrastructure group and teamed up with EIG, a US-based energy investor. They used their subsidiary, Mid-Ocean to offer just under $9 for each Origin share, valuing the putative takeover at $18.7 bn. The proposal requires approval of 75% of the shareholders at a GM. AustralianSuper, Australia's biggest superannuation company which holds a 13.68% stake in Origin and has rejected the bid based on the issues referred to above:

> arguing that the offer grossly undervalues the energy producer and the valuation report's assumptions are far too low. AustralianSuper's stance on the Origin Energy takeover bid is driven by a fresh perspective on valuation, one that capitalizes on the ongoing global energy transition.[138]

AustralianSuper 'believes the ongoing energy transition, as we move towards net zero by 2050, has further enhanced the value of strategic energy transition platforms, such as Origin'. The portfolio of assets in the energy transition towards renewables included the fact that

> Origin has the potential to become Australia's leading energy supplier, drawing lessons from its 20% shareholding in UK-based Octopus Energy, a fast-growing renewable energy-focused provider. Additionally, through APLNG (the Queensland LNG project), Origin is well-positioned to access

138 Geeta Pillai, 'AustralianSuper's Rejection of Origin Energy Takeover Signals New Valuation Paradigm', BNN Breaking, 31 October 2023.

> gas for its Energy Markets business and benefit from strong global demand for LNG.[139]

This 'new lens for valuation' is supported by Frontier Economics, which specialises in the energy industry. Smaller shareholders have also 'joined the chorus of dissatisfaction'. The key point is that valuing companies will be increasingly dependent on their net zero credentials and this provide a new lens for valuation. As AustralianSuper notes 'Origin has a unique portfolio of market-leading energy assets and an advantaged position to capture value from the energy transition.'[140] If REST super was the case study in AustralianSuper's funds being slow to factor in long-term climate risk, AS is the prime example of a superfund seeking to benefit from the premium for assets with high transition value.

5.5 Implications of the McVeigh corporate case study for corporate law theory, risk, and governance

5.5.1 Corporate risk and the role of directors

Directors are required to be vigilant about risk. Its clearest form is financial. This carries consequences within the formal Australian corporate law. Risk comes in other guises, too, including reputational and cultural. These may not necessarily embed legal consequences but they do give rise to significant business-related issues. The emerging risk now is climate risk. It is potentially multifaceted in that it harbours different types of risk such as financial and reputational elements. The Hutley Opinions confirm this growing trend. The spectre of climate risk is growing exponentially. Its complexity and multi-faceted nature is clear from the longitudinal perspective of five years over which the three Opinions span.

5.5.2 Commercial techniques, legitimate and otherwise, for boards dealing with climate risk

Justice Hayne refers to the political characterization of climate change:

> A response often seen in Australian political discourse is that 'The issue is large; Australia is comparatively small; nothing we do will affect the outcome if the big emitters do not act.' That is, the response is 'We can do nothing that will help'. By making that response, we are
>
> persuading ourselves that we are helpless.[141]

139 Finance News Network, Sharecafe, 'Uncertainty looms over $18.7billion Canadian-US bid for Origin Energy', 31 October 2023.

140 AustralianSuper, 'AustralianSuper rejects Brookfield and EIG bid for Origin Energy', Media Release, 31 October 2023.

141 Justice Hayne, 2019 CPD Roundtable, n 87, 3.

By contrast, corporate boards do not enjoy the same convenient ability to sidestep their legal responsibility. He notes that:

> Boards will reinforce that sense of helplessness if they put climate risk into a bucket marked 'non-financial risks'. And boards might think that they can do that if they see the risk as not being immediately realised in the next financial period.[142]

This invites potential misuse of various commercial techniques, including moving current liabilities and risks into the long term or shifting financial risk into the non-financial category. As well as being highly problematic, they do not obviate legal risk:

> As recent events in the financial services industry should have shown, the notion of 'non-financial' risks can be very misleading. The distinction between financial and non-financial risk to the entity is anything but clear. Conduct and regulatory risk were seen by some financial services entities as non-financial risks less important than other risks to the financial performance of the entity. But the realisation of conduct and regulatory risks has had large and continuing effects on, not only the reputation of the entities, but also their profitability.[143]

These admonitions by Justice Hayne should not be surprising to legal advisers. They are part of the long-established difference between form on the one hand, and substance on the other. The labels or categories given to items by the parties may not in the end count. It is the underlying legal substance which is critical and determinative of legal rights and responsibilities.

5.6 Conclusion: long-term investment risk and board accountability

The McVeigh case is clear evidence of the advent of climate litigation in Australia informed by new terminology. These concepts and definitions are informed by the international documents discussed in this chapter. This model, whilst still not fully configured, has at its core issues of ecological limitation, a keen evidential stance as regards climate science, and an evolving standard of climate risk for directors. Taken together, these elements move the law in Australia as regards corporations from its 19th-century anchor, and 20th-century developments into a particular 21st-century ambit. The emerging operating model—however it is labelled—whether as doughnut, ecological, or scientifically informed, represents a rupture from the past. Economic growth and the primacy of profits are no longer theoretically abundant concepts if the science of ecological limits is accepted. Profits and growth are contingent and conditional, and intrinsically linked to the climate-related concepts

142 Justice Hayne, 2019 CPD Roundtable, n 87, 3.
143 Justice Hayne, 2019 CPD Roundtable, n 87, 3-4

outlined in the McVeigh case, including climate change, physical impacts, and transition impacts. These are propositions which will increasingly frame climate-related litigation in its various manifestations. For example, in relation to negligence, breach of statute, and so on. These broader concepts will be sharpened as the scientific consensus continues to emerge. The convergence of international scientific around IPCC and other large-scale reports evidences this phenomenon. Deploying these foundation definitions, litigation will also focus on the particulars relevant to the defendant in question. This is to adopt the technique used in the McVeigh case. The bundle of relevant climate risks pertaining to the defendant were defined in a paragraph with three sub-points and were collectively referred to as 'REST'S Climate Change Business Risks'. The point is that this will become a form of litigation. The concept of '[The Defendant's] Climate Change Business Risks' will increasingly be a standard component of pleadings in court filings.

References

Amended Concise Statement, *Mark McVeigh v Retail Employees Superannuation Pty Ltd*, 24 September 2018. http://climatecasechart.com/climate-change-litigation/wp-content/uploads/sites/16/non-us-case-documents/2018/20180921_NSD13332018_complaint-1.pdf

Concise Statement, *Mark McVeigh v Retail Employees Superannuation Pty Ltd*, 26 July 2018. http://climatecasechart.com/climate-change-litigation/wp-content/uploads/sites/16/non-us-case-documents/2018/20180723_NSD13332018_complaint-1.pdf

Final Report, Royal Commission into Misconduct in the Banking, Superannuation and Financial Services Industry, 1 February, 2019, 1–530. https://treasury.gov.au/sites/default/files/2019-03/fsrc-volume1.pdf

Financial Stability Board. https://www.fsb.org/

Justice Kenneth Hayne, Centre for Policy Development, Climate Change Round Table, 21 November 2019 in Sydney, 1–5, 1. https://cpd.org.au/2019/12/full-text-of-kenneth-hayne-ac-qc-remarks-to-cpd-climate-roundtable/

Noel Hutley SC and Sebastian Hartford-Davis, 'Supplementary Memorandum of Opinion, Climate Change and Directors' Duties,' 26 March 2019. https://cpd.org.au/wp-content/uploads/2019/03/Noel-Hutley-SC-and-Sebastian-Hartford-Davis-Opinion-2019-and-2016_pdf

Noel Hutley SC and Sebastian Hartford- Davis, 'Memorandum of Opinion, Climate Change and Directors' Duties,' 7 October 2016. https://cpd.org.au/wp-content/uploads/2016/10/Legal-Opinion-on-Climate-Change-and-Directors-Duties.pdf

Noel Hutley SC and Sebastian Hartford Davis, 'Climate Change and Directors' Duties' *Further Supplementary Memorandum of Opinion*, The Centre for Policy Development, 23 April 2021. https://cpd.org.au/wp-content/uploads/2021/04/Further-Supplementary-Opinion-2021-3.pdf

Noel Hutley SC and JE Mack, Memorandum of Opinion, *Superannuation Fund Trustee Duties and Climate Change Risk*, Environmental Justice Centre, 15 June 2017. https://www.envirojustice.org.au/sites/default/files/files/20170615%20Superannuation%20Trustee%20Duties%20and%20Climate%20Change%20(Hutley%20%26%20Mack).pdf

Noel Hutley SC and JE Mack, Memorandum of Opinion, *Superannuation Trustee Duties and Climate Change*, Environmental Justice Centre, 16 February 2021. https://equitygenerationlawyers.com/wp/wp-content/uploads/2021/04/Hutley-SC-Mack-Superannuation-Trustee-Duties-and-Climate-Change-Memo-2021.pdf

Michael E. Mann, *The New Climate War: The Fight to Take Back Our Planet*, Scribe, 2021.

Guy Pearse, *Green Wash: Big Brands and Carbon Scams*, Black Inc., 2012.
Kate Raworth, *Doughnut Economics: Seven Ways to Think Like a 21st Century Economist*, Penguin, 2017.
Sabin Centre, Columbia Law School, Columbia University, New York, Climate Change Litigation Databases. Sabin Climate Law Centre. http://climatecasechart.com/climate-change-litigation/
United Nations Climate Change, Conference of the Parties 21, Paris December 2015. https://unfccc.int/process-and-meetings/the-paris-agreement
United Nations, Social Development Goals. https://sdgs.un.org/goals

6 The corporate climate IV

Litigation risk, the extension of the duty of care within the climate context, and stranded assets

6.1 The case study: the Sharma litigation against the Commonwealth Environment Minister

The Sharma litigation involved the following salient facts. The protagonist company was Vickery Coal Pty Ltd.[1] It was seeking to have approved a major extension of its coal mining operation in the north-west of New South Wales. For this purpose, it required the approval of the federal Minister for the Environment under sections 130 (timing of the decision on approval) and 133 (granting of approval by the Minister after an assessment process) of the Environment Protection and Biodiversity Conservation Act 1999 (Cth).

The plaintiffs comprised school-aged children led by the then 16-year-old, Anjali Sharma. Given the relevant rules of litigation for access to the Federal Court, they needed to be represented in the action by an adult. Hence, they acted through a litigation representative, Sister Marie Brigid Arthur.

The case was brought before Judge Bromberg in the Federal Court of Australia. The plaintiffs sought a declaration and an injunction. The declaration was that the Minister owed a duty of care to the children to not cause them physical harm in the form of personal injury from climate change. The injunction was to restrain an apprehended breach of the duty of care by the Minister. The declaration was granted on the basis that the Minister did owe a duty of care at common law. The applicant's case was based on scientific evidence presented to the court. This evidence was not challenged within the court process by the government by way of cross-examination or by the government presenting its own scientific evidence. It essentially met the scientific evidence with political action.

The claimants constructed a set of linked scientific arguments. Some concerned climate change in general. Others were specific to the impacts over the 25-year

1 A pty ltd company in Australia is proprietary limited. The shareholder liability is by reference to the amount unpaid on the shares. Such companies are defined by s.113 of the Corporations Act 2001 (Cth) in terms of size and scale. They can have a minimum of 50 non-employee shareholders. That is, they can have employee shareholders and a limited and proscribed segment of the public on their share register. This is by contrast to public companies and public listed companies which have access to raising funds from the public via Chapter 6D of the Corporations Act 2001 (Cth).

DOI: 10.4324/9781003263746-7

lifetime of the Vickery project. A third set of factors were relevant to the harm to be done to Australian children by reference to the other factor sets.

6.1.1 Climate change: the relevant general factors pleaded by the plaintiffs

There were three basic points pleaded by the plaintiffs as regards climate change:

- Human emissions of carbon dioxide in the atmosphere are largely responsible for the warming of the Earth's surface temperature.
- Average surface temperatures are increasing; the scientific consensus is that this century they will be two degrees above pre-industrial level.
- Increased surface temperatures in Australia will produce a series of impacts such as drought and sea-level rise.

6.1.2 The Vickery Project: the factors specific to the twenty-five-year duration of the project

The proposed 25-year project is an expansion of the existing mine. It will involve 33 million tonnes of coal being extracted. When burned, this will generate 100 million tonnes of carbon dioxide. This has, it was pleaded, a global impact; it will cause 'a tiny but measurable increase in global average surface temperatures'.[2] This would help push average global temperatures beyond the two-degree threshold referred to above.

6.1.3 The risk of harm by way of personal injury to the children of Australia

The risks were set out in detail:

- An estimated one million Australian children will at a point in future suffer a heat stress episode requiring hospitalization.
- There will be many thousands who die prematurely as result of heat stress or bushfire smoke.
- Many locations in Australia will be difficult to inhabit.
- Large areas will suffer from climate related impacts including water shortages and become unviable for long-established activities such as agriculture.
- Australian children are vulnerable to these distinct and measurable 'severe harms'.

As Bromberg noted of Australian children:

2 Mike Hales and Edward Fearis, 'The Sharma case- a false start for climate change negligence litigation in Australia', *International Bar Association*, Tuesday 13 December 2022, https://www.ibanet.org/the-sharma-case-false-start-for-climate-change-negligence-litigation-in-Australia.

> they bear no responsibility for the unparalleled predicament which they now face. That innocence is also deserving of recognition and weight in a consideration of the relationship between the children and the government they look to for protection.[3]

6.1.4 The decision at first instance: Bromberg J's finding of a duty of care

As such, Bromberg found that 'there was a real, significant and foreseeable risk of harm for Australian children arising from a continued increase in global surface temperatures, to which the Vickery Project would contribute if it proceeded'.[4] His Honour noted that the duty of care concept must evolve to 'meet contemporary social conditions and community standards.'[5] It does not, however, cover property damage and pure economic loss.[6]

By contrast, the government argued that the Minister had broad discretion under the EPBC Act. The statutory scheme provided the basis of the decision. To impose a duty at common law was inconsistent with the EPBC Act. It would amount to

> effectively 'foreclosing' the exercise of the Minister's broad discretion to approve a project by elevating the avoidance of harm to Australian children through climate change to a 'mandatory and paramount consideration' and dictating a particular outcome (in this case refusal of the Vickery Project).[7]

The government's argued, accordingly, that the finding of such a duty of care made the law '"incoherent" and contrary to public policy.'[8]

In Australia, the then federal government and ministerial response was that the proposed extension of the common law duty of care in this setting is both 'speculative'[9] and 'novel',[10] words well established means by which to characterize the weakness of a legal opponent's argument. The government has also argued that establishing a duty would give rise to incoherence of the law[11] and indeterminate

3 *Sharma by her litigation representative Sister Marie Brigid Arthur v Minister for the Environment* [2021] FCA 560, para 312, ttps://climatecasechart.com/wp-content/uploads/non-us-case-documents/2021/20210527_VID-389-of-2021-2021-FCA-560-2021-FCA-774-2022-FCAFC-35-2022-FCAFC-65_judgment.pdf.

4 Norton Rose Fulbright, Elisa De Wit, et al., 'Landmark Climate Change Decision: Sharma decision has significant implications for developments and activities with climate change impacts', June 2021, https://www.nortonrosefulbright.com/en/knowledge/publications/a2f31ca9/landmark-climate-change-decision.

5 Norton Rose Fulbright, n 4,

6 Norton Rose Fulbright, n 4.

7 Norton Rose Fulbright, n 4.

8 Norton Rose Fulbright, n 4.

9 The Australian Government Solicitor, *Sharma v Minister for the Environment*, Concise Statement in Response, 29 October 2020, paragraph 24, https://climatecasechart.com/non-us-case/raj-seppings-v-ley/.

10 ibid, paragraph 25.

11 ibid, paragraphs 26–8.

liability.[12] In particular that it would be 'incoherent with the Environment Protection and Biodiversity Conservation Act 1999 (Cth) and more generally with public law principles'.[13] The government's argument was that 'imposition of the alleged duty of care would involve the Court in consideration of the merits of the decision'.[14] As such, this would be 'neither sourced in, nor consistent with, the principles of administrative law'.[15]

6.1.4.1 The centrality of the coherence, or not, of the law in question

The federal government went on to argue at first instance that 'recognition of the alleged duty would be inconsistent with the limited role of the courts in supervising the legality of statutory decision-making'.[16] The government concluded its arguments regarding this point by claiming, essentially, that the concept of coherence is overarching. As such, 'coherence of the law is a consideration having such significance as to outweigh any other relevant feature that might favour recognition of the alleged duty of care'.[17] The concept of coherence has assumed an increasing profile in Australian negligence law in the last several years.[18] Coherence can be comprised of disparate elements. It may be presented as objective and impartial but it can also be seen as essentially determined by reference to particularity and a confined point of view. In this regard, analytical points arise. For whom is it that the law is characterized as coherent or otherwise, and by whom is it determined to be such? A statute may be coherent to the drafters, but incoherent to the applicants. The common law may be considered coherent at a point in time, but may become incoherent, given new circumstances. The claimed objective stability of coherence is highly problematic, given these shifting grounds.

6.1.5 The appeal by the Commonwealth Government to the Full Court of the Federal Court

The then federal government appealed its loss in the case to the Full Federal Court, comprising three justices.[19] The appeal by the government succeeded on the basis, essentially, that matters of public policy are best left to governments and to legislation rather than common law intervention by the courts.

Adopting an approach taken in the New Zealand Appellate Courts, Allsopp CJ noted that the courts and the deployment of causes of action in tort law, should not

12 ibid, paragraphs 29–30.
13 ibid, paragraph 26.
14 ibid, paragraph 27.
15 ibid, paragraph 27.
16 ibid, paragraph 27.
17 ibid, paragraph 27.
18 See for example, Andrew Fell, *MULR*.
19 Minister for the Environment v Sharma [2022] FCAFC 35, https://climatecasechart.com/non-us-case/raj-seppings-v-ley/.

be the forum for changing public policy about climate change. He characterized the litigation in a narrow sense as private, as opposed to public law, even though it directly affected the governed and the government. Key points included the finding that the matters referred to were of high public policy and reserved for the government. There was also a lack of factors—control, special vulnerability, proportionality to be able to invoke a duty of care. As such, the duty of care was rejected based on the factorial test relevant in Australia. Beach and Wheelahan JJ also found no duty, so that the first instance case was unanimously overturned.

6.1.5.1 The Sharma litigation—no appeal to the High Court of Australia

It has been opined that 'Australia is recognised as one of the most plaintiff-friendly jurisdictions for climate change litigation. This has kept Australia at the forefront of developments in climate change law'.[20] Despite this broader context, the Sharma plaintiffs did not appeal their loss in the Full Federal Court to the High Court of Australia:

> Somewhat surprisingly, the children did not seek special leave to appeal the Full Court's decision to the High Court of Australia (Australia's highest court). The proceedings are therefore at an end. As noted, before the primary judge the Minister chose not to call any expert evidence as to climate change or even to cross-examine the children's experts, no doubt for political reasons. The Full Court implicitly criticised this approach and it resulted in obvious strategic disadvantages for the Minister. However, it is difficult to see the Minister taking a different approach in the future, particularly given the recent defeat of the conservative Coalition government and the election of the more liberal Labor government together with a record number of climate change-motivated independent and Greens candidates.[21]

6.1.5.2 The legacy of the Sharma case: the climate science is established in the Federal Court

As such, the case may be viewed in the future as the beginning of a new chapter whereby the science in relation to climate change is no longer being challenged by governments (and possibly also corporations) in Australia. This would be consistent with the approach that governments and corporations are otherwise adopting in relation to climate change.

20 Hales and Fearis, n 2.
21 Hales and Fearis, n 2.

6.1.5.3 The limitations of negligence as a legal remedy to combat climate change

The case demonstrated the difficulties in connecting a particular emission source to a particular harm. The science is developing in this area, though, and as it does an applicant's prospects in future, similar cases will improve.

> Negligence law in Australia has traditionally struggled with the issue of multiple potential causative factors in relation to particular harm. For example, in mesothelioma cases courts historically struggled with (but seem to have resolved) how to address the issue of a plaintiff having had multiple exposures to asbestos from a range of defendants or other persons. As climate change negligence law develops, it could be expected that a similar resolution could be reached.[22]

Beach J implicitly invited the High Court to clarify the common law:

> It is for the High Court not us to engineer new seed varieties for sustainable duties of care, modifying concepts such as "sufficient closeness and directness" and indeterminacy to address the accelerating complexity, multiple links and cross-links of causal relations. Such concepts in their present form may have reached their shelf life, particularly where one is dealing with acts or omissions that have wide-scale consequences that transcend confined temporal boundaries and geographic ranges, and where more than direct mechanistic causal pathways are involved.[23]

While, as noted, the children did not seek special leave to appeal the Full Court's decision, it seems almost inevitable that the High Court will likely be required to grapple with the relevant issues in any relevant emerging context.

6.2 The background to and context of the Sharma case study

6.2.1 The evolutionary nature of the Australian common law

We can argue that common law is constantly evolving. It may have threads of historic and long-standing principle, but it is a living system of law required to address contemporary issues. The rule of law, at its heart, reflects this innate flexibility.[24] In the Australian context, the High Court as the apex court, is the guardian of the common law which is not 'frozen in time' as the High Court determined in the Mabo case.[25]

We can discern strands of the common law's adaptive capacity in the context of commercial and corporate law. In case law in Australia, for example, the courts

22 Hales and Fearis, n 2.

23 Hales and Fearis, n 2.

24 Tom Bingham, *The Rule of Law*, Penguin, 2010.

25 Mabo v Queensland [No 2] - [1992] HCA 23 - 175 CLR 1; 66 ALJR 408.

have referenced community standards and expectations as providing the underlying basis for developing or amending existing common principles.[26]

6.2.2 The traditional approach in Australia: a narrow view of standing in environmental law

Climate change litigation is very recent. In terms of longitudinal trends, the relevant legal tradition in Australia has been narrowly cast within the environmental prism, and by reference to constricting rules of access for putative plaintiffs, such as the rules regarding standing.

Cases have been founded in causes of action arising in environmental law. As such, the law has been seen as liminal and essentially specialist. Environmental law is a law school elective subject. By contrast, corporate law is a long-standing core unit. This is reflected in climate change litigation. The major development is that climate litigation is focused on and via the activities of corporations.

Perhaps the best-known summation of the historically narrow and restricted approach in which the courts explicitly cut off access to the courts arises from the judgment of Gibbs CJ in the High Court case *Australian Conservation Foundation (ACF) v Commonwealth 1980*.[27] The ACF was seeking a right to be heard in the case. The High Court denied standing to the ACF, and in doing so, then Chief Justice Sir Harry Gibbs held that:

> I would not deny that a person might have a special interest in the preservation of a particular environment. However, an interest, for present purposes, does not mean a mere intellectual or emotional concern. A person is not interested within the meaning of the rule, unless he is likely to gain some advantage, other than the satisfaction of righting a wrong, upholding a principle or winning a contest, if his action succeeds or to suffer some disadvantage, other than a sense of grievance or a debt for costs, if his action fails. A belief, however strongly felt, that the law generally, or a particular law, should be observed, or that conduct of a particular kind should be prevented, does not suffice to give its possessor *locus standi*. If that were not so, the rule requiring special interest would be meaningless. Any plaintiff who felt strongly enough to bring an action could maintain it.[28]

The phrase centrally deployed by Gibbs CJ was that a plaintiff have a 'mere intellectual or emotional concern'. This positions the plaintiffs as child-like, and the defendant as essentially adult, sensible, and coherent. The neoliberalism writ large in this approach is obvious in hindsight. An economic interest would, by contrast, be substantial and potent. By 1983, the High Court had deliberated in arguably the

26 *ASIC v Rich &Ors*, [2003] NSWSC 85; (2003) 44 ACSR 341.

27 *Australian Conservation Foundation Inc v Commonwealth* (1980) 146 CLR 493, 531 (ACF v Commonwealth).

28 ACF v Commonwealth, n 27.

most famous environmental law case in Australia to date, the so-called Tasmanian Dam case.[29] By this point, Gibbs CJ's view no longer ascendant. He commenced his lengthy dissenting judgment as follows:

> No lawyer will need to be told that in these proceedings the Court is not called upon to decide whether the Gordon below Franklin Scheme ought to proceed. It is not for the Court to weigh the economic needs of Tasmania against the possible damage that will be caused to the archaeological sites and the wilderness area if the construction of the dam proceeds. The wisdom and expediency of the two competing courses are matters of policy for the Governments to consider, and not for the Court. We are concerned with a strictly legal question—whether the Commonwealth regulations and the Commonwealth statute are within constitutional power.[30]

This observation and in particular the reference to a 'strictly legal question' bookends the comments from the ACF case three years earlier. For Gibbs CJ, there was a clear-cut and unshakeable distinction between purely legal issues of substance, and the quicksilver equivalent of merely emotional items.

The litigation which was based on examination of the external affairs power in the Commonwealth Constitution has ongoing relevance. In particular, the Tasmanian Dam case 'had enormous significance for the extent of Commonwealth powers to make laws under the Australian Constitution, including its power to make laws to protect the environment'.[31] As such,

> Today, large parts of Australia's main national environmental law, the Environment Protection and Biodiversity Conservation Act 1999 (Cth) (EPBC Act), depend for their constitutional validity on the decision in the Tasmanian Dam Case regarding the external affairs power.[32]

In the Sharma case, one of the matters underpinning the litigation is the role played by the government in the near four decades between the Tasmanian Dam litigation and the Sharma case. In the Tasmanian Dam case, the then Labor government, led by Prime minister Bob Hawke, was the plaintiff seeking to protect heritage wilderness in the state of Tasmania in opposing the state government. Largely because of, and response to, that case, the Environment Protection and Biodiversity Conservation Act came into force. The Sharma case, by contrast, involves the restriction and proscription of the EPBC Act by the government in its capacity as a defendant to legal proceedings.

29 *Commonwealth v Tasmania* ("Tasmanian Dam case") [1983] HCA 21; (1983) 158 CLR 1 (1 July 1983).

30 Commonwealth v Tasmania, n 29, Gibbs CJ, paragraph 2.

31 Environmental Law Australia, 'Tasmanian Dam Case', http://envlaw.com.au/tasmanian-dam-case/.

32 Environmental Law Australia, n 31.

6.2.3 Negligence law in Australia; the complexity of establishing a duty of care.

Another contextual barrier for plaintiffs in climate litigation is to prove that a duty of care exists. The relative simplicity of the tests in the 1980s has been replaced by a multi-factor approach. This makes the arguments for the parties more difficult and so whilst the plaintiffs in Sharma succeeded at first instance on this point, they lost comprehensively on appeal.

6.3 Post case study events

6.3.1 The climate-related assertion of a duty of care: will it move from the margins to the mainstream?

Whilst the duty of care was described and rejected as novel in the Sharma litigation by the Full Court of the Federal Court, the concept of legal novelty is prone to wearing off quickly, if there are follow-up cases with new plaintiffs pursuing claims and courts hearing and determining the merits. The glass ceiling of novelty begins to crack and splinter over time and then the floodgates open. Justice Beach used an interesting alterative metaphor of the High Court as being akin to a seed bank, and as such, it rested upon that institution to 'engineer new seed varieties for sustainable duties of care'.[33] The use of the seed bank idea and of the term 'sustainability' are ironically fashioned and appropriate, given the use of plant saving storage, and the widespread recognition that the Anthropocene is causing the 6th mass extinction.

6.3.2 Evolving litigation strategies: governments calling no evidence regarding the assertion of climate change

Components of climate change evidence are rapidly evolving. This is affecting litigation techniques. The current scientific baseline of human-induced climate warming is being established by plaintiffs via expert witnesses. In the Sharma case, the esteemed climate scientist, Professor Will Steffen, was the key expert. The evidence included projections about future trends and likely scenarios. The Commonwealth as defendant adopted a particular strategy. It did not cross-examine the evidence, nor did it call its own evidence. As the IBA notes,

> before the primary judge the Minister chose not to call any expert evidence as to climate change or even to cross-examine the children's experts, no doubt for political reasons. The Full Court implicitly criticized this approach and it resulted in obvious strategic disadvantages for the Minister.[34]

33 Gilbert and Tobin, 'No 'Duty of Care' but risks of climate litigation continue to grow- insights from the Sharma decision,' 21 March 2022 https://www.gtlaw.com.au/knowledge/no-duty-care-risks-climate-litigation-continue-grow-insights-sharma-decision.

34 Hales and Fearis, n 2.

The point of political realism was sheeted home by the fact that the then Minister for the Environment 'had granted approval to the expansion of the coal mine between the date of the primary judge's decision and before the hearing of the appeal'.[35]

The government's approach was redolent of a crossroads strategy. It adopted a defensive, if not siege mentality, to the litigation but by boldly approving the mine extension in the meantime, it was effectively proclaiming political hegemony. This approach, in the round, is inherently unstable.

6.3.3 Fitting the climate change concept into traditional legal categories

The Sharma case also foundered at the appeal stage as regards the traditionally deployed limitation device of indeterminacy. This was related to the 'nature of climate change, which is not limited to a single catastrophic event' and as such 'impacted the nature and extent of prospective liability'.[36] This is part of the mystique and challenge of climate change as forming the basis of the determination of any rights and liabilities of the parties within a litigation context. Climate change is clearly not a single event. It is beyond temporal or easy characterization. Hence, to describe climate change as not fitting the old legal wineskin of single event accident or catastrophe is to realise there is a paradigm shift required. Traditional legal analysis and sequencing does not speak to or recognize the rapidly evolving nature of the context being determined within the court rooms of the nation. In this sense, though, the Australian judiciary and the High Court in particular, have demonstrated the capacity for a quantum leap to radically update the litigation context. The most famous decision of the Australian High Court in the last three decades bears out this point. The High Court of Australia in the Mabo case of 1992 made the fundamental point that the common law approach to claims of native title could not be kept 'frozen in an age of racial discrimination'.[37] In the course of the six to one majority, the common law orthodoxy as regard colonial conquest developed and enshrined in the 18th and 19th centuries, was swept away by Australia's apex court. This type of quantum leap is within the gift of the High Court. The climate emergency demands a new legal epoch. The hyper nature of climate change should be the catalyst for determining a new duty of care, not a reason to obscure it behind historical, inadequate, and narrow legal constructions of a single event. In summary, the nature of climate change may make it challenging for the courts to establish duty, whilst at the same time making it inevitable that further cases will follow.

35 Hales and Fearis, n 2.
36 Gilbert and Tobin, n 33.
37 Mabo, n 25.

6.4 Related climate change legal action arising within the Australian context

6.4.1 Pabai Pabai v Commonwealth of Australia, *2021*

The clearest example of a case following in the footsteps of the Sharma litigation is *Pabai Pabai v Commonwealth*.[38] It is a class-action brought in the Federal Court on behalf of Torres Strait Islanders (whose traditional lands and waters are in the far north of Australia).

It seeks to impose a duty of care on the federal government. The litigation was commenced on October 22, 2021, Wadhuam Paul and Wadhuam Pabai, First Nations leaders from the Gudamalulgal Nation of the Torres Strait Islands, filed a case in the Federal Court of Australia challenging the Government's failure to sufficiently cut emissions. The plaintiffs argue that this failure to act will mean that TSI communities will be required to vacate their long-standing ancestral country and be required to move en masse to new areas. This is a First Nations claim for loss of access to country and the clear trauma associated with that dislocation. It could have global implications for traditional owners, particularly those whose country is contiguous to the seas and oceans. It is long-term in nature. It is based in negligence but carries far wider consequences such that the Federal Court has advised:

> Given the significant public interest in this matter, the Court has adopted a publicly available Online File. Documents will be placed onto the Online File when they are considered both by the Court and the parties to be publicly accessible.[39]

In the Amended Statement of Claim, the plaintiffs claim as follows:

> B4. Commonwealth Duty of Care to Torres Strait Islanders
>
> 20. The Commonwealth owes a duty of care to Torres Strait Islanders to take reasonable steps to protect them from the harms caused by climate change. In fulfilling its duty, the Commonwealth must have regard to the best available science in relation to climate change.
>
> 21. Alternatively, the Commonwealth owes a duty of care to Torres Strait Islanders to take reasonable care to avoid causing property damage, loss of Ailan Kastom, loss of Native Title rights, and harm to Torres Strait Islanders arising from a failure to implement reasonable adaptation measures in the Torres Strait Islands.[40]

By way of remedies, the applicants seek:

38 Federal Court of Australia, Online File, *Pabai Pabai v Commonwealth of Australia* VID622/2021, https://www.fedcourt.gov.au/services/access-to-files-and-transcripts/online-files/pabai-v-australia.

39 Federal Court of Australia, n 38.

40 Federal Court of Australia, n 38, Amended Statement of Claim, lodged 11 October, 2022.

- A declaration that the Commonwealth owes a duty of care to Torres Strait Islanders to take reasonable steps to protect them, their way of life and the marine environment of the Torres Strait from the current and projected impacts of climate change.
- A declaration that the Commonwealth is in breach of this duty of care.
- An injunction requiring the Commonwealth to implement measures to protect the land and marine environment from greenhouse gas emissions, reduce greenhouse gas emissions, and otherwise avoid injury and harm to Torres Strait Islanders from greenhouse gas emissions; and damages.[41]

Even though a four-week trial had been listed to commence in June 2023,[42] at the start of 2024 it has not yet commenced and the case remains in the pleadings stage. The current federal Labor government has pleaded similar arguments to those pleaded by the previous Conservative government in Sharma's case. It has rejected owing the petitioners a duty of care:

> The Respondent does not owe the novel duty of care or alternative duty of care alleged. The duty and alternative duty as pleaded are framed at too high a level of abstraction and, as noted, would involve the Court in assessing at the point of breach questions of policy-making unsuited to judicial determination. The duty and alternative duty must be rejected for those reasons. Further, consideration of the relevant salient features point overwhelmingly against recognition of the duty and alternative duty.[43]

6.4.2 The Torres Strait Eight petition to the UN

In a broader international context, First Nations people in Australia are taking their claims to UN forums and seeking the ethical admonition of such bodies. Given Australian law requires that domestic law be passed to enforce the rulings of such bodies, this does not of itself give rise to a set of rights enforceable within Australia. It carries three important consequences. It shines a spotlight on some of those people and citizens most vulnerable to the effects of climate change, it sets up an intense focus by the international community of comparative national standards and evolving benchmarks, and it requires a tangible response (public or otherwise) from the government.

In May 2019, eight Traditional Owners living in the Torres Strait Islands submitted a petition with the UN Human Rights Committee. The group refer to

41 Federal Court of Australia, n 38, Amended Statement of Claim, lodged 11 October, 2022.

42 Hales and Fearis, n 2.

43 Respondents Amended Concise Statement in Response, 29 May 2023, para 13, https://www.fedcourt.gov.au/__data/assets/pdf_file/0005/110858/Respondents-Amended-Concise-Statement-in-Response.pdf.

themselves as the Torres Strait8.[44] The legal proceedings lodged by the Torres Strait 8 are supported by ClientEarth, an environmental law charity.[45] The complaint is decribed as a 'world-first'.[46] The Committee decides issues on the papers. The defendant is the Australian government. The petitioners allege breaches of fundamental human rights under the International Covenant on Civil and Political Rights (ICCPR). In August 2020, the Australian government asked the UN Committee to dismiss the petition.

In their final response, the Morrison government has pushed for the case to be dismissed on the basis that any one country cannot be held legally responsible for climate change.

Australia's last official response to the UN Human Rights Committee in Geneva states that Australia is already doing enough on climate change. Furthermore, the government states that the future impacts of climate change are too uncertain to require it to act.

The petitioners submitted a formal response with the United Nations on 29 September 2020 arguing that Australia failed to address climate change, and this has impacted the human rights of communities in Torres Strait Island. The conservative LNP government denied the claims.[47]

They argued that Australia has failed to acknowledge that significant climate impacts—such as advancing erosion, coral bleaching, and the extinction of regional plant and animal species—are happening now and have already impacted the human rights of Torres Strait Island communities.[48]

The United Nations' Human Rights Commission published its findings in November 2022. These were to the effect that the UN Charter of Civil and Political Rights had been breached by the Australian government and to compensate the communities. Despite this, the formal response by the government is pending. There have been calls for various measures to be put in place including compensatory damages, reparations, and the installation of infrastructure including sea walls. No compensation has been paid, despite the UN findings.[49]

44 https://ourislandsourhome.com.au/homepage/?_ga=2.135782833.1682823304.1637034502-1835110639.1637034502#torresstrait8.

45 https://ourislandsourhome.com.au/legal2/?_ga=2.206971667.1682823304.1637034502-1835110639.1637034502.

46 Teisha Cloos, 'Government denies responsibility for climate change in reply to Torres Strait Eight', *National Indigenous Times*, 30 September 2021, https://nit.com.au/30-09-2021/2386/government-denies-responsibility-for-climate-change-in-reply-to-torres-strait-eight.

47 Cloos, n 46.

48 ClientEarth, https://www.clientearth.org/latest/latest-updates/news/torres-strait-islander-group-submits-response-in-historic-climate-case/.

49 ClientEarth, 'One year on from historic Torres Strait UN climate victory- no compensation despite legal finding', 25 Sept 2023, https://www.clientearth.org/latest/press-office/press/one-year-on-from-historic-torres-strait-un-climate-victory-no-compensation-despite-legal-finding/.

6.4.3 The investment future for 'natural gas and litigation risk'

Methane gas is seen as a transition fuel and has long been marketed in Australia as both clean and 'natural'. However, there is widespread scientific consensus that methane produced by gas is longer-living and more potent than CO_2 emissions. As such, its claimed social licence will be keenly contested in future, particularly in terms of new projects and extensions of current projects.

Despite the scientific evidence, gas has been championed by the recently defeated LNP government in Australia as the key transition source of energy. During the COVID pandemic, a government-appointed economic advisory body was made up of members, several of whom were strongly aligned with the gas industry.

The concept of transition is a useful device to impose delays on innovations away from fossil fuels. A case which opts for a long and open-ended transition reliance on fossil fuels, whilst at the same time questioning the reliability of renewables, provides an effective braiding of the arguments for maintaining the fossil fuel status quo.

The variables will be the scale of renewables innovation and the foreshortening of time taken on the transition to renewables. If these occur, it will likely see an increasingly steep decline in the resort to 'natural gas' projects. The corporate orthodoxy given these unpredictable end times is to propose projects of unprecedented scale as the next two case studies indicate.

6.4.3.1 Conservation Council of WA v Woodside: the failure to properly consult

The Scarborough Gas Basin Development being undertaken by Woodside is one such example. This is specific and project-based. Woodside is seeking to develop this large gas-field off the northwest coast of Western Australia. This will test the arguments put, in this context, in relation to a listed corporation. The company wanted to conduct seismic testing for gas off the Pilbara coast.

The Conservation Council of WA has issued proceedings against Woodside in the Federal Court of Australia on behalf of a Traditional Owner, Raelene Cooper, because 'the seismic blasting would affect areas of cultural significance to Aboriginal people'.[50] The Federal Court imposed the condition that consultation be substantive and meaningful. It was imposing lessons from the gaps in the Rio case covered in Chapter 4.

6.4.3.2 The Australasian Centre for Corporate Responsibility v Santos Ltd

The Australasian Centre for Corporate Responsibility commenced proceedings against Santos Ltd for misleading and deceptive statements under Australian consumer law. There were two claims by Santos which were disputed. The first

50 Conservation Council of WA, 'Another set back for Scarborough as Woodside missteps pile pressure on investors', 28 Sept, 2023, https://www.ccwa.org.au/another_set_back_for_scarborough.

being that natural gas provides clean energy. The second that the company has a plan for net zero emissions by 2040.

> On August 25, 2021, Australasian Centre for Corporate Responsibility (ACCR), a shareholder advocacy NGO, sued Australian oil and gas company Santos over its claims that it provides clean energy natural gas and has a plan for net zero emissions by 2040. According to news reports, ACCR raised two major claims. First, ACCR alleges that Santos' claims that natural gas is 'clean fuel' that provides 'clean energy' misrepresents the true effect of natural gas on the climate, including the large releases of CO_2 and methane during extraction and burning. Second, Santos' claims that it has a clear and credible plan to achieve net zero emissions by 2040 are misleading. ACCR alleges that Santos plans to expand its natural gas operations and their plan depends on undisclosed assumptions about the effectiveness of carbon capture and storage processes. The suit alleges that these misrepresentations are in violation of Australian consumer protection and corporations laws.[51]

The status if the case is noted as pending.[52]

6.4.4 Related international developments in climate litigation

6.4.4.1 Litigation in Holland involving Royal Dutch Shell as defendant

Litigation in Holland occurred in 2021 in the same week the Federal Court found in favour of the plaintiffs in the Sharma litigation. In the case, judgment was issued against Royal Dutch Shell, the transnational oil company.[53] The salient facts were that in:

> a landmark judgment, the Hague District Court ordered Royal Dutch Shell (Shell) to drastically reduce its carbon dioxide emissions by 45% (compared to 2019 levels) by 2030. The reduction applies throughout Shell's global energy portfolio and across Scope 1, 2 and 3 emissions - covering emissions from Shell's own operations, its suppliers and customers. Shell was ordered to implement this reduction target with immediate effect, irrespective of any appeal. This class action was brought against Shell by environmental groups and supported by over 17,000 individuals. Notably, Shell had already committed to net-zero emissions by 2050. The Hague District Court considered those plans as inadequate, noting the significance of Shell's contribution to global emissions. The ruling marks that the largest greenhouse gas emitters are expected to bear a commensurately greater burden in taking

51 *Australasian Centre for Corporate Responsibility v Santos Ltd,* https://climatecasechart.com/non-us-case/australasian-centre-for-corporate-responsibility-v-santos/.

52 Australasian Centre for Corporate Responsibility v Santos, n 51.

53 *Mileudefensie et al v Royal Dutch Shell Plc*, Hague District Court C/09/571932/HA ZA 19-379 (English) (26 May 2021).

> action, irrespective of how challenging that might be for business models established upon carbon heavy industry. The judgment marked a significant precedent that companies, not just countries, can be compelled to reduce their greenhouse gas emissions in line with the Paris Agreement.[54]

6.4.4.2 Litigation in New Zealand involving Fonterra and others as defendants

Another ongoing example is the litigation in the Supreme Court of New Zealand brought by Maori elder, Mike Smith, against a group of seven the country's largest corporate greenhouse gas emitters, including Fonterra, New Zealand's largest company and responsible for about 30% of the world's total diary exports and the respondents collectively re also responsible for 30% of NZ's greenhouse gas emissions.[55] Mike Smith has put his claim within three causes of action arguing that 'the activities and effects of the corporate defendants amount to three forms of "tort" or civil wrong: public nuisance, negligence, and a new form of civil wrong described as a "proposed climate system damage tort"'.[56]

Whilst the negligence claim is reminiscent of the Sharma litigation in Australia, the proposed climate system damage tort is novel and that is why the world is watching the case closely. As Vernon Rive observes:

> A major issue for the Supreme Court (and now the High Court, where this claim will proceed) was whether longstanding rules and principles of tort liability should be adjusted in light of the contemporary, existential challenges presented by climate change. This might involve adapting established tort categories of public nuisance and negligence. It might also involve fashioning an entirely new 'climate system damage' tort. A key plank of the corporate emitters' argument was that the courts 'are ill-suited to deal with a systemic problem of this nature with all the complexity entailed'. They argued the courts should leave those inherently political issues to the politicians. The Supreme Court rejected that argument. Unless parliament has, through statute, clearly displaced civil obligations—and the court found that it had not—a judicial pathway is 'open for the common law to operate, develop and evolve'.[57]

The case law in the climate field is now becoming international in reach because climate litigation is testing the boundaries of long-held restrictions within national jurisdictions and these events observed in real time are able to be adapted and

54 King and Wood Mallesons, Will Heath et al, 'Insight: A big week for the fossil fuel sector: climate activism hits global courts and boardrooms', 1 June 2021, https://www.kwm.com/au/en/insights/latest-thinking/climate-activism-hits-global-courts-and-boardrooms.html

55 Vernon Rive, *The Conversation*, 'One of NZ's most contentious climate cases is moving forward. And the world is watching', 13 February 2024. One of NZ's most contentious climate cases is moving forward. And the world is watching (theconversation.com).

56 Rive, n 55.

57 Rive, n 55.

tested in similar national contexts. As Daniel Street from law firm DLA Piper notes of the Fonterra case:

> Previously, tort law has been closed off to these sorts of claims. This particular claim has been one of much interest internationally, so there have been a number of my international colleagues and international NGOs and climate activist groups who've been following this case closely, and I suspect similar arguments being run in numerous cases offshore. The getting past the strikeout stage means you get that detailed consideration and then if Mr Smith was successful on the main elements of this claim, then you get the question of, well, what is the appropriate relief in a case such as this.[58]

The acceleration of climate litigation on a jurisdiction-by-jurisdiction basis is recorded by the Sabin Centre at Columbia Law School.[59] Around the world, putative defendants including companies and governments are on notice. In Australia, more than one 130 climate related case have been recorded,[60] making Australia a leading jurisdiction in the field.

6.5 Implications for corporate law, theory, risk, and governance

6.5.1 The evolving relevance of the duty of care concept to companies and boards

As the law firm Gilbert and Tobin have noted, 'climate change litigation remains a key trend in Australia'.[61] The litigation has involved public law defendants such as governments, but private actors such as companies will be enmeshed and soon. This is already happening on a trickle basis; it is not yet a flood. It may involve the assertion of a duty of care, but there are other legal strategies to investigate. They advise that 'companies should be aware that stakeholders have other legal avenues to pursue climate change actions'.[62]

Similarly, the law firm Norton Rose Fulbright noted that:

> the decision in Sharma fundamentally alters the liability landscape in the context of climate change. Potentially, the recognition of the duty, if supported by other courts, could operate to condition the ability of not only governments but also *private entities* to undertake new developments and projects, including infrastructure and energy projects, and also conceivably

58 RNZ, New Zealand Business, 'Mike Smith's case against major NZ emitters garners international interest, lawyer says', 8 Feb 2024, Mike Smith's case against major NZ emitters garners international interest, lawyer says | RNZ News.

59 The Sabin Centre for Climate Change Law, Columbia Law School, Columbia University, climatecasechart.com/non-us-case/australasian-centre-for-corporate-responsibility-v-santos/#:~:text=ACCR%20alleges%20that%20Santos%20plans,consumer%20protection%20and%20corporations%20laws.

60 The Sabin Centre, n 59, https://climatecasechart.com/non-us-jurisdiction/australia/.

61 Gilbert and Tobin, n 33.

62 Gilbert and Tobin, n 33.

> any business activity that may lead to appreciable risk of harm arising from the contribution of that activity to net carbon emissions.[63]

The interests of different putative classes of powerful well-resourced defendant are conflating. As Gilbert and Tobin note:

> we expect that Australian governments and companies- particularly those in energy and consumer-facing industries- will increasingly be a target for litigants including class action litigants bringing novel climate-related claims.[64]

These observations by major commercial law firms reveal the alignment of interests in the Australian corporate sector seeking to buttress traditional shareholder primacy norms in a way like the discussion regarding the Rio Tinto case study in Chapter 4.

6.5.2 Companies moving into a state of readiness as regards climate change litigation

Litigation regarding climate change risk is developing rapidly and beyond the historical limitations of damages as a remedy. The McVeigh case discussed in Chapter 5 saw the advent of litigation to influence corporate behaviour and governance with regard to long-term investment decisions. The Sharma case in this chapter focused on an investment decision by the board to expand an existing project. The fact is this litigation is intensifying and covering an increasingly wide array of strategies. As the Australian-trained, London-based environmental lawyer, Tessa Khan, has argued:

> At key moments in history, courts around the world have helped to accelerate social change .... It should therefore come as no surprise that they are being called on to help resolve the biggest social and environmental crisis of our time: the climate emergency. Lawsuits are not a panacea. It takes significant public vigilance and pressure to ensure that judgments translate into real change. But litigation is one of the most powerful tools we have for claiming our rights and making clear what's at stake—and the stakes have never been higher.[65]

The formal political and legal tropes in Australia are being outflanked by regulatory, financial, and long-term risk which reflect the rapidly evolving reality of the climate

63 Norton Rose Fulbright, n 4.

64 Gilbert and Tobin, n 34.

65 Tessa Kahn, 'Litigation is a powerful tool in the environmental crisis', *The Guardian Australia*, 16 August, 2020, https://www.theguardian.com/lifeandstyle/2020/aug/16/tessa-khan-litigation-is-a-powerful-tool-in-the-environmental-crisis.

emergency. This challenge is global in scale and necessitates comparative national analysis as between nations.

At least in the realm of climate litigation, Australia is seeing rapid development. It is a leader, not a laggard within this domain. This is not because the law on the books has changed, but because the world around the law has moved on at considerable pace. Not least of these are the vectors referred to above—these include the advances in scientific consensus on a global scale facilitated by the UN, the regulatory framework and the stance of regulators, the availability of finance and insurance, and the evolving nature of broad-based tests of legal liability.

The fact that the reasonable director tests sit at the heart of Australian corporate law in s.180(1) provides both broad coherence and innate flexibility. As the 2016 Hutley Opinion confirms, its component parts combine both objective and subjective elements. The critical point is that it is not a provision which is frozen in time. It is not time-bound but alive to developments. It can be broadly applied to the current state of knowledge (scientific and otherwise). It works within a similarly expansive conception of current community expectations. More specifically, by reference to the field of climate change, it is adaptable to the emerging scientific consensus, and its effect on the legal content of the term 'climate risk'. In this respect, the clear trend is that the standard enunciated within s.180(1) Corporations Act 2001 (Cth) is shifting in line with community expectations.

Climate risk has emerged rapidly and with increasing clarity. Directors and trustees cannot plead ignorance or attempt obfuscation. It could be argued that formal corporate law is being by-passed or, alternatively, that key provisions of formal law provide for change and flexibility given wider contextual changes. Whichever of these hypotheses is correct, the liability of directors and of boards is materially different over a period to date of five years in so far as climate risk is concerned. Claims of ignorance or indifference will not suffice. Nor will inactivity and the stance of being reactive.

The practical changes rendered to the legal responsibility of directors means that the content of corporate law is changing apace, irrespective of new law on the books or new theories of corporate law. In this respect, broad based legislative provisions struck in terms of general principles, are providing a particularly efficient gateway to change and evolution of the law of companies in Australia.

The prediction that climate change was on the horizon in 2016 has proven correct. It has come with increasing intensity. It affects corporations through their directors and others such as trustees.

Putative defendants to climate change, whether directors, boards, or governments, need to be aware of the range of vectors they face which may appear chaotic but are increasingly strategic.[66] In terms of climate litigation worldwide, there have been

66 Shannon Gibson, 'From throwing soup to suing governments, there's strategy to climate activism's seeming chaos- here's where it's headed next', *The Conversation*, 3 Feb 2024, https://theconversation.com/from-throwing-soup-to-suing-governments-theres-strategy-to-climate-activisms-seeming-chaos-heres-where-its-headed-next-219545.

more than 2,000 climate-change cases commenced in the last five years with most seeking 'to compel government and corporations to reduce their emissions or keep fossil fuels in the ground'.[67]

Law firm Gilbert and Tobin provide four practical steps for companies to implement to mitigate the risk of climate litigation.

- Identify particular activities within the organization with heightened risk.
- Ensure the accuracy of climate-related claims and statements.
- Establish governance structures with oversight of climate risk.
- Develop an action plan to proactively engage with stakeholders and to deal with and manage risk if a climate-related dispute arises.[68]

Australian companies operate in a high-risk context given the national and international standing of the nation. Australia is a wealthy country and a member of the G20 with an advanced legal system. In terms of if its economy, however, it is very simple in relative terms coming in at 93rd place as the Harvard Atlas of Complexity rankings confirm.[69] This simplicity is predicated on the fact that Australia is one of the highest carbon emitters by reference to population and is a major contributor to international scope 3 emissions. These factors are based on the nation's strong dependence on fossil fuel exports. The totality of this national matrix—the wealth, the simplicity, the narrowly focused economy, with a well-resourced dispute system—combines to also put Australia near the top of countries with active climate litigation; the nation has created a Petri dish of factors giving rise to this activity and this means high exposure to companies and boards.

6.5.3 The potential exposure of companies, their boards, and directors

Companies will need to adopt high level strategies, proactive measures, and detailed operational plans subject to regular review to deal with climate risk. They face myriad points of exposure:

- Setting weak long term or interim emissions targets, for example for 2030, or 2050.
- The lack of a rigorous, costed plan to meet targets.
- Exposure to the emerging principle of proportionality—if a company is a high carbon emitter it needs a more robust strategy.
- Litigation for greenwashing and using marketing spin to claim climate credentials without underlying legal substance.

67 Gibson, n 66.

68 Gilbert and Tobin, n 33.

69 Harvard University Centre for International Development (CID), Atlas of Economic Complexity, 'Country and Product Complexity Rankings', https://atlas.cid.harvard.edu/rankings. This Atlas of Economic Complexity was discussed in Chapter 3 and referred to in Chapter 4.

- Litigation for negligence under s.180 Corporations Act 2001 (Cth).
- Litigation for breach of a duty of care owed in common law.
- Litigation for breach of the duty to act in the best interests of the company.
- Litigation seeking to influence corporate behaviour and governance.
- Litigation seeking to increase disclosure of investment strategy, for example long-term super fund allocations.
- Facing resolutions at general meetings to stop or protest executive remuneration or to block the appointment of, or to vote off board members.
- Disinvestment by major institutional shareholders in a company, for example by superannuation funds.
- Sale of problematic high emissions company assets to third parties.
- Setting up subsidiary companies to house problem assets.
- Problems and delays with obtaining finance, insurance, and government licences or approvals.
- No weak or incomplete scope three emissions disclosures, whether at domestic or international levels.

6.5.4 Boards pushing back? The case of Exxon Mobil

Historically, decisions about strategy, investment, and risk have been the exclusive province of the c-suite and reserved for the corporate board. The term 'activist' can and is applied to current members or to third parties seeking to disrupt this historically evolved role of the board. It is the sole body privileged with stewardship of the business entity. The techniques of climate litigation will test the fortress like mentality of boards in unprecedented ways. A new defensive corporate technique is becoming apparent. Companies are seeking to push back against the encroachment of activism, for example in the litigation involving Exxon Mobil.

Arjuna Capital of Massachusetts and Follow This, an Amsterdam-based climate activist group, lodged a shareholder proposal involving climate change. In response, Exxon filed the lawsuit in January 2024 against Arjuna Capital and Follow This, aiming to block their shareholder proposal. Arjuna Capital and Follow This withdrew their proposals. Exxon continues its lawsuit, despite this withdrawal. In its filing Exxon:

> repeated accusations that the activists hope to constrain its business rather than increase shareholder value, and that they seek to 'micromanage' company business. Without a ruling in its favour, Exxon wrote, the groups or others could file a similar proposal in future years. 'There is no good reason to believe they will stop'.[70]

70 Reuters, Jody Godoy and Ross Kerber, 'Exxon shareholder proposal withdrawal may end lawsuit: judge', 6 Feb 2024, https://www.reuters.com/legal/exxon-shareholder-proposal-withdrawal-may-end-lawsuit-judge-2024-02-05/.

The case reveals a further move away from traditional remedies within the climate change context. Plaintiffs seek remedies other than damages; defendants seek to pursue rulings even when the matter complained of has been withdrawn as in the Exxon Mobil case. US District Judge, Mark Pittman, has written:

> As it stands now, the Court struggles to see what the ongoing case or controversy is in this matter given the only relief sought from the Court was a declaration that Exxon may exclude Defendants proposal from its annual shareholder meeting[71].

Corporate law Professor Eric Talley from Columbia University said the strategy by ExxonMobil:

> now looks like an attempt to garner a ruling to wield against other similar proposals I can imagine a law firm that represents a lot of these companies that get shareholder proposals wouldn't mind having a holding on the books saying this is excludable.[72]

The litigation exposes an important emerging battleline between companies and activists. The corporate argument is founded on the unfettered, sole province and privilege retained by the board to increase shareholder value, such that any attempted interference with this principle, including micromanagement and the assertion of the right to 'question everything' is illegitimate. It is an approach based on established corporate principles pre-eminent and perfected in the 20th century.

Against this view is the hyperobject nature of climate change, the climate emergency, and climate risk. This complex new terrain requires a 'whatever it takes' approach to disrupting hegemonic norms, such as boardroom pre-eminence. It looks to disrupt corporate principles and to replace them with innovative solutions fit to meet the challenges of the emergency of the next three decades. For corporate law and governance, this will be a battle of seismic proportions. In this sense, the informal practice, if not principle, of necessity will be important, just as it was in underwriting corporate behaviour by the East India Company between 1600 and 1870 which later gave rise the codification of basic corporate law principles, and later still retrofitting the theory to the practice.

6.6 Conclusion

Climate change risk will be litigated in many guises. It will encompass long-held commercial law tactics and techniques including contract law and tort law with particular focus on negligence. The defendants in such claims will be corporations and other forms of for-profit business entities. The most common of these is likely the listed public company, given their economic reach and business scale.

71 Reuters, 70.
72 Reuters, n 70.

Indeed, there is increasing recognition that a select few companies are responsible for disproportionate CO_2 emissions. As a result, climate risk will become a core concern of commercial law and corporate law.

6.6.1 A new chapter in relation to climate change in Australia

This evolving situation completes another chapter of the narrative constructed over the last several years framed within the Australian context by the sequence of Opinions by Hutley SC, and within the international realm by the work of the UN and other bodies. That narrative has shifted distinctly from one in which climate change was incipient, liminal, and theoretical for boards to where it is now a clear, compelling, and ever-present consideration and central risk factor. Boards have had to shift their approach from a position of benign passivity to necessarily being in a state of readiness. Climate change litigation is no longer a mere theoretical abstraction which happens elsewhere. It is present and increasingly pervasive within the realms of Australian litigation.

Of the Sharma case, members of the International Bar Association have noted of the Sharma case that it

> may be viewed in the future as the beginning of a new chapter whereby the science in relation to climate change is no longer being challenged by governments (and possibly also corporations) in Australia. This would be consistent with the approach that governments and corporations are otherwise adopting in relation to climate change.[73]

6.6.2 Timelines and the interim 2030 target: the urgency of avoiding intergenerational negligence

As the newly appointed federal climate change Minister, Chris Bowen notes, the government has committed to a 43% reduction in carbon emissions by 2030. This is 'a floor, not a ceiling.'[74] He goes on to note that:

> this being the first day of the month, 2030 is just 84 months away. As the Climate Change Authority advice makes clear, to achieve this target we will need to achieve the same emissions reduction in the next eight years that has been achieved in the last eighteen. [75]

The Climate Change Minister also notes that 'Australia is highly vulnerable to the impacts of climate change, including bushfires and floods, so the stakes are

73 Hales and Fearis, n 2.

74 Shiloh Payne, 'We don't have a second to waste, Climate Change Minister says', ABC News, 1 December 2022, abc.net.au/news.

75 Payne, n 74.

extremely high. Not acting would be an unforgivable act of intergenerational negligence'.[76]

Directors face twin threats of negligence. The first is statutory negligence embedded within s.180 of the Corporations Act 2001 (Cth), and the second is the potential (for now, at least not realized) of negligence in common law. This second limb has the potential to be broad ranging and high impact. Fossil fuel companies and businesses with high greenhouse gas emissions will be particularly exposed to liability. As NRF noted

> failure to ensure projects and business activities are 'climate friendly' and minimize emissions could lead to liability in negligence. While the trajectory of this form of liability will be very much in a state of development in coming years … the foundation stone has been potentially set firmly in place. At the very least, this decision sounds a warning bell to those who wish to pursue developments or activities that could be said to have climate change impacts.[77]

In Australia, this focuses on some of the biggest corporations which have long been blue-chip listed entities. Extraction activities focused on the big three fossil fuels—coal, gas, and oil—will be the focus of much scrutiny. Proposals involving long-term investments in these areas of industrial and export activity will be the subject of potential class actions by mass claimants, as well as scrutiny by activist groups and research centres. The shape of climate risk for corporations will accelerate in parallel with the wider societal journey within Australia to net zero by 2050. It is axiomatic to state the case: corporations have been at the crux of creating climate warming; they must be present and accountable in terms of solutions and innovation to help turbo-charge the reduction, reversal, and sequestration of greenhouse gases so that planetary health does not continue to spiral towards an unliveable endgame.

6.6.3 'Staying with the trouble': the hyperobject of climate change for companies from this point onwards

As NRF notes, 'climate change is, in particular, a matter that reflects the concerns of the vast majority of Australians'.[78]

There is a composite effect taking place. It is multi-faceted. It includes the increasing cost of insurance for climate risk and the clear and present prospect of litigation against directors and boards of companies. Such litigation may arise from several quarters including class actions from multiple claimants, institutional investors, and climate action groups. The baseline in corporate law has been established. It is not the more pervasive and unpredictable common law concept of negligence that hovers over companies and other for-profit and not-for-profit actors.

76 Payne, n 74.
77 Norton Rose Fulbright, n 4.
78 Norton Rose Fulbright, n 4.

The stage is set for action. It needs to prevail. Companies and boards must be alive to the opportunities rather than waylaid by the various flag falls of inaction. New firms will be well placed. Established firms may require fundamental engineering.

The climate change emergency requires a joined-up approach. It requires strategy, careful response, dedicated effort, and long-term thinking. Each of these is anathema to the Australian political federal system which requires elections every three years. The timing within the three years is within the gift of the Prime Minister of the day and this has factor, the intra party climate wars, and deep personality clashes have given way to prolonged instability. Australia has had eight Prime Ministers in 15 years between December 2007 and the end of 2023.[79]

By contrast, the Australian states have fixed-term elections every four years. The states have certainty whereas the federal government does not. Business has been well ahead of the federal government in terms of responses to climate change. Business has sought policy certainty and a legislative and regulatory framework which is beyond the political divide. Long-term planning is not at all easy in a short-term politicized environment. Campaigns are frenetic. Policy gets lost in tribal politics. This context or lack of rules of the game makes life complex for corporations.

6.6.4 Climate change risk as salient to boards and central to companies

The salient point is that as climate risks grows and becomes increasingly relevant to boards of directors, the litigation will move from arguably more esoteric issues such as the external affairs power in the constitution to mainstream domestic commercial law. The province of the company, its strategy, its operations, and its navigation of future and long-term risk, will be indelibly marked by concerns for climate change. In this sense, the nature of climate change as a hyperobject will be a constant presence for the consideration of boards.

References

Australasian Centre for Corporate Responsibility v Santos Ltd. https://climatecasechart.com/non-us-case/australasian-centre-for-corporate-responsibility-v-santos/

Australian Conservation Foundation Inc v Commonwealth (1980) 146 *CLR* 493, 531 (ACF v Commonwealth).

Tom Bingham, *The Rule of Law*, Penguin, 2010.

Commonwealth v Tasmania ("Tasmanian Dam case") [1983] *HCA* 21 (1983) 158 CLR 1 (1 July 1983).

Federal Court of Australia, Online File, *Pabai Pabai v Commonwealth of Australia* VID622/2021. https://www.fedcourt.gov.au/services/access-to-files-and-transcripts/online-files/pabai-v-australia

Jhon Gardner, 'The Many Faces of the Reasonable Person,' *Law Quarterly Review*, 131, 2015, 563–584.

79 Australia's prime ministers since late 2007 are John Howard, Kevin Rudd, Julia Gillard, Kevin Rudd (again), Tony Abbott, Malcolm Turnbull, Scott Morrison, and Anthony Albanese.

Saul Griffith, *The Big Switch: Australia's Electric Future*, Black Inc., 2022.
King and Wood Mallesons, Will Heath et al, 'Insight: A big week for the fossil fuel sector: Climate activism hits global courts and boardrooms,' 1 June 2021, https://www.kwm.com/au/en/insights/latest-thinking/climate-activism-hits-global-courts-and-boardrooms.html
Michael Legg, *Regulation, Litigation and Enforcement*, Lawbook Co, 2011. http://www.environment.gov.au/epbc
Mabo v Queensland [No 2] - [1992] HCA 23–175 CLR 1; 66 ALJR 408.
Sharma by her litigation representative Sister Marie Brigid Arthur v Minister for the Environment [2021] FCA 560, para 312. https://climatecasechart.com/wp-content/uploads/non-us-case-documents/2021/20210527_VID-389-of-2021-2021-FCA-560-2021-FCA-774-2022-FCAFC-35-2022-FCAFC-65_judgment.pdf
The Sabin Centre for Climate Change Law, Columbia Law School, Columbia University. climatecasechart.com/non-us-case/australasian-centre-for-corporate-responsibility-v-santos/#:~:text=ACCR%20alleges%20that%20Santos%20plans,consumer%20protection%20and%20corporations%20laws

7 The emergence of climate risk and the end of shareholder primacy?

7.1 The historical dominance of shareholder primacy in Australia

The risk for the owners of companies has in Australia, for the two centuries corresponding with the European settlement, been focused largely on controlling agents, such as directors and senior employees, who are, given their insider status, endowed with more knowledge about the company's choices, strategy, and day-to-day challenges than the owners and shareholders who are often remote, and problematically distant, in terms of communication, geography, and access. This delineation of ownership, risk, delegation, and trust embodies both the ingenuity and the challenge inherent in the corporate form. The company is, and has only ever been, a creature of statute. It is metaphorical in its basic guise. It is somewhat anthropomorphic, described as being 'like' an adult person,[1] and it requires such adult people to act for and on its behalf. The corporate form needs to invest its trust in the directors, and it is only able to act and to contract and to proceed in the legal landscape through and by the agency of such people. Without their actions, the company is a stationary legal vehicle without a key. It is dormant and without effect.

7.1.1 The Australian **sui generis** *case: the co-extensive rise of the company and of the modern industrially based economy*

As noted in Chapter 3, the attribute of limited liability was emerging in the 19th-century UK parliament at the same time as the nascent, industrial base of the then colonies of Australia were emerging.

Australia's modern industrial base remains stubbornly simple, making it vulnerable to international price shocks and so-called 'Black Swan' events. It relies on growing animals, plants, and crops and it is highly dependent on the extraction and export of minerals, fossil fuels and the like with little value-adding. It has been sustained in its luck, for when the world successively wanted wool, iron ore, and precious materials and minerals, Australia could produce all of them in abundance. Luck and complacency, though, go hand in hand.

1 Section 124 of the Corporations Act 2001 (Cth) makes the point in specific terms.

DOI: 10.4324/9781003263746-8

Extraction's long ascendancy has also stymied the role of corporate reform. In terms of company law in Australia, it closely followed UK developments until the Second World War and more latterly has ascribed to US-style issues. A mistaken assumption deployed in the US as identified by Kent Greenfield is that 'the common law and the laissez faire marketplace are pre-political, neutral, and insulated from government regulation'.[2] This type of analysis has been used to promote an economic rationalist approach to corporate law development in Australia in which 'the private law of contract is now the dominant, and quite powerful, metaphor used to explain corporate law'.[3]

7.1.2 The reinforcing influence of the Anglosphere

The fact that Australia shares much of the 'history, culture and practice'[4] of corporate law with the UK necessarily binds the nation to these origins. Shareholder primacy is a product of these issues. The law underpins the rights of shareholders, and the nature of directorial reporting is first about profit and second, shareholder returns. These factors are exacerbated by the fact that both countries have degrees of institutional share ownership, and that the UK stands out in this regard within the European geographical marketplace because 'institutional investors play a leading role'[5] in the company law and securities markets. This connects the share market with the superannuation industry and pension funds. Of influence in both countries has been the corporate governance project commenced in the UK in the early 1990s with the Cadbury Report and then the Greenbury Report. The Hampel Report of 1998 has been of clear and enduring influence, particularly in Australia. The Committee noted that a central goal was 'to consider the aims of those who direct and control companies'.[6] The Hampel Report concluded decisively its approach:

> The single overriding objective shared by all listed companies, whatever their size or type of business, is the preservation and the greatest practicable enhancement over time of their shareholders' investment. All boards have this responsibility and their policies, structure, composition, and governing processes should reflect this. A company must develop relationships relevant to its success. These will depend on the nature of the company's business; but they will include those with employees, customers, suppliers, credit providers, local communities and governments. It is management's

2 Kent Greenfield, *The Failure of Corporate Law: Fundamental Flaws and Progressive Possibilities*, The University of Chicago Press, 2006, 29.

3 Greenfield, n 2, 30.

4 John Farrar, Corporate Governance: Theories, Principles, and Practice, 2nd ed, Oxford University Press, 2006, 462.

5 Eddy Wymeersch, 'A status report on corporate governance rules and practices in some continental European states', in Hopt, Klaus J, Hideki Kanda, Mark J Roe, Eddy Wymeersch and Stefan Prigge, (eds) *Comparative Corporate Governance: The State of the Art and Emerging Research,* Clarendon Press, 1998, 1045–199, 1173.

6 The Hampel Report, 1998, para 1.16, 11.

> responsibility to develop policies which address these matters; in doing so they must have regard to the overriding objective of preserving and enhancing the shareholders' investment over time.[7]

The risk investment of shareholders is pre-eminent. Relationships beyond the owners are acknowledged but they serve the greater purpose of long-term owner returns. This relegates stakeholders to a distant secondary position within the dominant corporate paradigm. The ethos of the Hampel Report has been of clear influence in the Corporations Act 2001 (Cth) and the iterations of the ASX Corporate Governance Principles and Recommendations.

7.1.3 Companies as the embodiment of private arrangements

As such 'the contractual model sees the corporate form not as a juridical person created by the legislature, but a legal form created through a multitude of private contractual relationships'.[8] This has corresponded in a weak regulatory corporate environment, and an architecture with low expectations. Whilst s.124 of the Corporations Act 2001 (Cth) describes the corporation as having the capacities and powers of an individual— essentially, an adult person—it is silent on setting-out correlative obligations. Given this silence, and the dominant view that corporations are 'only an embodiment of private arrangements'[9] it logically follows that companies are 'incapable of having social or moral obligations much in the same way that inanimate objects are incapable of having these obligations'.[10] This view put forward by US scholar, Daniel Fischel, in the early 1980s has been ascendant for more than four decades.

By contrast, the influence of corporate social responsibility is correspondingly weak 'because the corporation is a particular type of firm formed by individuals acting voluntarily and for their mutual benefit, it can far more reasonably be viewed as the product of private contract than as a creature of the state'.[11] Mainstream corporate scholarship in Australia reflects these views. Shareholder primacy and contractarian supremacy provide a powerful and abiding contextual binary. They are not neutral concepts but important implicit political and economic constructs of modern corporate law.

7.1.4 Climate risk in Australia: clearly emerging legal contours

Climate risk has now assumed the centrality of being a financial risk. It is therefore incumbent on directors to take it into account, to plan for it, and to invest time and resources in developing strategies which take it very seriously, which are detailed,

7 Hampel Committee on Corporate Governance, Final Report, 1997, The Committee on Corporate Governance and Gee Publishing, 1–65, 11–2, para 1.16.

8 Greenfield, n 2, 30.

9 Greenfield, n 2, 30.

10 Daniel Fischel, 'The Corporate Governance Movement', 35 *Vand. L. Rev.*, (1982) 1259, 1273.

11 Fischel, n 10, 1273–4.

achievable, and backed by the proper allocation of resources. Climate risk shows just how quickly new forms of financial risk can emerge from the fringes to the centre stage as it has done in Australia. In 2016, the first of the Hutley Opinions characterized climate risk as liminal; just five years later in 2021 by the publication of the third of the sequence of three, publicly available Opinions—surely as influential as High Court judgments, climate risk was central.

And within the timeline of a particular company, the hegemony of shareholders may give way to other stakeholders, including the creditors. This is the case with companies in financial distress. The attention given to creditors is at least as great, if not greater than that afforded to shareholders. This change in dynamic may be very rapid. As soon as a company has going concern issues, or questions going to its solvency,[12] the directors need to turn on a dime and act. Creditors are overnight the foremost stakeholders in their minds. The sightlines for the directors are therefore potentially quixotic within the realm of the single business. Risk may swing within the course of a single business day from the members to the creditors, so adaptability about risk is an inherent for directors. Considering the competing interests of the stakeholders within the situational realm of the company is a fundamental component of a director fulfilling her duty in law.

If new forms of corporate risk can arise (and retreat) over time, and risk within the corporate context can focus on different stakeholders, depending on the point in the company's lifecycle, can the fundamental nature of companies in Australia, which is to serve first and foremost the interests of shareholders, also be altered over time?

7.1.5 The role of the apex court in Australia: the High Court

In a common law democracy like Australia, this can only occur in two basic ways. One is by the judges of apex courts. Another is by sovereign parliaments. Perhaps a third mode can be added, for the sake of completeness and that is the rule making function of the listed market, in Australia that being the Australian Securities Exchange with its ability to set another layer of architecture for companies enjoying the benefits, privileges, and obligations of access to capital markets and phenomenal potential scale in terms of size, revenue, and shareholder reach.[13]

7.1.6 Corporate law in a world of climate crisis

The challenge of the climate crisis is its multi-dimensional shape and influence. As noted, the assertion of shareholder primacy has been an enduring feature of Australian corporate law. Current shareholders and would-be shareholders share the ideological belief that to the investor go the spoils, the promise of the sky being the limit. This is a form of incantation from letting the free market decide. The

12 See s.95A Corporations Act 2001 (Cth).

13 CBA has approximately 800,000 shareholders.

point, though, is that the market is never free. There is legislation. There are rules and checks and balances. Corporate law even in its most acutely Anglo-spherical emanations, balances the rights of shareholders against those of creditors. And in times of crisis, emergency, and war, the economy may be more directional in nature, giving rise to a collective and collaborative 'war effort'. Meeting the crisis of war has been the impetus for several of the most successful and enduring family companies.[14]

7.2 The emergence of climate-based financial risk

Is the challenge of meeting the climate change crisis and delivering net zero carbon emissions going to involve the diminishment of shareholder primacy and will it be challenged as the current preeminent corporate orthodoxy in Australia? The answer to these questions will rely largely on the evolving nature of corporate financial risk. The deployment of risk capital will still lie at the heart of corporate activity. However, the activities that companies undertake, and how they undertake them will be newly subject to scrutiny and reflection. The assumptions, often long-held and therefore judged reliable or predictable, may in due course be subject to profound disruption and turbulence.

7.2.1 Scenario setting until 2050

There will be one of three irreducible scenarios which emerges by 2050. These are first, that net zero carbon emission will not be met; second, that net zero will be met; or third, that the net zero target will be bettered. Companies will clearly need to be one of the central pieces of the actions, solutions, and innovations implicit in scenarios two and three. Companies will also be central as regards the failure to achieve the target envisioned in the third scenario.

7.2.2 Tracing the elements of climate risk

The company is the most ubiquitous business and mercantile vehicle in advanced economies such as Australia and the UK. As such, corporate law will play a vital role in meeting the challenge to mitigate global CO_2 emissions. As early as 1911, the US philosopher and President of Columbia University, William Murray Butler, said:

> I weigh my words, when I say that in my judgment the limited liability corporation is the greatest single discovery of modern times, whether you judge it by its social, by its ethical, by its industrial or, in the long run, — after we understand it and know how to use it,—by its political, effects. Even steam

14 David S. Landes, *Dynasties: Fortunes and Misfortunes of the World's Great Family Businesses*, Viking, 2006.

> and electricity are far less important than the limited liability corporation, and they would be reduced to comparative impotence without it.[15]

Corporate law and the modern market economy are inextricably linked. Corporate law theory will be pivotal to reconceptualizing the role of the corporation in relation to climate change. The company as the most popular mercantile entity in the modern, global, market economy. As such it is integral to answering the question: how to develop 'sustainable business models' within the wider 'revolution in sustainability'?[16]

Theoretical approaches to the corporation include concession theory, aggregate theory, economic theories, natural entity theory, organizational theory, feminist theory, corporate social responsibility (CSR), and environmental social governance (ESG). This monograph will suggest and identify the types of reforms or changes, major or otherwise, needed for corporate law to respond to the climate crisis being faced by governments and economies globally.

The emerging economy for risk is exemplified by the recent decision by Svergies Riksbank, the Swedish central bank, to divest from Australian-based bonds. As Richard Gluyas notes:

> The decision by the Swedish central bank to dump its holdings of Queensland and West Australian bonds because of inaction on climate change and high greenhouse gas emissions might be world first but it should come as no surprise. For global investors, it's just the latest in an increasingly regular stream of market and regulatory signals on climate risks that date back thirty years. It's only in recent years, however, that central banks have accepted that the changing climate is a threat to financial stability. Natural disasters can damage property and disrupt trade, and the transition from fossil fuels to renewables has the potential to create stranded assets. Svergies Riksbank, the Swedish central bank, hold 500 billion Swedish krona ($75bn) in foreign exchange reserves for contingency purposes, the majority of which is invested in highly liquid US government bonds. Australian and Canadian bonds represent about 8 per cent of the portfolio and are held to achieve a higher yield and reduce financial risk. In the words of deputy governor Martin Floden, the two countries are 'not known for good climate work,' with emissions per capita among the highest in the world and varying considerably between states.[17]

Directly relevant to corporate law, Martin Foo, an analyst with Standard and Poors, has noted that 'central banks are increasingly showing an interest in incorporating environmental objectives into their reserve portfolios.'[18] Clearly, it is time for Australian companies to pay attention.

15 http://conversableeconomist.blogspot.com/2017/07/the-limited-liability-corporation-is.html.

16 David Attenborough, *A Life on our Planet*, Penguin, 2020, 2C3.

17 Richard Gluyas, *The Australian: Business*, Swedish bond withdrawal may be the thin end of the wedge', 19 November, 2019, 21.

18 Gluyas, n 17.

7.3 The potential end of shareholder primacy?

7.3.1 The contemporary critique of capitalism and the 'war' on corporate profits

Greta Thunberg is arguably the best-known climate activist in the world. Her view is that:

> Saving the world is voluntary. You could certainly argue against that statement from a moral point of view, but the fact remains: there are no laws or restrictions in place that will force anyone to take the necessary steps towards safeguarding our future living conditions on planet Earth. This is troublesome from many perspectives, not least because—as much as I hate to admit it—Beyoncé was wrong. It is not girls who run the world. It is run by politicians, corporations and financial interests—mainly represented by white, privileged, middle-aged, straight cis men. And it turns out most of them are terribly ill suited for the job. This may not come as a big surprise. After all, the purpose of a company is not to save the world—it is to make a profit. Or, rather, it is to make as much profit as it possibly can in order to keep shareholders and market interests happy.[19]

This is an eloquent but simplistic view. Companies are designed to make a profit, it is part of corporate law, it is a focus of director's duties and of claims by creditors. It is at the forefront of the regulatory process. All the interested players—shareholder, employees, creditors, and managers—are focused on the balance sheet. It symbiotically links the interests of retail shareholders to institutional shareholders. Profit is an intrinsic part of the modern market economy.

This approach is widespread amongst all business entities, whether they are incorporated or not. Companies are designed to make a profit, but so too is a not-for-profit entity, and a for-purpose entity. Loss making is not, by statutory design or member concern, an aim for any entity.

This deeply held aim to make profit may be a core part of human DNA and encapsulates the ideas of risk and reward. The first writing was a fragment of a contract; a crop yield. The delivery of value and reciprocity. Profit is not just an emanation of the Industrial revolution. It is not just part of the modern parlance of Adam Smith. It is age-old and foundational.

What is the alternative to profit? The problem is that the reduction of climate damage through the net zero target is a global problem. It requires the capacity and genius of profit-making, but it also an unprecedented set of coordinated plans. It is a one-world emergency requiring a one-world approach. On their own, neither hyper-capitalism nor redux-socialism is the answer.

19 Greta Thunberg, Greta Thunberg on the Climate Delusion: 'We've been greenwashed out of our senses. It's time to stand our ground', *The Guardian*, 8 October 2022, https://www.theguardian.com/environment/2022/oct/08/greta-thunberg-climate-delusion-greenwashed-out-of-our-senses.

7.3.2 Seeing profit seeking as part of the solution to the hyper problem

The green economy is a response to the hyper problem of climate change. The hyper problem gives rise to hyper solutions. An array of companies and business entities will be involved in the collective effort of carbon reduction. Some plans will work spectacularly well. Start-ups will grow at a scale reminiscent of the tech industry. Others will not. Some will involve greenwashing and mere speculation about the future. Others will involve failed reinventions by established companies.

7.3.3 Profit, self-interest, and the tradability of shares: part of the corporate DNA

Corporate law internationally carries within it five common features. The five markers of a corporation[20] taken together encode a fictional agency or legal entity. It is increasingly clear this has allowed for excess and the exploitation of human and natural resources with limited responsibility. They are:

- Legal personality, that is, it is a legal entity with powers equivalent to an adult person. As such, the company has the power to enter contracts, to be bound by promises, and to assume liability. This breadth of legal autonomy gives the company the ability to grow as a business entity.
- Delegated management under a board structure, as noted above at point one, the company as an artificial legal entity needs to be activated by people, particularly the board of directors. The board has responsibility for the legal (and ethical) acts of the company. These concepts will be examined and expanded.
- Limited liability, a chief reason for the popularity of the company as a business entity is that ownership of the company, which rests with the shareholders, involves limited liability on their individual part.
- Transferable shares: the shares held by the owner/member/shareholder are transferable.
- Investor ownership, this is a device for increasing the number of owners, spreading risk, and raising investment capital.

It is these basic markers of the corporation which give rise to unusual licence and freedom for an agent before the law that will increasingly need to fit within the realms of allowable corporate activity. This may necessarily be more interventionist than the wide activity model which operates in Australian. As global and social pressures build, incentives and disincentives to better shape corporate activity will emerge. The boundaries for what is legal will come into sharper focus. For instance, the realm of what is illegal corporate behaviour may need to include those activities which are simply not sustainable in evidential or scientific

20 Reinier R. Kraakman, Paul Davies, Henry Hansmann, Gerard Hertig, Klaus J. Hopt, Hideki Kanda, and Edward B. Rock, *The Anatomy of Corporate Law: A Comparative and Functional Approach*, Oxford University Press, 2005.

terms. In this way, the urgency of climate change will quite possibly necessitate a fundamental redeployment of the power, skills, and capacities available to the corporation.

These features contrast with collective responsibility, a broad sense of overlapping interests, or sustainability of the corporation.

7.3.4 Nudge economics and the power of corporate law

The Corporations Act 2001 (Cth) is replete with references to different types of corporations and the channelling of effort into the corporate form. For example, partnerships of a certain size must become corporations. The NL or no liability company is a mining only entity. Not-for-profit legislation is a patchwork of state legislation and thereby limited in terms of generating nationally consistent principles; as such, it makes not-for-profits unnecessarily complex and small, and it limits their growth. Trade unions cannot incorporate. The power of the legislature is clear. It can do what it wishes to do with the corporate form. It can also solve problems which were intractable at common law. This includes pre-registration contracts, providing for reductions of share capital, enabling the criminal liability of companies, and largely removing the complexities caused by the ultra vires doctrine. As such, key legislation like this can shift corporate behaviour and do so quickly and at scale.

7.3.5 The various types of companies able to be incorporated and registered in Australia

There are two types of proprietary (pty) ltd and four types of public company able to be registered in Australia. The company limited by shares is the most popular form of business entity in Australia. In mid-2023 there were some 2.6 million companies of this type in operation. This corporate form ascertains the shareholder's liability by reference to the amount unpaid on the relevant shareholding.

The company limited by guarantee finds form in the CA 2001 and these are public companies and not for profit entities. They cannot issue shares or pay dividends. Member liability is set by reference to a guaranteed amount.

CORPORATIONS ACT 2001 - SECT 112

Types of companies

(1) The following types of companies can be registered under this Act:

Proprietary companies	Limited by shares Unlimited with share capital

Public companies	Limited by shares Limited by guarantee Unlimited with share capital No liability company

7.3.6 Australian specialist companies: to enable mining and extraction

Australian commercial conditions and the political context have given rise to at least two examples of corporate forms. This demonstrates that legislation and regulation can overtly direct and modify corporate behaviour to suit local and national conditions.

7.3.6.1 No Liability (NL) companies

Section 112 of the Corporations Act 2001 provides that:

No liability companies

(2) A company may be registered as a no liability company only if:

a) the company has a share capital; and
b) the company's constitution states that its sole objects are mining purposes; and
c) the company has no contractual right under its constitution to recover calls made on its shares from a shareholder who fails to pay them.

(3) A no liability company must not engage in activities that are outside its mining purposes objects.
(4) The directors of a no liability company must not:

a. let the whole or proportion of a mine or claim on tribute; or
b. make any contract for working any land on tribute;

unless:

(c) the letting or contract is approved by a special resolution; or
(d) no such letting or contract has been made within the period of 2 years immediately preceding the proposed letting or contract.

"mining purposes" means any or all of the following purposes:

a) prospecting for ores, metals or minerals;
b) obtaining, by any mode or method, ores, metals or minerals;
c) the sale or other disposal of ores, metals, minerals or other products of mining;
d) the carrying on of any business or activity necessary for, or incidental to, any of the foregoing purposes;

whether in Australia or elsewhere, but does not include quarrying operations for the sole purpose of obtaining stone for building, roadmaking or similar purposes. ***"minerals"*** means minerals in any form, whether solid, liquefied or gaseous and whether organic or inorganic.Further in s.9, the Corporations Act provides as follows:

CORPORATIONS ACT 2001 - SECT 9
Dictionary

Unless the contrary intention appears:

"no liability company " means a company that is registered as, or converts to, a no liability company under this Act.

Note 1: A no liability company can be registered under section 118 or 601BD. A company can convert to a no liability company under Part 2B.7.
Note 2: A no liability company must have solely mining purposes and have no contractual right to recover unpaid calls (see subsection 112(2)).

The no-liability company is a variant of the company limited by shares and the company limited by guarantee. It is a form of public company.

The no-liability company is specifically designed with no liability being borne on the part of the shareholder. This type of company is an Australian invention in the 19th century. By reference to mainstream analysis, it was designed to encourage investment in the mining sector. As Lipton et al. note,

> companies engaged in mining have always had a speculative character because of the nature of the industry. This has especially been the case in Australia. Victoria was the first Australian State to specially cater for such companies and introduced the no liability company in 1871.[21]

This was achieved in Victoria via the Mining Companies Act 1871 (Vic).

Risk-taking is a necessary feature of the mining sector, given the capital-intensive nature of the industry at each stage of a project. This is particularly the case in the exploration phase which may well turn out to be less promising than projected forecasts. Confirmation of the financial viability of new ventures is a central feature of the industry. It is a sector with high risk and potentially high reward, and long-time lags between the two phases. It is highly contingent and somewhat speculative. Hence, this entrepreneurial spirit was underwritten by rules specific to this specialist type of company.

Alternative research about the advent of NL companies is that they were a:

> response to the problem of 'dummying', a practice whereby shareholders in speculative mining ventures were registered under fictitious names to avoid

21 Phillip Lipton, Abe Herzberg, and Michelle Welsh, *Understanding Company Law,* 20th ed, Thomson Reuters, 2020, 88.

> having to pay unpaid amounts on their shares. There is debate about whether this legislation was a creative move to encourage investment in speculative mining ventures.[22]

As such the NL company was in fact 'a backward-looking, short-term expedient to the problems created by the lack of an effective corporate enforcement mechanism in the colonies'.[23] Further 'whatever view is taken of its history, this category of incorporation is now restricted to companies with share capital whose sole object (as stated in the company constitution) is mining purposes'.[24] This restriction is set out in s.112(2) and the company cannot engage in activities outside this purpose (s112(3)). This demonstrates that corporate regulation in the formal of legislative rules can take various shapes and strategies.

The Corporations Act 2001 (Cth) requires that NL companies state that mining is their sole purpose in their rules or corporate constitution. By contrast most companies do not require constitutions. Additionally, the ultra vires doctrine has, for the most part, been eviscerated by s.125 (emphasis added):

> **CORPORATIONS ACT 2001 - SECT 125**
> **Constitution may limit powers and set out objects**
>
> (1) If a company has a constitution, it may contain an express restriction on, or a prohibition of, the company's exercise of any of its powers. *The exercise of a power by the company is not invalid merely because it is contrary to an express restriction or prohibition in the company's constitution.*
> (2) If a company has a constitution, it may set out the company's objects. *An act of the company is not invalid merely because it is contrary to or beyond any objects in the company's constitution.*

By contrast, s.112 of the Corporations Act 2001 (Cth) keeps in place ultra vires type restrictions on NL companies (by reference to paragraph (b) highlighted below):

> **CORPORATIONS ACT 2001 - SECT 112**
> **Types of companies**
>
> (2) A company may be registered as a no liability company only if:
>
> (a) the company has a share capital; and
> (b) *the company's constitution* states *that its sole objects are mining purposes*; and
> (c) the company has no contractual right under its constitution to recover calls made on its shares from a shareholder who fails to pay them.

22 Stephen Bottomley, Kath Hall, Peta Spender and Beth Nosworthy, *Contemporary Australian Corporate Law*, Cambridge University Press, 2018, 103.

23 R McQueen, 'Limited Liability Company Legislation: The Australian Experience', *Australian Journal of Corporations Law*, 1991, 22, 36.

24 Bottomley et al, n 22, 103.

The NL company, an Australian variant of the corporate form, is an example of directional capitalism and regulation because the legal rules extant in the Corporations Act 2001 (Cth) have been designed to guide commercial activity along a certain pathway within a set context. This demonstrates that legal rules can be specific, can underpin economic consequences, and can drive allocations of capital in certain required directions.

The legislature can provide a series of incentives, or mandates or other devices which can promote commercial activity in a particular direction. The legislature can set the rules if it chooses to do so. If the rules are simple and meet their intended purpose, they will be used. If a benefit is outweighed by a detriment (which might be in the form of complexity of competing rules etc) then the idea will be little used or become redundant. Over time it will be dormant, a footnote in obscure legal history.

The NL company in Australia has become a case study in regulatory complexity and is hence little used. However, it points the way: a regulatory scheme that was simple, compelling, and worked in alignment with incentives would nudge the market towards a preferred result. The take-up would be a choice for the market based on a host of factors.

7.3.6.2 CATSI corporations

In Australia, a particular type of corporation is the so-called CATSI corporation. These are corporations specially designed and set up by and for Aboriginal and Torres Strait Islander people. There is specific Commonwealth legislation dealing with these corporations, the Corporations (Aboriginal and Torres Strait Islander Act 2006 (Cth) (CATSI Act) which provides a bespoke set of rules, guidelines, and relevant corporate law oversight. The Indigenous business sector is one of the fastest growing in Australia, around 12,000–16,000 Australian businesses are Indigenous-owned, and Indigenous self-employment rates suggest this number will grow by around 2,200 by 2026.[25] CATSI corporations require five members, unless the Office of the Registrar of Indigenous Corporations (ORIC) approves a smaller number. Members need to be at least 15 years of age, be Aboriginal or Torres Strait Islander, and can be required to live in a particular Indigenous community. The members are not liable for the debts of the corporation.

7.3.7 The political fault lines of Australian corporate law

Perhaps the clearest expression of an ideological barrier in the CA2001 is the fact that trade unions cannot take advantage of incorporation status in Australia. This is set out in s.116 which bluntly states:

25 National Indigenous Australians Agency, The Indigenous Business Factsheet, 1–4, 1, https://www.niaa.gov.au/sites/default/files/publications/ibss_factsheet.pdf.

CORPORATIONS ACT 2001 - SECT 116
Trade unions cannot be registered

A trade union cannot be registered under this Act.

7.3.8 The ubiquity of Australian corporate law as regards business entities

Partnership law in Australia is a matter for each of the states and territories. They each have a Partnership Act which is based to some degree on the UK Partnership Act 1890. The fact that partnership law is a state and territory matter has not, however, precluded corporate legislation from setting out various directives. The question of the permissible size and scale of partnerships is somewhat curiously a matter set out in the Corporations Act 2001 (Cth). As to the possible size of a partnership or firm in Australia, s.115 of the Corporations Act 2001 (Cth) provides a nationally applicable set of criteria as follows:

CORPORATIONS ACT 2001 - SECT 115
Restrictions on size of partnerships and associations

(1) A person must not participate in the formation of a partnership or association that:

(a) has as an object gain for itself or for any of its members; and
(b) has more than 20 members;

unless the partnership or association is incorporated or formed under an Australian law.
Note: For the effect of a contravention of this section, see section 103.

(2) The regulations may specify a higher number that is higher than the number specified in paragraph (1)(b) for the purposes of the application of that paragraph to a particular kind of partnership or association.
(3) An offence based on subsection (1) is an offence of strict liability.

The default limit is 20 partners. Section 115(2) refers to regulations specifying the number of partners in different partnership contexts:

CORPORATIONS REGULATIONS 2001 - REG 2A.1.01
Size of partnerships or associations

(1) For paragraph 115(1)(b) of the Act, the number prescribed for a kind of partnership or association is the number specified in the following table for that kind of partnership or association:

Item	*Kind of partnership or association*	*Number*
1	(a) Actuaries, medical practitioners, patent attorneys, sharebrokers, stockbrokers or trademark attorneys (b) Partnerships or associations of the kind specified in subregulation (2)	50
2	Architects, pharmaceutical chemists or veterinary surgeons	100
3	Legal practitioners	400
4	Accountants	1 000

Different professions are afforded different levels of flexibility. For example, legal partnerships can comprise 400 partners; accountants by contrast, can have up to 1,000 partners. This configuration can be significant for international and global businesses. The so-called Big Four accounting firms[26] are examples of global businesses with significant Australian 'branches'.

If a partnership gets too big to meet these definitions, it needs to incorporate. Hence, the rules promote the corporate form over all other choice of business entity.

7.4 The durability and persistence of shareholder primacy

The dominance of shareholder primacy is also established by reference to historical conditions and innovations. These include the ongoing prevalence of limited liability for shareholders and the fact that they are not liable for the debts of the corporation as a separate entity, together with the highly liquid nature of investments on the public stock exchange, so that investors can reduce risk by trading out of such stocks they deem too risky.

7.4.1 The important foundation corporate benefit: the possibility of perpetual succession

Corporations though have the intrinsic advantage of perpetual succession. They are set up with the long term, at least theoretically, in mind. They can carry on through and survive the quirks and foibles of successive generations of managers, stakeholders, and owners. When this occurs, it will inevitably involve a good deal of skill, luck, and happenstance. A few rare companies survive from one century to another, and in Australia's corporate landscape, Westpac (which began as the Bank of NSW in 1817, the first bank established in the then colony less than 30 years after the commencement of European colonization in 1788) and the power company Australian Gaslight Company (AGL) established in 1837 are two such corporate rarities.

26 The four global accounting firms (KPMG, Ernst & Young (EY), Deloittes, and Pricewaterhouse-Coopers (PwC)) have large operations in Australia audit, assurance services, taxation, management consulting, advisory, actuarial, corporate finance and legal services.

7.4.2 The use of the corporate group to limit risk and delineate problematic businesses.

7.4.2.1 The concept of the corporate group of companies

The law on corporations and corporate groups provides salient lessons. In the rush to decarbonize, intensively polluting businesses such as major mining corporations will increasingly seek to hive-off problematic carbon-intensive parts of their conglomerate businesses. The group structure offers two key supports—the separate entity status of each of the companies within the group and the limited liability for shareholders, to enable these strategies.

These pillars of Anglo-Australian corporate law, established in the mid-19th century, provide the bedrock certainty for companies and groups of companies in Australia. They are problematic, however, in terms of delivering real action on climate change. They allow a conglomerate to essentially seal-off divisions or chambers of its business. However structured, these divisions may prove unprofitable and house stranded assets.

7.4.3 The centrality of providing capital and income to corporate owners

The board of directors face regular tests of their ability to deliver shareholder returns. This includes the annual issue of dividends and the longer-term issue of capital appreciation. Directors need also to be vigilant about solvency issues as regards the creditors.

Quite legitimately, shareholders purchase shares with self-interest in mind. In the main, they owe only themselves consideration or duty. This may alter if they hold a strategic or significant shareholding which carries with it a layer of legislated responsibilities or codified expectations.

The relevant provision regarding the payment of dividends is s.254T of the Corporations Act 2001 (Cth):

CORPORATIONS ACT 2001 - SECT 254T
Circumstances in which a dividend may be paid

(1) A company must not pay a dividend unless:

(a) the company's assets exceed its liabilities immediately before the dividend is declared and the excess is sufficient for the payment of the dividend; and
(b) the payment of the dividend is fair and reasonable to the company's shareholders as a whole; and
(c) the payment of the dividend does not materially prejudice the company's ability to pay its creditors.

Note 1: As an example, the payment of a dividend would materially prejudice the company's ability to pay its creditors if the company would become insolvent as a result of the payment.

> Note 2: For a director's duty to prevent insolvent trading on payment of dividends, see section 588G.

Whilst shareholders may seek rights of participation, particularly as regards voting, they expect dividends which are competitive within the given market and they seek both short-term income and long-term accrual of capital value. Against this expectation, directors need to bear in mind the tripartite test set out in s.254T.

7.4.3.1 Rio Tinto in 2024: the resumption of shareholder primacy

Nearly four years on from Juukan Gorge, Rio Tinto is a corporate success story. It has made some adjustments by downplaying the role of iron ore and promoting the phrase 'the transition to the low carbon economy':

> We continue to progress important growth opportunities and projects, to bring to market materials critical to the transition to a low-carbon economy: copper, lithium and iron ore, among others. We have a strong portfolio of assets across 6 continents. Many of our products are essential for the energy transition, and our focus is on growing our business while decarbonising, providing products to our customers that support the transition to a low-carbon economy. And looking to the future, the demand will only grow—driven by ongoing urbanisation and the energy transition. The demand we will face through to 2035 will grow around 3.9% per year, with around half stemming from the energy transition.[27]

Growth is intrinsic to the Rio Tinto corporate model:

> our portfolio is well-placed to meet the commodity needs of future generations, but we also need to build a pipeline of organic and inorganic growth opportunities and establish a strong track record of capital-efficient delivery. We are broadening our approach to developing our pipeline of growth options and are testing innovative ways of bringing projects online faster. Through it all, we will maintain our absolute commitment to capital discipline and only pursue opportunities that create value. We are also focused on further building our capabilities in business development and project execution.[28]

The Rio share price has gone from about \$80 in 2020 to \$120,[29] and the historical dividend yield is between five and nine%. By any measure it is a successful company predicated on shareholder primacy and a business suffering few after-effects from the crisis of May 2020. If shareholder primacy was briefly questioned, it is now back in the driving seat.

27 Rio Tinto, Growth, https://www.riotinto.com/en/about/growth.

28 Rio Tinto, n 27.

29 Rio Tinto Ltd, Share Price History.

7.5 Conclusion: the powerful vested interests upholding shareholder primacy

There are many long-term and powerful vested interests which are deeply immersed in upholding current and established corporate law techniques, which are in turn intent on bolstering, strengthening, and reinforcing the norms of shareholder primacy. Company law in Australia reflects this approach. Set and forget has become the basic premise. Shareholder primacy is a victim of its own success and is championed by the Australian Securities Exchange and the Australian superannuation industry. These forces were on display in Australia when the 4th edition of the ASX Corporate Governance Principles and Recommendations was up for debate in 2018–9, as discussed in Chapter 4. Shareholder primacy is a dominant feature of the neoliberal, fossil fuel economy of Australia. It is advocated for and supported by corporate advisers, it is defended by key group such as law and accounting firms. It is the dominant narrative thread of the Corporations Act 2001 (Cth). Conservative think-tanks such as the Institute of Public Affairs and the Business Council of Australia advocate for shareholder primacy. There is a lack of specialist law reform regarding corporate law since the Corporations and Markets Advisory Committee (CAMAC) was disbanded in 2018 after having been established in 1989.[30] As such, the conditions seem ripe for fossil fuel companies to keep promoting shareholder primacy as the guiding light for Australian boards.

References

David Attenborough, *A Life on our Planet*, Penguin, 2020.

Stephen Bottomley, Kath Hall, Peta Spender and Beth Nosworthy, *Contemporary Australian Corporate Law*, Cambridge University Press, 2018,

John Farrar, *Corporate Governance: Theories, Principles, and Practice*, 2nd ed, Oxford University Press, 2006.

Daniel Fischel, 'The Corporate Governance Movement', *Vanderbilt Law Review*, 35, 1982, 1259.

Kent Greenfield, *The Failure of Corporate Law: Fundamental Flaws and Progressive Possibilities*, The University of Chicago Press, 2006.

Hampel Committee on Corporate Governance, Final Report, 1997, The Committee on Corporate Governance and Gee Publishing, 1–65.

Klaus J Hopt, Hideki Kanda, Mark J Roe, Eddy Wymeersch and Stefan Prigge (eds) *Comparative Corporate Governance- The State of the Art and Emerging Research*, Clarendon Press, 1998.

David S. Landes, *Dynasties: Fortunes and Misfortunes of the World's Great Family Businesses*, Viking, 2006.

Phillip Lipton, Abe Herzberg, and Michelle Welsh, *Understanding Company Law*, 20th ed, Thomson Reuters, 2020.

30 Australian Government, The Treasury, Corporations and Markets Advisory Committee (CAMAC), https://treasury.gov.au/policy-topics/business-and-industry/CAMAC. The Abbott conservative LNP government made the decision to abolish CAMAC in the 2014-15 Federal budget.

Reinier R. Kraakman, Paul Davies, Henry Hansmann, Gerard Hertig, Klaus J. Hopt, Hideki Kanda, and Edward B. Rock, *The Anatomy of Corporate Law; A Comparative and Functional Approach*, Oxford University Press, 2005.

David S. Landes, *Dynasties: Fortunes and Misfortunes of the World's Great Family Businesses*, Viking, 2006.

R McQueen, 'Limited Liability Company Legislation- The Australian Experience,' *Australian Journal of Corporations Law*, 22, 1991, 36.

Eddy Wymeersch, 'A Status Report on Corporate Governance Rules and Practices in Some Continental European States,' in Hopt, Klaus J, Hideki Kanda, Mark J Roe, Eddy Wymeersch and Stefan Prigge (eds) *Comparative Corporate Governance- The State of the Art and Emerging Research*, Clarendon Press, 1998, 1045–1199.

8 Recasting corporate law theory

Emerging possibilities in the epoch of the climate emergency

8.1 Corporate law theory: its efficacy in the quest for net zero

8.1.1 The context for investigating corporate theory

The events of the 21st century should mark a paradigm shift in discussion of corporate theory. Gone is the hegemony of the corporation within the stand-alone nation state. Multinational companies have long made the case for international consideration. Acknowledgment of the limits of the natural world and its resources means there is an emerging one world-view which will need to be grappled with. Navigating scarcity and ensuring just distribution will be endemic challenges—not necessarily, but as time goes by. The role of the state vis-à-vis the corporate sector generally and individual companies more specifically will need be necessary precursors to corporate debate.

8.1.2 The elusive nature of corporate law theory

As Bottomley et al. note,

> One difficulty in discussing corporate theory is that theories tend to remain submerged beneath the text of the statute or judicial decisions; they are not always expressly acknowledged or explained. Nevertheless, lawyers, legislators and judges rely implicitly upon these different theories whenever they prefer one decision over another, argue for one interpretation of a section over another, resolve an ambiguity in legal principle one way rather than another, or urge one type of legal reform rather than another (or opt for no reform at all). In different ways, these theories attempt to explain and justify the exercise of corporate power, as well as the exercise of power within the corporation.[1]

1 Stephen Bottomley, Kath Hall, Peta Spender, and Beth Nosworthy, *Contemporary Australian Corporate Law,* Cambridge University Press, 2018, 45.

DOI: 10.4324/9781003263746-9

8.1.3 The range of corporate law theories

There are many theories of the corporation but they variously resort to techniques and strategies that are syllogistic. The company is an artificial legal entity and simulacrum (particularly concerning the claim that the company is somehow anthropomorphic).

The existence of many theories belies the fact that little regard is paid to them within given systems. It is as if they are original and historic artefacts. They are of little importance in the day-to-day cut and thrust of commercial and corporate activity. In a corporate system like Australia's, it is essentially a closed loop. The history of corporate law is largely from the UK and more latterly from the US. As such, Australia's system of corporate law is overwhelmingly organized around the concept of shareholder primacy. It may not invoke a theory but its practice is all encompassing and pivotal. Keeping shareholders content is the modus operandi of the board. Profits distributed to shareholders in the way of dividends or extra shares are the currency of the corporate realm. In turn, capital appreciation in the value of the shares is a lodestar for the company. This is Posner's 'shoot for the stars' paradigm. Companies best seek to do so. The basic binary with the shareholder is with stakeholder systems which are seen as maverick. They may be relevant to countries such as Germany and Japan where employees reign prominently, if not supreme, within the corporate environment, but these modalities are exotic and little else.

There are numerous other ways to invest in and classify corporate theory. We can refer to four basic types of theory. First, fiction or concession theory, second realist or natural entity theory, third economic or contractarian theory, and fourth progressive or communitarian theory.[2] These theories overlap and intersect. They are generally consigned to the first few or last few pages of company law textbooks. They are rarely treated the same by authors on company law. This is the problem of malleable (if not slippery) definitions and terms which is the hallmark problem often of legal scholarship. In the Australian commercial context, for instance, there is no agreed definition of SME or small- and medium-sized enterprise. There are different views and applications, depending on the context. For instance, the Australian Tax Office (ATO), the Australian Bureau of Statistics (ABS), and the corporate regulator, the Australian Securities and Investments Commission (ASIC), each adopt different approaches to this basic concept inherent within commercial activity.

Another approach to corporate theory is to list the various theories.[3] These include concession theory, aggregate theory, economic theories, natural entity theories, organizational perspectives, and corporate social responsibility. Within each of these theories there are, in turn, strands and subcomponents. The challenge

2 See, for example, Jason Harris, *Company Law: Theories, Principles and Applications*, LexisNexis, 2012, 12–27.

3 See, for instance, the approach adopted by Stephen Bottomley, Kath Hall, Peta Spender, and Beth Nosworthy, *Contemporary Australian Corporate Law*, Cambridge University Press, 2018, 44–66.

of the climate crisis and the nature of that urgency for corporations is an opportunity for reconceptualizing the theory and the role of the corporation in the 21st century.

It may be an artificial legal entity but that artifice should not extend to corporate theory often being sidelined and held to little account within the neoliberal orthodoxy of the incumbent economic model.

8.1.4 Corporate law theory and climate change

There are two ways to proceed with this type of discussion. If climate change is seen as minor, as liminal, then the economic model and the corporation and corporate theory within that model continue. The neoliberal model continues. Climate change denialism is an ongoing precondition of this viewpoint.

If, by contrast, climate change is seen as a fundamental disruption to the orthodox economic model, this has inevitable flow-on consequences for the operation and theory of the corporation. This chapter, and indeed this book, proceeds based on this fundamental assumption which was sketched in Chapter 5. That is, climate change is fundamental in that it is redrawing the economic, political, and social landscape. By its nature, it will have profound impacts on the economic model, theory and practice of corporations, and the role of owners and other stakeholders.

Climate change will invoke new ways of governing and regulating. It will challenge the orthodoxy of growth for its own sake. It will render conscious the distribution of goods, services, and profit within an essentially fixed global system of finite capacity. One of the opportunities of the climate change crisis, within this emerging wider context, is the necessary reimagining and re-theorizing of the company. What has been implicit and liminal will need to be explicit and central. There will be a necessary re-examination of the fundamental question, 'from where corporations derive their political and social legitimacy?'[4] To these historically significant criteria will be added contemporary ones including scientific, economic, and international.

8.1.5 Re-examining some corporate law theories in the epoch of the climate emergency

The historical order of corporate law development has been practical mercantile developments, followed by legal principles, and backed up by theoretical understanding. Addressing the climate crisis provides the opportunity to invert this order of doing things.

8.2 Concession theory and the public nature of the corporation

Within the debates that inform contemporary corporate law and theory are two questions. First, should the role of corporate law 'merely be to facilitate the capacity

4 Bottomley et al., n 1, 45.

of people to form and operate corporations, or should it be more interventionist and regulatory?' Second, 'whether corporations are to be regarded as private economic and social actors, or as a significant part of the public dimension of social and economic life?'[5]

Prior to the recent escalation of concern about the climate emergency in recent years, and particularly following the 2018–9 bushfire emergency and the widely held scientific consensus that there is a decade to make significant cuts to CO_2 emissions, these questions may have remained as theoretical tensions not requiring resolution.

Presently, however, it is arguable that in each case, the answer is firmly in the second category, and this aligns with the central thesis of the book. That is, in fundamental terms, the corporation, corporate law, and its theory as we now know it, will undergo unprecedented challenges. Corporate law will likely be more interventionist and regulatory and corporations will increasingly be recognized as part of the public dimension of social and economic life. We need therefore to reimagine corporate law theory to better understand how corporations will navigate this fundamental shift.

The scope of what companies can do, the activities they undertake, and the goods and services they produce will be constrained by the emerging point of scientific limitation; that will reference CO_2 and other greenhouse gas emissions, including methane and nitrous oxide. This necessarily means that concession theory, a long-standing framework of corporate law that has been somewhat liminal, may be reconceptualized and made pivotal to the debate. Concession theory posits that the state grants the corporation a licence to operate via the registration process. Until now, what the company does has been a matter for the shareholders and has been prescribed by the company's constituent documents. In essence, if it is not illegal, then the activity can go ahead. Now there is a growing need to develop a new comprehensive theory of concession which promotes climate solutions, discourages enterprises which cannot provide climate bona fides, and prevent businesses which will do further harm and exacerbate the climate crisis. Environmental sustainability and climate change mitigation are likely to be central drivers of what companies can and should be encouraged to do.

This book posits that foundations will remain; that is, for-profit companies, companies as separate entities, and providing limited liability of members. These are the cornerstones of the modern corporation. The scope, however, of what is socially acceptable and 'legal' as pursuits of the company may increasingly need to be informed by science.

Examining the nature of corporate law theory allows for this new imaginative realm. In particular, a reinvigorated concession theory which looks anew at the scope of what companies are able to do within risk constraints will be a component of the new climate-directed corporate activity.

5 Bottomley et al., n 1, 65.

8.2.1 Versions of the concession theory

The mild or weak version of concession theory is that the state, having issued a certificate of incorporation marking the existence of the corporation as an artificial legal entity, thereafter takes a minimal approach. The company is free to pursue whatever business opportunities its board of directors recommend and owners approve. The role of the state is very light-touch. It will receive any reports and only police allegations of impropriety or illegality under the relevant corporate statutes. It is under no obligation to regulate the company any more than this. It is a moment in time contact between state and entity; once incorporation has passed, the company is free to proceed, save for acts of potential legislative illegality. This *de minimis* model fits neatly within a neoliberal economic approach. The Salomon case is an example of this version of concession theory. The company incorporated by Mr Salomon met the foundation requirements; thereafter, the state was little interested in its oversight. As Bottomley et al, note, 'under this version of concession theory, there is a presumption in favour of government regulation, but it is not a mandate: governments *may* regulate corporate activity'.[6]

By contrast, the strong or demarcated view of concession theory is that the state has an active role in overseeing and regulating the company. The company has been given the privilege of incorporation—a public power conferred on a legal entity—and this is an ongoing legacy for the company. The price of its incorporation and profit-making capacity is to be held accountable to rules made by the state.

It is a creature of statute and hence created by the state. The state is entitled and indeed required to oversee the company.

8.2.2 Controlling corporate activity

As Bottomley et al. note:

> By controlling corporate activity, concession theory has the capacity to emphasize the wider public interest over the private interests of individuals involved in the corporation.[7]

Whether the state can, should or must regulate companies is bound up in the concession theory. The challenge of tackling the climate change emergency means that the strong view of concession theory needs to be revisited and that mandated forms of regulation need to be overseen and enforced.

8.2.3 The ultra vires doctrine: weak control and third-party issues

The ultra vires doctrine gave shape and substance to the more rigorous view of concession theory because a company was required to act within the scope of

6 Bottomley et al, n 1, 47.
7 Bottomley et al, n 1, 47.

its stated objectives. The original power of this position was diluted by the legal device of drafting omnibus provisions so that a company's objects were manifest in a broad array either through many listed items, through a catch all type of provision or via both techniques.

The ultra vires doctrine was a central part of corporate law in Australia until the advent of s.125 of the Corporations Act 2001 (Cth) which recognized that the nature of fixed objects and corporate purposes had become a fiction through these various drafting techniques. These matters were discussed in Chapter 7. It is worth repeating s.125(2) for current purposes:

> **CORPORATIONS ACT 2001 - SECT 125**
> **Constitution may limit powers and set out objects**
>
> (2) If a company has a constitution, it may set out the company's objects. An act of the company is not invalid merely because it is contrary to or beyond any objects in the company's constitution.

The ultra vires doctrine had at least indirectly given the state some degree of control over corporations. Corporations want to be unfettered, or to be restricted as little as possible. The freedom to contract and to carry on business lay at the heart of its removal, at least from the corporations' perspective. Its removal provided clarity for third parties.

Alongside the removal of ultra vires, the Act endows companies with adult status:

> **CORPORATIONS ACT 2001 - SECT 124**
> **Legal capacity and powers of a company**
>
> (1) A company has the legal capacity and powers of an individual both in and outside this jurisdiction

It could be argued that for companies the legislative terms have become too generous. The removal of ultra vires gives a company the ability to act with impunity as regards its stated objects. Couple this with the fact that companies have the powers of an adult person and together, these two features theoretically provide a company with untrammelled power, bearing little responsibility in return. An adult without responsibility is an unlikely concept. How then will corporate law lay the groundwork for the adult company operating responsibly in the climate emergency?

8.3 Identifying the socially informed elements of the corporation

There are both private and public law aspects to the duty of directors, just as there are private and public aspects to incorporation. There are privileges afforded on incorporation (for example, limited liability) and there are obligations extracted (for example, the mandatory nature of reporting to ASIC).

Directors are enabled to run the company profitably, subject to the internal rules of the constitution, the guardrails provided by Ch 2D CA2001) and any relevant general law. These is not a simple one-sided equation. Instead, there is a binary or set of correlatives, the right to act tempered by the obligation to do so within the rules.

The irony is acute that the corporate sector and its loyal adherents railed against the notion of the social licence to operate being explicitly embedded in the ASX 4th edition. This obscures the immense political and *social power* wielded by large corporations, as an inherent aspect of their armoury. John Parkinson notes that large companies, especially valuable companies which are publicly listed on the stock exchange and who employ many people, are different from other interest groups in society because they have real 'social decision-making power' or influence in two ways:

- Directly through interest groups to make representations to government to influence government policy.
- Structurally because of the crucial role boards and managers exercise over production, investment and employment decisions which shape the economic and political environment within which Governments make policy.[8]

These factors give large corporations enhanced bargaining power and influence.[9] These listed public entities are the most powerful corporate actors in Australia They have access to lobbyists and government; they comprise the membership of key groups such as the ASX CG Council. As part of their economic footprint, they have access to global capital markets and to the full suite of behind-the-scenes power and influence. The current *de minimis* law on the books is in their favour. It seeks little and demands nothing. They daily define and use considerable social power to advance their agenda, ideology, and strategy. If, on the other hand, social licence is inverted, and imposed on them, they very effectively counter this argument. They will, in effect, refrain from being accountable for any understanding of social obligation.

The rebuttal is carried out both directly and by proxies. It is sustained and persistent. The role played by major law firms and the peak body, the Law Council of Australia, provide signal examples of this representative and advocacy model.[10] Indeed the Law Council of Australia is one of the 19 members of the ASX Corporate Governance Council.[11] The connections, links, and overlaps run deep and wide.

8 Parkinson, J.E., *Corporate Power and Responsibility: Issues in the Theory of Company Law*, Oxford University Press, 1993, 19.

9 Parkinson, n 8, 20.

10 ASX Corporate Governance Council Launch of The 4th Edition of The Corporate Governance Principles & Recommendations, Address by The Chair of The ASX Corporate Governance Council Elizabeth Johnstone, 27 February 2019, https://www.asx.com au/content/dam/asx/about/corporate-governance-council/ej-speech-press-version.pdf

11 ASX Corporate Governance Council Launch, Address by The Chair, n 11.

8.3.1 The economic licence to operate and correctives: ESG, CSR, and SLTO

The economic licence (indeed, mandate) to operate is the bulwark against which an alternative narrative is increasingly being developed. The role of social licence to operate is a mechanism which provides the foundations for demanding ethical and constructive behaviour of corporations, rather than simple technical legal compliance. It can enable reinvestment of 'the personal'—and consideration of social and environmental consequences—directly into the core of the corporate entity. The role of the company in the 21st century will be increasingly examined in terms of the pertinent theories, namely the social licence to operate (SLTO), corporate social responsibility (CSR), and—more generally—environmental social governance (ESG).

Despite the potential theoretical niceties of a company acting with justice in mind, the practical notion of a money-making entity for owners or shareholders is the dominant operating paradigm. For large, multi-national companies, such as Rio Tinto, and indeed the trillion-dollar technology companies,[12] this is an extension of the idea of the company as global behemoth profiteering out of sight and out of mind in distant lands in the 19th century even if distance between perpetrator and owner is collapsed within the corporate structure. Today, acts of malfeasance may occur in plain sight, yet are given fiat by entrenched formal corporate theories and interests.

In the climate emergency economy, corporate success will be vital to solving the climate crisis, but it won't simply reflect corporate law theory as it currently stands. The predominance of shareholder primacy needs to be examined via the rapid emergence of competing interests and stakeholders. This will likely move CSR, SLTO, and certain other corporate theories from the margins to the mainstream.

8.4 Social Licence to Operate (SLTO)

The concept of social licence to operate may be, somewhat conveniently, regarded by its critics as problematic due to being it being characterized as amorphous, or as hard to define.[13] It has been described as 'a concept in search of a definition and boundaries'.[14] Although it needs to be noted that the context to these types of criticisms is relevant. This characterization of SLTO by David Bursey, a Canadian resources lawyer is the essentially pejorative opinion emanating from the mining and resources sector and its proxies. It is remarkably similar in this regard to opposition to the ASX 4th edition. It simultaneous makes out the proposition is

12 In 2020, at least four of these businesses have surpassed market valuation more than $1 trillion US. These include Apple, Alphabet (parent of Google), Amazon, and Microsoft.

13 Rosemary Teele Langford, 'Social Licence to Operate and Directors' Duties: Is there a Need for Change?' *Company & Securities Law Journal 37,* (2019), 200–18, 200.

14 David Bursey, 'Rethinking Social Licence to Operate: A concept in Search of Definition and Boundaries', Business Council of British Columbia, *Environment and Energy Bulletin*, Vol. 7, Issue 2, May 2015.

vague ('a concept in search of definition') and also that it also requires immediate containment and limitation ('a concept in search of....boundaries.')[15] Despite this dual line of attack, it is a concept increasingly to the fore in corporate debates.

8.4.1 Greenwashing in sport, the arts and community organizations

Greenwashing appears to be the new normal for fossil fuel companies, whether it is logos on the jumpers of sports teams,[16] platinum sponsorship deals (discussed below as regards Australian netball) and further afield, or the Royal Shakespeare company's sponsorship deal with British Petroleum (BP) which was ended by a public campaign:

> The Royal Shakespeare Company is to end its sponsorship deal with BP amid growing opposition to fossil fuel companies' sponsorship of many of the UK's leading cultural institutions. The RSC announced that after months of deliberations and a vociferous campaign from artists, the public and environmentalists, it had decided to curtail its eight-year relationship. Jess Worth, the co-director of the campaign group Culture Unstained, said the decision was 'fantastic news' that signalled the end of fossil fuel sponsorship of the arts. 'The RSC has understood that a climate emergency means that business as usual cannot continue, and we congratulate them for showing leadership.'[17]

In Australia corporate greenwashing occurs on an industrial scale:

> Fossil fuel interests have signed more than 500 sponsorship deals with Australian arts, sport, education and community organisations, prompting accusations they are 'engineering a social licence to operate' in the face of growing public pressure on coal, gas and oil. The oil and gas company Woodside Energy was the most frequent entrant on a list of 535 sponsorship agreements, having signed 56 deals, including with AFL team the Fremantle Dockers and the West Australian Nippers surf lifesaving program. Santos, another oil and gas business, had 41 known sponsorships. BHP, which maintains coal interests but this year sold its petroleum assets to Woodside, had 44 and was linked to another seven through an associated entity, the BHP-Mitsubishi Alliance.[18]

15 Bursey, n 14.

16 For example the Woodside logo prominent on the guernseys of the AFL side, the Fremantle Dockers.

17 Matthew Taylor, 'Royal Shakespeare Company to end BP sponsorship deal', *The Guardian*, 3 Oct 2019, https://www.theguardian.com/stage/2019/oct/02/royal-shakespeare-company-to-end-bp-sponsorship-deal.

18 Royce Kurmelovs, 'Fossil fuel interests revealed to have sponsored more than 500 Australian community organizations', *The Guardian*, 27 Dec 2022, https://www.theguardian.com/environment/2022/dec/27/fossil-fuel-interests-revealed-to-have-signed-more-than-500-sponsorship-deals

It is a pervasive corporate technique and 'depending on the organization and the type of partnership, some are thought to be worth a few thousand dollars. Others, including naming rights deals on major venues or events, can run into the millions.'[19]

The deals are about building brand influence and turning negative perceptions around by obfuscation:

> It's a subtle way of trying to engineer social support, or continued social support, for these polluting products. Most of these companies don't sell to the general population. There's no reason for them to be spending millions of dollars on sports and arts sponsorships. What they're trying to do is sell their brand.[20]

The strategies adopted by companies with their sports sponsorship deals are clearly aimed at winning over sceptics, building social licence, and providing a competing narrative over which they have control. In this way, SLTO is constructed over time. However, it can be disrupted, if not ruptured, by a sudden event. This was the case with Rio Tinto essentially oblivious in the lead up to the explosions it set off in the Juukan Gorge. Another corporate case study out of WA is illustrative.

8.4.2 Roy Hill and the Australian Diamonds national netball team

This involved the national netball team and its sponsor, a mining company. The Australian Diamonds is a reference to the national netball team who have been very successful on the global stage for many years. The team has only ever had three indigenous players. The current indigenous player, recently selected, comes from WA which is where the sponsoring company Roy Hill's business is based. The chairman of the company is Gina Rinehart, a wealthy second generation miner. Her father, Lang Hancock was the company founder. In 1984, he made deeply racist and offensive comments regarding indigenous people. As such, in 2022, the newly selected indigenous player did not want to wear the uniform with the sponsor's name on it. This was personal, singular, and specific. The rest of the team, on finding out these facts, joined their team-mate in an act of solidarity.

The company mischaracterized the issues and adopted an overtly political narrative; it was clearly using sport to broaden its appeal and its public perception. Instead, the company tried to portray the sports team as being used for shallow and insincere social purposes:

-with-australian-bodies#:~:text=Fossil%20fuel%20interests%20have%20signed,on%20coal%2C%20gas%20and%20oil.

19 Royce Kurmelovs, 'Fossil fuel interests revealed to have sponsored more than 500 Australian community organizations', *The Guardian*, 27 Dec 2022, https://www.theguardian.com/environment/2022/dec/27/fossil-fuel-interests-revealed-to-have-signed-more-than-500-sponsorship-deals-with-australian-bodies#:~:text=Fossil%20fuel%20interests%20have%20signed,on%20coal%2C%20gas%20and%20oil.

20 Kurmelovs, n 19.

> Hancock and its executive chairman Mrs Rinehart consider that it is unnecessary for sports organisations to be used as the vehicle for social or political causes ... there are more targeted and genuine ways to progress social or political causes without virtue signalling or for self-publicity.[21]

The company alluded to it being the most successful private company in the nation:

> Hancock, and similarly Roy Hill, embarked on these proposed partnerships in good faith and on the basis of representations and its resulting understanding that Netball Australia and the sport's key stakeholder. groups including the Australian Diamonds, were united in their support of one of West Australia's preeminent mining companies becoming their principal sponsor. Particularly given Hancock is the most successful private company in Australia, indeed in Australia's history, and the Australian Diamonds strive to be a highly successful Australian netball team.[22]

Rather than apologize and deal with the issue in a culturally sensitive manner, the company abruptly ended its sponsorship. Under the heading 'seeking a scapegoat' the company noted that:

> Rinehart, who has funded charities providing schooling, scholarships, and employment opportunities for Indigenous youth through Hancock Prospecting, declined to be blamed for her deceased father's words, and has pulled the plug on Hancock's $15 million sponsorship.[23]

In a convoluted defence, Roy Hill noted that:

> Contrary to recent media, Hancock has not insisted that its name be worn by the Australian Diamonds in the current Constellation Cup series when overseas and was advised that the netballers had no concerns in wearing the name on the team dress for the series. Further, Hancock does not support gambling or smoking.[24]

This curiously returns to the list of problematic industries, including gambling, identified by the ASX as discussed in Chapter 4.

21 *The Guardian*, Australia Associated Press, 'Netball Australia boss says sport must balance "social conversations" with "commercial realities"', 23 October 2022 https://www.theguardian.com/sport/2022/oct/23/netball-australia-boss-says-sport-must-balance-social-conversations-with-commercial-realities#:~:text=Netball%20Australia%20boss%20says%20sport,realities'%20%7C%20Netball%20%7C%20The%20Guardian.

22 Roy Hill, 'Hancock Prospecting withdraws netball support: Announcement comes after Australian Diamonds players raised concerns', *News*, 23 Oct 2022, https://www.royhill.com.au/hancock-prospecting-withdraws-netball-support-announcement-comes-after-australian-diamonds-players-raised-concerns/.

23 Roy Hill, 'Cult-of-victimhood – Netball Australi vs Gina Rinehart', Roy Hill, 3 Nov 2022, https://www.royhill.com.au/cult-of-victimhood-netball-australia-vs-gina-rinehart/.

24 Roy Hill, *News*, n 22.

8.4.3 Beyond the SLTO realm—the case of the casinos—can gambling ever hold onto a fully operative social licence?

There are basically three business formats in terms of the association with SLTO. This includes its case for possession, its case for keeping, and its case for retaining on terms conducive to business success. Some industries are problematic in terms of SLTO in any form, and by reference to any manner of conducting the business. Other business arenas may obtain and keep SLTO, if they act in a certain way and channel their business structures, strategies, and operational plans in a deliberative manner. At the core of the concept, exist some industries which have, and can demonstrate, a natural connection with, and affinity for, the SLTO concept.[25]

Gambling sits in the narrow channel category. The industry is regulated, and the level of regulatory compliance is supposedly critical because the costs of failure are high: addiction, people in huge debt, money laundering, and so on. The industry survives despite regular damning reviews; it is symbiotically linked with government coffers and the revenue it produces silences effective arm's length oversight. The concept in Australia of people having a punt or a 'flutter'—on the horses, or the 'pokies'—is part of cultural and social folklore. Indeed, even ANZAC day, the national time of mourning for war victims and their sacrifice, is accompanied by games across the nation of two-up with old fashioned coins. The Melbourne Cup two-mile horse race has long been immortalized as the race that stops a nation and is also the day on which national gambling peaks.

8.5 Corporate Social Responsibility (CSR)

The arguably more established CSR movement has promoted a range of stakeholders beyond shareholders. This may include employees, consumers, and environmental concerns. CSR is referred to as 'a description of what is required or desired of companies, whereas social licence to operate is a description of the legitimacy of a company and its permission or reception by society'.[26] In this sense, CSR is the wider aspirational term of goals and aspirations in a broad sense, and SLTO is the more specific emanation of those goals. This is the notion of a concept embedded within a broader methodology.

Alternatively, it has been argued there is a linear relationship linking the goal of CSR with the outcome of SLTO. For instance, David Bursey notes that 'project developers often talk about social licence as the outcome of a commitment to corporate social responsibility'.[27] Bursey offers another view where he notes that 'others often expect something deeper, akin to demonstrable community acceptance'.[28]

25 The Body Shop 1975–2024 was in this core category with its innovations, including eschewing animal testing on its products which created a global trend.

26 Rosemary Teele Langford, n 13, 204.

27 Bursey, n 14.

28 Bursey, n 14.

That is, companies gain their initial licence to operate from the government, but SLTO means that they may forfeit that licence or legitimacy within the community in which they operate (and putatively serve). It speaks to a symbiotic relationship between corporation and context. Whilst it is a developing and contested concept, mapping its contours will be a key part of 21st-century law. In essence, shareholders are educating themselves, talking back, and holding the company to account.

It has been a convenient side system, the feel-good aspect of the business. Well-resourced companies can do this adeptly and do so. It can usefully distract and deflect from businesses which would otherwise be subject to more robust scrutiny.

> If CSR is to be a useful concept in our context, this would require first of all that CSR must encompass both the level of legal compliance and action beyond minimal legal standards. Second, CSR must go beyond community and charitable contributions to deal with the core business of the company, how that is conducted, and the social and environmental impacts of that business. Furthermore, CSR must entail an integration of environmental (and social) concerns in the decision-making of the company in such a way as to lead to an internalisation of costly externalities.[29]

In any event, the UK has shifted to a model of enlightened shareholder value, departing from the simplicity of shareholder primacy. As Brenda Hannigan observes of the UK context:

> Of course, corporate social responsibility (CSR) is now an important issue in its own right to which large companies, in particular, pay considerable regard. To some extent, therefore, this aspect of s.172 has been overtaken by events. Ideas which seemed radical (eg the disclosure of CSR-type activities) … are now commonplace … At one level, it may be said that the law is playing catch-up with a developing business culture which does look to a much wider agenda and broader constituencies than merely a company's own shareholders.[30]

8.5.1 Companies central to the fossil fuel economy have relied on economic success to avoid scrutiny and wider accountability

This model, first developed and perfected by the East India Company in its 270-year operational 'reign' is still relevant, in a political economy such as Australia. The nation provides an intensely loyal version of shareholder primacy. This is part of its industrial and historical DNA as Judith Brett forcefully demonstrates.[31] It

29 Beate Sjafjell and Benjamin J Richardson, 'The Future of Company Law and Sustainability', in Beate Sjafjell and Benjamin J Richardson (eds), *Company Law and Sustainability: Legal Barriers and Opportunities*, Cambridge University Press, 2019, 315.

30 Brenda Hannigan, *Company Law*, 3rd edn., OUP, 198.

31 Judith Brett, 'The Coal Curse: Resources, Climate and Australia's Future', *Quarterly Essay*, Black Inc. Books, Issue 78, 2020, 1–78.

gives rise to a national narrative and crucially in turn to what is measured, valued, and celebrated. Economic might and success are the pre-eminent yardsticks by which a host nation, such as Australia, views sectors of the economy and the companies making them up. As noted, they are prominent listed companies, and make relentless claims social capital and corporate responsibility by pointing to schools and hospitals that their activities, they claim, underwrite. They assiduously countenance the support and loyalty of the local communities in which they operate.[32]

8.5.1.1 Santos at the COP26, Glasgow, November 2021

This may be valid enough, but it needs to be seen in its fuller context. It should not buy opacity or a lack of accountability. Just as a balance sheet examines both sides of the corporate equation, social capital allocation by a company needs to be viewed against the broader context of what the company does, its core activities, and how it generates its revenues and profits. If they are problematic, the CSR and ESG initiatives need to be seen within that wider context. Fossil fuel companies are very good at seeking that only their CSR issues are examined. If their CSR credentials are questioned, they can become very sensitive. An example of this was the withdrawal of support for Netball Australia.[33] Such companies boast their CSR credentials and this can be enabled and underwritten by government approval and largesse; perhaps the best example in the Australian government context is COP26 in Glasgow where the conservative, Morison-led LNP government allowed Santos, the gas producer to occupy the key site for the nation in the international pavilion. The government allocated to a corporation producing high levels of methane gas, the ability to spruik its climate credentials with unproven technologies such as CCS carbon capture and storage. The for-profit business was able to conflate its views and advocacy with that of the nation. The danger with CSR is that it can misprized to this extent. Hence the Climate Council campaign to end fossil fuel sponsorship from 'sports, arts, and events'.[34]

The current left-wing Labor government is not much advanced on this stance. The increasingly irrefutable point for governments seeking to prove they take the science of the unfolding climate catastrophe seriously is to step in and put in place a clear-cut moratorium on new coal and gas projects and on the requests for extensions in time, scope, or scale of current and existing projects. No other market signal will be more effective. If this 'say no' campaign was in place, changes to directors' duties and so forth could follow. As the *Global Tipping Points Summary Report* makes clear 'countries should reassess their highest possible ambitions

32 Royce Kurmelovs, n 19.

33 Roy Hill, News, n 22.

34 Climate Council of Australia Ltd, Fossil Fuel Free Sponsorship Code, 'Calling Time: How to remove fossil fuel sponsorship from sports, arts, and events', 2023, 1–51, https://www.climatecouncil.org.au/wp-content/uploads/2023/06/CC_MVSA0356-CC-Report-Fossil-Fuel-Free-Sponsorship-Code_V5-FA-Screen-Single.pdf.

… particularly *wealthy, high-emitting nations*' (emphasis added).[35] Australia is an exemplar of this definition. There needs to be in evidence a strong policy and regulatory stand from the top to establish the point of principle; change can then cascade downwards.

8.5.2 The BHP Samarco dam disaster

The formal law as regards directors' duties is necessarily conducted via a courtroom or other evidence based proceeding, such as an ASIC investigation, often years after the salient events. It is necessarily a narrow retrospective analysis of a director's behaviour often years after the event through a thicket of documents, meeting notes, and incomplete recall. Resorting to shareholder primacy and the need to make a profit can blunt such investigations.

By contrast, ESG or CSR can be seen as prospective checklists for doing business, and as retrospective checklists for business carried out. They do not preclude shareholder primacy, but they set it within a broader operating context. It may be a *primus inter pares* approach to make profit and to distribute it where possible, but how the profit is made and how the firm's reputational index is improved can be just as important, especially in the case of ecological and human disaster. This was the dilemma for BHP, the Australian mining company, regarding the Samarco dam disaster in Brazil in 2015 as a result of the joint venture between BHP and Brazilian mining behemoth, Vale:

> The collapse of the Fundao dam in 2015 caused 40 million cubic metres of mining waste to pour downstream into the villages of Bento Rodrigues and Paracatu de Baixo, killing 19 people. It is the worst recorded environmental disaster in the industry, both in terms of the volume of tailings dumped and the magnitude of the damage, with pollution stretching for 668 kilometres from the Doce River to the Atlantic Ocean.[36]

Litigation is ongoing. Adopting a stakeholder approach is also increasingly how big complex matters are settled:

> London-based law firm Pogust Goodhead says the claim could amount to £36 billion ($67 billion) and have sent representatives to meet this week with major investors and federal Environment Minister Tanya Plibersek. Tom Goodhead, the law firm's global managing partner and chief executive, said court action was only one element in its strategy of pursuing BHP over the deadly 2015 disaster. 'I've come here to speak to people in BHP's

35 Global Tipping Points, Summary, University of Exeter, 6 December 2023, https://global-tipping-points.org/summary-report/narrative-summary/.

36 Tom Rabe, 'Lawyers behind BHP class action warn of investor risk', Financial Review, 15 May 2023, https://www.afr.com/companies/mining/lawyers-behind-bhp-class-action-warn-of-investor-risk-20230515-p5d8h3.

> backyard .... As a lawyer, there's only so much you can actually do in the courtroom on this, to be honest,' he said in Perth on Monday, before flying to Melbourne, Sydney and Brisbane to meet with superannuation funds, MPs and trade unions. 'Unless you really engage in politics and in the financial markets in particular, especially with a company like BHP, then you're never really going to see an effective resolution to something like this.'[37]

It also points to the fact the global businesses cannot insulate their legal liabilities to national jurisdictions of their choice. Tom Goodhead said of the class action:

> the company should not be insulated in Australia from its conduct overseas, and pointed to the ramifications faced by Rio Tinto executives after the Juukan Gorge destruction. I think the way that BHP has treated Indigenous communities in Brazil, in particular, stands in complete contrast to anything that they ever could have got away with here in Australia or in Canada or in the United States. Imagine this had happened in the UK or imagine this had happened in Australia. With it happening in Brazil as well, not happening in the UK or Australia, the public awareness of it has diminished over time. BHP is obviously an Australian national icon. I think that the message is really that we would seek that government, that shareholders and that civil society encourage BHP to do the right thing. [38]

BHP faces multiple ongoing lawsuits, and has recently been ordered by a Brazilian court to pay, together with Vale, nearly $15bn in damages.[39] This ongoing delay and reticence in tackling climate change is damaging to Australia's social fabric and economic capacity.[40] As Judith Brett notes, Australia risks 'being boycotted by global capital and marginalised.'[41] Australian economic and corporate law policies urgently require a fundamental reset. Adherents of fossil fuel extraction/climate denial cling to their 'beliefs', despite the clear scientific and financial evidence. As such, defining the contours of the social licence to operate and the scope of corporate responsibility informs the essential corporate law and governance debates of the 21st century, and yet hegemonic Australian fossil fuel seeks to defer this advance and to variously ignore or belittle its intent. In an interconnected but historically informed world, the example of the UK stands in distinct, if not stark, contrast to Australia's current corporate paucity.

The provocation for corporate law in Australia, therefore, is to move from the periphery to the centre in this debate; principle 3 in the ASX 4th edition is an

37 Rabe, n 36.

38 Tom Rabe, n 36.

39 The Guardian, 'BHP and Vale ordered to pay $15bn un damages for 2015 Brazil dam collapse,' 26 Jan 2024, https://www.theguardian.com/world/2024/jan/26/brazil-dam-collapse-mariana-bhp-vale-samarco-15bn-damages-payout.

40 This adherence to times past and 20th century economics has been referred to as displaying 'a comical degree of self confidence,' referencing Robert Manne, Brett n 31.

41 Brett n 31, 70.

example of conveniently deferring the issue. It will not, however conveniently vanish, as the Rio Tinto episode confirms. The company as a legal entity able to meet the expectations of its stakeholders in their various realms—whether social, political, and economic—requires nothing less.

As such, this is as much a challenge to corporate law, as it is for companies and what they do. The law, with its divisions and categorizations based on historical causes of action, has to date not found a way to deal holistically with the immense and rapidly evolving challenges of climate change. Global heating calls into question all the hitherto specialist areas of law to address the issue. Environmental law, for example, has largely focused to date on marginal issues of licencing and so forth. By contrast, corporate law has the capacity to go to the very issues of the efficient, fair, just, and sustainable allocation of capital.[42] Corporate law can and should, therefore, simultaneously enunciate high principles of corporate behaviour and be able to provide a vital prism through which the forces of climate change can be met head-on. The theory and the practice of the modern company as responsible, effective, and intergenerational in meeting its myriad contexts need to be grappled with as never before. Reforms which are fit for purpose for the 21st century are the simply stated aim of what is required.

8.6 The emerging factors controlling corporate behaviour

8.6.1 The example of the world's biggest investment business

The corporate law and governance are being deployed as devices to enable this continuation, and to defer debate and reform. With global heating now fundamentally altering the nature and outlook of international capital flows away from fossil fuels and carbon emitting extractive industries as Blackrock—the world's largest investor—has done.[43] Blackrock's sheer size and global reach matters according to economist John Quiggin:

> The announcement matters, in part because of Blackrock's sheer size. It is the world's largest investor, with a total of $US7 trillion in funds under its control. Its announcement it will 'put climate change at the center of its investment strategy' raises questions about the soundness of smaller financial institutions that remain committed to coal and to a carbon-based economy.[44]

Larry Fink is accused by the US right of conducting some sort of Marxist plot:

42 Joanna Partridge, 'BlackRock votes against 49 companies for lack of climate crisis progress: World's largest asset manager reveals votes against directors on environment issues', *The Guardian,* Fri 18 Sep 2020, https://www.theguardian.com/business/2020/sep/17/blackrock-votes-against-49-companies-for-lack-of-climate-crisis-progress.

43 John Quiggin, 'BlackRock is the canary in the coalmine. Its decision to dump coal signals what's next', *The Conversation,* 16 January 2020, https://theconversation.com/blackrock-is-the-canary-in-the-coalmine-its-decision-to-dump-coal-signals-whats-next-129972.

44 Quiggin, n 43.

So what explains this fantastical rhetoric about ESG being the road to Marxist tyranny? In my view, it shows just how much the intellectual foundations of conservatism and liberalism have been debased in a media marketplace that favours reactionary emotionalism over tempered thought. Economic conservatism (rooted in the belief in free markets, globalisation and small government) has become disconnected from social and political conservatism (especially as related to climate activism, social justice and diversity and inclusion).[45]

8.6.2 *The ramifications for wider business reform*

This chapter has examined some of the theoretical and political bases of corporate law given the challenge that can be expressed as a question: How to achieve corporate and business innovation that delivers both reductions in carbon emissions and provides business with sufficient incentives to participate in an ongoing and sustained manner, given the totality of the rules of the game? The will of governments to act and to use their wide legislative and regulatory powers is key. They set the rules of the game. In terms of theories, some of these such as the concession theory intersect with political action or inaction. The rights and privileges granted to companies are in the gift of the legislation, in just the same way as are the costs and responsibilities.

There are two related challenges for the Australian government in terms of the business and corporate sector. First, has there been the unwitting creation in Australia of a business monoculture, given the popularity of the pty ltd company, at the expense of unincorporated business entities? Second, how to enable the rise of the not-for-profit entity, and the 'for purpose' entity and the 'rewilding' for a more varied and robust business habitat? Unfortunately, these two issues are beyond the scope of this present work.

8.7 Conclusion: what have companies railed against?

Well-resourced companies will lobby hard when required. What concerns such companies are those matters by which they get exercised, absorbed, or fixated. Often this may be behind the scenes and hard to trace. By contrast, sometimes this takes on the guise of a campaign and is obvious and on the public record. These are the issues that they put resources into challenging, defending, and defeating either directly or through proxies such as peak bodies, professional advisors, and the like. This pattern of activity demonstrates what concerns them.

Mainstream formal corporate law has not changed in relation to the challenge of climate change. It could, but it is still focused on rules and predicated on free

45 Carl Rhodes, 'No, BlackRock is not leading a Marxist assault on capitalism', *The Conversation*, 6 April 2023, https://theconversation.com/no-blackrock-is-not-leading-a-marxist-assault-on-capitalism-203042.

market orthodoxy. There is a lack of political will. The short-term winner takes all nature of the Australian political cycle means that insufficient time and attention is given to a full—and proper—time dimension to 2050. In the case of Australia, three decades is the equivalent of ten, three-year political terms. The challenge is to develop a coordinated and consistent plan for this period informed by clear rules and backed by cogent regulation. The ideal would be an apolitical approach.

As Kent Greenfield notes, a model of corporate law can recognize the legitimate interests of shareholders without deifying them:

> I believe that the best corporate model is one that gives due regard to the goal of realizing the preference of shareholders but also does not deify those preferences at the expense of other stakeholders, the firm as a whole, or society in general. If what we care about are the concerns of all the corporation's stakeholders, then a 'stakeholder model' is likely to be more efficient in achieving that goal than a model that focuses on shareholders and managers only.[46]

In the last several years in corporate Australia one issue has stood out. It involved the proposed introduction of a social licence provision in the 4th edition of the Australian Securities Exchange listing rules and caused a flurry of activity and intense opposition. The symbolic nature of that localized issue is likely to be minor as climate action takes effect.

By contrast, the issue that will fundamentally alter corporate behaviour is encapsulated in the new international accounting standards for financial disclosure as regards climate change and sustainability. These standards as they will apply in Australia are discussed in Chapter 9.

References

Stephen Bottomley, Kath Hall, Peta Spender, and Beth Nosworthy, *Contemporary Australian Corporate Law*, Cambridge University Press, 2018.

Judith Brett, 'The Coal Curse: Resources, Climate and Australia's Future', *Quarterly Essay, Black Inc. Books*, 78, 2020, 1–78.

David Bursey, 'Rethinking Social Licence to Operate- A concept in Search of Definition and Boundaries,' *Business Council of British Columbia, Environment and Energy Bulletin*, 7(2), May 2015, 1–3.

Janet Dine, *The Governance of Corporate Groups*, *Cambridge Studies in Corporate Law*, Cambridge University Press, 2000.

Kent Greenfield, *The Failure of Corporate Law: Fundamental Flaws and Progressive Possibilities*, The University of Chicago Press, 2006.

Jason Harris, *Company Law: Theories, Principles and Applications*, LexisNexis, 2012.

Rosemary Teele Langford, 'Social Licence to Operate and Directors' Duties: Is there a Need for Change?' *Company & Securities Law Journal*, 37, 2019, 200–218.

Michael Legg, *Regulation, Litigation and Enforcement*, Lawbook Co, 2011.

46 Kent Greenfield, *The Failure of Corporate Law: Fundamental Flaws and Progressive Possibilities*, The University of Chicago Press, 2006, 27.

J.E. Parkinson, *Corporate Power and Responsibility: Issues in the Theory of Company Law*, OUP, 1993.

Guy Pearse, 'Quarry Vision: Coal, Climate Change and the End of the Resources Boom,' *Quarterly Essay* 33, 6 March 2009.

John Quiggin, 'Blackrock is the canary in the coalmine. Its decision to dump coal signals what's next,' *The Conversation*, 16 January 2020.

Carl Rhodes, 'No, BlackRock is not leading a Marxist assault on capitalism', *The Conversation.* https://theconversation.com/no-blackrock-is-not-leading-a-marxist-assault-on-capitalism-203042

Beate Sjafjell and Benjamin J Richardson, 'Chapter 8, The Future of Company Law and Sustainability,' in Beate Sjafjell and Benjamin J Richardson (eds) *Company Law and Sustainability: Legal Barriers and Opportunities*, Cambridge University Press, 2015, 312–340.

Rosemary Teele Langford, 'Social Licence to Operate and Directors' Duties: Is there a Need for Change?' *Company & Securities Law Journal*, 37, 2018, 200–218.

Raymond Williams, *Key Words: A Vocabulary of Culture and Society*, Croom Helm, 1976.

9 The sustainable corporation in the epoch of net zero

9.1 Identifying the elements of the 'sustainable corporation'

Critically thinking about the role and purpose of companies and the scope and efficacy of corporate law theory is central to the work demanded in this decade. Reconceptualizing the corporation and challenging the long-held hegemonic model of the company is necessary and important. Corporate law may not be able to simply stand for maintaining the status quo, for vested interests, and for the incumbency mindset. It will need to be adaptive, responsive, and reflexive. Gordon Brown, the former UK Prime Minister and Chancellor, observes in reviewing Bill Gates' new book (Bill Gates, *How to Avoid a Climate Disaster*, Penguin, 2021) as regards the challenge for corporate law:

> new corporate laws should be agreed, to be applied worldwide, that ensure global companies disclose their carbon footprints, adopt impact-weighted accounting that would reveal the full environmental cost of their operations, and break with business-as-usual by publishing transition plans to a zero net carbon economy.[1]

The reference to worldwide corporate laws also recalls the convergence debate and the so-called end of corporate law history thesis.[2] We are entering an era where business-as-usual in corporate law and governance is at an end, or at least must generate new beginnings. As Sir David King, the former UK Chief Scientific Advisor, observes 'what we as humanity together do over the next four to five years may well determine the future of humanity for the next few thousand years'.[3] This imperative, driven by science, requires disciplines such as corporate law to examine

1 Gordon Brown, 'How to Avoid a Climate Disaster by Bill Gates review why science isn't enough', *The Guardian*, Review, 17 Feb 2021.

2 Henry Hansmann and Reinier Kraakman, 'The End of History for Corporate Law', 10 March 2000, *Yale Law School Working Paper No. 235; NYU Working Paper No. 013; Harvard Law School Discussion Paper No. 280; Yale SOM Working Paper No. ICF - 00-09.*

Hansmann, H and Kraakman, R, 'Towards a Single Model of Corporate Law?' in McCahery, Joseph A, Piet Moerland, Theo Raaijmakers and Luc Renneboog (eds), *Corporate Governance Regimes: Convergence and Diversity*, Oxford University Press, Oxford, 2002, 56–82.

3 ABC, 7.30 Report, https://iview.abc.net.au/video/NC2101H061S00.

DOI: 10.4324/9781003263746-10

and critique fundamental precepts. Corporate law can be a progressive force for change. As Ross Garnaut argues, a country like Australia could be a leader, not a laggard and this is a challenge to the corporate sector. This is encapsulated by the prescient observations made by Christopher Wright and Daniel Nyberg in 2015 which are as urgent as ever:

> Our message is that many of the corporate world's responses to climate change, despite representing a profoundly significant influence, can more accurately be described as narratives or, better still, myths. Like Plato's original Noble Lie, they function to further an agenda and maintain the status quo. It is easy enough to condemn these myths. It is easy to become angry about them and to rail against the self-serving short-termism they epitomise. But until we fully appreciate quite how brilliantly they satisfy their purpose, until we grasp how sublimely they protect the interests of their instigators and risk betraying those of everyone else, the meaningful alternatives that are so desperately required will remain disturbingly elusive. Our hope is that our overall argument will encourage and support a double-movement of much-needed regulation and more local and democratic responses.[4]

Reference will also be made to dealing with so-called wicked corporate law problems. These include limited liability and its effects on corporate groups, multinational conglomerates, and how to avoid the widespread use of corporate greenwashing as a form of 'box-ticking' in place of substantive action. The issue to be explored is how these established mechanisms and legal constructs can be effective within the wider need for economic, social, and environmental sustainability. It is posited that whilst advanced economies such as Australia and the UK will still have a focus on profit and GDP, post-GDP measures will be increasingly prominent and demand navigation.

9.1.1 The characteristics of corporations within a sustainability context

By contrast to a time reference, an alternative way of analyzing the concept of sustainability is in terms of what the company does. What is its business model, and what are the practices that a particular company adopts on a day to day and on a strategic basis, that could be collectively characterized as adding a quantum of sustainability? This secondary lens is to view the company, not in terms of its lifespan, but in relation to its carbon footprint. In this guise, companies and other organizations should be able to aspire to the goal of net zero, and for many, to be able do so relatively quickly. Achieving, measuring, and confirming this aim may involve renegotiating the equilibrium between various internal and external stakeholders, but it is theoretically and practicably achievable if there is some goodwill and common purpose. A correlative outcome of the pursuit of net zero

4 Christopher Wright and Daniel Nyberg, *Climate Change, Capitalism, and Corporations: Processes of Creative Self-Destruction,* Cambridge University Press, 2015, 27.

may in fact be higher profits, such that the economic case of 'doing well' links to the environmental precept of 'doing good'.

The five characteristics widely found companies (discussed in Chapter 7.3.3) are legal personality, delegated management, investor ownership, transferable shares, and limited liability can be applied through a sustainability lens. Whilst they are basic characteristics common to companies, analyzing how successful companies optimize them to the advantage of their shareholders and stakeholders is informative in the era of the climate challenge. For example, a company successful in the next three decades is likely to have strong corporate social responsibility and social licence to operate, have fluidity of shares with strong demand, and have boards with a broad range of skills.

Potential investors are key are potential key stakeholders as shareholder in waiting.

9.1.2 The possibility of sustainability enabled by the theory of perpetual succession

Companies are attributed or gifted by statute particular foundation benefits.

The power of statute is immense. It can include retrospectivity. It can change rights, duties, and obligations. It can bestow advantages and impose penalties. It can deal with the market as a whole or segment the market.

Companies are in a pre-eminent position to deliver innovation, longevity, and profit in the emerging new green economy. Their advantages attributed by statute and a range of interlocking mechanisms give them prime position status to deliver net zero solutions.

With the net zero target three decades away, companies have the inherent ability to start now, be there at the time, and carry on beyond that time point.

Corporations, whilst vested in theory with perpetual succession and the ability to go on infinitely, in practical terms rarely make it beyond the middle years equivalent of a modern human life span in a modern economic nation.[5] This is the orthodox view put by the organizational learning expert Peter Senge.[6] Senge notes that:

> In most companies that fail, there is abundant evidence in advance that the firm is in trouble. The evidence goes unheeded, however, even when individual managers are aware of it. The organization as a whole cannot recognize impending threats, understand the implications of those threats, or come up with alternatives. Perhaps under the laws of 'survival of the fittest,' this continual death of firms is fine for society. Painful though it may be for the employees and owners, it is simply a turnover of the economic

5 At the time of writing the global brand started in 1975, The Body Shop, is in the process of appointing administrators; the business is not yet fifty years old.

6 Peter M. Senge, *The Fifth Discipline: The Art and Practice of The Learning Organization*, Random House, 1990, 17.

> soil, redistributing the resources of production to new companies and new cultures.[7]

This narrative fits neatly with shareholder primacy where the market relentlessly chases return on capital. This was the basis of the post war economic model, but the climate crisis gives rise to fundamental new challenges.

9.1.3 Corporate sustainability in the age of climate change

Peter Senge's premise of the short-lived nature of companies, even US Fortune 500 companies was based on work done by Arie de Geus,[8] a longtime employee of Royal Dutch Shell who started in 1951 and retired in 1989 as group planning coordinator, the fossil fuel company and prominent in the world's top 20 carbon emitters since 1965.[9]

The survey was conducted by De Geus on behalf of his employer Shell. De Geus noted that:

> our survey identified several that were still vigorous at 200, 300, and even 700 years of age. What made the difference? Why are some companies better able to adapt? Sociologists and psychologists tell us it is pain that makes people and living systems change. And certainly corporations have their share of painful crises, the recent spate of takeovers and takeover threats conspicuously among them. But crisis management—pain management—is a dangerous way to manage for change. Once in a crisis, everyone in the organization feels the pain. The need for change is clear. The problem is that you usually have little time and few options. The deeper into the crisis you are, the fewer options remain. Crisis management, by necessity, becomes autocratic management. The positive characteristic of a crisis is that the decisions are quick. The other side of that coin is that the implementation is rarely good; many companies fail to survive. The challenge, therefore, is to recognize and react to environmental change before the pain of a crisis. Not surprisingly, this is what the long-lived companies in our study were so well able to do. All these companies had a striking capacity to institutionalize change. They never stood still. Moreover, they seemed to recognize that they had internal strengths that could be developed as environmental conditions changed.[10]

Of the long-lived companies De Geus notes that:

7 Senge, n 6, 17.

8 Arie De Geus, *Harvard Business Review*, 'Decision Making and Problem Solving: Planning as Learning', March 1988, 1-14, 3, https://hbr.org/1988/03/planning-as-learning.

9 Matthew Taylor and Jonathon Watts, The Guardian, 'Revealed: the 20 firms behind a third of all carbon emissions', 9 Oct 2019, https://www.theguardian.com/environment/2019/oct/09/revealed-20-firms-third-carbon-emissions.

10 Arie De Geus, n 8, 3.

> Some years ago, the planning group at Shell surveyed 30 companies that had been in business for more than 75 years. What impressed us most was their ability to live in harmony with the business environment, to switch from a survival mode when times were turbulent to a self-development mode when the pace of change was slow. And this pattern rang a familiar bell because Shell's history is similarly replete with switches from expansion to self-preservation and back again to growth.[11]

The only reference is to 'the business environment', not to the environmental or social constraints. This was no doubt the overriding business approach of the 1950s to 1980s spanning De Geus' career with Shell. He refers to the challenges in the company's corporate history at the start of the 20th century:

> Early in our history, for example, there was a burst of prosperity in the Far East and we dominated the market for kerosene in tins and 'oil for the lamps of China.' Survival became the keynote, however, when Rockefeller's Standard Oil snatched market share by cutting price. In fact, it was the survival instinct that led in 1907 to the joining of Royal Dutch Petroleum and the Shell Transport and Trading Company—separate businesses until then and competitors in the Far East. This, in turn, paved the way for Shell's expansion into the United States in 1911 with a new product, Sumatran gasoline—also a reaction to Standard Oil's activities.[12]

This is the narrative of a powerful global corporation seeking market reach in the boom industries connected with the internal combustion engine. An alternative global history may have seen these types of companies as associated with electric vehicles but they are much simpler to run given their fuel source, so Shell's alternative history may have been as lithium producer or battery maker. As John Naughton observes:

> The internal combustion engine spawned a huge ecosystem of auxiliary industries – garages, service centres, refineries, tankers, filling stations and so on – supply chains created to cater to the needs of a 19th-century technology based on heavy machinery, oil, gasoline and exhaust fumes. EVs, by comparison, are relatively simple machines – basically big skateboards with wheels driven by electric motors and controlled by software. They need less maintenance and different skills to minister to them.[13]

De Geus' learning narrative about Shell is within the paradigm of this fossil fuel ecosystem. It was one of the growth industries, if not 'growth engines', at the heart

11 De Geus, n 8, 1.

12 De Geus, n 8, 1.

13 John Naughton, *The Guardian* and *The Observer*, 'Forget range anxiety: we should really worry about China's global dominance in the electric car market', 11 Feb 2024, https://www.theguardian.com/commentisfree/2024/feb/10/china-global-dominance-electric-car-market-ev-trade-war.

of the lexical and economic commons. The 20th century was powered by such fossil fuel companies. Even in popular culture, the admonition and advice to young people was to go into an industry like 'plastics, son'.[14]

In the 21st century companies like Adani still claim they are keeping the lights on in villages in India. The incumbency narrative of companies like coal is at the heart of the 20th century of industrial development. Shell's view of the world and De Geus's methodologies have dominated business schools and strategy setting. De Geus was a powerful advocate for understanding diverse national cultures within a global corporate structure, and so Royal Dutch Shell became an early by-word for corporate cultural sensitivity within the myriad host nations it operated. We can look back and say this was a form of greenwashing by a company benefitting from government largesse and favourable treatment, but it was very effective for building the brand, nevertheless. Formerly lauded corporations like Shell must be finding the new learning regime required to address the climate crisis disconcerting and challenging.

9.1.4 Harmony between the generations of owners and managers

In practice, a sustainable company can survive despite succession generations of owners and managers. It is a business entity able to take practical advantage of the theoretical opportunity of perpetual succession. In the 21st century and its third to fifth decades, the definition will take on a crucial additional dimension. It will allow the company to attract employees, customers, finance, and so on that either aligns with net zero targets or is not seen as an outlier and a company attracting attention as a high climate risk. Financing new thermal coal mines is already a market segment of this type. Attracting finance at market-competitive rates will be the issue. It is the signature of the stranded asset. What has been valuable and bankable for more than two centuries is undergoing a seismic shift in the compressed decades of the 21st century.

Sustainable corporations will be of two basic types. Firstly, they will be new corporations, including those that don't yet exist, taking advantage of opportunities which may still be nascent. They will be underpinned by delivering climate solutions—delivering net zero carbon goods or services, or better still sequestering carbon and removing it from the atmosphere. Secondly, they will be adaptable existing companies with sufficient insight into the problem and capacity to be solution driven.

There will of course be many companies which will profess to be outside the economy for climate. These companies will have the pressure of being net zero in the way they do their business.

14 Film: The Graduate, 'One word: plastics' 1967 https://en.wikiquote.org/wiki/The_Graduate.

9.2 The unsustainable corporation

9.2.1 Entropy is the practical outcome for most corporations

Whilst the law allows for perpetual succession, the reality for most corporations, even family businesses, is that that they come to an often-messy end. After three generations or less, typically, the unsustainable and untenable business model takes hold.

Companies are easy to set up and register and they are provided, in theory, with the great benefit of perpetual succession. That is, they can carry on from a micro base indefinitely and well beyond the founders, originators, or current members and board. As a matter of evidence, and in fact and law, they either exist or they do not. There is no doubt about their status in almost all cases. There may be issues as to preregistration contracts and dormant companies, but these are at the margins. In any event, companies have the benefit of the umpire/regulator to ascertain and clarify such issues, should they arise. The statutory powers of the regulator are significant. The statute is comprehensive, and the rules of the game are being regularly, if not continually, revised, upgraded, and made fit for contemporary market conditions. Statute has overlaid itself over and above the historical common law development. The starting position is both implicitly and explicitly statute. The rules from cases, from common law principle, and equitable rules and considerations, and colour and light, but they are secondary to the statutory provision. The provision is clear on its terms is the law.

9.2.2 The legislative demise of other entities in the Australian business ecosystem: the case of partnerships

By contrast, other entities that have a common law foundation tended to have remained largely in the common law realm. These include partnerships, trusts, and cooperatives. Whether such entities exist will often be a significant preliminary barrier. The question of whether there is or has been a partnership in operation may not be clear-cut. What has been the assumption of the parties? This is a relevant consideration, but not determinative. There may be evidence adduced one way or the other.

A partnership does not need to be registered nor is it required to have a written agreement. Similarly, a pty ltd does not require internal rules but putting them in place is supported in three distinct ways which are not available to a partnership. There are replaceable rules which can be readily adopted; there is a comprehensive and up to date piece of corporate legislation and other related pieces of legislation, and there is a regulator tasked with compliance issues.

To protect themselves from potential dissolution, partnerships need clearly drafted provisions. If they want certainty of duration, they require a time frame and other bespoke clauses. If they want to avoid being characterized as partnerships, they will need to make this clear. If they want pre-emption rights, valuation mechanisms, and other centrally important control devices, they need to spell this out. There is much work to be done to come into existence and to stay in operation.

Whilst the historical common law hovers over partnerships, the partnership acts in Australia are creaky, 19th-century relics and not fit for contemporary purpose. They provide a self-perpetuating limit on the popularity of partnerships as a business vehicle. For example, dissolution and closure are hallmarks of the Partnership Act 1958 (Vic). This is the opposite to the arrangement in the Corporations Act 2001 (Cth) which contains the assumption of perpetual succession for the corporate form. The spectre of entropy lurks in the Partnership Act 1958 (Vic). In the 128 sections, the word 'dissolution' appears no less than 40 times. Division Four of the Partnership Act 1958 (Vic) is entitled Dissolution of Partnership. It covers sections 36 to 48 inclusively and specifically deals with dissolution issues. For instance:

> **36 Dissolution by expiration or notice**
>
> Subject to any agreement between the partners a partnership is dissolved—
>
> (a) if entered into for a fixed term by the expiration of that term;
> (b) if entered into for a single adventure or undertaking by the termination of that adventure or undertaking;
> (c) if entered into for an undefined time by any partner giving notice to the other or others of his intention to dissolve the partnership.
>
> In the last-mentioned case the partnership is dissolved as from the date mentioned in the notice as the date of dissolution or if no date is so mentioned as from the date of the communication of the notice.

Triggering the notice period is a simple matter:

> **30 Retirement from partnership at will**
>
> (1) Where no fixed term has been agreed upon for the duration of the partnership any partner may determine the partnership at any time on giving notice of his intention so to do to all the other partners.
> (2) Where the partnership has originally been constituted by deed a notice in writing signed by the partner giving it shall be sufficient for this purpose.

This type of provision could decimate the value for the business. The parties can draft an agreement which overrides these clauses but doing so may be expensive, particularly at the outset of the arrangement.

9.2.3 Electric vehicle policy in Australia: a set of vectors creating inaction

Cars and SUVs are part of the 'getting around' component of CO_2 emissions, to adopt the terminology used by Bill Gates and others.[15] They are one of the five major areas of emissions along with heating and cooling, what we grow, electricity and making

15 Bill Gates, *How to Avoid a Climate Disaster*, Penguin, 2021.

things. The 'getting around' component comprises about 16% of total annual global emissions. Emissions from cars and sports utility vehicles (SUVs) etc are about half of the 16%, or 8%. Given the geography of Australia this is a major issue and EVs should be an advanced solution. Instead, they make up just a few percent of new car sales. The reasons for this low take-up are legion as the following list provides:

- High prices and the lack of subsidies and other incentives provided by governments.
- High price and the imposition of taxes to make prices even higher; for example, the Victorian government's road tax on EV owners which was eventually successfully challenged in the High Court as a tax which states did not have the power to impose.
- The price of EVs and the politics of envy; just as NZ has had what conservative parties have labelled the 'ute tax', the former government in Australia went so far as to allege that EVs would 'destroy the weekend'.
- No national emissions standards so that Australia has been seen as a car backwater and international dumping ground for vehicles no longer fit for purpose in more progressive countries which impose emission and related vehicle standards. The nation's vast network of roads and highways carries a very high proportion of older vehicles fitted with diesel and lead petrol engines. Many of these means of transport would be referred to as 'gas guzzlers' and 'clunkers' in other countries. This is another example, like its concentration on fossil fuel production, where Australia is an anomalous outlier as a G20 economic member.
- A complex set of state-by-state laws, rather than simplified, uniform, national rules.
- The geography of long distances and sparse populations, particularly outside the major centres.
- Related to the point above is the lack of charging infrastructure. This is exacerbated by range issues limited currently to about 500km between recharging, given the typical current battery technology.
- The lack of a local car manufacturing industry since about 2013 when international makers such as Ford, GM, and Toyota closed their local branches in Victoria and South Australia, traditionally manufacturing heartlands of the nation. Car-making is a major economic platform for R&D, employment, and widespread economic impact. The closure of car-making branches involved losing frontline expertise and a whole ecosystem of specialist trades and skills. It is highly consequential. It becomes very difficult politically to resurrect abandoned industrial capacity. It is also expensive and uncertain, given the intensity of international competition. It requires a coordinated national approach regarding necessary educational, training, investment, and long-term commitments. This is not an area Australia has done well in. It can take a generation or more, and several three-year political cycles to reboot this type of lost capacity. Hence, it requires intergenerational bipartisan political support.

Unfortunately, governments tend to erase policy they inherit from their predecessors than build on it, and this has been the wicked problem in Australian federal politics, particularly as regard climate policy (unlike defence policy).

- The secondhand market for cars and SUVs has been limited to this point, given that such vehicles currently need to be imported, and this is an expensive exercise, given the shipping and freight costs relevant to 'the tyranny of distance' that sea travel to Australia entails. Additionally, governments in Australia have been slow to purchase new fleets of EVs. If they were to be purchased in bulk order, they could then be turned over for resale, thereby creating supply for a domestic secondhand market. This would send a clear policy signal to the wider commercial market. Were it to be done at scale by the federal government, it would also deliver an effective message to State and Territory governments.

Each of these vectors has created a sclerotic market for EVs. This has been a problem for governments of both stripes. Where Australia has failed in EVs, there is hope that the nation can do better in solar, wind, and wave technology. But EV technology would be a game changer for Australia. A home-grown EV car industry using solar power would solve a wicked problem. Branch office international corporations and start-up local corporations could impact an activity that sits at the core of the national DNA. Australia has become a largely overlooked market for EVs because there is no manufacturing hub (in contrast to China) or import incentives (in contrast to Europe):

> The European Commission says that China's share of EVs sold in Europe has grown to 8% and could hit 15% in 2025, on the basis of prices that are often 20% below EU-made models. To Europeans this looks suspiciously like dumping and may require imposing punitive tariffs "to protect European Union producers against cheaper Chinese electric vehicle (EV) imports [that] are benefiting from state subsidies". Underpinning this potential crisis is a strange dichotomy: the EU (and indeed the UK) has been subsidising the consumption of EVs, while China, struggling with a consumer economy stricken by the collapse of its property market, is massively subsidising EV production to boost exports and compensate for falling domestic demand.[16]

Australia has become the clunkers vehicle market at the bottom of the known world. This may begin to change with the belated introduction of national emissions standards.

16 John Naughton, n 11.

9.2.3.1 The Victorian government—challenged in the High Court for imposing a road users tax on EVs

The nadir of EV policy in Australia was achieved by Victoria.

The state government state imposed a tax on electric vehicles by reference to distance covered; the matter was taken up by EV drivers who took the matter to the High Court in Canberra. The Court held that the state tax was not constitutional.

9.2.3.2 The case of car registration payments in the ACT. light at the end of the tunnel?

By contrast to Victoria, that ACT government has provided free registration for EVs.

Linked to fuel emissions, rather than weight

> The ACT Government is offering 2 years of free registration for new or used zero emissions vehicles in the ACT that have been purchased or acquired from 24 May 2021 and before 30 June 2024. If you are eligible, the waiver will only apply to the registration component of vehicle registration fees. All other relevant fees, charges, or levies related to registering a vehicle will remain, such as the annual cost of Motor Accident Injuries Insurance.[17]
>
> **'Eligible vehicles include:**
>
> - new or used passenger and goods carrying vehicles under 4.5t that have an electric motor powered by electricity alone or cars powered by a hydrogen fuel cell
> - vehicles that have been converted from a different power source into one of the above vehicle configurations and certified as registrable on or after 24 May 2021 and before 30 June 2024
> - second hand zero emissions vehicles imported into Australia that meet the above requirements. [18]

EV policy has stymied a whole sector in Australia. Corporations have been slow to embrace an area where governments have hindered innovation. This contrasts with nations such as Sweden with long- established car makers able to quickly develop capacity in the manufacture of EVs as the case of Polestar demonstrates.

17 'Two years free registration for zero emissions vehicles,' https://www.energy.gov.au/rebates/two-years-free-registration-zero-emissions-vehicles.

18 Ibid, n 17.

9.3 Case studies in sustainable corporations

9.3.1 Polestar: a sustainable EV corporation?

By contrast to Australia, Sweden has retained a valuable car manufacturing sector. This has allowed new EV manufacturers to emerge, or as offshoots of iconic brands. Polestar is a Swedish automotive brand established in 1996 by Volvo Cars' partner, Flash/Polestar Racing, and acquired in 2015 by Volvo, which itself was acquired by Geely in 2010. It is headquartered in Torslanda outside Gothenburg, Sweden with vehicle production taking place in China. Polestar shares began trading on the Nasdaq exchange under the symbol PSNY on June 24, 2022. It wants to be leader in bidirectional charging ability:

> Most home electric vehicle chargers are adept at taking power off the grid and delivering it to your car, but what if the vehicle could also automatically keep the lights on during blackouts and offset electricity costs by returning power to its source during high-demand times?[19]

Hence the concept of bidirectional charging ability. This includes V2V vehicle to vehicle and V2H vehicle to home. This involves two private assets. It is not communal per se. It also includes V2G or vehicle to grid. This becomes more complex and problematic particularly given the market reach and vested interests of electricity providers. Polestar has indicated bidirectional charging will be available on the next generation of their vehicles:

> A Polestar would send energy back into the grid (potentially reducing the owner's electric bills) to help sustain the integrity of the system during peak usage. This is especially relevant when the house has solar panels and is generating more electricity than the house is using. The car would also be a backup battery during power outages.[20]

This kind of innovation is only possible when there is an active car manufacturing base; Australia's car industry closed in 2017 when General Motors' local Holden division folded in the wake of Ford, Mitsubishi, Toyota, and others.

9.3.2 OZ Minerals Ltd: a takeover target for BHP

Whilst BHP has been divesting coal assets, it has made forays into companies with critical minerals. In 2022, BHP made an indicative offer for OZ Minerals. The OZ Minerals Managing Director and Chief Executive Officer, Andrew Cole, said:

19 Jim Motavalli, Tech Crunch, 'Are bidirectional EV chargers ready for the home market?,' 29 April 2022, https://techcrunch.com/2022/04/28/are-bidirectional-ev-chargers-ready-for-the-home-market/.

20 Roberto Baldwin, Tech Crunch, 'Polestar CEO sees value in EVs, even when they are parked,' 22 August 2022, https://techcrunch.com/2022/08/21/polestar-ceo-sees-value-in-evs-even-when-theyre-parked/.

> We have a unique set of copper and nickel assets, all with strong long-term growth potential in quality locations. We are mining minerals that are in strong demand particularly for the global electrification and decarbonisation thematic and we have a long-life Resource and Reserve base. We do not consider the proposal from BHP sufficiently recognises these attributes.[21]

As to the trading price of critical minerals the board took a long-term view:

> Whilst the copper price has weakened recently, the medium to long-term outlook remains strong for minerals linked to the renewable energy industry, like copper and nickel. Our focus for 2022 remains on safely delivering our operational targets, advancing our current growth projects and adding new growth options to the portfolio while we continue to strengthen our unique company culture, placing us in a positive position against forecast demand trends.[22]

The analysis by OZ Minerals as to BHP's offer was comprehensive:

> The Board has carefully assessed the Indicative Proposal including with the assistance of its financial and legal advisers. The Board has unanimously determined that the Indicative Proposal significantly undervalues OZ Minerals and, as such, is not in the best interests of shareholders. In coming to its decision, the Board considered that the Indicative Proposal does not adequately compensate shareholders for:
>
> - the unique nature of OZ Minerals' core business which represents a high-quality portfolio of copper and nickel assets, located in a Tier-1 mining jurisdiction with long mine lives, first quartile cost positioning and extensive strategic optionality;
> - the unique investment proposition which OZ Minerals provides as the only primary copper company in the ASX100;
> - The low carbon intensity of OZ Minerals' assets relative to its peers with a defined and market leading plan for further decarbonisation to meet our target of net zero Scope 1 and 2 operational emissions by 2030;
> - the high-quality nature of OZ Minerals' growth projects which include the West Musgrave Project (FID scheduled for H2 2022), the Carrapateena Block Cave and the Prominent Hill Extension which together are expected to generate significant production growth over the next 5 years;
> - the strong long-term outlook for both the copper and nickel markets underpinned by increasing geological scarcity, global electrification and

21 ASX Release, 8 August, 2022, OZ Minerals rejects Indicative Proposal from BHP, https://www.ozminerals.com/ArticleDocuments/435/220808%20OZL%20ASX%20Release%20OZ%20Minerals%20rejects%20indicative%20proposal%20from%20BHP.pdf.aspx?Embed=Y

22 ASX Quarterly Release, 2nd Quarter Report 2022, Andrew Cole, MD and CEO Ozmin, 22 July 2022, https://www.ozminerals.com/ArticleDocuments/435/02544768.pdf.aspx?Embed=Y.

accelerating decarbonisation, to which OZ Minerals is highly leveraged; and

- the strong and consistent returns that the OZ Minerals management team has delivered with a total shareholder return of ~145% over the past 5 years.[23]

Less than a year later in April 2023, BHP completed its takeover of OZ Minerals. OZ Minerals is now part of the BHP group of companies.

The BHP CEO, Mike Henry, said:

> This acquisition strengthens BHP's portfolio in copper and nickel and is in line with our strategy to meet increasing demand for the critical minerals needed for electric vehicles, wind turbines and solar panels to support the energy transition. Combining our two organisations will provide options for growth, bring new talent and innovation to unlock these resources in a sustainable way, and deliver value to shareholders and communities.[24]

Where a company offers a compelling business case for success in the climate change epoch, it will be the subject of intense speculation by a larger company.

9.3.3 Plastics recycling in the UK: Milspeed

James Milhench, Business Development manager at Milspeed, based in the Cotswolds, said:

> We are thrilled to be involved in this revolutionary net reprocessing scheme where we are able to utilise our 20+ years of reprocessing expertise creating high-performing pellets from 'tricky to re-use' polymers. We have been incorporating ocean waste into our footwear products for four years now but we look forward to using this scheme to upscale and encourage the use of ocean waste in a variety of industries. I believe it is localised synergies like this which will prove vital in creating a more sustainable future.[25]

This might be argued to perpetuate the production of plastic.

> The scheme has been made possible thanks to funding from Scottish Power Foundation and the Squire Charitable Trust to set up systems at zero cost to local authorities, fishing companies or other organisations working with the fishing industry. [26]

23 ASX Release, 8 August, 2022, n 21.

24 BHP, News Media Centre, 'Completion of OZ Minerals acquisition', https://www.bhp.com/news/media-centre/releases/2023/05/completion-of-oz-minerals-acquisition.

25 Fish Focus, 'Fishing Nets Recycled in the UK for the First Time', 2 Nov 2022, https://fishfocus.co.uk/fishing-nets-recycled-in-the-uk-for-the-first-time/

26 Focus, n 25.

Similarly, it might be characterized as greenwashing or balance-sheet carbon offsetting.

Solutions and innovation will come in myriad forms. Cleaning up long-run historical problems is inevitably part of the spectrum.

9.3.4 Steel recycling companies: exemplars of the circular economy

The Canadian-based climate and business group, Corporate Knights, ranks companies by sustainability.[27] Of the 2023 ranking, the group announced:

> The annual ranking, now in its 19th year, is based on an assessment of more than 6,000 public companies that report more than US$1 billion in revenues. In the 2023 list, one-fifth of the most sustainable corporations are based in the US and 11% in Canada. Europe still leads the way with 44%, while 22% are located in the Asia Pacific region.28

On this basis, fifty of the World's Most Sustainable Companies in 2023 were nominated. Occupying top spots Schnitzer Steel Industries Inc (US)—a steel recycling business with an A+ rating, and Vestas Wind Systems A/S (Denmark)—a wind farm business with an A rating. Two Australian metal recycling companies made the list: Brambles Ltd with an A and Sims Ltd with an A- rating.

9.3.5 Australian-based start-ups seeking to innovate

In Australia, sustainable companies are reported to be in the following sectors:[29]

- Reusable or biodegradable packaging, eco-friendly packaging.
- Rooftop solar.
- The use of non-toxic chemicals.
- Repurposing recycled plastic e.g. into dog leashes.
- Avoiding single use coffee cups.
- Tree planting as a carbon offset mechanism.
- Reducing fast fashion; ethical clothing manufacturing.
- The use of natural products such as bamboo.

These examples, whilst laudable, focus on improving the environment and reducing waste by reference to the circular economy, and of extending end of product

27 Corporate Knights, Mike Scott, '100 most sustainable companies of 2023 still flourishing in tumultuous times', 18 January 2023, https://www.corporateknights.com/rankings/global-100-rankings/2023-global-100-rankings/2023-global-100-most-sustainable-companies/.

28 Earth.ORG, 'The World's 50 Most Sustainable Companies in 2023', https://earth.org/sustainable-companies-2023/

29 Our Trace, Business and Partnerships, '23 Sustainable Companies in Australia Doing Great Things', June 2021, https://www.our-trace.com/blog/23-companies-in-australia-doing-great-things-in-sustainability.

lifecycles. But they do not address the fundamental causes of carbon dioxide in the atmosphere. And they are niche businesses rather than business at scale and at the core of the issue.

9.3.6 Smart technology solutions for a dry continent: water into wine

The question is simple and fundamental: when to irrigate crops and how much water to apply? These are issues that 'horticulturalists have battled with for years'.[30]

The company Athena IR-Tech has developed 'technology that detects whether a plant is water-stressed up to a week before it starts to wilt'.[31] The company's website notes that the business 'was born out of novel research in determining optimal irrigation recommendations using proximal IR (InfraRed) devices'.[32]

9.4 Creating the conditions for sustainable corporations

9.4.1 Recognising the power of governments

The COVID-19 Pandemic gave rise to new versions of government power; 'they demonstrated they have almost unlimited regulatory and economic power to rebuild economies by fast-tracking spending on renewable energy to create clean and sustainable jobs'.[33] Governments have unique powers. They can set the scene for both for-profit and not-for-profit sectors. They can direct companies by motivating and by guiding.

In corporate law, there were rapid changes made to insolvency provisions as business liquidity dried up and supply chains were fundamentally disrupted.

The economy switched into online mode with education online, every distillery making hand sanitizer which could.

Changes can take place if there is political will and social agreement that there is an emergency. This was medical emergency but the climate crisis as a hyper emergency has the capacity to include multiple simultaneous dimensions causing disruption, if not chaos. These include:

- The economic and human toll of climate disasters, sea level rise, flood, fire, and drought.
- The health particularly the elderly, the vulnerable, and the displaced.
- Food security.

Governments can act quickly and at scale. Their power and remit give them unique resources.

30 Kellie Hollingworth, 'NSW vineyard installs water-sensing technology to save waste and improve quality', ABC Rural, 1 December 2022, abc.net.au/news.

31 Hollingworth, n 30.

32 AthenaIR-Tech, About Us, https://athenairtech.com/about-us/.

33 Ian Goldin, *Rescue: From Global Crisis to a Better World*, Sceptre, 2021, 210.

9.4.2 The EIC as the prototype model for many of the features of the modern shareholder primacy economic model

The only corporation to come close to the power of contemporary governments, at least in the democratic, market-based economies was the EIC which was a corporate behemoth like no other, given its unique combination of factors:

- Its experimental origins and foundational DNA as a venture of 1599.
- Its adoption of a nascent international branch office system.
- Its geographical advantage from London to Luxor.
- The high trust but slow accountability model it was able to manipulate.
- Its loosely worded original charter which was a lawyer's gift of imprecision and gaps leading to an essentially unfettered operational modality.
- The same discretionary loopholes in successive 15-year charters.
- Extant to its mercantile power was its influence, deal making and lobby; it had platinum political access before lobbying was a calling; it arguably invented the guile and craft of the art.
- The EIC's standing army of more than 250,000. This makes the modern Wagner group look like a platoon alongside it.

The EIC was so commercially successful, so relatively quickly that the governance lapses, cracks, and deficiencies were papered over. Rampant commercial success trumped scrutiny and concerns about governance and related shortcomings. The success of the EIC was conflated with the success of the emergent modern nation state of the UK. Both were the most successful empire builders in their respective categories of corporation as a national ruler and a small geographic nation as building the first truly global empire in geographic terms, both projects being underwritten by nautical technology allowing sailing ships for the first time to be able to reach all points of the globe, and travel to the 'ends of the earth'.

Contented investors at home will forgive many a sin aboard. BHP and RIO are two examples where this distancing is now a problematic fig leaf to charges of corporate malfeasance.

9.4.3 Positive change societal tipping points: based on 3% of people with strong commitment to a shared cause

Just as there are negative tipping points in climate science, the climate scientist, Prof Tim Lenton, also advocates that there can be positive social tipping points through collective action.[34] Lenton's great grandmother was a suffragette in the

34 Professor Tim Lenton, University of Exeter, 'Positive tipping points through collective action', 7 Dec 2023, You Tube, https://www.google.com/search?q=tim+lenton+tipping+points&rlz=1C1VDKB_enAU1086AU1086&oq=tim+lenton+tipping+points&gs_lcrp=EgZjaHJvbWUyDggAEEUYORhDGIAEGIoFMgcIARAAGIAEMggIAhAAGBYYHjIICAMQABgWGB4yDQgEEAAYhgMYgAQYigUyDQgFEAAYhgMYgAQYigUyDQgGEAAYhgMYgAQYigXS

early 20th century. The suffragette movement rose quickly and powerfully to bring about voting rights for women. Within a decade, fundamental change was achieved. He also points to photographs of New York in the early 20th century; within a decade, horses were replaced by motor vehicles.

In Australia, we see the rapid take-up of solar on rooftops and induction stoves in kitchens; gas in stoves to induction in stoves; power from the grid to power from the rooftop solar. These changes can be gradual and organic and then become rapid and irreversible. The latter features are part of a tipping point; the status quo shifts and is not returned to. There is a new equilibrium and an emergent paradigm. Greta Thunberg's school strike for climate is an example in the climate movement. Within months it was a global action strategy. Erica Chenoweth, the Harvard based academic, has proposed the so-called '3.5% rule' whereby:

> Nonviolent protests are twice as likely to succeed as armed conflicts—and those engaging a threshold of 3.5% of the population have never failed to bring about change.[35]

This small number of dedicated people can produce a powerful catalytic effect.

9.4.3.1 Cleaning up plastic pollution in Sydney Harbour

Wading through the shallows of Sydney Harbour on a daily basis is a retired schoolteacher. Andy Orr was appalled by the 'swamp of plastic'. His is currently a one-person effort. Into an abandoned builder's bucket he also retrieved from the water, he collects thousands of pieces of plastic and rubbish in a session. It is an industrial-scale problem with a human entry point to begin the fix.[36] Orr said:

> I thought someone's got to do something about this,' Mr Orr says. Westerly winds direct a steady tide of plastic into small harbour inlets like Hermit Beach in Vaucluse. 'It's only 50 metres long that beach bed [but] it'll take me two hours, three hours and I'll get 5,000 pieces of plastic—7,000 pieces of plastic in three hours, and then I'm exhausted'.[37]

There may be the start of a world-wide network of guardian environmentalists like Orr, given that plastic now inundates beaches in the most remote parts of the world's oceans including places such as Lord Howe Island, 600 kilometres off the

---

AQg3MTU3ajBqN6gCALACAA&sourceid=chrome&ie=UTF-8#fpstate=ive&vld=cid:86aea97c,vid:KmJWaCRJnl0,st:0.

35 Harvard Kennedy School, Carr Center for Human Rights Policy, 'The 3.5% rule: How a small minoritycan change the world', 13 May 2019, https://carrcenter.hks.harvard.edu/publications/35-rule-how-small-minority-can-change-world.

36 ABC Radio Sydney, Rosemary Bolger and Danielle O'Neal, 'Inheritance allows "Guardian of Sydney Harbour" to quit his job and pick up plastic every day', 11 Feb 2024, https://www.abc.net.au/news/2024-02-11/sydney-harbour-guardian-inheritance-pick-up-plastic-beaches/103419966.

37 ABC Radio Sydney, n 33.

east coast of Australia.[38] This approach to taking tangible action where a single person makes an initial stand is also what occurred with Greta Thunberg and the school strike for climate movement.

The Sydney Harbour plastic pollution scourge issue points to the perverse allocation of social capital; the council in the wealthy harbourside suburb apparently do not have sufficient funds to fix the systemic problem of plastic pollution in their local waterways.

9.4.3.2 Battery storage at household level

Another social movement will be the take up of battery storage in the home. This will create a virtuous circle potentially heating, cooling, cooking, growing things for a house (with the unfortunately named greenhouse), and transport via EVs, such that this accounts several of the main areas of greenhouse-gas emissions at the household level. Bottom-up social movement and top-down policy initiatives can together provide powerful capacity for systemic change.

9.4.4 The clarity provided by government rules

Only national governments can set clear nation-wide priorities. They can create the conditions and the rules for doing business on a sector-wide basis. Governments can give the market certainty. They have important rule-setting functions. Government policy determines what companies can and can't do. It is the baseline for activity setting.

It does not necessarily need leadership or permission from central governments, as long as those governments do not actively set up obstacles to progress. Jean-Sebastian Jacques, formerly CEO of Rio Tinto noted:

> we always welcome smart supporting policies from governments. Anything that can help develop (low carbon) technology is more than welcome. But I am not going to wait for governments. We welcome good government policies but we need to keep on moving. Canada is a good example. It is one of the countries trying to show leadership. The governments there are very pragmatic. They are putting money in the bucket to develop the technology (for green aluminium).[39]

Multiple governments, whether internationally or within a federation, can provide an elaborate ecosystem of competitive innovation. This can occur between state governments in federations, for example with California in the US in terms of

38 Jennifer Lavers, 'Plastic in the Pacific', in Cameron Muir, Kirsten Wehner and Jenny Newell (eds), *Living with the Anthropocene: Love, Loss and Hope in the Face of Environmental Crisis* ', NewSouth, 2020, 198–200.

39 Glenda Korporaal, 'The Jacques Solution', *The Australian: The Deal*, Issue 121, March 2020, 10–11.

climate change and Delaware in terms of corporate law efficiency. This can also occur between cities where attracting talented, diverse, and creative people can be advantageous and long lasting. [40]

9.5 Identifying effective corporate market regulation

Regulation is conceptually broad. It is usually predicated on economic factors. Social factors, by contrast, are less common reasons to invoke it. The problem with climate change is that it is a hyperobject. It does not fit neatly within either a social or economic paradigm. It encapsulates both sets of issues. The traditional model of regulation as enunciated by Michael Legg is that 'regulation seeks to govern, direct or alter human behaviour in particular areas of endeavour, for example, by requiring the payment of taxes, making anti-competitive conduct illegal and defining how securities may be dealt with'.[41] This is narrow and economically focused. As Legg notes 'the act of regulating has been defined as controlling or directing by rule, principle or method. Rules and principles enable regulators to prohibit or allow certain conduct, communicate expectations and provide guidance as to what is required or allowed'.[42]

A more relevant model for dealing with the climate emergency is the notion of regulation focused on social policy. As Michael Legg notes:

> Regulation based on social policy involves a regulator who is charged with advancing some conception of the public welfare and meeting human needs for such things as education, health, safety and a clean environment. The aim of the regulation is to attempt to improve the wellbeing of individuals and societies by focusing on such factors as quality of life. As a result regulation aimed at social policy tends to cut across industry or sectors of the economy as a society-wide outcome is desired. The regulation may seek to directly intervene in societal affairs or indirectly shape social behaviour.[43]

This broad-based approach comes closer to encapsulating the wide parameters of the challenge represented by climate change. It is first and foremost a social challenge. It has clear economic implications, too. As Legg observes 'some regulation may have both social policy and economic rationales for its adoption. For example, regulation addressing pollution may be regarded as necessary to both address externalities and to foster human health'.[44] This observation, published in 2011, is prescient in terms of the much larger concept of climate change. Pollution was viewed as a relatively simple stand-alone concept. The climate emergency

40 Richard Florida, 'Cities and the Creative Class', 2003, https://creativeclass.com/rfcgdb/articles/4%20Cities%20and%20the%20Creative%20Class.pdf.

41 Michael Legg, *Regulation, Litigation and Enforcement*, Lawbook Co, 2011, 1.

42 Legg, n 41, 1.

43 Legg, n 41, 4.

44 Legg, n 41, 5.

links many concepts within a macro social and economic framework. In the post-Paris, post-2016 context, the interconnectivity of formerly discrete concepts is key. As Legg notes 'regulation may be embodied not just in legislation and regulations, but also in standards, policy statements, rulings, codes of conduct and the like'.[45]

9.5.1 Australia's systems of regulation: often ineffective oversight

The effectiveness of regulation is correlated with the effectiveness of the regulator. As Legg notes, 'central to ensuring that regulation is complied with is an effective enforcement strategy'.[46] As Baldwin and Cave observe 'astute enforcement can remedy design defects in regulatory mechanisms and ill-enforcement can undermine the most sophisticated designs of regulation'.[47]

9.5.1.1 The regulatory environment: the imperative for clarity-banking and ANZ

Shayne Elliott, the CEO of ANZ Bank, has observed that 'what business wants is clarity—they want clarity in direction, they want clarity in the rules of the game, and businesses have learned to operate in almost any environment'.[48]

9.5.1.2 Sectoral inefficiencies: the regulation of mining ventures

The myriad state and commonwealth laws allowed Rio to take advantage of this complex, inconsistent web of laws, rules, and regulations.

9.5.1.3 Effective climate and CO2 regulation in Australia?: the lack of informed expression of sovereign political will

Tony Shepherd, former president of the Business Council of Australia and CEO of Transfield observes that

> I think it's fair to say we have found it extremely difficult in Australia to get an integrated national policy on climate change, so we have each state going in its own direction, we have the commonwealth going in its own direction.[49]

45 Legg, n 41, 1.
46 Legg, n 41, 1.
47 Legg, n 41, 1.
48 Brad Norington, 'Corporate leaders hit back over climate attack', *The Australian*, Wed 1 June 2022, 5.
49 Norington, n 48, ibid.

9.5.1.4 Nant Whisky: barrels of whisky were not securities

ASIC did not have jurisdiction because barrels of whisky were not considered as securities. It was a pyramid or Ponzi scheme promising returns of near 10% per annum.

9.5.1.5 Grey Wolf Resources NL: promises of a public listing which never eventuated

Promises were made to shareholders that the company would list and exploit billions of dollars-worth of lithium and other minerals that were meaningless and without merit have gone unexamined by ASIC. This was a promise to list that never eventuated. First-time shareholders ploughed much of their pensions into the prelisting price of one cent per share. There were given glossy share certificates. A level of naivety was present in each case. The asymmetry between the promoter and the duped investors was clear. The problem is that the promoter has gone on to set up another company. Reinvention of the corporate guise is a clear gap in the legal setting which is apparently easy to exploit for persistent corporate charlatans.

9.5.2 The regulation model in Australia: the legacy of post war gaps in oversight

The post-war theories of regulation 'provide generalised descriptions of the socio-political context which gives rise to and affects the progress of regulation. These descriptions do not of themselves tell us how regulation should affect the world'.[50] This observation, whilst apt, in the mid-1980s is even more prescient today. In September 1984, it was noted that 'market-based societies bring with them the need for systems of business regulation both to protect businesses from the excesses of unrestrained competition and to protect the public from business abuses'.[51] This neoliberal view of regulation as primarily aimed at the rules of competition between participants and consumer protection finds voice in the ACCC.

It reflects a narrow prism and a former time. These instincts remain pertinent in the era of climate change but the challenge is far more whole of society and longer term in nature than the relatively limited gauge of the debate in bygone decades. It is a whole-of-society challenge. It is three decades in the making. It is prospective in nature. The nearest equivalent is the war footing of the Second World War. It was global in scale. It mobilized all of society. It was an existential emergency. Its end- date and outcome were uncertain. Hence, there are some similarities, but the net zero by 2050 global strategy as a scientifically informed, future-oriented project is essentially unique in world history. It is both quintessentially modern and unprecedented. The role of corporate regulation will be critical in the evolution of corporations striving to be part of the solution. The basic binary of incentives and

50 Gerard C Rowe, 'Economic Theories of the Nature of Regulatory Activity,' in Tomasic, R. (ed), *Business Regulation in Australia*, CCH Australia Ltd, 1984, 147–73, 169.

51 Roman Tomasic (ed), *Business Regulation in Australia*, 1984, CCH Australia Ltd, Preface, v.

mandates will need to be reconceptualized. The theory, regulation, and governance of the company will all warrant critical attention.

For regulation to be affective it needs to identify and operate within the relevant socio-political context. That context is unfolding in real time in the 2020s. The imposed post-war orthodoxy of stability in broad economic, political, and cultural terms is no longer a stable, reliable, or efficacious platform upon which to base regulatory theory or practice.

9.6 Regulatory techniques which could be applied to Australian corporations

9.6.1 Effectively measuring and reporting carbon emissions

The continued exploitation of fossil fuels and carbon emission gives rise to several potential corporate techniques. A company can be set up or an asset exploited within the given corporate structure. A conglomerate organization can devolve a carbon intensive product or business area to a separate company within the group. The company can divest the asset. All of these techniques produce more carbon emissions. This is where regulation needs to be clear and explicit.

9.6.2 Outlawing the use and abuse of accounting, balance sheet, and other measures

One of the major obstacles emerging as regards the efficacy of the journey to net zero is deployment of the ubiquitous business strategy; reversion to balance sheet analysis. The problems with this approach are legion. Centrally, the issue is problematic numbers and their presentation within the confines of a balance sheet. The wicked problem emanates from the concept of 'net' zero, or overall zero. The balance sheet is a long-standing visual device with two sides to the equation. Producing more carbon needs to be offset by carbon reduction or abatement.

As such, the potential accounting and political perfidy of the target of net zero carbon emissions by 2050 needs to be part of the enforcement regime by governments and regulatory specialists.

The accounting device of the balance sheet and the legal protections afforded the corporate group provide an enduring mechanism for companies seeking to continue with business as usual. They can do this via a range of perfectly legal means. They can park problematic carbon production in technically separate corporations. This provides the perfectly legal licence or permission to keep emitting carbon. They can purchase carbon credits, no matter how discredited those financial instruments are. They can sell assets.

Both the law and accounting disciplines provide succour for this range of techniques without any apparent moral suasion.

The fact is, however, that these matters are embedded within deeply historicized and hence normalized economic and political codes. These tectonic plates include neoliberalism, economic rationalism, consumerism, and so forth.

9.6.3 Regulating corporate groups

Companies can quite legitimately devise and use well-known techniques. For a group company, this can be the creation of a subsidiary to house the problematic assets or business. Alternatively, it can be a sale of a problematic asset or business. This does not take the assets or business out of circulation. It is simply transferring the problem sideways.

As Margaret Blair has noted, the:

> field of sustainable corporate governance must address is the fact that corporations can organise themselves in business groups, as sprawling collections of subsidiaries and affiliates and supply chains, spread out over many countries, and financed through hundreds of different securities issued in dozens of countries, so that no one jurisdiction can easily regulate the whole. Corporations can (and do) thereby hide their 'dirty' business in the places that are the hardest to regulate.[52]

9.6.4 Strengthening the continuous disclosure regime for corporations

ASIC has 'noted the importance of the continuous disclosure regime for ensuring that market investors remain informed and confident'.[53] As Luke Hastings has noted 'it follows that appropriate and effective enforcement of the continuous disclosure regime is also critical'.[54] The parties enforcing the regime vary from private shareholders seeking to enforce their rights to the corporate regulator Australian Securities and Investment Commission (ASIC) or ASX Limited as the operator of the Australian Securities Exchange may also enforce the relevant listing rule.

As ASIC notes:

> The continuous disclosure obligations in the Corporations Act 2001 are fundamental to maintaining the integrity of the market by ensuring transparency and equal access to information. Listed companies must disclose material price sensitive information on a timely basis and comply with listing rules of the relevant market. ASIC can issue infringement notices for breaches of these obligations.[55]

These are legal issues for well-resourced, listed companies; the accounting standards discussed below will have much wider remit.

52 Margaret Blair, Foreword to Beate Sjafjell and Christopher M. Bruner (eds), *The Cambridge Handbook of Corporate Law, Corporate Governance and Sustainability*, 2019.

53 Luke Hastings, 'Enforcing the Continuous Disclosure Regime: Three Case Studies,' in Michael Legg, *Regulation, Litigation and Enforcement*, Lawbook Company, 2011, 133-149, 133.

54 Hastings n 53, 133.

55 ASIC, Handling Corporate Information- Continuous disclosure, https://asic.gov.au/regulatory-resources/corporate-governance/handling-corporate-information/.

9.7 The development of international financial reporting standards for corporations

International Financial Reporting Standards provide a coordinated approach to the singular project of net zero emissions. They treat the problem as measurable and mathematical.

Companies are one element in a chain of causality with international will and documentation, followed by national projections and accountability, and then corporate sequencing.

International bodies must stay focused—they are stakeholders in multiple ways. They are invested in compliance; they need to set aspirational standards and demonstrate the BlackRock effect of market leadership.

At the political level since 2022, the federal government has contemplated a carbon reporting mechanism for companies across all three of the 'emissions scopes', so as provide investors with details about risk the detail investors require to make judgements about the risk profile of companies themselves.

In 2023, the International Sustainability Standards Board (ISSB) a body set up as part of the International Financial Reporting Standards (IFRS) produced global sustainability disclosure standards expecting nations to adopt them domestically.

As the Climatework Centre notes:

> The International Sustainability Standards Board (ISSB) issued two new standards in June 2023. The standards are designed to form a baseline for sustainability (IFRS S1) and climate-related (IFRS S2) disclosures around the world. They consolidate numerous reporting frameworks and are structured around the TCFD's elements of governance, strategy, risk management, and metrics and targets. Jurisdictions are able to adapt the standards to their local needs whilst maintaining interoperability with international financial markets. Treasury's proposal signals Australia's intent to follow many other jurisdictions in introducing mandatory climate-related disclosures closely aligned with the ISSB's climate-related standard (IFRS S2). Under Treasury's proposal, companies will have to disclose their current and anticipated climate-related risks over the short, medium and long term. This represents a significant change from previous financial reporting by requiring substantial forward-looking information.[56]

As to the details, disclosure requirements include:

56 Climateworks Centre, News Blog, 'Mandatory climate-related financial disclosures for Australian companies, explained', 30 October 2023, https://www.climateworkscentre.org/news/mandatory-climate-related-financial-disclosures-for-australian-companies-explained/#:~:text=Under%20Treasury's%20proposal%2C%20companies%20will,requiring%20substantial%20forward%2Dlooking%20information.

- Greenhouse gas emissions from all sources—scope 1 (direct emissions generated by operations), scope 2 (indirect emissions from energy purchased and used) and scope 3 (indirect emissions along the wider value-chain).
- climate resilience of strategy and business models, informed by scenario analysis.
- responses to anticipated material climate-related physical and transition risks and opportunities.
- any climate-related targets, offset contributions, and transition plans.[57]

This is a precursor to major change:

> Mandatory climate-related disclosures represent a key first component of a wider sustainable finance system that is capable of facilitating and accelerating economy-wide decarbonisation. As the disclosures are implemented, a wealth of new data will enter the market that decision-makers throughout the economy will be able to use to support company, sector and national transitions to net zero in line with Paris Agreement goals.[58]

New Zealand has already incorporated the international standards into its reporting regime, and Australia is in the process of consultation as regards the exposure draft legislation with some companies required to disclose:

> climate-related information as part of their general financial reporting, starting as early as July 2024 for some companies. Australian Security & Investments Commission chair Joe Longo described the shift as the 'biggest change to corporate reporting in a generation.[59]

The Financial Services Council based in Sydney noted in its submission:

> The Financial Services Council (FSC) is a peak body which develops policy for more than 100 member companies in one of Australia's largest industry sectors, financial services. Our Full Members represent Australia's retail and wholesale funds management businesses, and superannuation funds. The FSC is supportive of the climate-related financial disclosure regime. *It is appropriate that fund managers and superannuation funds are required to prepare climate-related financial disclosures given their importance to stewarding the savings of millions of Australians. It is also important that members of these funds understand the climate-related risks and opportunities to their portfolios.*[60] (emphasis added)

57 Climateworks Centre, n 56.

58 Climateworks Centre, n 56.

59 Climateworks Centre, n 56.

60 Financial Services Council, FSC Submission, 'Climate-related financial disclosure: exposure draft legislation', 9 Feb 2024, file:///C:/Users/andre/Downloads/FSC%20Submission_Climate%20Related%20Financial%20Disclosures%20Exposure%20Draft_090224%20(1).pdf.

This reveals the extent to which the financial services industry has accepted the nature of long-term climate risk; it vindicates the legal action taken by Mark McVeigh against REST Super, discussed in Chapter 5.

Competition between companies can generate innovation and inventions at scale. Companies being in competition with one another explicitly sits at the core of this rapidly emerging climate strategy:

> Companies should act now to integrate climate and other sustainability considerations into their overall strategy to better prepare for further developments, including the upcoming release of Treasury's sustainable finance strategy. Companies that do this successfully will demonstrate a competitive advantage and value to investors and customers in a decarbonising economy.[61]

The epoch of carbon accounting has arrived; as Catherine Long, CEO of Trace, a software company providing SMEs with the tools to measure their carbon emissions and proactively reduce them notes:

> Carbon accounting is no longer a climate strategy, but a financial one. I am convinced that in five years' time carbon accounting will be as commonplace as financial accounting.[62]

Esoteric questions about the effectiveness of potential legal regulation have been replaced by the ubiquitous practical nature of mandatory financial reporting. This international change has occurred in rapid time and fundamentally alters the business outlook at a local and national level. This will be the key driver of climate compliance and solution-seeking corporate behaviour.

9.8 Conclusion: new interdisciplinary studies into the nature of capitalism

There is an increasing body of literature on the nature of capitalism arising from a range of disciplines and making unexpected links and connections. For example, the anthropologist Anna Lowenhaupt Tsing refers to capitalism as having several defining features:

> In collecting goods and people from around the world, capitalism has the characteristics of an assemblage. However, it seems to me that capitalism *also* has the characteristics of a machine, a contraption limited to the sum of its parts. This machine is not a total institution, which we spend our lives inside; instead, it translates across living arrangements, turning worlds into assets.

61 Climateworks Centre, n 56.

62 Chartered Accountants Australia and New Zealand, 'How to add carbon accounting to your skill set', *Acuity Magazine, Australian Edition*, Feb/March 2024, vol. 11, Issue 1, 28, www.acuitymag.com.

> But not just any translation can be accepted into capitalism. The gathering it sponsors is not open-ended. An army of technicians and managers stand by to remove offending parts- and they have the power of courts.[63]

Note the reference to litigation; as such corporations can ensure that 'some commitments are sustained, through force'.[64] Companies as bundles of contracts have ready access to the courts. Two of the commitments underpinning companies are alienation and accumulation, respectively, as Tsing observes:

> alienation is that form of disentanglement that allows the making of capitalist assets. Capitalist commodities are removed from their life-worlds to serve as counters in the making of further investments. Infinite needs are one result; there is no limit on how many assets investors want. Thus, too, alienation makes possible accumulation- the amassing of investment capital .... Accumulation is important because it converts ownership into power. *Those with capital can overturn communities and ecologies*.[65] (emphasis added)

In referring to communities and ecologies, Tsing echoes some of the theoretical ground of ESG and CSR. Beyond capitalism being like an assemblage and a contraption, Tsing posits that 'capitalism is a translation machine for producing capital from all kinds of livelihoods, human and not human'.[66] Corporations are the vital cogs within this machine.

The arguments, therefore, about corporations have correlative obligations to and responsibility for the ecologies and communities from which they benefit, and in whose midst, they prosper, will only become more intense in the interconnected epoch of climate litigation. Indeed, 'totally unexpected connections can be made between the economy, culture, biology, and survival strategies'.[67]

Dealing with the Anthropocene and finding climate solutions requires new ways of decoding the world. Delineating the nature of capitalism and the role of corporations will involve analysis (whether welcome or not) from a novel range of disciplinary approaches beyond the narrow, traditional sources of law and economics.

Tackling climate change and finding solutions at scale will reset the economic and conditions for many companies, industries, and sectors. Arguably this may be widespread and part of a socially demanded tipping point if climate risk becomes exponentially important. This sets a fundamental challenge for governments in their capacity as legislators and regulators. The resultant rules will be bifurcated. They will entail both positive steps (in the form of incentives) and negative interventions

63 Anna Lowenhaupt Tsing, *The Mushroom at the End of the World: On the Possibility of Life in Capitalist Ruins*, Princeton University Press, 2015, 133.
64 Tsing, n 63, 133.
65 Tsing, n 63, 133.
66 Tsing, n 63, 133.
67 Bruno Latour, review of Tsing, n 63.

(in the form of penalties). These will be variously set, imposed, maintained, and supervised by differential levels of government.

References

Ian Ayres and John Braithwaite, *Responsive Regulation Transcending the Deregulation Debate*, Oxford University Press, 1992.

Julia Black, *Rules and Regulators*, Clarendon Press, 1997.

Margaret Blair, 'Foreword,' in Beate Sjafjell and Christopher M. Bruner (eds) *The Cambridge Handbook of Corporate Law, Corporate Governance and Sustainability*, Cambridge University Press, 2019.

Bill Gates, *How to Avoid a Climate Disaster*, Penguin, 2021.

Ian Goldin, *Rescue: From Global Crisis to a Better World*, Sceptre, 2021.

Hansmann, H and Kraakman, R, 'Towards a Single Model of Corporate Law?' in Joseph A McCahery, Piet Moerland, Theo Raaijmakers and Luc Renneboog (eds) *Corporate Governance Regimes: Convergence and Diversity*, Oxford University Press, 2002, 56–82.

Henry Hansmann and Reinier Kraakman, 'The End of History for Corporate Law,' 10 March 2000, Yale Law School Working Paper No. 235; NYU Working Paper No. 013; Harvard Law School Discussion Paper No. 280; Yale SOM Working Paper No. ICF - 00-09.

Jeremy Heimans and Henry Timms, *New Power: How Power Works in Our Hyperconnected World- and How to Make it Work for You*, MacMillan, 2018.

Michael Legg, *Regulation, Litigation and Enforcement*, Thomson Reuters, 2011.

Bronwen Morgan and Karen Yeung, *An Introduction to Law and Regulation*, University of Bristol, 2007.

Tony Prosser, *Law and the Regulators*, Clarendon Press, 1997.

Margaret Blair, 'Foreword,' in Beate Sjafjell and Christopher M. Bruner (eds) *The Cambridge Handbook of Corporate Law, Corporate Governance and Sustainability*, University of Oslo, 2019.

Ian M Ramsay, 'Models of Corporate Regulation: The Mandatory/Enabling Debate,' in Ross Grantham and Charles Rickett (eds), *Corporate Personality in the 20th Century*, Hart Publishing 1998, 215–270.

Gerard C Rowe, 'Economic Theories of the Nature of Regulatory Activity,' in Tomasic, R. (ed), *Business Regulation in Australia*, CCH Australia Ltd, 1984, 147–173.

Peter M. Senge, *The Fifth Discipline: The Art and Practice of The Learning Organization*, Random House, 1990.

Beate Sjafjell and Benjamin J Richardson, 'Chapter 8, The Future of Company Law and Sustainability,' in Beate Sjafjell and Benjamin J Richardson (eds) *Company Law and Sustainability: Legal Barriers and Opportunities*, Cambridge University Press, 2015, 312–340.

Roman Tomasic (ed) *Business Regulation in Australia*, CCH Australia Ltd, 1984.

Anna Lowenhaupt Tsing, *The Mushroom at the End of the World: On the Possibility of Life in Capitalist Ruins*, Princeton University Press, 2015.

Christopher Wright and Daniel Nyberg, *Climate Change, Capitalism, and Corporations: Processes of Creative Self Destruction*, Cambridge University Press, 2015.

10 Conclusion

The challenge for corporate law in the age of the climate emergency

10.1 The three prisms through which climate change debate has been conducted

Australia's entrenched extraction and monetization model is now at a crossroads in the face of global climate change action and particularly following the Paris Climate Change Agreement.[1] The government has been accused of not taking climate damage seriously, and supporting coal and fossil fuel extraction as what seems to be a matter of ideological fixation.[2] This was particularly the case after Australia's arguments at the Madrid update conference in 2019,[3] where Australia sought to support mining by justifying the use of carry-over credits from the Kyoto Protocol in 2005,[4] some 14 years previously. As a G20 country with an advanced economy and regulatory framework, this is seen as setting a dangerous precedent, fostering an out-of-date argument, and one distinctly lacking in merit,[5] likely to be emulated by developing economies.

Australia's grappling with climate change reflects three prisms of its social and economic fabric. First, it is one of the world's major producers and exporter of fossil fuels. Second, it has a highly concentrated press and media with major corporate interests occupying a dominant position in the national discourse. That media position has led to the rise of populism. In this mode, the media has become an adherent of scepticism when it comes to accepting climate science and the existence of the climate emergency. It sets out to undermine the public's confidence in the need for radical solutions, and thereby to sequester climate science to the peripheries as a concern of elites as confected and bogus, and perhaps most effectively of all, as an attack on the lives and livelihoods of working

1 The Paris Climate Agreement, 2016, https://unfccc.int/process-and-meetings/the-paris-agreement/the-paris-agreement.

2 For techniques used by the electricity and coal sector, see Guy Pearse, *Greenwash: Big Brands and Carbon Scams*, Black Inc, 2012, 70–6.

3 COP25, Madrid December 2019, https://www.carbonbrief.org/cop25-key-outcomes-agreed-at-the-un-climate-talks-in-madrid.

4 United Nations Climate Change, 'What is the Kyoto Protocol?', 2005, https://unfccc.int/kyoto_protocol.

5 Criticism of carry-over credit techniques https://www.carbonbrief.org/cop25-key-outcomes-agreed-at-the-un-climate-talks-in-madrid

DOI: 10.4324/9781003263746-11

families. The EV scenario of low take-up combined with the political discourse of combining greed and envy is a case in point. The high uptake of household rooftop solar power solutions is, by contrast, an argument for optimism. The third prism is that the climate debate is dominated by political and economic narratives. In broad terms, the Left seeks to be more ambitious, the Right less so, but there is at play an implicit and powerful reversion to the mean. For instance, both sides have approved new coal and gas projects in recent times and there is a hesitance to break with the status quo. The fact that fossil fuels still receive approximately ten billion dollars in subsidies is illustrative.

10.1.1 Delayed political action driven by denial of the climate science

Whilst Australia was essentially in a denialist-loop about the climate crisis until the May 2022 federal election, such that the incumbent right-wing government drove home the message that the climate crisis was a phantom of, and fantasy perpetuated by, green-left parties. Even though the worst elements of denialism are thankfully behind us, the new, highly contested political terrain is what to do between now and 2050. The political acrimony between left and right has been doubled down to the extent that the right, now in opposition, cannot shift its mindset from the political fray, and refuses to characterize the climate crisis as urgent in various dimensions, as national, as global, and as requiring policy initiatives beyond the three-year political cycle.

10.1.2 Political gridlock and corporate confusion

Whilst ever this obsessional gridlock with the politicizing every aspect of climate science-based solutions remains in place, as opposed to finding common cause, and given the unending internecine warfare mindset of the federal sphere, it is very difficult for corporations to deliver the necessary creativity, innovation, and tangible solutions. Australia has this century been poor at providing the legislative conditions, the political will and regulatory simplicity, and the commercial certainty for companies to take risks and to make big bets on the future. Corporate law has become less adventurous and reform-minded in an era dominated by political and economic concerns, rather than social and environmental issues.

Individual companies and corporate risk takers, even the wealthiest participants, can only go so far. They need to know the rules of the game, and they require long and stable horizons. Those are, paradoxically, the same parameters required to meet net zero by 2050. The calumny of the Australian polity is short termism and timidity exacerbated by the nominal three-year electoral cycle, but which is often foreshortened. In this shallow and uncertain terrain, it is difficult for start-up companies to grow and prosper, especially when they are in industries replete with well-resourced, long-standing participants whose interests are well served, implicitly or not, by keeping new competitors at bay.

10.1.3 Corporate law within the broader political economic paradigm

In one sense, Australian corporate law fits neatly within the economic paradigm. It is an important but subsidiary part of the neoliberal, profit-seeking paradigm, as exemplified by the backlash suffered by the ASX as regards the social license that it unwittingly set in train in seeking to review the CGP&R 4th edition, as discussed in Chapter 4. Major law firms and peak body stakeholders played a major role as part of the corporate law ecosystem in vehemently opposing the introduction of the concept of social licence. In this regard economic and political factors overwhelmed references to social and environmental factors. The damage of a social licence variety suffered by Rio Tinto in 2020 has been short-term and not deleterious to the share price which now sits in record territory.

Companies will be important actors within a new and dynamic economic, political, cultural, and social matrix. Company law theory, as it emerges in the post-emergency (and ideally steady-state or sustainable) economy, will be quite different to the 19th-conception of the company. The ways in which it will vary, potentially, will be subject to conjecture and contest. A critical component which was referred to earlier is the scope and range of what companies can and should do. The realm of activity will necessarily be more interdisciplinary. It will not simply be underpinned by law and economic considerations, but also by science, including eco-systems, environmental science, and sustainable engineering. In this way, the epoch of the corporation acting out of sight and out of mind in the pursuit of profits (the model of which emanates from the British East India Company) requires fundamental recalibration. This debate focuses on the corporate climate: the conditions, theory, and practices of the corporation. Sustainable corporations will play an integral role. This book explores the tensions inherent in an evolving economy of ideas and proposes that the sustainable corporation will be the new benchmark within just a few years.

10.1.4 The climate crisis and the quest for corporate sustainability

Recognition of the climate crisis has inextricably linked the health of the natural world with anthropological wellbeing. The ongoing modern day industrial experiment rendered on the Australian continent is a prime example of this. Agricultural, livestock, and mining corporations have been exponents of the exploit-at-all-costs mentality for much of the nation's recent history. Monetization of the landscape has been the fundamental driver of the Australian economy, and in turn, the Australian corporation. The First Nations notion of reasonable balance is now manifest in the climate related term, sustainable balance. This requires companies to think long term, to embrace stakeholders beyond short-term profit for shareholders, and for corporations to be part of the communities they serve, and able to demonstrate this through tangible endeavours such as CSR, and SLTO which is investigated in the Chapter 4 case study involving Rio Tinto. Companies need to demonstrate sustainability in the face of the climate crisis:

- Board which are representative of the community.
- Stakeholder engagement.
- True triple bottom line thinking that meshes profit, the environment, and social aspects.
- Where possible, climate driven solutions, including carbon reduction and thinking beyond the balance sheet mechanics of net zero.

10.2 The evolution of complex corporate law and sophisticated climate science

10.2.1 The last three decades: from the Holocene to the Anthropocene

The hockey-stick graph visually represents:

> what people now call the 'great acceleration' in climate change, and, at a longer time scale, the brusque shift from what geologists have named the Holocene- the almost straight horizontal line for the last 12,000 years- to the Anthropocene- the other straight but vertical line, that keeps drilling through all those charts scientists are so tired of commenting on and their audiences so terrified to look at.[6]

Companies are disembodied constructs. They are artificial legal entities. They don't have a soul or a conscience. Sheeting home criminal culpability is fraught. We need to populate and humanize the company. This would increase accountability and responsibility. We witness the same phenomenon in a global environment of scarce resources. This is sheeted home by the work of the Global Footprint Network and the concept of the Earth Overshoot Day.[7]

In 2020, Australia uses its fair share of resources by 30 March, just a quarter of the way into the year. By contrast, Indonesia does not do so until December 18. Australia was 8th worst economy for overshoot. This means that for nine months of the year Australians are living beyond their allocation of the planetary envelope and the Earth's resources.

This skewing is borne out by Bruno Latour's set of observations:

> None of the nation states composing Globalizations' map occupies only the official space inside its borders and frontiers. China, Europe, the United States- all occupy other territories in many ways, either forcibly or through the partially hidden means of 'ghost acreage' to use Kenneth Pomeranz's powerful expression (in Pomeranz, The Great Divergence: China, Europe and the Making of the Modern World Economy, Princeton University Press, 2000. This is what Pierre Charbonnier calls the 'ubiquity of the moderns'

6 Bruno Latour, 'Seven Objections against landing on Earth,' in Bruno Latour and Peter Weibel (eds), *Critical Zones: The Science and Politics of Landing on Earth*, ZKM, 2020, 12-19, 15.

7 Earth Overshoot Day, 'Earth Overshoot Day 2023 fell on August 2', https://overshoot.footprintnetwork.org/.

> to underline that there is no correspondence whatsoever between the shape of nation states in the legal sense and the widely distributed sources of the wealth its citizens benefit from. Belonging to a territory on such a planet is a sure way of being misled and lost: your wealth, or your misery, comes from places that are invisible on the administrative map of your land.[8]

10.2.2 The emergence of a clear legal schematic of climate risk for corporations

Economics and politics have until recently dominated debate in Australia leaving little room for other narratives or areas of concern. Since the Paris Climate Agreement 2016,[9] a range of new concerns have coalesced. Climate science, the emergence of financial risk, and the clarification of legal liability principles have emerged. Climate concerns have moved beyond environmental law and public law, and into the realms of corporate law, governance, and regulation. This has changed how directors need to view the future, especially the long-term. As Justice Kenneth Hayne, formerly a Justice of the High Court of Australia, observed extrajudicially in 2019:

> Directors must act in the best interests of the company. "Best interests" is not one-dimensional – it is not determined *only* by share price movement or "total shareholder return" over a period. "Best interests" does not present a binary choice between the interests of shareholders and the interests of others (whether customers, employees, or society more generally). *The longer the period of reference, the more the interests of all affected by a company's actions will converge in pursuit of the long-term financial advantage of the enterprise.* (Italics added)[10]

This reference to the longer term is apposite, given the goal of net zero by the middle of the 21st century. The wicked problem of how climate risk will be navigated by directors is coming into increasing focus in Australia as the result of litigation. The reference to 'society more generally' includes the social, environmental, and ecological parameters relevant to a corporation's business. The 'social' dimension—whether part of corporate social responsibility (CSR), environmental social governance (ESG), or the Social Licence to Operate (SLTO) will move from the periphery to the centre, from the liminal edges to the core.

8 Bruno Latour, '"We don't seem to live on the same planet": A fictional planetarium', in Bruno Latour and Peter Weibel (eds), *Critical Zones: The Science and Politics of Landing on Earth*, ZKM, 2020, 276–81, 276.

9 Paris Climate Agreement 2016, n 1.

10 Centre for Policy Development, CPD Roundtable on Climate and Sustainability, 21 November, 2019, 1-5, 1, https://cpd.org.au/wp-content/uploads/2019/12/Ken-Hayne-remarks-to-CPD-Roundtable.pdf

10.2.3 The evolution of the investment landscape to account for climate risk

It is clear from an analysis of Australian developments, that there is an emerging set of legal principles which are based around climate risk. These are founded on an ever more sophisticated scientific consensus, particularly focused on climate science. This provides a model of the world based on ecosystems and planetary boundaries.

What does this mean for business law and mercantile activity more generally, and the role of business entities such as companies, more specifically? Activity will have to be guided. Regulation will have to be more directional, both in terms of outlining incentives and disincentives.

This will require a reassessment in neoliberal economies such as Australia about the realm of corporate law theory. Concession theory currently supposes that a company can engage in absolutely any activity unless it is narrowly defined as illegal. The organic theory—that companies are like humans—needs to be given fuller meaning in terms of societal and contextual obligations, rather than the focus on privilege and power. An ecologically informed version of concession theory will be a requisite piece of reform. More broadly, convergence of global benchmarks will mean that more cooperation is required.

10.3 Reasons to be pessimistic about reaching net zero carbon emissions by 2050

10.3.1 The need for advocacy regarding the facts of climate science

Dr Joelle Gergis, who was an Australian representative on the UN's 6th Intergovernmental Panel on Climate Change has written of her role and that of climate scientists:

> As a climate scientist at this fraught point in our history, the most important thing I can offer is clear-eyed and compassionate look at the facts.[11]

Even overtly scientific entities like the Bureau of Meteorology (BoM) can be swamped by concerted campaigns of climate denialism. Ideology and belief must give way to observable, measurable, and verifiable data findings, but this takes time and resources:

> A small band of sceptics have long claimed a conspiracy, without evidence, that the bureau deliberately used homogenisation in its centrepiece dataset of 112 weather stations—known as the Australian Climate Observations

11 Dr Joelle Gergis, 'The Terrible Truth of Climate Change', in Cameron Muir, Kirsten Wehner and Jenny Newell (eds), *Living with the Anthropocene: Love, Loss and Hope in the face of Environmental Crisis*, NewSouth Publishing, 2020, 29–34.

> Reference Network—Surface Air Temperature (Acorn-Sat)—to make the heating of the continent's climate appear worse.[12]

Former BoM boss, Rob Vertessy, who left the agency in 2016, has said:

> the attacks were pushed by an organised 'fever swamp' of climate science denial. Every minute a BoM executive spends on this nonsense is a minute lost to managing risk and protecting the community. It is a real problem.[13]

The politicization of science has been led by fossil fuel interests and lobby groups, including sections of the media. Much time has been spent on distracting issues, including:

- The long-running electricity wars in Australia.
- The pervasive use of greenwashing by fossil fuel companies.
- The capture of language; the status quo is enabled, prolonged, and given licence by the elastic concept of 'transition'.
- 'Carbon capture and storage' also referred to as carbon sequestration—a fantasy technology perpetuated by the fossil fuel industry.
- The often obscure but penetrating use of so-called 'independent' think-tanks.

10.3.2 The political and economic challenge of climate change: dealing with paradigms of entrenched power

Corporate law will continue to occupy a central place in neoliberal economies. These economies will be forced to pivot towards the emerging ecological model of society imposed by climate science and the recognition of hyperobject which is climate change and global warming. This will impact every feature of society, including the operation and scope of corporations.

The fact that much of the world is now signed up to the simple sounding declaration—net zero by 2050, provides a nearly three-decade time frame into the future.

This necessarily means that societies, economies, and companies must operate in the present, but also in the imaginative realm provided this three-decade window. Is it an opportunity or a burdensome inconvenience? Is it a Darwinian race to the bottom, or the start of the new green revolution? Is it Lord of the Flies and dystopian, or will it be generative of grand visions such as the universal wage in some countries?

12 Graham Readfearn, 'Climate scientists first laughed at a 'bizarre' campaign against the BoM- then came the harassment', *The Guardian*, 7 May 2023, https://www.theguardian.com/science/2023/may/07/climate-scientists-first-laughed-at-a-bizarre-campaign-against-the-bom-then-came-the-harassment.

13 Graham Readfearn, *The Guardian*, n 12.

10.3.2.1 Legal history and common law incrementalism

The common law of Australia, based on the English system is historically informed and generally cautious. Its abiding modus operandi in the apex court of Australia has been incrementalism. The urgent challenge of the next three decades is essentially unique. It is a global point in time, and global convergence will become more important. Even within a single nation state, the common law is not a sufficient instrument to lead the way on driving climate solutions. Litigation is an important tool but not paradigm changing in sufficient scale as it deals with facts on a case by case basis

10.3.2.2 The privilege of self-regulation: reserved for the powerful few

The power for a company to judge itself against a set of guidelines is a powerful privilege. The individual taxpayer gets no such right or honour. It is, paradoxically enough, a privilege often afforded to well-resourced and often powerful participants within a given market. It is the resources base which means the firm can, in theory, oversee its compliance as a properly resourced project. Therein lies the rub. The resources at hand can also be deployed to game the system. To avoid the strictures and spirit of the set of rules and guidelines extant to the industry.

In Australia, nowhere is this more the case than with the Australian Media and Communications Authority (ACMA) and the technology and media industry where:

> Online misinformation in Australia is self-regulated, with the tech peak body Digital Industry Group Inc—whose members include Google, Apple, Meta, Twitter and TikTok—responsible for drawing up the voluntary code of conduct.[14]

10.3.3 The disavowal: the claimed exceptionalism of the Australian political economy

Exceptionalism of the Australian political economy with its reliance on percentages to argue we have done our fair share.

Australia has been during 'extractive capitalism' since its modern foundation. This entails 'resource mobilization'. The 'history of labor and capitalism' and its connection to 'Earth and planet' is explored by Bruno Latour and Dipesh Chakrabarty.[15] This extraction directly affects the health of the biosphere. The example of the Sharma litigation is a case in point. The school student plaintiffs

14 Paul Karp, 'WhatsApp and other messaging services left out of new Australian misinformation code, regulator says,' *The Guardian (Australia)*, Mon 9 Jan 2023.

15 Bruno Latour and Dipesh Chakrabarty, 'When the Global Reveals the Planetary: Bruno Latour Interviews Dipesh Chakrabarty,' in Bruno Latour and Peter Weibel (eds), *Critical Zones: The Science and Politics of Landing on Earth*, ZKM, 2020, 24–31, 24.

founded their claim in negligence and asserted that a duty of care was owed on the basis that the Galilee/Jubilee mine extension of coal extraction would generate more than 100 million tonnes of carbon dioxide into the Earth's atmosphere.

The hegemony of the status quo, and the untrammelled power of the incumbents is revealed by the fact that the five biggest oil and gas companies in Australia in 2020 were: [16]

- BHP Billiton Limited, at no. 3 on the ASX 300 (and in 2024, ranked first).
- Woodside Petroleum Ltd, at no. 17.
- Origin Energy Ltd, at no. 39.
- Santos Ltd, at no 49.
- Caltex Australia Ltd, at no 51.

These are five companies in the top 50 or within the top 1/6th (that is, within the top 16%) of the most powerful sector of the market. Put alternatively, they are five businesses within the elite, high-end strata by reference to market value and influence. By any view, they represent a substantial segment of Australia's most powerful corporations.

10.3.4 The corporate concentration of CO_2 emissions globally

This concentration is not unique to Australia. It is a feature globally of greenhouse gas emissions. In 2019, it was reported that just 20 large corporations have been responsible for more than 35% of the world's carbon dioxide and methane pollution between 1965 and 2020, equivalent to a total of 480bn tonnes of carbon dioxide.[17] These findings were calculated by reference to the companies' annual reports and supply-chain data. Eight of the companies were investor-owned entities, and 12 were state-owned enterprises with the biggest, Saudi Aramco, producing neatly 60bn tonnes of carbon dioxide equivalent to '4.38% of the global total on its own'.[18] The investor-owned corporations included Chevron and Exxon, each having produced more than 40bn tonnes, and BP and Shell, each having produced more than 30bn tonnes.

The list also included Australia's BHP which between 1965 and 2020 produced 9.8 billion tonnes of carbon dioxide. The fact that 12 of the 20 companies (60%) were state-owned companies indicates how enmeshed governments are with the global fossil fuel market. Expecting states to be effective regulators as regards investor-owned corporations is problematic, given this context. The US climate scientist, Michael Mann, observed of these findings:

16 Jake Powell, Australia's Top Five Oil and Gas Companies, 18 May 2020, https://blog.iseekplant.com.au/blog/biggest-oil-and-gas-companies-australia.

17 Matthew Taylor and Jonathon Watts, 'Revealed: the 20 firms behind a third of all carbon emissions,' *The Guardian*, 9 October, 2019, https://www.theguardian.com/environment/2019/oct/09/revealed-20-firms-third-carbon-emissions.

18 Taylor and Watts, n 17.

> The great tragedy of the climate crisis is that seven and a half billion people must pay the price—in the form of a degraded planet—so that a couple of dozen polluting interests can continue to make record profits. It is a great moral failing of our political system that we have allowed this to happen.[19]

The fact that so few companies have done so much of the damage is alarming. What makes it more disturbing is the fact that they have known about the catastrophic dangers of excessive carbon emissions since December 1954.[20] The date against which they should be held morally culpable, if not legally responsible, goes back further in time as new research emerges from corporate archives via painstaking research conducted by climate think-tanks. Previously it was thought that the corporate knowledge could be attributed to the 1980s, then back to the 1970s, and further back to the 1960s. The fact that the scientific knowledge now traces back to December 1954, just nine years after the end of World War 2 in September 1945, reveals that the post-war industrial boom in fossil fuel production was in full swing and this clearly underwrites the three-decade period of heightened prosperity between 1950 and 1980. These decades were historical outliers in terms of western-world growth and prosperity.[21]

In 1954, the major fossil fuel and car companies in the US 'funded some of the world's most foundational climate science as early as 1954'[22] via a group referred to as the Air Pollution Foundation.

10.3.5 The partisan nature, even now, of climate policy

10.3.5.1 The New Zealand example—the winding back of hard-won climate policy

To wind back hard-won climate policy can still be politically expedient and popular in the short-term in nations such as Australia and New Zealand. Policy that can have taken years to put in place, can take just weeks to wind down and eliminate.

In terms of the electric vehicle sector, New Zealand Government policy under the former Labor government offered generous discounts and rebates to buyers of zero- and low-emissions vehicles—and taxed utes and SUVs at higher rate to pay for the scheme known as the Clean Car Rebate will be scrapped after a change of government and the election of the conservative National party.[23] The scheme used a sliding-scale to provide financial incentives of up to NZ$7,015 ($6,519) for

19 Taylor and Watts, n 17.

20 Oliver Milman, '"Smoking gun proof": fossil fuel industry knew of climate danger as early as 1954, documents show', *The Guardian*, 31 January 2024, https://www.theguardian.com/us-news/2024/jan/30/fossil-fuel-industry-air-pollution-fund-research-caltech-climate-change-denial.

21 Thomas Piketty, *Capital in the 21st Century*, Belknap, 2014.

22 Milman, n 20.

23 Ben Zachariah, 'Newly-elected New Zealand Government to scrap 'ute tax', electric-car rebates – report', *DRIVE*, 18 October 2023, https://www.drive.com.au/news/new-zealand-government-to-scrap-ute-tax-electric-car-rebates/.

buyers of electric cars and hybrids, while those purchasing vehicles with higher emissions were taxed up to a maximum of NZ$6,900 ($6,412).[24]

According to a report from New Zealand's Autocar, 'the newly-elected government has announced it will scrap the 'carrot and stick' approach—referred to locally as the "ute tax"—which was meant to be self-funding but has instead wracked up a NZ$279 million ($259 million) loss since it was introduced in 2021'.[25]

The new government's political attack was typical of the critique of EVs as high-priced luxury purchases:

> [The party] does not believe New Zealanders who can afford to buy a brand-new electric car need a subsidy from hardworking taxpayers to pay for it. [26]

Similar critiques have been levelled at EVs and their owners in Australia.

10.4 Reasons to be optimistic about corporate action as regards the climate emergency

10.4.1 Emergence of a UN-led international consensus

The UN Conference of the Parties held in December 2023 (COP 28) was said by the UN to be:

> particularly momentous as it marked the conclusion of the first 'global stocktake' of the world's efforts to address climate change under the Paris Agreement. Having shown that progress was too slow across all areas of climate action—from reducing greenhouse gas emissions, to strengthening resilience to a changing climate, to getting the financial and technological support to vulnerable nations—countries responded with a decision on how to accelerate action across all areas by 2030. This includes a call on governments to speed up the transition away from fossil fuels to renewables such as wind and solar power in their next round of climate commitments.[27]

The issue of fossil fuels was addressed:

> COP 28 closed with an agreement that signals the 'beginning of the end' of the fossil fuel era by laying the ground for a swift, just and equitable transition, underpinned by deep emissions cuts and scaled-up finance. As COP 28 President Dr. Sultan Al Jaber said: 'We have language on fossil fuel in the (COP) final agreement for the first time ever.' It clearly points to

24 DRIVE, n 23.
25 DRIVE, n 23.
26 DRIVE, n 23.
27 United Nations Climate Change, 'COP28: What Was Achieved and What Happens Next?' 13 December 2023, https://unfccc.int/cop28/5-key-takeaways#end-of-fossil-fuels.

> the direction of travel in the energy transition, and that the scale and pace of change can't be stopped or reversed.[28]

The UN Climate Change Executive Secretary, Simon Stiell, in his closing speech at COP28 said:

> Whilst we didn't turn the page on the fossil fuel era in Dubai, this outcome is the beginning of the end. Now all governments and businesses need to turn these pledges into real-economy outcomes, without delay.[29]

By contrast, climate scientist, Dr Friederike Otto, at Imperial College London and co-founder of the World Weather Attribution group, reacted strongly to the COP28 deal:

> The lukewarm agreement reached at Cop28 will cost every country, no matter how rich, no matter how poor. Everyone loses. It's hailed as a compromise, but we need to be very clear what has been compromised. The short-term financial interests of a few have again won over the health, lives and livelihoods of most people living on this planet. With every vague verb, every empty promise in the final text, millions more people will enter the frontline of climate change and many will die. At 1.2C of warming, we're already seeing devastating climate impacts that disrupt economies, destroy livelihoods, and claim lives. Climate change is driving instability. Nearly every country wants stability, but until fossil fuels are phased out, the world will continue to become a more dangerous, more expensive, and more uncertain place to live.[30]

10.4.2 Exemplars of good practice: the US suspending new permits for natural gas

Gas is promoted as a transition or bridging fossil fuel between coal and renewables both in Australia and the US. President Biden has belatedly suspended new permits for natural gas terminals. This announcement has been welcomed by US environmentalist Bill McKibben who writes that a US President saying 'no to big oil' is 'remarkable, and almost without precedent'.[31]

28 United Nations Climate Change, n 27.

29 Simon Stiell, UN Climate Change Executive Secretary at COP 28 Closing Address, 'We didn't turn the page on the fossil fuel era, but this outcome is the beginning of the end', 13 December 2023, https://unfccc.int/news/we-didn-t-turn-the-page-on-the-fossil-fuel-era-but-this-outcome-is-the-beginning-of-the-end-un-0.

30 Jonathon Watts, 'COP28's winners and losers: from fossil fuel firms to future generations', *The Guardian*, 14 Dec 2023, https://www.theguardian.com/environment/2023/dec/14/cop28-winners-and-losers-fossil-fuel-climate-crisis.

31 Bill McKibben, 'Joe Biden just did the rarest thing in US politics: he stood up to the oil industry', The Guardian, 7 Feb 2024, https://www.theguardian.com/commentisfree/2024/feb/07/joe-biden-big-oil-lng-permits#:~:text=The%20Biden%20administration%20suspended%20new,of%20this

The Biden administration has:

> halted the granting of new permits for building liquefied natural gas (LNG) export terminals, something Washington had been handing out like M&Ms on Halloween for nearly a decade. It's a provisional 'no'—Department of Energy experts will spend the coming months figuring out a new formula for granting the licenses that takes the latest science and economics into account—but you can tell what a big deal it is because of the howls of rage coming from the petroleum industry and its gaggle of politicians. [32]

McKibben argues that:

> We now live on a planet where the cheapest way to produce power is to point a sheet of glass at the sun; there's no reason not to go straight from coal to renewable energy, with no intermediate stop at gas. The idea that it's a 'bridge fuel' is a decade out of date, but it's an argument that big oil wants to extend four or five decades into the future.[33]

This political initiative is an example of national leadership on climate action but given the US's standing as still the world's biggest economy, it has international potency for other nations to follow. In this way, it is like the European Union's CBAM proposal. As a regional coalition of nations making up the largest trading bloc in the world, this too carries significance for other nation states.

Whether the US political stance on oil translates to Australian conditions is the moot point. Gas was lauded as the COVID-19 transition fuel of choice by the Morrison government right up until its election loss in 2022. The other political reality is that the likely Republican candidate for the November 2024 US Presidential election has made repeated reference to his signature fossil fuel policy summed up by the slogan 'drill, baby, drill',[34] a phrase used by the Republican Party since 2008.[35]

10.4.3 Sovereign parliaments exercising political will

Regulation can be imposed on sector-wide corporations by governments willing to act. It can synchronously affect a wide range of market participants. In addition to regulation there are variously taxes, incentives, penalties, and subsidies (TIPS) that

---

%20kind%20of%20backbone%3F&text=Ten%20days%20ago%20Joe%20Biden,said%20no%20to%20big%20oil.

32 McKibben, n 31.

33 McKibben, n 31.

34 Julianne Geiger, 'Trump Promises to 'Drill, Baby, Drill' if Elected', OIlPrice.Com, 11 May 2023, https://oilprice.com/Latest-Energy-News/World-News/Trump-Promises-To-Drill-Baby-Drill-If-Elected.html.

35 Raylene Rogers, 'Drill, Baby, Drill', Trust Company Oklahoma, https://www.trustok.com/drill-baby-drill/.

can form part of a policy setting. Providing subsidies and incentives can set in place positive change; taxes and penalties can limit negative change.

10.4.4 The existence of practical plans and ideas to tackle the climate crisis

In the Australian context of dealing with the climate emergency, two books stand out. The first is Ross Garnaut's *Superpower*[36] setting out the case for Australia's economy to pivot from fossil fuel champion to global leader in renewables, given the geographical and geological bestowed by nature on the island continent. The second book, which provides practical advice at the household level is Saul Griffith's *The Big Switch.*[37] It is described by climate entrepreneur, Mike Cannon-Brookes, as 'an actual plan written down that can be executed and financed. In a decarbonised world, Australia is a winner. The opportunity now is ours for the taking'[38]. Climate science, economic possibilities, and technology breakthroughs can set up companies to be at the forefront of the solutions era.

10.4.5 Positive social tipping points

Climate science has revealed several harmful tipping points in the natural world.

Climate scientists are beginning to refer to positive social tipping points, where profound change can occur rapidly:

> The current approach of linear incremental change favoured by many decision makers is no longer an option. Existing governance institutions and decision-making approaches need to adapt to facilitate transformational change. Crucial to achieving this transformational change are positive tipping point opportunities, where desirable changes in society become self-propelling. Concerted actions can create the enabling conditions for triggering rapid and large-scale transformation. Human history is flush with examples of abrupt social and technological change. Recent examples include the exponential increases in renewable electricity, the global reach of environmental justice movements, and the accelerating rollout of electric vehicles.[39]

Perhaps more significantly is the growing awareness of the connection between positive social tipping points potentially reducing the impact of negative climate impacts, given that 'negative tipping point threats could be mitigated if there was a vast effort to trigger other positive tipping point opportunities'.[40] For example, 'targeted actions by innovators, governments, investors and companies have created

36 Ross Garnaut, *Superpower: Australia's Low-carbon Opportunity*, La Trobe University Press, 2020.

37 Saul Griffith, *The Big Switch: Australia's Electric Future*, Black Inc., 2022.

38 Griffith, n 37.

39 Global Tipping Points, Summary, University of Exeter, 6 December 2023, https://global-tipping-points.org/summary-report/narrative-summary/.

40 Global Tipping Points, Summary, n 39.

economies of scale that are now propelling the exponential uptake of renewable energy worldwide, which has reached or exceeded cost parity with fossil fuel power generation'.[41]

10.5 The role of the corporation in the epoch of the climate emergency

10.5.1 Reflecting on the four corporate case studies

10.5.1.1 Adani, Chapter 3

Whilst the Adani case study was ostensibly about investments in thermal coal and the possibility of stranded assets, the case matter is highly political. The fact that corporate law can be political is reflected in leading texts on Anglo-US corporate law literature.[42] The for-profit entity is a creature of statute and public law and private law are co-extensive in the essential architecture and purpose of the corporation. As Kent Greenfield notes, 'corporate law should be seen not as a narrow, private-law field for the acolytes of law and economics. Rather, it should be debated as if it were part of large social and macroeconomic policy'.[43] Given the context of the climate emergency, political discussions regarding corporations will be inescapable.

10.5.1.2 Rio Tinto, Chapter 4

Chapter 4 analyzed a particular action by the Rio Tinto corporate group in May 2020, and the ongoing fallout from this event. It involved the destruction by explosion by the company, whilst extracting iron ore for export, of ancient rock shelters, paintings, and drawings located in the Juukan Gorge of the Pilbara in the north-west of Western Australia. It brought to the surface of debate the social license to operate debate. This was not long after the ASX's struggle with the SLTO issue. After the Juukan destruction, SLTO was important in the short term, but its lack of political and economic traction over a longer period has been apparent; Rio's share price now sits at a record high.

SLTO will be important in climate litigation and will hover in the debate concerning the forthcoming 5th edition of the ASX Corporate Governance Principles and Rule.

41 Global Tipping Points, Summary, n 39.

42 See, for instance, Mark Roe's *Political Determinants of Corporate Governance: Political Context, Corporate Impact*, OUP, 2003, and John Parkinson, Andrew Gamble and Gavin Kelly (eds), *The Political Economy of the Company*, Hart Publishing, 2000.

43 Kent Greenfield, *The Failure of Corporate Law: Fundamental Flaws and Progressive Possibilities*, The University of Chicago Press, 2006, 27.

10.5.1.3 McVeigh, Chapter 5

Chapter 5 examined long-run investment decision-making and the spectre of intergenerational stranded assets. It provided impetus to the changing nature of financial risk. Climate change is a financial risk and will be critically important to corporate viability. This chapter also, more broadly, traced the contours of a nascent fault line between the long-established, neoliberal economy, of which Australia has long been a demonstrable adherent, and the emerging green or sustainable economy, with reference to climate risk. The steady accumulation of international factors, evidencing the emergence of this new and paradigm-shifting economic model, were outlined.

10.5.1.4 Sharma, Chapter 6

Chapter 6 examined litigation risk, the prospect of stranded people, land masses, and nation states. It examined the coming decades through the perspective of young people who will be left with the legacy damage.

By contrast to legislation, the common law will not provide climate solutions quickly, or on its own. Litigation can assist as part of a broader movement, comprising a positive social tipping point. It is part of the set of factors which can shift behaviour, and it may lead change in specific instances, but the broad push needs to come from the political and legislative sectors.

10.5.2 Embracing the concept of 'what is possible?' in a time of crisis

Just as the 19th century gave rise to innovations in Australian specific corporate structures, and regulation reflected this, the 21st century and the climate emergency gives rise to a similar challenge.

As the year 2023 ends, one is reminded of the hourglass and time passing relentlessly between the annual UN COPs, and the fact it is just seven years to 2030 and the compliance with, or otherwise, of major interim targets, and just 27 years until there exists a transformed global ecosystem in some sort of stable balance at net zero emissions or better.

COVID-19 was a case study in what was possible in short time if there was political will and commercial focus. Australia rapidly became a land of hand-sanitizer manufacturers where distilleries and other infrastructure switched purpose in short order to assist with the national and international health emergency.

Corporate laws were also changed to allow more time for corporate solvency issues to be overcome, just as supply chains and business cashflows dried up in the volatile and dystopian markets of 2020–2. This demonstrated that if political will and commercial resolve align, much can be achieved in short order.

However, the aftermath of COVID has also been a period of insularity. Nation states guard their borders ever more vigilantly. Voters are sceptical of government involvement and activity, and the capacity of elected officials to solve problems at scale. There is a persistent anti-science segmentation of the population which has coalesced around the issues of vaccines. This has given rise to widescale vaccine hesitancy and in a growing number of people, an obdurate refusal on their part, and for those they care for to be vaccinated. This has emanated in courts in Australia, particularly in remote and regional Magistrates Courts with the steep recent rise in the number of self-represented so called 'sovereign citizens' claiming they are not bound by the court's jurisdiction.

Currently, science has never been more important. It provides the best objective data and evidence to support policy, whether it be health measures, vaccine mandates, or the climate science revealing the scale of the issue.

10.5.3 The re-emergence and persistence of political and economic conditions favouring weak corporate law

This disregard for science gives rise to a new form of politics of confected populism and misleading simplicity, which drives an economic model foregrounded on the individual rather than the collective good, which in turn create the perfect conditions for shareholder primacy in corporate law. Social licence is critiqued as the dead hand of a socialist dystopia.

As such, the political Right can succinctly characterize its case for the status quo. By contrast, the Left has a much more complex case to make for just change. With weak laws and a poorly resourced regulator, the behemoth companies effectively rule the business landscape unchallenged.

10.5.4 Returning to a mindset of corporate law reform to enable corporate capacity

If corporations are to be part of an integrated national solution, we need to envision what corporate law could possibly be, and how the regulator could be fully involved as a well-resourced litigant. The law on the books is porous and inadequate; net zero by 2050 requires both political will and regulatory capacity.

Some of the changes involving corporate law and governance are set out below:

- The legislature needs to be clear and explicit about the need for companies to be seriously engaged in delivering net zero.
- ESG, CSR, and SLTO are already here; they need to be given full voice and structure.
- Regulation needs to be a serious and sought after career path; working in AIC should be prestigious in the way that working in the SEC in the United States has been considered.
- Regulators need prime funding and to have no conflict-of-interest issues.
- Policies to encourage positive social tipping points need to be explicit, for example with EV policy.
- Companies need to be held to account for greenwashing. Corporate fines need to deliver immediate behaviour change and brands, whatever their size and iconic status, need to be called out for recalcitrance.

- Market leader behaviour should be celebrated and seeded more widely. It requires tangible support.
- Directors need to be held accountable via litigation for climate-related negligence and misrepresentation. Penalties need to carry significant deterrent effect in the wider business community. Fines and disqualifications need to tangible, substantial and meaningful.
- Sections 180 and 181 of the Corporations Act 2001 (Cth) need to be expanded and aligned with international best practice.
- Section 181 is too weak and looks backwards; it is not fit for purpose.
- Australia should look to adapt a stronger version of the UK's s.172 Companies Act 2006.

Boards of public companies need to bear some form of collective legal responsibility, rather than the traditional model of examining the board's role individual by individual. This is a convenient fiction baked into the system to render the task of holding boards to account nugatory.

Corporate groups need to be held accountable on a group basis to reflect commercial reality. The atomizing tendency in Australia pervades corporate law. A simple reform would be to embrace a collective and more joined-up approach; the net zero target demands it. Hence, there could a new form of social citizenship or collective individualism which sits at the core of corporate law and practice.

The ASX needs to include social licence in its principles and to drive improvement.

The continuous disclosure rules under the Corporations Act 2001 (Cth) need to align with this approach.

The ASIC Act 2001 and Corporations Act 2001 (note that both were enacted in 2001) need to be revised and fully aligned to be fit for purpose for the challenge of the next three decades.

Any reforms should have regards to super funds with their long-term investment horizons, and to major corporations involved in carbon-intensive production, including sectors such as the mining and production of fossil fuels. The corporate market needs clear legislative signals.

10.5.4.1 Reviving the corporate law project in Australia

The corporate law on the books has not undergone significant change this century. This is despite the Asian Financial Crisis in the late 1990s, the Global Financial Crisis of 2008–10, or COVID-19 which stretched from 2019–22 as a public discourse and continues in the background to wreak havoc. Three major crises have barely shifted the dial.

Meanwhile the mechanisms for corporate policy change and reform like CAMAC has been abolished.. As such, Australia needs to reintroduce CAMAC or a specialist corporate law reform body.

New approvals for certain types of activity need to change and governments need to stop relying on the elastic comforter concept of a long and undefined 'transition period'. If there is an emergency, and governments have the will to act, the market can adapt at rapid speed. This was the best lesson from COVID for corporations to carry forward to deliver climate solutions.

There must be an embracing of a new bold reformist version of corporate law underpinned by climate science, informed by the climate emergency, having core regard to environmental and social values, and providing innovative solutions at scale. Nothing less is required.

References

Ross Garnaut, *Superpower: Australia's Low-carbon Opportunity*, La Trobe University Press, 2020.

Kent Greenfield, *The Failure of Corporate Law: Fundamental Flaws and Progressive Possibilities*, The University of Chicago Press, 2006.

Saul Griffith, *The Big Switch: Australia's Electric Future*, Black Inc., 2022.

John Parkinson, Andrew Gamble and Gavin Kelly (eds), *The Political Economy of the Company*, Hart Publishing, 2000.

Thomas Piketty, *Capital in the 21st Century*, Belknap, 2014.

Mark Roe, *Political Determinants of Corporate Governance: Political Context, Corporate Impact*, OUP, 2003.

Index

Made in the USA
Las Vegas, NV
19 September 2026

3ad7cfc0-63f2-46d9-8aac-74de81fb05a0R01